JOHN, QUMRAN, AND THE DEAD SEA SCROLLS

Society of Biblical Literature

Early Judaism and Its Literature

Judith Newman
Series Editor

Number 32

JOHN, QUMRAN, AND THE DEAD SEA SCROLLS

JOHN, QUMRAN, AND THE DEAD SEA SCROLLS:

SIXTY YEARS OF DISCOVERY AND DEBATE

Edited by

Mary L. Coloe and Tom Thatcher

Society of Biblical Literature
Atlanta

JOHN, QUMRAN, AND THE DEAD SEA SCROLLS

Library of Congress Cataloging-in-Publication Data

John, Qumran, and the Dead Sea scrolls : sixty years of discovery and debate / edited by Mary L. Coloe and Tom Thatcher.
    p. cm. — (Society of Biblical Literature : early Judaism and its literature ; no. 32)
  Based on papers originally presented at the Society of Biblical Literature Annual Meeting, 2007, San Diego, Calif.
  Includes bibliographical references and index.
  ISBN 978-1-58983-546-7 (paper binding : alk. paper)
  1. Bible. N.T. John—Criticism, interpretation, etc.—Congresses. 2. Dead Sea scrolls—Relation to the New Testament—Congresses. 3. Dead Sea scrolls—Congresses. I. Coloe, Mary L., 1949- II. Thatcher, Tom, 1967- III. Society of Biblical Literature. Meeting (2007 : San Diego, Calif.)
  BS2615.52.J655 2011
  226.5'06—dc22
                              2011008948

Printed in the United States of America on acid-free, recycled paper conforming to ANSI/NISO Z39.48-1992 (R1997) and ISO 9706:1994 standards for paper permanence.

CONTENTS

Preface:
New Light on John and Qumran

Mary Coloe and Tom Thatcher

The discovery of the Dead Sea Scrolls has dramatically expanded our knowledge of Late Second Temple Judaism and the early period of Christian origins. The scrolls have given scholars access to biblical manuscripts that are centuries older than the Masoretic Text and have made us aware of previously unknown Jewish documents contemporary with the emerging Christian movement. To date, at least nine hundred manuscripts have been recovered from the Judean desert. With the texts now widely available in their original languages and in translation, the past decade has seen a renewed interest in the many questions raised by the scrolls. Who wrote and/or published these documents? Why were they hidden in the wilderness caves? How are the scrolls related to the ancient complex at nearby Khirbet Qumran and what was the nature and worldview of the community that lived there? What trends do Qumran and the scrolls reflect in the history of Jewish thought? What can they reveal about Christian origins and how can they inform our understanding of the New Testament and the social world of Late Second Temple Judaism?

To commemorate the sixtieth anniversary of the discovery of the scrolls, the 2007 annual meeting of the Society of Biblical Literature in San Diego featured a number of special sessions on recent developments in scrolls research. The essays in this book reflect the deliberations of a session that considered the past and potential impact of the scrolls on Johannine Studies, jointly sponsored by the John, Jesus, and History Group and the Johannine Literature Section. This special session sought to make Johannine scholars aware of recent developments in scrolls research and to open new avenues of exploration, in view of the somewhat surprising fact that the scrolls have played no significant role in discussions of the Johannine literature over the past several decades. Specifically, the many questions noted above have garnered little notice in Johannine circles, despite a growing interest in the historical roots of the Johannine tradition and an emerging reevaluation of the origins and nature of the "Johannine community" and its relationship to mainstream Judaism. The panelists for the special session, including experts on the scrolls and Johannine scholars, were asked to reflect on the significance of the scrolls in past research and, more significantly, to point to future avenues of inquiry. The results of their work appear in the chapters to follow.

The volume opens with two essays that review recent developments in research on John and the scrolls. First, Eileen Schuller's essay, a transcript of her remarks that opened the SBL session, offers an informative overview of the past decade of Qumran scholarship. She lists the major documents that have recently become available, noting that "over three hundred of the approximately nine hundred known scrolls have been published in a scholarly *editio princeps* in this past decade [1997–2007]" (p. 6). In some cases, the quantity of material now available has made it possible to compare multiple copies of texts, leading to new questions about the history of their recension. In addition to these new manuscripts, there are also new reference works. New literary and social-scientific methodologies are adding to understandings of the scrolls and the community that produced them. Following Schuller's observations, Paul Anderson focuses more specifically on the impact of the scrolls on the study of the Gospel of John over the past sixty years. At the beginning of the twentieth century, the provenance of the Fourth Gospel was considered to be Hellenistic, not Jewish; with the discovery of the scrolls, the roots of the Johannine tradition now find their place among other forms of Palestinian Judaism. Anderson's article helpfully traces some of the major moments in this gradual reversal and highlights ways that the scrolls have influenced the shift in consensus.

These introductory essays are followed by a number of "case studies" that examine instances in which the desert manuscripts may help shed light on expressions, themes, and concepts in the Johannine literature and/or on the history and character of Johannine Christianity. These articles clearly suggest that future scholarship will be interested not only in connections between the Gospel of John and the scrolls but also in Qumran Judaism and Johannine Christianity as parallel religious movements. These chapters forecast the many and diverse avenues of potential future research on John and Qumran.

John Ashton's essay focuses on a puzzling expression in the scrolls. What is meant by the term רז נהיה? Does it correspond to any known concept in first-century Judaism or Christianity? Ashton argues that the idea behind this expression is not unique to Qumran but has parallels with contemporary apocalyptic writings in which life is shaped by the revelation of a "mystery" in the process of actualization. Ashton's work has implications for understanding Johannine eschatology and what the New Testament literature calls the "reign of God."

For many years, scholars have sought to explain the similarities between the Gospels of John and Luke. George Brooke's essay revisits one proposal that suggests a Judean provenance for some of the traditions common to both Gospels. Brooke believes that this hypothesis can be strengthened by considering new material from the scrolls. The Qumran literature reflects ideas within Palestinian

Judaism that may have provided a common source of concepts for both Luke and John.

Brian Capper draws on social-science models to discuss the wide-ranging impact of the Essenes on pre-70 C.E. Judean village life. He points out that an overemphasis on celibate Essenes may lead one to overlook a much larger number of married members of the sect who lived communally in Judean villages. His intriguing study proceeds to consider two sites mentioned in the Fourth Gospel—Bethany and the location of Jesus' final meal in Jerusalem—where the Essenes may have been active. John's interest in and awareness of these locations may also reflect an awareness of Essene thought and, thus, of the type of thinking preserved in the scrolls.

A number of recent discoveries have shed new light on ancient Jewish purity rituals, the topic of Hannah Harrington's essay. Within Judaism, water rituals were associated with, and carried out in anticipation of, the gifts of the Holy Spirit and new life. Previous scholarship tended to view the Fourth Gospel's conceptual connections among water, life, and Spirit as a peculiar development within the Johannine tradition that had no clear precedent in ancient Judaism. The scrolls challenge the notion that John's outlook was unique and establish a much richer understanding of the broader Jewish theological context from which Johannine thought emerged.

Loren Stuckenbruck considers ancient Jewish prayers for protection from demonic powers. His essay examines not just the Late Second Temple texts themselves but also the brand of piety that lay behind them, a piety that sought divine protection from personified forms of evil. Prayers of this type shed light on Jesus' final prayer in John 17, in which he notably asks the Father to keep his disciples "from the evil one" (17:15).

Following these focused studies, the volume concludes with reflections by James Charlesworth, a preeminent authority on both the Johannine Literature and the scrolls. Charlesworth's essay sets a program for future study by noting a number of points at which John and the scrolls speak from a similar, if not common, milieu. He rightfully insists that the scrolls must be given consideration in any attempt to re-create the historical Jesus or early Christianity. When read in light of the scrolls, the Fourth Gospel no longer need stand apart from the early traditions that gave shape to the Synoptics, nor does it look to a Hellenistic provenance. The scrolls reveal a Palestinian form of Second Temple Judaism in which the seeds of Johannine Christianity may have first sprouted.

The editors thank all who participated in the "John and the Scrolls" 2007 SBL session,[1] including those whose essays appear in this publication and also

---

1. Since the SBL special session in 2007, scrolls study has continued to make rapid progress. A 2009 issue of *Dead Sea Discoveries* (16, no. 3) examines questions concerning the communities connected with the scrolls, and John J. Collins' recent book, *Beyond the Qumran*

Professor Jörg Frey, who graciously served as a discussion panelist. We also thank our colleagues on the steering committee of the John, Jesus, and History Group, whose planning and organization made this session possible—Paul Anderson, Jaime Clark-Soles, Alan Culpepper, Felix Just, and Moody Smith—along with Colleen Conway of the Johannine Literature Section for her helpful advice and support. Finally, we are most grateful to Bob Buller and Billie Jean Collins from the Society of Biblical Literature and to Judith H. Newman, the editor of the Early Judaism and Its Literature Series, for their support, critical comments, and patient assistance, which has made publication of these essays possible.

Community (Eerdmans, 2009) considers other communities involved in this movement. Both these volumes raise issues that connect with Brian Capper's essay in this volume. Similarly, John Ashton's analysis of the term *raz nihyey* could not take into consideration work by Matthew Goff, "Recent Trends in the Study of Early Jewish Wisdom Literature: The Contribution of 4qInstruction and Other Qumran Texts," *Currents in Biblical Research* 7 (2009): 376–416, or Sam Thomas, *The "Mysteries" of Qumran: Mystery, Secrecy, and Esotericism in the Dead Sea Scrolls* (SBLEJL 25; Atlanta: Society of Biblical Literature, 2009).

Abbreviations

AB	Anchor Bible Commentary
ABRL	The Anchor Bible Reference Library
AGSU	Arbeiten zur Geschichte des Spätjudentums und Urchristentums
ANRW	*Aufstieg und Niedergang der römischen Welt*
ASBT	Acadia Studies in Bible and Theology (Baker Books)
AVTRW	Aufsätze und Vorträge zur Theologie und Religionswissenschaft
BA	*Biblical Archaeologist*
BAFCS	The Book of Acts in Its First-Century Setting (Eerdmans)
BAZ	Biblische Archaologie und Zeitgeschichte (Brunnen)
BBB	Bonner biblische Beiträge
BBR	*Bulletin for Biblical Research*
BETL	Bibliotheca ephemeridum theologicarum lovaniensium
BibSem	Biblical Seminar Series (Sheffield Academic)
BIS	Biblical Interpretation Series
BJS	Brown Judaic Studies
BNTC	Black's New Testament Commentaries
BRLJ	Brill Reference Library of Judaism
BSac	*Bibliotheca sacra*
BZNW	Beihefte zur Zeitschrift für die neutestamentliche Wissenschaft
CB	*Cultura Bíblica*
CBQ	*Catholic Biblical Quarterly*
CQS	Companion to the Qumran Scrolls (T&T Clark)
CRAI	*Comptes rendus de l'Académie des inscriptions et belles lettres*
CSCO	Corpus scriptorum christianorum orientalium
CTSRR	College Theology Society Resources in Religion (University Press of America)
DJD	Discoveries in the Judean Desert
DSD	*Dead Sea Discoveries*
DSS	Dead Sea Scrolls
DSSCOL	The Dead Sea Scrolls and Christian Origins Library (Bibal Press)
EBib	*Etudes bibliques*
ECDSS	Eerdmans Commentaries on the Dead Sea Scrolls
EKKNT	Evangelisch-katholischer Kommentar zum Neuen Testament

ErIsr	*Eretz Israel*
EstEcl	*Estudios eclesiásticos*
ETL	*Ephemerides theologicae lovanienses*
EvQ	*Evangelical Quarterly*
ExpTim	*Expository Times*
FB	Forschung zur Bibel
FRLANT	Forschungen zur Religion und Literatur des Alten und Neuen Testaments
HBS	Herders Biblical Studies
HeyJ	*Heythrop Journal*
HTKNT	Herders theologischer Kommentar zum Neuen Testament
HTS	Harvard Theological Studies
IEJ	*Israel Exploration Journal*
IJSCC	*International Journal for the Study of the Christian Church*
IOS	*Israel Oriental Society*
IRT	Issues in Religion and Theology
JB	Jerusalem Bible
JBL	*Journal of Biblical Literature*
JJS	*Journal of Jewish Studies*
JSJ	*Journal for the Study of Judaism in the Persian, Hellenistic, and Roman Period*
JSJSup	Journal for the Study of Judaism: Supplement Series
JSNTSup	Journal for the Study of the New Testament: Supplement Series
JSOT	*Journal for the Study of the Old Testament*
JSOTSup	Journal for the Study of the Old Testament: Supplement Series
JSP	*Journal for the Study of the Pseudepigrapha*
JSPSup	Journal for the Study of the Pseudepigrapha: Supplement Series
JSSSup	Journal of Semitic Studies: Supplement Series
JTS	*Journal of Theological Studies*
LNTS	Library of New Testament Studies
LSTS	Library of Second Temple Studies
NCBC	New Century Bible Commentary
NICNT	New International Commentary on the New Testament
NovT	*Novum Testamentum*
NovTSup	Novum Testamentum Supplements
NTOA	Novum Testamentum et Orbis Antiquus
NTS	*New Testament Studies*
NTTS	New Testament Tools and Studies
PTSDSSP	Princeton Theological Seminary Dead Sea Scrolls Project
RB	*Revue Biblique*
RBS	Readers in Biblical Studies (Brill)
RelSoc	Religion and Society
RevQ	*Revue de Qumran*

SBAB	Stuttgarter biblische Aufsatzbände
SBFLA	*Studii biblici Franciscani liber annus*
SBL	Society of Biblical Literature
SBLABS	Society of Biblical Literature Archaeology and Biblical Studies
SBLAcB	Society of Biblical Literature Academia Biblica
SBLDS	Society of Biblical Literature Dissertation Series
SBLEJL	Society of Biblical Literature Early Judaism and Its Literature
SBLMS	Society of Biblical Literature Monograph Series
SBLRBS	Society of Biblical Literature Resources for Biblical Study
SBLSymS	Society of Biblical Literature Symposium Series
SBS	Stuttgarter Bibelstudien
SBT	Studies in Biblical Theology
SDSSRL	Studies in the Dead Sea Scrolls and Related Literature (Eerdmans)
SHJ	Studying the Historical Jesus (Eerdmans)
SJLA	Studies in Judaism in Late Antiquity
SNTSMS	Society for New Testament Studies Monograph Series
StBibL	Studies in Biblical Literature Series (Peter Lang)
STDJ	Studies on the Texts of the Desert of Judah
StudLit	*Studia Liturgica*
SUNT	Studien zur Umwelt des Neuen Testaments
SVTP	Studia in Veteris Testamenti pseudepigraphica
TBei	*Theologische Beiträge*
TBN	Themes in Biblical Narrative (Brill)
TJT	*Toronto Journal of Theology*
TLZ	*Theologische Literaturzeitung*
TRE	*Theologische Realenzyklopädie*
TRu	*Theologische Rundschau*
TTS	Theologische Texte und Studien
VT	*Vetus Testamentum*
WUNT	Wissenschaftliche Untersuchungen zum Neuen Testament
ZNW	*Zeitschrift für die neutestamentliche Wissenschaft*
ZTK	*Zeitschrift für Theologie und Kirche*

Note on Citations

The following format is used throughout this volume for citations of the Dead Sea Scrolls and related documents. Note that the Dead Sea Scrolls are cited by column and line numbers in the original manuscripts, not by "verses."

> cave number/Q(umran)/manuscript number column.line

Or, in the case of fragments of documents:

> cave number/Q/manuscript number "frag." fragment number column.line

In the case of fragments, a single number following the fragment number refers to the relevant line in the fragment—many smaller fragments do not have distinct "columns."

> Example: "1QS 1.10" refers to line 10 in column 1 of the Community Rule, which is catalogued under the heading "1QS."

> Example: "4Q177 frag. 3 8" refers to line 8 in fragment 3 of 4Q177.

> Example: "4Q417 frag. 2 1.11–13" refers to lines 11 through 13 in column 1 of fragment 2 of 4Q417, which is popularly titled "4QInstruction^c."

> Example: "4Q163 frags. 4–7 2.10-12" reflects an instance where multiple fragments have been combined to reconstruct the original document. In this case, fragments 4 through 7 of 4Q163 have been combined to reconstruct the original text. The citation here refers to lines 10 through 12 in column 2 of the reconstruction.

Please note that, except where indicated, all citations of the Dead Sea Scrolls reflect the column, line, and fragment numbers indicated in the respective critical editions from the *Discoveries in the Judean Desert* (DJD) series (Oxford: Clarendon).

The Editors wish to thank Loren Stuckenbruck, Eileen Schuller, and Jeremy Penner for their tireless and patient assistance in the review of citations of the scrolls and the preparation of the index of citations.

PART 1
JOHN AND QUMRAN IN RECENT RESEARCH

THE PAST DECADE OF QUMRAN STUDIES: 1997–2007

Eileen Schuller

Let me begin by saying that I am honored to be invited to this evening's panel and that I congratulate you for holding this special session and for preparing a volume for publication on the sixtieth anniversary of the discovery of the Dead Sea Scrolls.

I will admit that, as an outsider to Johannine studies, I was initially somewhat skeptical about whether there is a need to have a presentation on current Qumran studies within the framework of this panel. Almost every introductory book on the Dead Sea Scrolls that I know of has a section on "John and Qumran" and assumes that the scrolls have something to contribute to the study of the Fourth Gospel. But recently I spent an afternoon browsing the "John section" in our university library, and in my completely unscientific survey of monographs and essay collections from the last decade or so I quickly became aware that, in much recent writing on the Fourth Gospel, there are few references to Qumran texts. Further, the scope of the documents cited is actually quite limited and key works of major Qumran scholars rarely make it into the bibliographies. I looked through the recent volume *What We Have Heard from the Beginning*,[1] where many of the "big names" of Johannine scholarship reflect in a personal way on their journey with John, and to my surprise the scrolls and/or Qumran were rarely mentioned—although Johannes Beutler did allow that "the time may have come for reconsidering these texts."[2] Hopefully, my comments and our session this evening will encourage and suggest some avenues for such a reconsideration.

The celebration of an anniversary usually occasions a look back to the past, and the history of scrolls research over the past six decades was one of the topics I was asked specifically to address here. I do not intend to devote too much time to this, since the fiftieth anniversary of the scrolls' discovery in 1947 occasioned

---

1. Tom Thatcher, ed., *What We Have Heard from the Beginning: The Past, Present, and Future of Johannine Studies* (Waco, Tex.: Baylor University Press, 2007).

2. Johannes Beutler, "In Search of a New Synthesis," in Thatcher, *What We Have Heard from the Beginning*, 27.

the publication of a number of fine surveys of Qumran scholarship, and I have made my own attempt to use a decade-by-decade schematization to lay out on a more popular level the progress of research.[3] In particular, two detailed fiftieth-anniversary surveys focused specifically on the use and contribution of the scrolls to the study of the New Testament—that of Jörg Frey and that of George Brooke,[4] the latter of whom playfully adapted Roland de Vaux's archaeological periods at Qumran (Ia, Ib, II) as a framework to lay out the various stages of scholarship. Although the terminology and precise divisions vary slightly in these and other surveys, the overall flow and flux of the research is clear and, I think, quite well known: the intense excitement of the first two decades, which generated an unprecedented amount of strong publication and creative thinking in a relatively short time; the "day of small things" (to quote the prophet), that is, the decades of the 1970s and 1980s; and the revitalization after the 1990 reorganization of the publication project under Emanuel Tov at Hebrew University, which was just beginning to show concrete results by the 1997 anniversary. In terms of Johannine and scrolls research, the volume of collected essays that has been standard in the field, *John and Qumran*, was published in 1972,[5] then reissued, virtually unchanged, in 1990, and there has been no comparable volume since. Somewhat ironically, it was in papers given within the framework of the fiftieth-anniversary celebrations that Richard Bauckham and David Aune called for caution against a too-eager linkage of Qumran and John, even in terms of such basic themes and motifs as light/darkness dualism, suggesting that we should pay more attention to the biblical books themselves and to the general Second Temple matrix rather than sectarian sources in our attempts to understand the Gospel of John.[6]

---

3. Eileen Schuller, *The Dead Sea Scrolls: What Have We Learned?* (Louisville: Westminster John Knox, 2006), 1–33.

4. Jörg Frey, "The Impact of the Dead Sea Scrolls on New Testament Interpretation: Proposals, Problems, and Further Perspectives," in *The Bible and the Dead Sea Scrolls: The Princeton Symposium on the Dead Sea Scrolls*, ed. James H. Charlesworth, 3 vols. (Waco, Tex.: Baylor University Press, 2006), 3:407–63; George Brooke, "The Scrolls and the Study of the New Testament," in *The Dead Sea Scrolls at Fifty: Proceedings of the 1997 Society of Biblical Literature Qumran Section Meetings*, ed. Robert A. Kugler and Eileen M. Schuller (SBLEJL15; Atlanta: Scholars Press, 1999), 61–78.

5. James Charlesworth, ed., *John and Qumran* (London: Chapman, 1972).

6. Richard Bauckham, "The Qumran Community and the Gospel of John," in *The Dead Sea Scrolls Fifty Years After Their Discovery, 1947–1997*, ed. Lawrence H. Schiffman, Emanuel Tov, and James C. VanderKam (Jerusalem: Israel Exploration Society and the Shrine of the Book, 2000), 105–15; see also idem, "Qumran and the Fourth Gospel: Is There a Connection?" in *The Scrolls and the Scriptures, Qumran Fifty Years After*, ed. Stanley E. Porter and Craig A. Evans (JSPSup 26; Sheffield: Sheffield Academic Press, 1997), 267–79; David E. Aune, "Dualism in the Fourth Gospel and the Dead Sea Scrolls: A Reassessment of the Problem," in *Neotestamentica et Philonica: Studies in Honor of Peder Borgen*, ed. David E. Aune, Torrey Seland, and Jarl Henning Ulrichsen (NovTSup 106; Boston: Brill, 2003), 281–303.

New Publications

But to turn now to the decade since the fiftieth anniversary, 1997–2007, I wish to highlight both the publication of previously unavailable materials and the adoption of new approaches to the texts that have been available for some decades already.

The amount of "new" Qumran-related material published in the last ten years is quite spectacular. This becomes obvious when we consider year by year the volumes of *Discoveries in the Judaean Desert* that have appeared.

1998	DJD XI, *Poetical and Liturgical Texts, Part 1*
	DJD XXVI, *Serekh Ha-Yahad and Two Related Texts*
	DJD XXIII, *Qumran Cave 11.II* (11Q2–18; 11Q20–31)
	DJD XXV, *Textes hébreux* (4Q521–528; 4Q576–579)
1999	DJD XXXIV, *Sapiential Texts, Part 2*, 4QInstruction
	DJD XXIX, *Poetic and Liturgical Texts, Part 2*
	DJD XXXV, *Halakhic Texts*
2000	DJD XXXVI, *Cryptic Texts,* and *Miscellanea, Part 1*
	DJD XXXVIII, *Miscellaneous Texts*
	DJD XVI, *Psalms to Chronicles*
2001	DJD XXI, *Calendrical Texts*
	DJD XXVIII, *Wadi Daliyeh II; Miscellanea, Part 2*
	DJD XXX, *Parabiblical Texts, Part 4; Pseudo-Prophetic Texts*
	DJD XXXIII, *Unidentified Fragments*
	DJD XXXI, *Textes araméens, première partie*
2005	DJD XVII, *1–2 Samuel*
2008	DJD XXXVII, *Textes araméens, deuxième partie*
2009	DJD XL, *1QHodayot^a with Incorporation of 4QH^{a-f} and 1QH^b*
2010	DJD XXXII, *Qumran Cave 1.II: The Isaiah Scrolls*

In addition to the publication of previously inaccessible manuscripts, the years 1997–2007 have seen the production of significant "auxiliary publications," an attestation to a certain consolidation and maturity in scrolls scholarship. At the turn of the millennium, the editors of the *Encyclopedia of the Dead Sea Scrolls* undertook to "present to scholars and interested lay people the results of this half century of research" on these texts "composed over two millennia ago."[7] One long-awaited scholarly tool was the complete word-in-context concordance, *The Dead Sea Scrolls Concordance,* two volumes of which have been available since 2003 covering all nonbiblical texts, with a third volume in 2010 covering

---

7. Lawrence H. Schiffman and James C. VanderKam, eds., *Encyclopedia of the Dead Sea Scrolls* (Oxford: Oxford University Press, 2000).

the biblical texts.[8] Although photographs of all of the scrolls (as well as many photographs from the archaeological excavations at Qumran) have been available on microfiche since 1993,[9] the past decade has seen the production of various electronic reference works of both texts and photographs—for example, as part of the Accordance Bible Software and *The Dead Sea Scrolls Electronic Reference Library*. A variety of study editions are now available in most modern languages, including, with Hebrew-Aramaic text and English, the multivolume *Princeton Theological Seminary Dead Sea Scrolls Project* series (edited by James Charlesworth) and the more compact *Dead Sea Scrolls Study Edition* and *Dead Sea Scrolls Reader*.[10] For English-only text, both Geza Vermes and Michael Wise, Martin Abegg, and Edward M. Cook have updated their translations to include most of the newer manuscripts.[11] Various ongoing series, such as *The Companion to the Qumran Scrolls* (T&T Clark) and *The Literature of the Dead Sea Scrolls* (Routledge) provide topical, book-length treatments of specific documents or genres and play an indispensable role in making specialized scrolls scholarship accessible to nonspecialists.

By my very rough count, over three hundred of the approximately nine hundred known scrolls have been published in a scholarly *editio princeps* in this past decade—though this prism is somewhat artificial, since many of these works had already been "known in part" in preliminary publications in the 1991–1997 era. But, to continue the biblical image, we are now seeing all this material "face to face," in scholarly editions that force us to confront all the problems, complexity, and often very basic questions of interpretation that remain unanswered. This is a large amount of text even for specialists in the field to absorb, a fact that explains why today it is simply no longer possible for most of us to be conversant with, much less expert in, the entire available corpus in a way that was still possible in the 1970s.

A quick glance at a few of the essays to follow in this volume will readily illustrate some of the different ways in which new questions are being posed and old assumptions reexamined in light of this expanded corpus of texts.

John Ashton explores concepts of mystery, revelation, and life and concludes that, in James Charlesworth's words, "the Jewish sectarians at Qumran—and

---

8. Martin G. Abegg Jr. et al., eds., *The Dead Sea Scrolls Concordance: The Non-biblical Texts from Qumran* (Leiden: Brill, 2003); *The Biblical Texts from the Judean Desert* (2010).

9. Emanuel Tov and Stephen Pfann, eds., *The Dead Sea Scrolls on Microfiche: A Comprehensive Facsimile Edition of the Texts from the Judean Desert* (Leiden: Brill, 1993).

10. Florentino García Martínez and Eibert J. C. Tigchelaar, eds., *The Dead Sea Scrolls Study Edition* (2 vols.; Leiden: Brill, 1997); Donald W. Parry and Emanuel Tov, eds., *The Dead Sea Scrolls Reader* (6 vols.; Leiden: Brill, 2004).

11. Geza Vermes, *The Complete Dead Sea Scrolls in English* (rev. ed.; London: Penguin Books, 1997); Michael Wise, Martin Abegg Jr., and Edward M. Cook, *The Dead Sea Scrolls: A New Translation* (rev. ed.; San Francisco: HarperSanFranciso, 2005).

the Johannine community—were apocalyptic both in the sense in which earlier scholars understood that term and in the more specific sense of living lives shaped by a revealed mystery" (p. 68). Ashton's interpretation of the expression רז נהיה, "the mystery that is coming to pass," draws heavily on new evidence from 4QInstruction, and it was precisely his work on this document that stimulated a rethinking of other long-known texts where the same expression appears.[12] Likewise, references to being "with the angels, among the godly ones" (especially in the Songs of the Sabbath Sacrifice and Daily Prayer/4Q503) lead Ashton to reexamine some of his former suppositions and to change his former opinion: he now agrees with scholars such as Hans-Wolfgang Kuhn and David Aune, who had read previously published texts in such a way as to find evidence that the sectarians claimed participation in the life of the angels even in this present age.[13]

George Brooke argues for the Judean/Qumranic provenance of at least some of the traditions in Luke's special material and some of the later redactional sections of the Fourth Gospel. He makes his case by calling upon a wide variety of texts, such as The Commentary on Genesis A, 4Q252;[14] the terminology "Son of God" and "Son of the Most High" in 4Q246, the so-called Aramaic "Son of God" text; negative references to the Samaritans in a poem in 4Q372; and the almost ninety references to Jacob that we now have in nonsectarian works. All of these documents have been published relatively recently, and some had not been previously brought into dialogue with the New Testament.

Hannah Harrington takes up a theme that was much discussed already in the 1960s and 1970s, that of purity/purification in the Fourth Gospel. She considers it now in the light of purification rituals attested in the scrolls and newer archaeological evidence, such as *mikva'ot* and stone vessels from both Qumran and elsewhere in Judaea.

In order to situate the prayer for protection "from the evil one" in John 17:15, Loren Stuckenbruck's essay surveys the large number and wide variety of Qumran texts that are concerned with demons, thus giving evidence of a worldview in which spirits, demons, and exorcism were much more important than we generally acknowledge.

These essays have all moved beyond the themes of dualism, predestination, love/hate, light/darkness, and so on that dominated the study of John and

---

12. For example, the hymn at the end of the Rule of the Community (1QS 11.13) and in 1QMysteries, one of the texts published in DJD I (1955).

13. Hans-Wolfgang Kuhn, *Enderwartung und gegenwärtiges Heil: Untersuchungen zu den Gemeindeliedern von Qumran, mit einen Anhang über Eschatologie und Gegenwart in der Verkündigung Jesus* (SUNT 4; Göttingen: Vandenhoek & Ruprecht, 1966); David E. Aune, *The Cultic Setting of Realized Eschatology in Early Christianity* (NovTSup 28; Leiden: Brill, 1972).

14. This text provides the number 153 in the flood narratives, identical to the Gospel of John's numbering of the miraculous catch of fish (21:11; cf. Luke 5:4–11).

Qumran in an earlier era precisely because modern scholars have access to manuscripts that were not available to previous generations of scholarship.

RETHINKING THE CORE DOCUMENTS

In addition to texts and resources newly published in the past decade, scholars are now substantially rethinking the foundational documents discovered in Cave 1: the Community Rule, the Thanksgiving Psalms, and the War Scroll. With the availability of multiple copies of these texts from Cave 4 and a few of the smaller caves, it becomes clear that the source and redaction history of each of these key documents is so much more complex, and the historical milieu in which they were generated so much less certain, than we had thought when we relied solely upon the single copy found in Cave 1. This is not the time or place to go into details, but I want to give several examples of the types of issues currently being discussed.

The Community Rule has been studied the most intensely, and two competing recensional reconstructions have been debated for almost a decade now. To summarize the argument: Does the order in which the manuscripts were copied (1QS the oldest, then 4QS[b,d], then 4QS[e] the youngest) reflect the order in which the different recensions were created (as proposed by Philip Alexander)?[15] Or, does 1QS give us a later, more developed version of this document, even though the copy itself is earlier (as argued by Metso)?[16] Any answer to this question has major consequences for reconstructing community formation and ideology. Are we seeing traces of movement from a priestly-dominated to a lay-led community, or was the movement in the opposite direction? Or, is the question itself wrongly formulated, with something else in fact going on? Perhaps, as Alison Schonfield has recently suggested, rather than assuming a linear development we need a different chronological-spatial model that would nuance more carefully questions of authorship, transmission, and ownership.[17]

When we turn to the multiple recensions of the Hodayot/Thanksgiving Psalms and the War Scroll, however, work is not so advanced. Scholars have not yet articulated a comprehensive hypothesis, let alone competing hypotheses, that can explain the significant differences between the various copies of the Hodayot, especially the divergent order of the psalms and extent of the collection as found in 1QH[a] and 4QH[b] versus the quite different collection in 4QH[a]

---

15. Philip S. Alexander, "The Redaction-History of Serekh ha-Yahad: A Proposal," *RevQ* 17 (1996): 437–56; see also Paul Garnet, "Cave 4 MS Parallels to 1QS 5:1–7: Towards a *Serek* Text History," *JSP* 15 (1997): 67–78.

16. Sarianna Metso, *The Textual Development of the Qumran Community Rule* (STDJ 21; Leiden: Brill, 1997).

17. Alison Schofield, "Rereading S: A New Model of Textual Development in Light of the Cave 4 *Serekh* Copies," *DSD* 15 (2008): 96–120.

and in what I suggest are shorter manuscripts, 4QH[c] and 4QH[f], that originally contained only the Hymns of the Teacher collection.[18] The division of the psalms into two groups, Hymns of the Teacher and Hymns of the Community (a division established by the Heidelberg "school" in the 1960s),[19] needs to be reexamined, especially now that Hartmut Stegemann and Émile Puech have reconstructed the original shape of the scroll as a whole and, in so doing, have established how various pieces fit together to reconstruct much more of the psalms found in cols. 4–8 and 21–26.[20] Hopefully the publication of this reconstructed scroll in DJD XL (2009) will stimulate a major reconsideration of this important collection. And with the War Scroll, we are still working out some of the most basic questions regarding differences between the Cave 1 copy and similar materials (4Q491–496, 4Q497, 4Q285, 4Q471, 11Q14) to determine what points to variant recensions and what are simply "War Scroll–like" materials.[21]

Of particular interest are the ongoing debates about "The Treatise on the Two Spirits" (1QS 3.13–4.26), which has played such a pivotal role in discussions on John and Qumran. Some scholars continue to argue that this block of material, with its distinctive perspective on dualism and predestination, was composed by the Teacher of Righteousness as an exposition of his central theological thought. Other scholars, particularly in the German world,[22] take it as a given that this is an Essenic but not specifically Qumranic treatise and emphasize similarities with other recently published texts—such as 4QVisions of Amran (4Q543–548), an Aramaic composition with similar dualism and terminology—thus situating such ideas in a much broader matrix. Sarianna Metso has suggested that there are a few poorly preserved fragments from these columns in 4QS[a] (and perhaps in 4QS[h]) that differ from 1QS, suggesting some process of redaction,[23] and manuscripts 4QS[b, d] do not contain this section. The Johannine scholar who wants to work with the "Treatise on the Two Spirits" can no longer simply turn to the standard articles from the 1960s and 1970s; the fundamental starting points of the discussion have changed.

---

18. Eileen Schuller, "4QHodayot[a–e] and 4QpapHodayot[f]: Introduction," in DJD XXIX, 69–75; see also the specific introductions to each of the manuscripts.

19. See, for example, Gert Jeremais, *Der Lehrer der Gerechtigkeit* (SUNT 2; Göttingen: Vandenhoeck & Ruprecht, 1963); Kuhn, *Enderwartung und gegenwärtiges Heil*.

20. Hartmut Stegemann, "The Material Reconstruction of 1QHodayot," in Schiffman, Tov, and VanderKam, *Dead Sea Scrolls Fifty Years after Their Discovery*, 274–84; Émile Puech, "Quelques aspects de la restauration du rouleau des hymnes (1QH)," *JJS* 39 (1988): 38–55.

21. For a description of the problems in terms of 1QM, see Jean Duhaime, *The War Texts: 1QM and Related Manuscripts* (CQS 6; London: T&T Clark, 2004), 14–44.

22. See, for example, Armin Lange, *Weisheit und Präedestination: Weisheitliche Urordnung und Präedestination in den Textfunden von Qumran* (STDJ 18; Leiden: Brill, 1995).

23. Sarianna Metso, *The Serekh Texts* (CQS 9; London: T&T Clark, 2007), 9.

METHODOLOGY

In the concluding section of my remarks, let me say something about issues of methodology. During the decades of producing first editions—from the formation of an international team of scholars in the 1950s up until the late 1990s—those involved in scrolls work primarily needed well-developed textual skills, paleographic expertise, and strong philological training, plus unlimited patience and dogged perseverance. But that era is at an end. At the fiftieth-anniversary SBL plenary session, George Nickelsburg set forth a challenge: Could new minds and hands be found for the next fifty years of scrolls research—in particular, scholars trained in social-scientific methods?[24] Nickelsburg acknowledged that some such work was already being done by individuals such as Jean Duhaime, who worked with relative-deprivation theory, and Albert Baumgarten, who drew on sociological studies of Puritan sectarians.[25] But such forays were often regarded as, at best, peripheral to "real" Qumran scholarship. In her affirmative response to Nickelsburg, Carol Newsom formulated the question this way: In the next decade, who would our conversation partners be?[26]

As the decade since the fiftieth anniversary has progressed, there has been a conscious attempt to talk to "different" people and to broaden the methodologies used in the study of the scrolls. For example, a major colloquium held in Bristol in September 2003 was postured as a "modest attempt to link into Qumran research some of the newer methodologies currently available to scholars working in related fields in the Humanities and Social Sciences, especially what is known as Biblical Studies."[27] The titles of the conference papers include references to sociology, narratology, and postcolonialism—words still infrequently heard at Qumran conferences. Closer to home, one of the sessions of the Qumran Section at this 2007 SBL meeting is devoted specifically to "Methods and Theories," and from this will come a published volume of papers exploring a variety of new methodologies and approaches.

Let me mention, very briefly, four such ways of approaching the scrolls, with some examples of specific studies. First, there is a move to a less historical, more

---

24. George W. E. Nickelsburg, "Currents in Qumran Scholarship: The Interplay of Data, Agendas, and Methodology," in Kugler and Schuller, *Dead Sea Scrolls at Fifty*, 79–99.

25. Jean Duhaime, "Relative Deprivation in New Religious Movements and the Qumran Community," *RevQ* 16 (1993–1995): 265–76; Albert I. Baumgarten, "The Rule of the Martian as Applied to Qumran," *IOS* 12 (1992): 121–42.

26. Carol Newsom, "A Response to George Nickelsburg's 'Currents in Qumran Scholarship: The Interplay of Data, Agendas, and Methodology,'" in Kugler and Schuller, *Dead Sea Scrolls at Fifty*, 119.

27. Jonathan G. Campbell, introduction to *New Directions in Qumran Studies*, ed. Jonathan G. Campbell, William John Lyons, and Lloyd K. Pietersen (LSTS 52; London: T&T Clark, 2005), 4.

literary reading of the scrolls, with more explicit use of current literary theory. This is best illustrated by the work of Carol Newsom, especially in her book *The Self as Symbolic Space: Constructing Identity and Community at Qumran.*[28] Building on a series of articles that she wrote in the early 1990s, Newsom models a socio-rhetorical way of reading sectarian texts that draws attention to how the discourse of a community creates an alternatively figured world and self-identity. Her dialogue partners include Michel Foucault, Fredric Jameson, Kenneth Burke, and M. M. Bakhtin. In a series of close studies of specific passages in the Rule of the Community and Thanksgiving Hymns, Newsom isolates elements that form a sectarian self-identity and subjectivity which she designates the "masochistic sublime"—her terminology for what Hans-Wolfgang Kuhn had called, in untranslatable German, *Niedrigskeitdoxologie.* For Johannine scholars, of special interest is Newsom's key chapter, "Knowing as Doing: The Social Symbolics of Knowledge in the Two Spirits Treatise of the *Serek ha-Yahad.*"

The tension between the scrolls as sources for historical reconstruction and as literary works that are to be understood within the parameters of their distinctive genres is not new. The question was already articulated by Philip Davies in *Behind the Essenes* (1987), specifically in reference to whether compositions such as Pesher Habakkuk and the Thanksgiving Psalms should or can be read as sources for historical information about a figure such as the Wicked Priest.[29] Nor is Newsom's methodological approach the only one possible. For example, Maxine Grossman's *Reading for History in the Damascus Document* turns to reader-response criticism and the New Historicism to supply an interpretive lens for reading the text.[30] Perhaps these two volumes (Newsom and Grossman) will function for Qumran studies in somewhat the same way that Alan Culpepper's *Anatomy of the Fourth Gospel* did for Johannine studies some twenty years earlier in signaling a far-reaching change of orientation.[31]

Second, Nickelsburg's call for a more *social-scientific approach* to scrolls study has already yielded concrete results. Many studies have employed the sociological category of "sect/sectarianism," especially as formulated by Bryan Wilson and Stark and Bainbridge, but theories of relative deprivation, the sociology of deviance, models of religious conversion, and the more anthropological approach of Mary Douglas have also been brought into play. Given that there has been a recent dearth of articles that treat John and Qumran together on the level of

---

28. Carol A. Newsom, *The Self as Symbolic Space: Constructing Identity and Community at Qumran* (STDJ 52; Leiden: Brill, 2004; repr., Atlanta: Society of Biblical Literature, 2007).

29. Philip R. Davies, *Behind the Essenes: History and Ideology in the Dead Sea Scrolls* (BJS 94; Atlanta: Scholars Press, 1987), 87–106.

30. Maxine L. Grossman, *Reading for History in the Damascus Document: A Methodological Study* (STDJ 45; Leiden: Brill, 2002; repr., Atlanta: Society of Biblical Literature, 2009).

31. R. Alan Culpepper, *Anatomy of the Fourth Gospel: A Study in Literary Design* (Philadelphia: Fortress, 1983).

shared ideas, vocabulary, and theology, it seems all the more significant that social scientists have continued to find it obvious and profitable to study Qumran and John together—one thinks, for example, of the influential work of Philip Esler on introversionist communities, and of the more recent monograph of Kåre Sigvald Fuglseth, *Johannine Sectarianism in Perspective*.[32] In the current volume, Brian Capper's essay pursues his distinctive claim that the sociological category "religious order"/*virtuoso religio* is more productive than "sect" for describing both Qumran and the Johannine community. Other recent studies have introduced a comparative dimension that had hitherto been lacking: for example, Capper's student Timothy Ling made use of ethnographic studies of modern-day Nepalese Sherpas to explain the restriction of Essenism to the heartland of Judea, and Eyal Regev turned to contemporary Christian religious movements—the Shakers, Mormons, and Amish—as parallels, drawing upon both their texts and ethnographic studies of these communities.[33]

Third, let me say something briefly about *the study of gender*. Although there has been a well-established trajectory of studies on the women in the Fourth Gospel, as well as reflection on Lady Wisdom/Logos, from an explicitly feminist perspective, it may seem as if this is an area where Qumran scholarship could have little to contribute. But Pliny's description of the Essenes as "without money, without women . . . , with only the palm trees for company" now must be placed alongside numerous passages in the scrolls that simply assume the presence of women, family, children, marriage, and sexual relations, especially in setting forth halakhic regulations. Initial studies—for instance, my own first venture into this topic at the New York conference back in 1991 and even for the 1997 Jubilee volume[34]—were still at the level of "gathering up the fragments" (to use an image that New Testament studies of women has often employed), that is, simply recognizing, collecting, and analyzing the texts that mention women. More-recent essays, such as Maxine Grossman's "Reading for Gender in the Damascus

32. Philip F. Esler, "Introverted Sectarianism at Qumran and in the Johannine Community," in *The First Christians in Their Social Worlds: Social-Scientific Approaches to New Testament Interpretation* (London: Routledge, 1994), 92–109; Kåre Sigvald Fuglseth, *Johannine Sectarianism in Perspective: A Sociological, Historical, and Comparative Analysis of the Temple and Social Relationships in the Gospel of John, Philo, and Qumran* (NovTSup 119; Leiden: Brill, 2005).

33. Timothy J. M. Ling, *The Judaean Poor and the Fourth Gospel* (SNTSMS 136; Cambridge: Cambridge University Press, 2006); Eyal Regev, *Sectarianism in Qumran: A Cross-Cultural Perspective* (RelSoc 45; Berlin: Walter de Gruyter, 2007).

34. Eileen Schuller, "Women in the Dead Sea Scrolls," in *Methods of Investigation of the Dead Sea Scrolls and the Khirbet Qumran Site*, ed. Michael O. Wise et al. (New York: New York Academy of Sciences, 1994), 115–32; idem, "Women in the Dead Sea Scrolls," in *The Dead Sea Scrolls after Fifty Years: A Comprehensive Assessment*, ed. Peter W. Flint and James C. VanderKam (2 vols.; Leiden: Brill, 1999), 2:117–44.

Document,"[35] have pushed the theoretical and methodological questions, and further study should expand the parameters to include all imagery related to women (such as the language of childbirth in the eschatological poem in 1QH^a 11). We are only beginning to ask what it would mean to read all the Qumran texts with the assumption, even heuristically, that they were addressed to a community of both men and women.[36]

Fourth and finally, although the focus in Qumran studies has been often on legal regulations and biblical interpretation, a third category of materials—the prayers, hymns, and psalms—is receiving increasing attention. Here, the field of *ritual studies*, particularly the work of Catherine Bell, has supplied some of the theoretical framework for preliminary studies by Rob Kugel and also for the more extensive monograph by Russell Arnold.[37] At an even more preliminary stage is the bringing of the questions and methods developed by scholars of mysticism (Jewish, Christian, philosophical, Eastern) to the language and form of texts such as the Songs of the Sabbath Sacrifice, which are so different from anything else in the scrolls.

In this era of expanding methodological approaches, I suspect that there is much that Qumran scholars can learn from Johannine scholars who, in my opinion, have been considerably more self-reflective and innovative in questions of theory and method over the past decades.

THE NEXT DECADE: THE SCROLLS AT SEVENTY

In addition to glancing back into the past, an anniversary celebration often closes with at least a gesture of looking forward into the future. When SBL gathers in 2017 to celebrate the seventieth anniversary of the discovery of the scrolls, how *might* we be summarizing the work of 2007–2017?

In 2017, for the first time, it is likely that the discussion of newly discovered texts will not predominate. Certainly there are some fragments, mainly held by private owners, which may become accessible in the next decade. But unless we find caves 12, 13, and 14, or major scrolls surface from other sources, the excitement of "brand new" materials will not be the focus when we meet to celebrate again. In the work of editing texts, I suspect that the focus will shift to the use of highly specialized scientific techniques, including advanced photographic cameras, digitization, and DNA identification to match fragments. Most of the

---

35. Maxine L. Grossman, "Reading for Gender in the Damascus Document," *DSD* 11 (2004): 212–39.

36. For an attempt to adopt this principle in reading one specific text, see Cecilia Wassen, *Women in the Damascus Document* (SBLAcB 21; Atlanta: Scholars Press, 2005).

37. Robert A. Kugler, "Making All Experience Religious: The Hegemony of Ritual at Qumran," *JSJ* 33 (2002): 131–52; Russell C. D. Arnold, *The Social Role of Liturgy in the Religion of the Qumran Community* (STDJ 60; Leiden: Brill, 2006).

innovative technological advances, many already announced at the time of the fiftieth anniversary, are still "in the works" and have not yet yielded, at least on any broad scale, the dramatic results promised.[38] Hopefully there will be more to report by the seventieth anniversary.

By 2017, I hope that we will see the production of the two scholarly resources now so sorely lacking: full-length commentaries on the major texts and dictionaries. Specific projects are already in the works. Commentaries on some of the major Qumran texts have been assigned in the prestigious Hermeneia series (Fortress Press); other shorter and less specialized commentary series are also planned.[39] Work has begun on two major dictionary projects: the predominately philological *Hebrew and Aramaic Lexicon of the Dead Sea Scrolls*, to be produced under the direction of Reinhard Kratz at the Qumran Institute, University of Göttingen, and *The Theological Dictionary of the Qumran Texts* to be produced by Heinz-Josef Fabry at the University of Bonn. Whether these will be completed and available by 2017 remains to be seen.

But will there even be a session on the Dead Sea Scrolls at SBL in 2017? Perhaps by then Dead Sea Scrolls research will be so much a part of the overall study of Second Temple–period Judaism that there will no longer be an obvious need to hold a separate session on the scrolls. Would this be a loss or a gain? More specifically here, by the seventieth anniversary, will the study of the Dead Sea Scrolls have become central, even indispensable, to the study of the Gospel of John? Or will Qumran specialists and Johannine scholars have gone their separate ways, leaving no impetus to hold another session like this one? Perhaps these essays and this discussion will give us some clues.

---

38. See, for example, Gregory H. Bearman, Stephen J. Pfann, and Sheila I. Spiro, "Imaging the Scrolls: Photographic and Direct Digital Acquisition," and Donald W. Parry et al., "New Technological Advances: DNA, Databases, Imaging Radar," both in vol. 1 of Flint and VanderKam, *Dead Sea Scrolls after Fifty Years.*

39. For instance, James R. Davila, *Liturgical Works* (ECDSS; Grand Rapids: Eerdmans, 2000). Although sixteen volumes are listed and assigned for this ambitious series, this is the only volume to have appeared to date.

John and Qumran: Discovery and Interpretation over Sixty Years

Paul N. Anderson

It would be no exaggeration to say that the discovery of the Dead Sea Scrolls was the most significant archaeological find of the twentieth century. As the Jesus movement must be understood in the light of contemporary Judaism, numerous comparisons and contrasts with the Qumran community and its writings illumine our understandings of early Christianity and its writings. As our knowledge of Qumran and the Dead Sea Scrolls has grown, so have its implications for Second Temple Judaism and early Christianity. Likewise, as understandings of Johannine Christianity and its writings have grown, the Qumran-Johannine analyses have also evolved. The goal of this essay is to survey the scholarly literature featuring comparative investigations of Qumran and the Fourth Gospel, showing developments across six decades and suggesting new venues of inquiry for the future.

At the outset, it must be said that the state of Johannine studies has probably evolved more over the last six decades than that of any other corpus within the New Testament.[1] If Rudolf Bultmann had written his monumental commentary on John a decade or more after 1947, would he have been able to posit his source theories in the same way, inferring stark tensions between Jewish and Hellenistic cosmologies during the first century C.E.?[2] In the pre-Qumran-discovery bed-

---

1. For reviews of Johannine secondary literature and its treatment of the Dead Sea Scrolls, see the extensive treatments by Robert Kysar, *The Fourth Evangelist and His Gospel: An Examination of Contemporary Scholarship* (Minneapolis: Augsburg, 1975), and *Voyages with John: Charting the Fourth Gospel* (Waco, Tex.: Baylor University Press, 2006), chs. 5–8. See also the reviews of Johannine research by Stephen S. Smalley, "Keeping Up with Recent Studies; XII. St John's Gospel," *ExpTim* 97 (1986): 102–8, and Paul N. Anderson, "Beyond the Shade of the Oak Tree: The Recent Growth of Johannine Studies," *ExpTim* 119 (2008): 365–73.

2. Indeed, Bultmann's inference of three non-Johannine sources underlying the Fourth Gospel, edited by an evangelist and reordered (wrongly) by a redactor, was built upon the assumption that the Revelation-Sayings Source reflected a Mandaean and Gnostic ideology and origin, as Judaism was thought to be pervasively monistic in contrast to Johannine dualism.

rock of Johannine scholarship, several foundation stones resisted assault. First, critical scholarship had drawn a sharp distinction between monistic Judaism and dualistic Hellenism. Given John's highly dualistic character, it was therefore assumed that the provenance of the Fourth Gospel was Hellenistic, not Jewish. As a result, the Johannine tradition was truncated from Palestinian Judaism, severed from the ministry of Jesus, and even distanced from Pauline Christianity in Asia Minor in favor of other settings, such as Alexandria. Second, pre-1947 New Testament research characteristically saw the theme of Jesus' "agency" within John's Christology as an element of the Gnostic Revealer-Myth. Bultmann exploited this perception in arguing for the existence of a Revelation-Sayings Source underlying the Johannine "I-Am" sayings, connected inferentially with John the Baptizer and his followers. Third, Johannine religious forms were typically portrayed as primarily non-Jewish, cultic ones rather than as socio-religious features of a Jewish-Christian group. A fourth tendency connected John's Logos Christology with Philo's treatment of the Logos motif, as well as Hellenistic speculation, driving a wedge between John's elevated theology and his mundane presentation of the earthly Jesus. Fifth, messianic Christological constructs tended to be viewed as somewhat monolithic rather than variegated. All these elements of pre-1947 approaches to Johannine studies have largely fallen by the wayside and have been replaced by other perspectives rooted in religious and historical developments largely furthered by the discovery of the Dead Sea Scrolls.

Since the discovery of the Dead Sea Scrolls, and under the influence of scrolls research, several new movements in Johannine studies have developed. First, given the light/darkness dualism of the Community Rule, the War Scroll, and other Qumran writings, Johannine dualism is seen to be perfectly at home within Palestinian Judaism. As a result, the Jewishness of John has been recognized, even to the extent that C. K. Barrett has come to view John as the most Jewish of all the Gospels.[3] Second, rather than seeing John's agency schema as Gnostic,

---

See Rudolf Bultmann, *The Gospel of John: A Commentary*, trans. G. R. Beasley-Murray, R. N. W. Hoare, and J. K. Riches (Philadelphia: Westminster, 1971). For an extensive analysis of the evidence for Bultmann's diachronic approach to John's composition, see Paul N. Anderson, *The Christology of the Fourth Gospel: Its Unity and Disunity in the Light of John 6* (WUNT 2.78; Tübingen: Mohr Siebeck, 1996). Even C. H. Dodd, who saw the Johannine tradition as having a far greater unity than Bultmann proposed, hardly referred to the Qumran literature at all in sketching the religious background of the Fourth Gospel, even after the initial discoveries had been published. While some awareness of Qumran writings is apparent in *Historical Tradition in the Fourth Gospel* (Cambridge: Cambridge University Press, 1963), only a few references are made, and Dodd believed the scrolls' impact on Johannine studies (and even on the background of John the Baptizer) to be negligible. See also his *Interpretation of the Fourth Gospel* (Cambridge: Cambridge University Press, 1953).

3. C. K. Barrett, *The Gospel of John and Judaism* (Philadelphia: Fortress, 1975); see also his monumental commentary, *The Gospel according to St. John*, 2nd ed. (Philadelphia: Westminster, 1978).

scholars have come to see it as closer to the *shaliach* motif within the Mosaic Prophet agency typology rooted in Deut 18:15–22.[4] Third, the social function of religious practice and identity has come under new focus, suggesting something of the history of the Johannine dialectical situation. As features of sectarian faith and practice have been illumined by findings at Qumran, greater light has been shed on the emerging Jesus movement, especially in its individuation from Judaism. Fourth, the Jewishness of John's Logos Christology has gained respect over against Hellenistic associations, implying connections with Gen 1 and Prov 8 rather than necessitating Gnostic cosmological speculation.[5] Fifth, a growing awareness of the rich diversity of Jewish and Christian Messianic expectations, as well as unity and diversity within emerging Christologies of the New Testament, has forced scholars to appreciate the dialectical character of early Christological developments rather than pitting one construct against another in needless dichotomies.[6] While not all of these changes in perspective were affected equally by the Qumran discoveries, it must be said that Qumran has played a significant role in these developments.

These changes can also be seen in the meaningful engagement of the leading Johannine commentaries with the Qumran writings in the several decades after the discovery of the scrolls. While C. K. Barrett argued in the second edition of his commentary (1978) that the original excitement of Qumran had not exactly revolutionized Johannine studies, he did list more than one hundred

---

4. Note, for instance, Juan Peter Miranda's *Der Vater, der mich gesandt hat: Religionsgeschichtliche Untersuchungen zu den johanneischen Sendungsformeln Zugleich ein Beitrag zur johanneischen Christologie und Ekklesiologie* (Europaische Hochschulschriften; Frankfurt: Lang, 1972), which connects the Johannine sending motif with Mosaic agency as found in Qumran (353–72); Jan-A. Bühner, *Der Gedandte und sein Weg in 4. Evangelium: Die kultur- und religionsgeschichtlichen Grundlagen der johanneischen Sendungschristologie sowie ihre traditionsgeschichtliche Entwicklung* (WUNT 2.2; Tübingen: Mohr Siebeck, 1977), carries the connection further, especially linking Deut 18:15–22 with John's agency formula. For eight specific links between the LXX rendering of Deut 18:15–22 and John, see Paul N. Anderson, "The Having-Sent-Me Father—Aspects of Agency, Irony, and Encounter in the Johannine Father-Son Relationship," in *God the Father in the Gospel of John*, ed. Adele Reinhartz, *Semeia* 85 (Atlanta: Society of Biblical Literature, 1999), 33–57.

5. Especially significant was the second appendix in the first volume of Raymond Brown's Anchor Bible commentary, which argues strongly for the Jewish background of the Fourth Gospel and its Prologue. See Raymond E. Brown, *The Gospel According to John*, 2 vols. (AB; New York: Doubleday, 1966–1970), 1.519–24.

6. Building on examples from Qumran, C. K. Barrett shows how the Fourth Evangelist, like other Jewish writers of his day, intentionally placed contravening notions side by side as a means of engaging the reader and drawing audiences into the dialectical thought of the narrator (*Gospel of John and Judaism*, 68–75).

references to Qumran writings in his index.[7] Raymond Brown's commentary connected the Qumran writings to the background of John, although he emphasized that the contacts are not close enough to imply literary dependence.[8] Likewise, while Rudolf Schnackenburg noted several significant similarities between John and Qumran, he did not think they were close enough to imply any sort of direct dependence. Nonetheless, he did not rule out the possibility that, if John the Baptizer had some contact with Qumran and his disciples became Johannine followers of Jesus, this indirect contact might have explained the connection between the Johannine ethos and that of the Essene community.[9] While Barnabas Lindars only provided a couple of pages on the contacts between John and Qumran, he did argue that this link in some ways "provides the closest parallel of the thought of Judaism at the time of Jesus." Thus, connections between John and the Manual of Discipline make the likelihood of some sort of Qumranic influence upon John "inescapable," although Lindars does not spell out specific possibilities.[10] These and other examples indicate the growing influence of the scrolls on mainstream Johannine research, even in the face of deeply entrenched assumptions.

Immediately upon their discovery, the new knowledge provided by the Dead Sea Scrolls began to be applied to related subjects. Whereas other archaeological discoveries had involved shopping lists and political correspondence, this set of writings was rich with religious significance and carried obvious implications both for Judaism and Christianity. The discovery of scrolls in a total of eleven caves continued through 1952, although ongoing quests for further archaeological and manuscript evidence will probably never be definitively concluded. While varying interests, levels of information, and aspects of expertise have led to a multiplicity of claims about the manuscripts and their implications for Johannine studies, one way to review the "findings" is to consider the types of claims that are made. Below I supply punctuation marks for claims made in scrolls literature. Beginning with the more significant and moving toward the more mundane, I punctuate some of the highlights of discovery and interpretation. It should be stated at the

---

7. Barrett, *Gospel according to St. John*, 34. Note the rejoinder, however, in James H. Charlesworth, "Have the Dead Sea Scrolls Revolutionized Our Understanding of the New Testament?" in *The Dead Sea Scrolls Fifty Years after Their Discovery*, ed. Lawrence H. Schiffman, Emanuel Tov, and James C. VanderKam (Jerusalem: Israel Exploration Society and the Shrine of the Book, 2000), 116–38. Charlesworth answers the question in the title of his essay with a resounding "yes."

8. See Brown, *Gospel according to John*, 1.lxii–lxiv.

9. Rudolf Schnackenburg, *The Gospel according to St. John*, trans. Kevin Smyth, 3 vols. (HTKNT; New York: Seabury and Crossroad, 1980–82), 1.128–35.

10. Barnabas Lindars, *The Gospel of John* (NCBC; Grand Rapids: Eerdmans, 1972), 36–38. More recently, Craig Keener's commentary, with its extensive engagement with ancient sources, provides one of the most helpful treatments of John's Jewish background, although its focus on the Dead Sea Scrolls is more incidental than pronounced (*The Gospel of John: A Commentary*, 2 vols. [Peabody, Mass.: Hendrickson, 2003], 1.171–232).

outset that the following lists make no attempt to be exhaustive in their treatment. Indeed, at least twenty thousand essays and books have been written on Qumran and related subjects. Roughly the same number have been written on Johannine studies over the last six decades as well, with hundreds of essays and books touching on the intersections between the two fields. This survey, however, attempts to outline at least a suggestive sample of some of the main contributions, concluding with questions for further research. I begin with the *exclamation marks*!

EXCLAMATION MARKS! NOTABLE CLAIMS,
BOTH NOTEWORTHY AND NOTORIOUS!

As with any momentous discovery, "exclamations" in research on the scrolls indicate the perceived significance of the event—both realized and anticipated. More-outrageous assertions include the claims that Jesus was "an astonishing reincarnation" of Qumran's Teacher of Righteousness;[11] that the monastery at Qumran was "more the cradle of Christianity than Bethlehem or Nazareth";[12] and that Jesus did not exist but was instead the hallucinogenic projection of a fertility cult experimenting with mind-expanding mushroom intoxicants.[13] Perhaps the grandest theory put forward is that of Barbara Thiering, who laid out an extensive hypothesis that the Gospel of John was actually *composed by Jesus himself* in 37 C.E. while living in Qumran.[14] While media outlets have covered fantastic reports

---

11. See André Dupont-Sommer, *The Dead Sea Scrolls: A Preliminary Survey*, trans. E. Margaret Rowley (New York: Macmillan, 1952), 99, who found many parallels between the presentation of Qumran's Teacher of Righteousness and Jesus: similar teachings; a challenge to the priestly establishment of Jerusalem; an untimely death; and the organization of the movement that emerged in his name.

12. Edmund Wilson, *The Scrolls from the Dead Sea* (New York: Oxford University Press, 1955), 98. Wilson argued that Jesus must have grown up in Qumran, where he returned after his ministry and was eventually buried sometime before 64 C.E. Accusing religious scholars and archaeologists of personal bias, Wilson apparently felt no need to cloak his own antireligious sentiments.

13. John Allegro, *The Dead Sea Scrolls and the Christian Myth*, 2nd ed. (Amherst, N.Y.: Prometheus Books, 1992); see also his more provocative *The Sacred Mushroom and the Cross: A Study of the Nature and Origins of Christianity within the Fertility Cults of the Ancient Near East* (Garden City, N.Y.: Doubleday, 1970). One of the original editors of the Dead Sea Scrolls, Allegro developed an imaginative set of implications for understanding the ministry of Jesus and the character of early Christianity. Following major rebuttals by scholars and former colleagues, however, he resigned from the University of Manchester in 1970 to devote himself to full-time writing.

14. While the media has paid special notice to Thiering's views, scholars have not. In understated terms, Geza Vermes responded to Thiering's critique of Vermes's earlier review of Thiering's *Jesus the Man* (New York: Doubleday, 1992): "Professor Barbara Thiering's reinterpretation of the New Testament, in which the married, divorced, and remarried Jesus, father of four, becomes the 'Wicked Priest' of the Dead Sea Scrolls, has made no impact on learned opin-

on the Dead Sea Scrolls with astounding popular appeal, striking exclamations from established scholars are still noteworthy.

"My Heartiest Congratulations on the Greatest Manuscript Discovery of Modern Times!"

William Foxwell Albright wrote these words in 1948 after receiving correspondence on the scrolls and sample photographs from John Trever.[15] While extraordinary as a claim, it is also true! No set of ancient manuscripts discovered within the last century has had a greater impact on our understanding of ancient Judaism and thus on the origins of Christianity. The way that the scrolls illuminate the ministries of Jesus and John the Baptizer, and also the Fourth Gospel, has been highly significant.

John the Baptizer Was Immersed in Qumran Essenism—A Possible Link between the Fourth Evangelist and Jesus!

One of the strongest sets of connections between the Qumran writings and early Christianity involves the great number of parallels between the ministry and message of John the Baptizer and Qumran: geographic intersections (John was baptizing across the Jordan, not far from Qumran); priestly lineages (Zadokite or otherwise); teachings regarding holy living and repentance from worldly compromise; prophetic warnings bolstered by threats of the axe "laid at the root of the tree"; emphases upon baptismal cleansings and purification; uses of Isa 40:3 ("the voice of one crying in the wilderness: 'Prepare the way of the Lord!'"); and challenges issued to religious leaders. Whether or not John was born in Qumran, Otto Betz and others have argued that he was raised there.[16] Plausibly, the Bap-

---

ion. Scrolls scholars and New Testament experts alike have found the basis of the new theory, Thiering's use of the so-called 'pesher technique,' without substance" (*The New York Review of Books* 41, no. 20, December 1, 1994). Of course, as Thiering suggests, Jesus *could have* been raised at Qumran, created a conflict (as the Wicked Priest) with John the Baptizer (the Teacher of Righteousness), married Mary Magdalene (divorcing and remarrying her again), married Lydia, been unsuccessfully crucified outside Qumran (between the bodies of Simon Magus and Judas), been buried and resuscitated in Cave 8, had four children, traveled with Peter and Paul to Rome, and died in Rome (ca. 64 C.E.). But does the textual evidence in the Temple Scroll and the Gospels confirm such, or even suggest it? For a more scholarly analysis of the use of the pesher method of interpretation at Qumran, see James H. Charlesworth, *The Pesharim and Qumran History: Chaos or Consensus?* (Grand Rapids: Eerdmans, 2002).

15. Cited by John C. Trever in *The Untold Story of Qumran* (Westwood, N.J.: Fleming H. Revell, 1965), 94.

16. Otto Betz, "Was John the Baptist an Essene?" in *Understanding the Dead Sea Scrolls: A Reader from the Biblical Archaeology Review,* ed. Hershel Shanks (New York: Random House, 1992), 205–14.

tizer's priestly heritage merged with his sense of prophetic and eschatological urgency, as reflected in the ministry of Jesus and eventually in the perspective of the Fourth Evangelist.

THE FOURTH EVANGELIST LIKELY DID SOME ABIDING AT QUMRAN!

As one of the leading British authorities on the Fourth Gospel, John Ashton's argument that the Fourth Evangelist spent time at Qumran is significant.[17] Attempting to ascertain the character and origin of Johannine dualism, Ashton inferred a direct association with Essene dualism rather than an indirect influence. Against Bultmann's inference that the Fourth Evangelist was a Gnostic, Ashton wondered if John might have encountered this sort of dualistic thinking within the Qumranic setting "from an early age, maybe from childhood." Thus, although firsthand contact with Qumran cannot be proven, the Fourth Evangelist "had dualism in his bones."[18]

QUMRAN COMMUNITY MEMBERS INFLUENCED THE PRODUCTION OF THE JOHANNINE GOSPEL!

As one of the leading experts on Qumran, the Fourth Gospel, archaeology, and Jesus, James Charlesworth argued that many residents of Qumran sought refuge in Jerusalem after the destruction of the complex by the Romans in 68 C.E. This influx might have coincided with the production of the first edition of the Gospel of John.[19] Given similarities in the dualistic paradigms of John and Qumran (especially evident in John 6, 12, 14, which Charlesworth calls *termini technici*) and that the Johannine Gospel possesses a good deal of firsthand archaeological knowledge of Jerusalem, Charlesworth poses that the Fourth Evangelist likely bolstered the story of Jesus by featuring the mission of John the Baptizer in John 1. If the first edition of John was written before 70 C.E., this would explain

---

17. See John Ashton, *Understanding the Fourth Gospel* (Oxford: Clarendon, 1991), 205–37. Ashton accused scholars such as Brown and Charlesworth of not going far enough in accounting for the Johannine-Qumranic similarities, although Charlesworth later questioned whether Ashton had fairly considered his analysis; see James H. Charlesworth, "The Dead Sea Scrolls and the Gospel according to John," in *Exploring the Gospel of John: In Honor of D. Moody Smith*, ed. R. Alan Culpepper and C. Clifton Black (Louisville: Westminster John Knox, 1996), 65–97. In Ashton's view, John's dualism was rooted not in "his receptiveness to new ideas but . . . his own gut reactions," which had been formed by his personal history of development (*Understanding the Fourth Gospel*, 237).

18. Ashton, *Understanding the Fourth Gospel*, 236–37.

19. James H. Charlesworth, "The Priority of John? Reflections on the Essenes and the First Edition of John," in *Für und wider die Priorität des Johannesevangeliums*, ed. Peter L. Hofrichter (TTS 9; Hildesheim, Germany: Georg Olms, 2002), 73–114.

why many of the Jerusalem topographical features are described as still standing (they had not yet been destroyed by the Romans in June of 70 C.E.). Charlesworth's proposal would also make the first edition of John the *first* Gospel—not only independent of the Synoptic traditions, but preceding them.

THE FOURTH EVANGELIST WAS AN ESSENE!

Did Essenes live *only* in Qumran, or did they live elsewhere in Palestine as well? Brian Capper's portrait of the Essene movement has been one of the most creative and suggestive of recent analyses, and his connection between the Essene ethos and the Johannine approach to community is provocative.[20] Based on Josephus's estimate that there were as many as four thousand Essenes in pre-70 Judea, Capper does not view the Essene movement as a reclusive sect but as a virtuoso religious movement of devout celibate males, inhabiting most Palestinian villages and caring for the social needs of local populations. Essenes therefore took in orphans and widows and addressed social concerns in Jewish communities. They cared for the needs of the poor and marginalized in their "houses of the community." If the Fourth Evangelist was a member of this sort of religious movement he may have seen Jesus as endorsing that sort of local social activism; therefore, the Johannine emphasis upon community deserves reconsideration as a movement of radical Jewish community concern.

THE JOHN–QUMRAN MARRIAGE TO BE DISSOLVED DUE TO IRRECONCILABLE DIFFERENCES!

While this exclamation might overstate Richard Bauckham's reluctance to make use of Qumran research for the advancement of Johannine studies, it comes close.[21] While Bauckham disagreed with Raymond Brown diametrically on a number of Johannine topics (including, notably, whether there *was* a Johannine community), he took Brown's modest assessment of Qumran-Johannine contacts further.[22] Due to the significant number of differences and inexact parallels, even regarding Qumran's modified dualism, Bauckham cautioned against finding the key to the Johannine tradition, and more pointedly the search for a Johannine community, in the literature from Qumran. According to Bauckham, "There is no

---

20. Aside from Capper's contribution to the present volume, see his "'With the Oldest Monks . . .': Light from Essene History on the Career of the Beloved Disciple?" *JTS* 49 (1998): 1–55; see also his "Essene Community Houses and Jesus' Early Community," in *Jesus and Archaeology*, ed. James H. Charlesworth (Grand Rapids: Eerdmans, 2006), 472–502.

21. Richard Bauckham, "The Qumran Community and the Gospel of John," in Schiffman, Tov, and VanderKam, *Dead Sea Scrolls Fifty Years after Their Discovery*, 105–15.

22. See Raymond Brown, "Qumran Scrolls and the Johannine Gospel and Epistles," in his *New Testament Essays* (Garden City, N.Y.: Doubleday, 1968), 102–31.

need to appeal to the Qumran texts in order to demonstrate the Jewishness of the Fourth Gospel's light/darkness imagery. This can be done more convincingly by comparison with other Jewish sources already available long before the discovery of the Dead Sea Scrolls."[23]

The "Johannine Community" Secedes from Sectarianism and Joins a Cult!

Breaking with the Martyn-Brown hypothesis regarding a Johannine "sectarian community" that sought to maintain separateness from the world, Kåre Fuglseth argues for a reappraisal of Johannine Christianity.[24] Here the Qumran-Johannine relationship becomes one of contrasts as well as comparisons, as the Qumranic-Johannine-Philonic continuum is revamped, with John closer to Philo than to Qumran. Especially taking issue with Wayne Meeks's sectarian approach to Johannine Christianity, Fuglseth shows some of the inadequacy of sect-like associations with the Johannine situation. If Johannine Christianity was part of a cosmopolitan setting, welcoming outsiders and maintaining contact with other religious institutions (as suggested by references to the temple and other groups), "sectarian" is the wrong designation. In contrast to Qumran's cutting itself off from the rest of the world and highly structured sectarian existence, Johannine Christianity is more permeable and less organized structurally. And, rather than being fixed upon its estranged parental group, Johannine Christianity engaged several fronts—Docetists, Samaritans, alleged Greeks and Romans, and other Christians. In these and other ways, the Qumran-Johannine relationship is as valuable for its contrasts as well as its similarities. According to Fuglseth, Johannine Christianity seems more cultic than sectarian.

Overall, while some "exclamations" about the Qumran writings call for a good deal of skepticism, others merit serious consideration. The above analyses show that biblical studies, and especially Johannine studies, have been influenced in unprecedented ways by the Qumran discoveries. Rather than seeing the Johannine writings against Hellenistic, Gnostic, or Hermetic backgrounds, the solidly Jewish parentage of the Johannine tradition—despite its later development in a Greco-Roman setting—raises inescapable issues for consideration.

In addition to exclamation marks, however, Johannine-Qumran dialogue also has its *periods*.

23. Bauckham, "Qumran Community," 115.

24. Kåre Sigvald Fuglseth, *Johannine Sectarianism in Perspective: A Sociological, Historical, and Comparative Analysis of the Temple and Social Relationships in the Gospel of John, Philo, and Qumran* (NovTSup 119; Leiden: Brill, 2005).

PERIODS. FULL STOPS, AND STARTS, IN THE
NEW TESTAMENT–QUMRAN DIALOGUE

The history of the New Testament-Qumran dialogue is punctuated by several major developments and projects, each of which contributes to ongoing discussions in particular ways. Often these "periods" are determined by actual discoveries (or lack thereof), leading to a periodization of the research. As well as being affected by archaeological discoveries, these periods are also shaped by particular scrolls being published, made available, or commented upon within larger conferences and publications. Whatever the case, these discoveries and their interpretations create the frameworks for chapters of development within the larger history of inquiry. Building upon the periodizations of George Brooke and Jörg Frey, the following outline of four periods of research emerges.[25]

PERIOD 1: FIRST DISCOVERIES AND PREMATURE ASSUMPTIONS (1947–CA. 1955)

As the first of the Dead Sea documents began to be noticed in 1947, great intrigue surrounded the discoveries, but primarily with regard to their implications for ancient Judaism. The pre-discovery era had already taken note of Ernst Renan's 1891 dictum that Christianity was an Essenism that had largely succeeded, and the Damascus Document of Cairo had been published in 1910.[26] However, with the discovery of the Great Isaiah Scroll A, the Manual of Discipline, the Habakkuk Pesher, the Thanksgiving Hymns, and the War Scroll, interest began to take off.[27] Karl Georg Kuhn produced several provocative essays analyzing parallels between the Qumran writings and the New Testament.[28] Especially

---

25. George J. Brooke, "The Scrolls and the Study of the New Testament," in *The Dead Sea Scrolls at Fifty: Proceedings of the 1997 Society of Biblical Literature Qumran Section Meetings*, ed. Robert A. Kugler and Eileen M. Schuller (SBLEJL15; Atlanta: Scholars Press, 1999), 61–76; repr. in his *Dead Sea Scrolls and the New Testament: Essays in Mutual Illumination* (Minneapolis: Fortress, 2005), 3–18. Brooke's periods of research, reflecting the archaeological history of Qumran, are described as "Pre-Qumran, Period IA (1948–1952)," "Period IB (1952–1977)," "Abandonment (1977–1991)," and "Periods II–IV (1991–the present)." Jörg Frey, "The Impact of the Dead Sea Scrolls on New Testament Interpretation: Proposals, Problems, and Further Perspectives," in *The Bible and the Dead Sea Scrolls: The Princeton Symposium on the Dead Sea Scrolls*, ed. James H. Charlesworth, 3 vols. (Waco, Tex.: Baylor University Press, 2006), 3:407–61. Frey's periods largely overlap with those of Brooke, but the dates and descriptions are more clearly spelled out.
26. See Brooke's analysis of the pre-Qumran era, *Dead Sea Scrolls and the New Testament*, 4.
27. Frey, "Impact of the Dead Sea Scrolls," 409.
28. See, for instance, Karl G. Kuhn, "Zur Bedeutung der neuen palästinischen Handschriftenfunde für die neutestamentlishce Wissenschaft," *TLZ* 47 (1950): 81–86, and his more fully developed "Die Sektenschrift und die iranische Religion," *ZTK* 49 (1952): 296–316, where he lays out a plausible view of the Iranian background of Qumran dualism, shedding important light on Johannine dualism.

significant was Kuhn's observation that the dualism of Qumran was not materialistic, but rather ethical and eschatological. Analyses of Qumran dualism bore special relevance to Johannine dualism, and this was a major factor in the movement away from seeing the Johannine literature as Hellenistic only, contributing to the recovery of an appreciation of its systemic Jewish character. During the early years, the interpretive promise of the scrolls as a resource for understanding the background of the New Testament grew as connections began to emerge between the Qumran writings and early Christianity.

PERIOD 2: THE CONTAGION OF "QUMRAN FEVER" (CA. 1955–1970)

Jörg Frey describes the next decade and a half as a period of "Qumran Fever." Launched by the discoveries of ten more caves containing thousands of fragments (1952–1956), this new phase saw both the production of solid work on the scrolls, with implications for Christian origins, as well as the expansion of speculation characterized above. The first volume of the *Discoveries in the Judean Desert* series appeared in 1955.[29] In addition to popular speculations on the scrolls and related subjects, an international group of New Testament scholars began to contribute its own analyses. French and German analyses began to make headlines in Europe,[30] and British and American advances soon followed. With the publication of the two-volume translation and introduction by Millar Burrows in 1955 and 1958, important New Testament themes were laid out, setting the template for further research to follow.[31] The translation of the scrolls into English by Geza Vermes and others led to a veritable avalanche of scrolls-related research. Alongside great optimism that the Qumran writings would revolutionize New Testament studies, however, doubts began to be expressed as to the exactness of the parallels and therefore their implications for the study of early Christianity. Rather than inferring direct connections among Jesus, John the Baptizer, Paul, and the Fourth Evangelist, analyses of parallels reflecting lines that

---

29. Now numbering forty assigned volumes (some still in production), the DJD series began with *Qumran Cave 1* (ed. D. Bartholélemy and J. T. Milik; Oxford: Clarendon, 1955). Volumes 2–5 were also published during this period.

30. See Jean Daniélou, *Les manuscrits des la Mer Mort et les origines du Christianisme* (Paris: Editions de l'Orange, 1957), translated as *The Dead Sea Scrolls and Primitive Christianity*, trans. Salvator Attanasio (Baltimore: Helicon, 1958). Note especially Daniélou's analysis, "St. John and the Theology of Qumran" (103–11).

31. Millar Burrows, *The Dead Sea Scrolls* (New York: Viking, 1955); idem, *More Light on the Dead Sea Scrolls: New Scrolls and Interpretations with Translations of Important Recent Discoveries* (New York: Viking, 1958).

never directly cross became an important interpretive approach.[32] In other words, the mere fact of parallels between writings need not imply actual contact.

PERIOD 3: STAGNATION AND ADVANCE (CA. 1970–1991)

While Frey and Brooke refer to this period as a time of stagnation or abandonment in Qumran archaeological research, it is one of the most aggressive periods of advance in Johannine-Qumran analysis. Due to a variety of factors, Qumran research slowed down considerably in the 1970s and the 1980s. The excavation work at Qumran was abandoned, and the dearth of new discoveries, coupled with the lengthy process of getting extant scrolls into print, led the media and the cutting edge of biblical scholarship to look elsewhere for subjects of interest. The publication of the Temple Scroll in Hebrew (1977) created some excitement,[33] but a growing awareness of the differences between Qumran and the New Testament writings had begun to sink in, pouring cold water on the fires of parallelomania.[34] Frustration was also growing as years, and even decades, passed without discovered texts becoming available to the broader world of scholarship. It was as though the failure to break new archaeological ground was matched by a failure to break new intellectual ground in interpreting the scrolls as resources for understanding either ancient Judaism or early Christianity. Regarding Qumran-Johannine research, however, some of the most significant advances were made during this period. Most notably, the essay collection *John and Qumran* gathered by James Charlesworth marks boundaries of this period with its first and second printings in 1972 and 1990, contributing to further explorations in significant ways. It is also during this period that some of the major commentaries and Johannine works were published, developing the Qumran-Johannine

---

32. F. F. Bruce, "Qumran and Early Christianity," *NTS* 2 (1955–1956): 176–90; Oscar Cullmann, "The Significance of the Qumran Texts for Research into the Beginnings of Christianity," *JBL* 74 (1955): 213–26. Daniel J. Harrington, S.J., also reminds us that, as in Euclidian geometry, parallel lines never do meet ("Response to Joseph Fitzmyer's 'Qumran Literature and the Johannine Writings,'" in *Life in Abundance: Studies of John's Gospel in Tribute to Raymond E. Brown, S.S.*, ed. John R. Donahue [Collegeville, Minn.: Liturgical Press, 2005], 134–37).

33. Between 1968 and 1992 only three volumes in the DJD project were published (vols. 6–8). Frey ("Impact of the Dead Sea Scrolls," 416) and Brooke (*Dead Sea Scrolls and the New Testament*, 10) note the importance of Yigael Yadin, *The Temple Scroll* (3 vols.; Jerusalem: Israel Exploration Society, 1977–83), which was the longest scroll to be discovered.

34. The truth of the 1961 SBL presidential address by Samuel Sandmel, "Parallelomania," *JBL* 81 (1962): 1–13, had begun to sink in for Qumran–Early Christianity studies. The mere determination of a parallel between two ancient texts need not imply derivation or a particular form of contact; caution should be used in determining the particulars of textual relationships.

connections further.[35] While archaeological discovery slowed down during this period, Johannine-Qumranic analyses flourished.

PERIOD 4: THE BLOSSOMING OF A NEW "QUMRAN SPRINGTIME" (1991–PRESENT)

Frey called the epoch since 1991 "a new 'Qumranic springtime,'" and indeed it has been, on several levels.[36] Especially significant was the marked increase in access to the Qumran writings. First, the publication of the texts of Cave 4 made accessible the most important of recent discoveries, facilitating the analysis of biblical and apocryphal texts as well as community writings. Second, the increased availability of these texts by microfiche, published photographs, and transcribed writings broke the logjam of limited access to manuscripts that were previously available only to small teams of scholars. Third, the publication of articles and books on particular topics began to take off in unprecedented ways, leading to a consensus opinion about Jesus and Qumran.[37] Fourth, symposia, anniversaries, and special collections provided the stimulus for new scholarship. Fifth, social-science developments within biblical studies produced new approaches to the Essene movement and the Qumran community as social and anthropological phenomena. New approaches to archaeology have also had an impact on Qumran studies. Analyses of skeletal remains, cloth, parchment, ink, fecal remains, pottery,

---

35. James H. Charlesworth, ed., *John and Qumran* (New York: Crossroad, 1972). For the 1990 second edition, the title was changed to *John and the Dead Sea Scrolls*. Brown's second volume, 1970; Barrett's second edition and monograph on John and Judaism, 1978 and 1975 respectively; Lindars's commentary, 1972; the translation of Schnackenburg's commentary into English, 1980–82; and Ashton's major analysis of John's dualism in his *Understanding the Fourth Gospel*, 1991.

36. Frey borrowed this term from Martin Hengel, who referred to the new "Qumranfrüh-ling" in "Die Qumranfollen undeder Umgang mit der Wahrheit," *TBei* 23 (1992): 233–37. From 1992–2002 publication of DJD volumes accelerated, with the release of twenty-eight of the forty commissioned volumes (most involving manuscripts from cave 4). In addition, the Princeton Theological Seminary Dead Sea Scrolls Project, founded in 1985 by James Charlesworth, published its first six volumes between 1994 and 2002.

37. In the forward to *Jesus and the Dead Sea Scrolls* (New York: Doubleday, 1992), James H. Charlesworth laid out sixteen elements of what he called a "critical consensus" regarding connections between Jesus and the Dead Sea Scrolls (xxxi–xxxvii). Essentially, the Qumran community members were a group of male, conservative Jewish religious covenanters, whose writings antedated Jesus and his followers but did not refer to any of them directly; this being the case, parallels are important but incidental. Comparative analysis is thus helpful in that it shows at least twenty-four similarities between Qumran and Jesus' movement and also twenty-seven major differences (see Charlesworth's own essay in the collection, "The Dead Sea Scrolls and the Historical Jesus," 1–74). For another impressive list of parallels involving similarities and differences, see Heinz-Wolfgang Kuhn, "Qumran Texts and the Historical Jesus: Parallels in Contrast," in Schiffman, Tov, and VanderKam, *Dead Sea Scrolls Fifty Years after Their Discovery*, 573–80.

and other materials have lent valuable insights into life in Qumran, illuminating some of the writings.

While this brief overview of the history of Qumran-John studies shows the ebb and flow of discovery and research, the boundaries between the periods are neither hard nor fixed. Sometimes discoveries in one period do not receive widespread notice until a later phase, so some of the chronological differences are simply a matter of timelines and incidental factors in the flow of publications. Overall, history reveals the emergence of more sensational claims, followed by more measured ones, leading finally to a more nuanced set of analyses that considers both similarities and differences between the New Testament and the Qumran writings. Most significant is the overall development of a keener sense of the Jewish background of all of the New Testament writings, including insights into the ministry of Jesus, the epistles of Paul, and the Johannine literature.

COLONS: SIGNIFICANT JOHN–QUMRAN DEVELOPMENTS

Of the many connections that have been drawn between the New Testament and the Dead Sea Scrolls, few have been as significant as the John–Qumran analyses. These studies have ranged in character from positive comparisons between the two sets of writings to observations of significant contrasts, and from assumptions of primary contact between Johannine Christianity and Qumran to assertions that the two communities were distinct. Sometimes a particular study made a significant impact, while at other times a cluster of studies created a wave of interest and furthered inquiry. Following are some of the major contributions to research on John and Qumran—not quite distinctive periods, but notable as *colons* in the larger flow of research.

EARLY EXPLORATIONS OF POSSIBLE CONNECTIONS

The year 1955 was significant in the blossoming of Qumran studies. It was also significant for the way several important analyses of the Qumran writings illuminated the religious background of the Gospel and Epistles of John.[38] At the same time, following the lead of Millar Burrows, scholars were coming to identify the Johannine literature as those New Testament writings bearing closest affinities with the Qumran writings.[39] Of particular importance were the early

---

38. In addition to Karl Kuhn's work on Qumranic dualism and the implications for Johannine interpretation (see n. 28 above), Lucetta Mowrey's essay "The Dead Sea Scrolls and the Background for the Gospel of John," *BA* 17 (1954): 78–97, focused early on the John–Qumran relationship.

39. See Burrows, *Dead Sea Scrolls*, 338–41; idem, *More Light*, 123–30. See also the early and extensive treatments by Leon Morris, *The Dead Sea Scrolls and the Gospel of John* (London: Viking, 1960; repr. in his *Studies in the Fourth Gospel* [Grand Rapids: Eerdmans, 1969], 321–58);

studies of Raymond Brown and William F. Albright, which identified impressive Johannine-Qumran parallels and argued for a closer connection with contemporary Judaism than with later Mandaean Gnosticism.[40] In addition to similarities, however, significant differences between John and the scrolls began to emerge. For instance, F. F. Bruce, after initially having noted significant parallels between John and the Qumran writings, soon thereafter expressed second thoughts.[41] Likewise, Howard Teeple, noting the many differences between the Qumran and the Johannine writings, concluded that there are not enough identical parallels to prove an indisputable connection between them, other than what would have been the case with any two sets of writings drawing on a common Jewish background.[42] Renewed interest in the relationship, however, was to be launched with a full volume dedicated to the subject by leading New Testament scholars.

John and the Dead Sea Scrolls

By far the most significant single volume in the history of John–Qumran analysis is a collection of essays edited by James Charlesworth in 1972 and republished in 1990.[43] Leading off with an overall analysis in "The Dead Sea Scrolls and the New Testament" (pp. 1–8), Raymond Brown covers nearly a quarter-century of research, calling for further investigation. In his more extensive "Light from Qumran upon Some Aspects of Johannine Theology" (pp. 9–37), James L. Price covers such themes as God the Creator, Johannine dualism, and the Teacher/Son as God's representative, revealer, and example. Within "The Johannine Paraclete and the Qumran Scrolls" (pp. 38–61), A. R. C. Leaney analyzes parallels among the Teacher of Righteousness, Jesus, and the Holy Spirit. In "The Calendar of

---

F.-M. Braun, "L'arrière-fond judaïque du Quartième Évangile et la Communauté de l'Alliance," *RB* 62 (1955): 5–44; M.-É. Boismard, "Qumrán y los Escritos de S. Juan," *CB* 12 (1955): 250–64; Gunther Baumach, *Qumran und das Johannes-Evangelium* (AVTRW 6; Berlin: Evangelische Verlagsanstalt, 1957).

40. Raymond E. Brown, "The Qumran Scrolls and the Johannine Gospel and Epistles," *CBQ* 17 (1955): 403–19, 559–74; repr. in *New Testament Essays*, 102–31. Albright showed how archaeology clearly suggests a Palestinian origin of the Johannine tradition. Later studies have not only confirmed but expanded that judgment (William F. Albright, "Recent Discoveries in Palestine and the Gospel of St. John," in *The Background of the New Testament and Its Eschatology*, ed. W. D. Davies and David Daube [Cambridge: Cambridge University Press, 1956], 153–71). See also Godfrey R. Driver, *The Judean Scrolls: The Problem and a Solution* (New York: Shocken Books, 1965), 544–62.

41. See F. F. Bruce, *Second Thoughts on the Dead Sea Scrolls* (Grand Rapids: Eerdmans, 1956).

42. Howard M. Teeple, "Qumran and the Origin of the Fourth Gospel," *NovT* 4 (1960): 6–24; repr. in *The Composition of John's Gospel: Selected Studies from "Novum Testamentum,"* ed. David E. Orton (RBS 2; Leiden: Brill, 1999), 1–20.

43. Charlesworth, *John and Qumran*, 1972. See n. 35 above for the full citation.

Qumran and the Passion Narrative in John" (pp. 62–75), Annie Jaubert seeks to resolve the differences between the Johannine and Synoptic datings of the Last Supper. Charlesworth himself contributed two essays: the first, "A Critical Comparison of the Dualism of 1 QS 3:13–4:26 and the 'Dualism' Contained in the Gospel of John" (pp. 76–106), outlines eleven significant parallels between the two; the second, "Qumran, John, and Odes of Solomon" (pp. 107–36), shows, on the basis of six parallels between these three bodies of literature, that the Johannine-Odes relationship was not an organic one, but rather that both had been influenced by Qumran. In "Qumran, John, and Jewish Christianity" (pp. 137–55), Giles Quispel shows how Jewish ideas and practices came to be expressed in Hellenistic categories as the Johannine tradition moved from Palestinian traditions toward their expression in an Asia Minor setting. Carrying the association further in "The First Epistle of John and the Writings of Qumran" (pp. 156–65), Marie-Émile Boismard attempts to identify aspects of Qumranic dualism within the Johannine community in Asia Minor. The discussion comes to a head in the essay by William H. Brownlee, "Whence the Gospel according to John?" (pp. 166–94), which connects Palestinian tradition with the work of the Apostle John finalized in a Hellenistic setting such as Alexandria. Noting the continued relevance of these essays for Johannine research in his new foreword to the 1990 reprint, Charlesworth concluded, "In summation, while the Dead Sea Scrolls cannot be used to prove the apostolic connection of the earliest layer of John or demonstrate the early date of the gospel, they do disclose the Palestinian origin and Jewish character of the Johannine tradition. The Gospel of John is perhaps the most Jewish of the canonical gospels."[44]

Anniversaries, Symposia, and Special Collections

After publication of the Charlesworth collection, the primary venues in which Johannine-Qumran studies have been carried out are larger collections, symposia, and special studies. For instance, Charlesworth contributed a significant essay on the subject to a *Festschrift* for Moody Smith in 1996, as did Joseph Fitzmyer and Daniel Harrington within the conference and volume of collected essays celebrating the contributions of Raymond Brown.[45] The fiftieth anniversary of the scrolls' discovery saw many more publications than any previous anniversary. A raft of Johannine-Qumran studies have appeared within the past

---

44. Charlesworth, *John and the Dead Sea Scrolls*, xv.

45. Charlesworth, "Dead Sea Scrolls and the Gospel," 65–97; Joseph A. Fitzmyer, S.J., "Qumran Literature and the Johannine Writings," in *Life in Abundance: Studies of John's Gospel in Tribute to Raymond E. Brown*, ed. John R. Donahue (Collegeville, Minn.: Liturgical Press, 2003), 117–33; Daniel J. Harrington, S.J., "Response," in Donahue, *Life in Abundance*,134–37.

decade or so.[46] The most significant collection on this topic appears in the proceedings of the second Princeton Symposium on the Bible and the Dead Sea Scrolls, in which significant direct and indirect treatments of John and Qumran abound.[47] The present book is the most recent example of this phenomenon. It is the only anniversary volume of which I am aware dedicated exclusively to Qumran and the Gospel of John.

What one can see in the first six decades of John-and-Qumran research is a set of movements, first toward degrees of specific influence and contact, and then away from them. Whereas the significant number of parallels between the Qumran and Johannine writings has led to inferences of a close relationship,[48] others have resisted inferring such close proximity. Indeed, influence can happen in a great number of ways, and even differences can be suggestive of contrastive analysis since they may reflect intertraditional contact, especially if a differing presentation is intended as an alternative. Current studies, beyond noting a similarity of worldview, seek to make use of growing knowledge of Qumran theology, sociology, psychology, and anthropology as a means of better understanding the Johannine writings and their settings. Only recently have the interdisciplinary approaches that have influenced biblical studies so extensively in recent decades begun to be applied to the Dead Sea Scrolls and their life settings. As those developments emerge, new venues of research will undoubtedly follow.

---

46. See, for example, Aage Pilgaard, "The Qumran Scrolls and John's Gospel," in *New Readings in John: Literary and Theological Perspectives: Essays from the Scandinavian Conference on the Fourth Gospel, Århus 1997*, ed. Johannes Nissen and Sigfred Pedersen (JSNTSup 182; Sheffield: Sheffield Academic Press, 1999), 126–42; Richard Bauckham, "Qumran and the Fourth Gospel: Is There a Connection?" in *The Scrolls and the Scriptures: Qumran Fifty Years After*, ed. Stanley E. Porter and Craig A. Evans (JSPSup 26; Sheffield: Sheffield Academic Press, 1997), 267–79; idem, "Qumran Community," in Nissen and Pedersen, *New Readings in John*, 105–15; Dietmar Neufeld, "'And When That One Comes,' Aspects of Johannine Messianism," in *Eschatology, Messianism, and the Dead Sea Scrolls*, ed. Craig A. Evans and Peter W. Flint (Grand Rapids: Eerdmans, 1997), 120–41.

47. Charlesworth, *Bible and the Dead Sea Scrolls*. See here especially Enno E. Popkes, "About the Differing Approach to a Theological Heritage: Comments on the Relationship between the Gospel of John, the *Gospel of Thomas*, and Qumran," 3.218–317; and James H. Charlesworth, "A Study in Shared Symbolism and Language: The Qumran Community and the Johannine Community," 3.97–152.

48. See especially John Ashton, who thinks John's dualism can only be explained on the basis of the Evangelist's direct contacts with the Qumran community (*Understanding the Fourth Gospel*, 205–37).

Semi-Colons; Denoting Significant Topics in Qumran–Johannine Research

Emerging from the above analyses are significant topical developments that punctuate the landscape of the study of John and Qumran. As broad themes, these subjects overlap with each other and with many other topics not covered in this essay. Therefore, this list is suggestive of some of the significant topics in Qumran-Johannine research, although not exhaustive. While the similarities involved are important, so also are the differences when seeking to understand a Johannine emphasis or approach.

Creation and the Workings of God

One of the striking parallels between the Fourth Gospel and the Qumran writings is the featuring of God's work in creation as a singular force in the cosmos.[49] This is an important feature, because the dualistic pairs of realities have their origins in God's sovereign work; therefore, Qumran dualism is a derived reality rather than an absolute one. Parallel to the creative work of the divine Logos in John 1:1–3, all that exists has come from God's creative power (1QS 3.15; 11.11, 17). Both positive and negative emphases are made in the Qumran writings (although less so in John): all has come into being through God's creative work, and nothing has come into being otherwise. In reflecting a belief in God's primacy in the universe, the Johannine Prologue (John 1:1–18) resonates with the Qumranic worldview, although both have their origin in Gen 1 and related texts. This confirms the Jewishness of the cosmology of the Fourth Gospel, providing an important backdrop for understanding the Johannine perspective and ethos.

Dualism

Given that God is the source of creation, how could things be so wrong in the world? In Qumranic terms, there are two Spirits, the Spirit of Truth and the Spirit of Deception, that draw humanity into two camps, the Children of Light and the Children of Darkness. This leads to cosmological warfare, wherein God calls the faithful—the Light of the World—to fight for the truth and the way of righteousness embraced by the community, against all opposition. Ironically, those targeted as the adversaries in this duel are largely fellow Jewish leaders in

---

49. See the treatment of theology in Qumran and the Gospel of John by James L. Price, "Light from Qumran upon Some Aspects of Johannine Theology," in *John and Qumran*, ed. James Charlesworth (London: Chapman, 1972), 9–37. Joseph Fitzmyer also begins his treatment of Johannine-Qumranic parallels with a focus on the work of God as Creator ("Qumran Literature and the Johannine Writings," 119–26).

Jerusalem, who are perceived as having compromised the ways of God in their dealings with the world. They will meet their doom at the hand of God's angels in warfare. The Johannine writings employ many of the same dualistic pairs and envision Jesus as the Light of the World, who illumines all (John 1:9). Darkness has not overcome the Light, and as many as receive Jesus as the Light receive the power to become the children of God (1:12). Following the way of Jesus is to be walking in the Light (8:12; 12:45), and the Holy Spirit convicts the world of both sin and of righteousness (16:8).

According to Charlesworth, the following dualistic pairs are found in the Qumran writings and also in John, a fact that had led some scholars to infer at least some sort of contact between those who formed the Johannine tradition and the ethos of the Qumran community.[50]

Fourth Gospel	1QS 3.14–4.26
the Spirit of Truth (14:17; 15:26; 16:13)	Spirit of Truth (3.18–19; 4.21, 23)
the Holy Spirit (14:26; 20:22)	the Spirit of Holiness (4.21)
sons of light (12:36)	sons of light (3.13, 24, 25)
eternal life (3:15, 16, 36; 5:24, *passim*)	in perpetual life (4.7)
the light of life (8:12)	in the light of life (3.7)
and he who walks in the darkness (12:35)	they . . . walk in the ways of darkness (3.21)
he will not walk in the darkness (8:12)	to walk in all the ways of darkness (4.11)
the wrath of God (3:36)	the furious wrath of God's vengeance (4.12)
the eyes of the blind (9:32; 10:21; 11:37)	blindness of eyes (4.11)
full of grace/fullness of grace (1:14, 16)	the fullness of grace/his grace (4.4, 5)
the works of God (6:28; 9:3)	the works of God (4.4)
their works (of men) were evil (3:19)	works of abomination/of a man (4.10, 20)

While there are significant similarities here, there are also differences. Brown's view that we have at least a common worldview articulated between these two movements within ancient Judaism is the best way forward. But if similarities do not imply direct contact, differences do not necessarily imply distance. Even the differences between the scrolls and the Gospel of John are significant for understanding more fully the Johannine ethos.

MESSIANISM

One of the striking things about perspectives on the Messiah in Qumran is the diversity of models that seem to be in play. The leading interpretation has

---

50. While Charlesworth outlines these technical terms elsewhere, his critical comparison is most fully laid out in his essay "A Critical Comparison of the Dualism in 1QS 3:13–4:26 and the 'Dualism' Contained in the Gospel of John," in Charlesworth, *John and Qumran*, 101–10; repr. from *NTS* 15 (1968–69): 389–418.

noted two "Messiahs" in the Qumran texts, that of "Aaron" and that of "Israel" (1QS 9.10–11), although a Prophet-like-Moses typology is also mentioned directly in that same context.[51] Initial discussions identified two messianic typologies in Qumran, one priestly and the other royal, but several objections have been raised. First, the reference to "Israel" is not necessarily a Davidic reference; it could be a reference to corporate Israel. Second, the two typologies could be seen as being fulfilled in the ministry of one person rather than referring to two different people.[52] Nevertheless, Craig Evans has suggested that the "two sons of oil" in 4Q254 frag. 42 and other passages argue for a diarchic view of the Messiah in Qumran involving a priestly figure and a royal figure,[53] reflecting a Qumranic embrace of two distinctive messianic leaders. Of course, the question is whether *only two* messianic typologies existed in Qumranic interpretation, or whether they accompanied additional associations.[54] In exploring not only these references, but also many others, Dietmar Neufeld argues for a vast proliferation of messianic typologies at Qumran, the sort of feature that is reflected in the vast number of messianic references in the Gospel of John.[55]

With relation to Johannine studies, three connections seem important. First, the great diversity of messianic presentation in the Fourth Gospel is not an anomaly; it is characteristic of messianic hope mingled with speculation as to how God might be working eschatologically in the redeeming of the world. Second, religious debates among characters in the Fourth Gospel as to whether Jesus was

---

51. On the "two Messiahs," see Karl G. Kuhn, "The Two Messiahs of Aaron and Israel," in *The Scrolls and the New Testament*, ed. Krister Stendahl (New York: Harper, 1957), 54–64; Raymond E. Brown, "The Messianism of Qumran," *CBQ* 19 (1957): 53–82; R. B. Laurin, "The Problem of Two Messiahs in the Qumran Scrolls," *RevQ* 4 (1963–64): 39–52; Emil A. Wcela, "The Messiah(s) of Qumran," *CBQ* 26 (1964): 340–49; Andrew Chester, *Messiah and Exaltation: Jewish Messianic and Visionary Traditions and New Testament Christology* (WUNT 207; Tübingen: Mohr Siebeck, 2007), 333–40. On Moses typology, see James E. Bowley, "Moses in the Dead Sea Scrolls: Living in the Shadow of God's Anointed," in *The Bible at Qumran: Text, Shape, and Interpretation*, ed. Peter W. Flint (Grand Rapids: Eerdmans, 2001), 159–81.

52. See George J. Brooke, "The Messiah of Aaron in the Damascus Document," *RevQ* 15 (1991): 215–30.

53. See Craig A. Evans, "'The Two Sons of Oil': Early Evidence of Messianic Expectation of Zechariah 4:14 in 4Q254 4 2," in *The Provo International Conference on the Dead Sea Scrolls: Technological Innovations, New Texts, and Reformulated Issues*, ed. Donald W. Parry and Eugene Ulrich (STDJ 30; Leiden: Brill, 1998), 566–75; "Diarchic Messianism in the Dead Sea Scrolls and the Messianism of Jesus of Nazareth," in Schiffman, Tov, and VanderKam, *Dead Sea Scrolls Fifty Years after Their Discovery*, 558–67.

54. D. L. Hurst sees the notion of "two Messiahs at Qumran" as a creation of modern scholars rather than a deduction from the evidence; see "Did Qumran Expect Two Messiahs?" *BBR* 9 (1999): 157–80.

55. Neufeld, "'And When That One Comes,'" 120–40. See also Anderson, *Christology of the Fourth Gospel*, 1–15.

indeed the Messiah (needing to have come from David's city, John 7:42; search-
ing the Scriptures but not having noted the one of whom Moses wrote, 1:45;
5:38–47) likely refer to real debates over the character and identity of the Messiah
in the ambivalent reception of Jesus and his mission. Third, the significance of
prophetic messianic typologies, including the Prophet-like-Moses (whose words
must come true; Deut 18:15–22) and the Prophet-like-Elijah (whose signs testify
to his authenticity), is pressing in both Qumranic and Johannine messianism. In
these ways, parallels between these two sets of messianic views are highly instructive for understanding the Johannine ethos and theology.

The Spirit of Truth

One of the interesting themes that emerges from Qumran-Johannine studies is the role of the Holy Spirit in John as prefigured by various images in the
Qumran writings. In the scrolls, the Spirit of Truth is contrasted to the Spirit of
Deception. The Holy Spirit, or Spirit of Righteousness, also denotes the means
by which God empowers the faithful to adhere to the way of the Torah, maintaining covenant faithfulness as opposed to falling short of full adherence. In
addition, the instructions of the Holy Spirit are the basis for community in Israel
(1QS 9.3), and God's enlightening work is a foundation for the Teacher of Righteousness and those who follow in his wake. In a creative synthesis of otherwise
disparate features, Otto Betz argued that the Qumranic presentation of the arch-
angel Michael, who communicates God's messages to the faithful and strengthens
them, serves as the religious backdrop for the Spirit/Paraclete that Jesus promises
to send.[56] From a slightly different angle, A. R. C. Leaney connected the original
advocacy and strengthening work of the Paraclete with that of the Father, which
the Son and the Holy Spirit carry out in their respective commissions.[57] Israel
Knohl drew particular connections between Menahem the Essene, described by
Josephus, and the leadership style of Jesus. Further, Knohl argues that the nouns
Menahem and *menahemim* mean "comfort/comforters" and implies that John's
presentation of Jesus and the ministry of the Holy Spirit, particularly the description of the Holy Spirit as "another" Paraclete (John 14:16), is rooted in stories of
Menahem, expressing "the unique concept of a *chain* of redeemers." If Jesus was a
second Menahem, the Holy Spirit is described in John as a third.[58] Finally, believ-

---

56. Otto Betz, *Der Paraklet: Fürsprecher im häretischen Spätjudentum, im Johannesevangelium und in neu gefundenen gnostischen Schriften* (AGSU 2; Leiden: Brill, 1963).

57. A. R. C. Leaney, "The Johannine Paraclete and the Qumran Scrolls," in Charlesworth,
John and Qumran, 38–61.

58. Israel Knohl, *The Messiah before Jesus: The Suffering Servant of the Dead Sea Scrolls*
(Berkeley and Los Angeles: University of California Press, 2000), 51–71, quote 71. See also A.
Shafaat, "Geber of the Qumran Scrolls and the Spirit-Paraclete of the Gospel of John," *NTS* 27
(1981): 263–69.

ers become commissioned as witnesses in the world, extending the agency of the Father by means of their faithfulness. In these and other ways, the Qumranic references to ways the Spirit of God interacts with humanity provide an important backdrop for understanding Johannine pneumatology and its implications for the faithful, as divine guidance is understood to be an important source of direction, effected by the Holy Spirit.

COMMUNITY DYNAMICS

One of the most important sets of insights to come from the Qumran writings is the sense of community life conveyed within this Jewish movement.[59] While the strict rules of joining and participating in this sectarian society probably did not apply in the same ways to the Johannine community in various phases of its development, some Quranic features do help us appreciate features that are distinctively Johannine. For instance, Jesus scholars have long noted the difference in the Synoptic Jesus' teachings about loving enemies and societal outcasts, whereas the Johannine Jesus commands his followers to "love one another" and to care for their own. This seems like an aberration—an inward-focused deviation from the outward-focused teachings of the Jesus of history. In the Community Rule, however, true followers of God are to "love everything He chose and to hate everything He rejected" (1QS 1.3) and "to love the Children of Light . . . and to hate the Children of Darkness" (1QS 1.9–10). Similarly in the Damascus Document, "Each one must love his brother as himself and support the poor, needy, and alien" (CD 6.20). While neither the Gospel nor the Epistles of John are as vehement in loving insiders and hating outsiders as the author(s) of 1QS, they seem to reflect a conventional set of concerns for members of one's religious community that was perfectly at home within contemporary Judaism, making the Johannine focus upon loving one another understandable. It is also a fact that the love of one's own does not preclude love for the outsider and alien (CD 6.20), so the Johannine silence on explicit commands to love one's enemies and neighbors should not be over-read.

SCRIPTURE AND ITS INTERPRETATION

One of the intriguing features of the Qumran writings is their reverence for Jewish Scripture, reflected in the many approaches to interpretation. While a good number of speculations have arisen which assume that a particular sort of

---

59. See Adriana Destro and Mauro Pesce, "The Gospel of John and the Community Rule of Qumran: A Comparison of Systems," in *Judaism in Late Antiquity, Part Five: The Judaism of Qumran, a Systemic Reading of the Dead Sea Scrolls*, ed. Alan J. Avery-Peck, Bruce Chilton, and Jacob Neusner, 2 vols. (Leiden: Brill, 2001), 2:201–29.

interpretation was characteristically in play, a more measured analysis of interpretive approaches to Scripture shows both the creativity and the real-life application exercised by the Teacher of Righteousness, followed by later generations of eschatological interpretation. Building on earlier analyses of forms of interpretation at Qumran, George Brooke outlined five types of biblical interpretation in the Qumran writings: legal, exhortatory, narrative, poetic, and prophetic.[60] Implications for Johannine studies are many. The Fourth Evangelist indeed shows a Jesus who challenges legal interpretations of Moses and the Law with his own (John 7:16–24); biblical themes are exposited by Jesus in exhortative ways (John 6:45 // Isa 54:13); narratives and events in Moses' day are appropriated by Jesus with relevance to his own mission (John 3:14 // Num 21:9); works of Moses are interpreted poetically (John 1:16–18); and biblical references are interpreted as prophecy fulfilled (John 19:32–37 // Ps 34:20; Zech 12:10). The relevance of this interpretive analysis of the use of Scripture in both the Qumranic and the Johannine writings is to invite the appreciation of the rich diversity of approach in both cases, helping interpreters avoid tendencies to overly generalize one particular approach or to insist on a singular pattern.

From these thematic parallels it is clear that there are a good number of topical similarities between the Johannine and Qumranic writings, and yet very few of them are exact parallels. They both have a monotheistic understanding of God as the source and destiny of the cosmic order while sketching the plight of humanity in dualistic terms. Challenges for humans are intensified by references to the workings of the two Spirits, leading either to truth or deception. While Qumranic dualism emphasizes divine judgment and violence far more intensely, the Johannine approach presents readers with a dualism of decision—to decide for or against the Revealer. In both sets of writings, a great diversity of approaches to messianic typologies and uses of Scripture can be seen, and this represents the creativity of contemporary Judaism of the day. With regard to community life, the Qumranic sociology has a far more sectarian character in contrast to the more permeable and boundary-bridging ethos of the Johannine situation. While Johannine community members (or even their mentors, if John the Baptizer played a role in forming the Johannine ethos) may have had some firsthand contact with Qumran society, such an inference is not required to account for the large number of parallels between the writings. Even in their differences and contrasts, however, these analyses are helpful for understanding the Johannine ethos and message.

---

60. George J. Brooke, "Biblical Interpretation at Qumran," in Charlesworth, *Bible and the Dead Sea Scrolls*, 1.287–319.

COMMAS, MUNDANE DETAILS, PHRASES, AND CONCEPTUAL CONSTRUCTS

In addition to topical themes, a variety of mundane details, phrases, and conceptual constructs deserve at least a brief consideration. The sheer number of parallels in particular details between the scrolls and the Johannine writings shows that individual intersections should not be viewed as anomalies. Again, while the relationship between the Qumranic and Johannine communities remains a question, these sets of connections remain suggestive for Johannine research. Whether the parallels are similar or dissimilar, they nonetheless are instructive for getting a better sense of the development of Johannine Christianity in its own trajectory. That being the case, both history and theology in John are affected by these comparisons and contrasts.

The minimal conclusion from the mundane parallels between the Qumranic and Johannine writings is that both operated from a similar perspective and worldview, drawing on Hebrew Scripture typologies and texts in addressing later religious challenges within their communities and beyond. While an exhaustive assessment of the particular relationship between the two compilations is beyond the scope of this essay, it might be helpful to be reminded of a digest of the various approaches to the question before looking briefly at several notable examples. In reviewing the various parallels in shared symbolism and language between the Qumranic and Johannine communities, James Charlesworth offers five "attractive hypotheses" as to how the Qumran Scrolls have influenced the Fourth Gospel.[61]

1. John the Baptizer had once been a member of the Qumran Community, Jesus was his disciple, and Jesus passed some of the unique Qumran terms on to his own disciples; or,

2. The Beloved Disciple, Jesus' intimate follower, had been a disciple of the Baptizer who had been a member of the Qumran Community, and he influenced Jesus and some of his followers; or,

3. Jesus met Essenes on the outskirts of towns and cities in Galilee and Judea, discussed theology with them, and was influenced by some of their ideas and terms; or,

4. Essenes lived in Jerusalem (or Ephesus) near the Johannine community and influenced the development of Johannine theology; or,

5. Essenes became followers of Jesus and lived in the Johannine School, shaping the dualism, pneumatology, and technical terms in the Fourth Gospel. This could have happened in numerous places, including Jerusalem.

In reflecting upon Johannine evidence for these approaches, the first two scenarios seem the most likely, accounting for the Qumranic material within the Johannine writings in an efficient and straightforward way. The Beloved Disciple,

---

61. James H. Charlesworth, "A Study in Shared Symbolism," 3.97–152.

if presented in John 1, may indeed have been one of the earliest disciples to leave their former master, the Baptizer, and follow Jesus. If the Baptizer was steeped in Qumranic ethos, that factor in itself could account for many of the ways the mission of Jesus is presented in cosmological terms—being cast in a struggle between light and darkness. Of course, the other theories of Jesus, the Johannine leadership, or the Johannine community having had contact with Essenes in Palestine and/or Asia Minor are entirely plausible, and there is no reason to discount their likelihood. Even informal contacts with Qumranic cosmology and ethos would have been "in the air" within first-century C.E. Judaism, and that would have included Palestine and surrounding regions, as well as Asia Minor, or whatever setting in which the Johannine community may have developed. Therefore, some combination of direct and indirect contacts between the Johannine tradition and Qumranic Judaism is likely, a reality that explains the numerous minor parallels between the Johannine writings and the scrolls.

Clues to the Baptizer's Ministry

From the beginning of the discoveries, Qumranic clues to the ministry of John the Baptizer have abounded, casting new light on the Johannine presentation of his ministry and his connection with both Jesus and the Fourth Evangelist. First, if John indeed was baptizing across the Jordan (John 1:28; 10:40) and was associated with Elijah (Matt 11:14; Mark 6:15; 8:28; Luke 1:17; but cf. John 1:21), this could locate his ministry just a few miles from Qumran. If he was or had been a member of the Qumran community, this might also account for his rugged appearance and unconventional diet. Second, the presentation of John's citing Isa 40:3 as the basis for his mission connects with the Qumranic description of the party of the Yahad (twelve laymen and three priests) who were to consecrate themselves for two years in the wilderness, grounding themselves in the way of truth by abiding in the law of righteousness (1QS 8.14; 9.19–20). This is entirely commensurate with John the Baptizer's claim to be a voice crying in the wilderness, making straight the way of the Lord (John 1:23). Third, John the Baptizer's teachings resemble many features of the ethos of Qumran, including his emphasis on righteousness (Matt 21:32) and baptizing as a call to repentance (Mark 1:4).[62] Fourth, John's baptism with water carries forth a central Qumranic concern with purification and cleansing, although it also is very different from Qumranic bathing. Rather than bathing twice a day, or having a ritualized approach to purification, John's baptism appears to have been a singular and pivotal experience.

---

62. In particular, his confronting of Herod for taking his brother's wife (Mark 6:18) reflects ethical concerns echoed in the Damascus Document (CD 4.21–5.1), where taking two wives is forbidden (in keeping with Jewish Scripture). Other aspects of keeping the Law rigorously are implied.

And, rather than simply continuing a standard process of purification, it appears to have been bestowed upon individuals who had already repented of their sins. These comparative and contrastive details confirm at least some sort of connection between John the Baptizer and the Qumran community, and the inference that he had probably spent some time there is by no means implausible.[63] Given this likelihood, the presentation of the Baptizer's followers becoming followers of Jesus in John 1:19–51 provides an important set of plausible contacts between the Johannine presentation of Jesus and the ethos and theology of Qumran.

Archaeological and Topographical Details

In addition to illuminating the ministry of John the Baptizer with implications for understanding better the interests of the Johannine Evangelist and the ministry of Jesus, a variety of other archaeological and topographical discoveries at Qumran are also significant. First, a historic clue to the five porticoes surrounding the Pool of Bethesda (also Beth-zatha) mentioned in John 5:2 is provided by the description of two pools in Jerusalem in the Copper Scroll. If "Beth Esdatayin" can be taken to refer to "the House of the Two Pools," four porticoes surrounded two adjoining pools with one portico separating them.[64] Confirmed by archaeological discoveries of such a site in Jerusalem, accompanied by Aesclepius images, this Johannine presentation of the Jerusalem healing setting is found to be more historical than it was earlier thought to be. Second, a clue to the six stone jars holding twenty or thirty gallons each in John 2:6 is provided in 11QTemple 50.10–19, where the impurity of clay jars is mentioned, suggesting the purity necessity of alternatives, such as stone vessels. A third archaeological clue to the Johannine presentation of Jesus and the Baptizer relates to the *mikva'ot,* the cleansing pools, found at Qumran. While theories vary as to which deep pools were used for drinking water storage and which ones were used for bathing, one pool in particular has three staircases coming up, with one going down, separated by a divider. The reason for this division is that if impurity was transmitted by touch, a bather coming up would not want to be contaminated

---

63. See, for example, James Charlesworth's explanation that, if John the Baptizer was indeed the son of a Zadokite priest, some sort of contact with this community with clear priestly associations is entirely plausible, although impossible to prove ("John the Baptizer and the Dead Sea Scrolls," in Charlesworth, *Bible and the Dead Sea Scrolls,* 3.1–35).

64. See Charlesworth, "Dead Sea Scrolls and the Gospel," 65–97; M. Baillet, J. T. Milik, and Roland de Vaux, eds., *Les 'petites grottes' de Qumrân* (DJD III; 2 vols.; Oxford: Clarendon, 1962), 1.214, 271–72; Joachim Jeremias, *The Rediscovery of Bethesda* (Louisville: Southern Baptist Theological Seminary, 1966), 11–12; John J. Rousseau and Rami Arav, eds., *Jesus and His World: An Archaeological and Cultural Dictionary* (Minneapolis: Fortress Press, 1995), 156. See also Urban von Wahlde, "Archaeology and John's Gospel," in *Jesus and Archaeology,* ed. James H. Charlesworth (Grand Rapids: Eerdmans, 2006), 560–66.

by the "unclean" state of ones coming down into the water. Therefore, gradations of removal from impurity are implied. This would have been similar in function to the purification pools one would have used in entering the temple area. That being the case, John the Baptizer's conjoining of ethical reform and washing in a noncultic setting appears to be a challenge to cultic purity, suggesting an alternative understanding of Jesus' early challenging of the temple system in the Fourth Gospel. Might Jesus be presented as taking further the Baptizer's challenge to ritual means of purity in the inaugural temple cleansing in the Fourth Gospel? While such a narrative interest cannot be confirmed or disconfirmed critically, the religious realism now disclosed by Qumran archaeology raises some interesting possibilities for consideration. These details not only bolster support for John's historicity but they also convey echoes of John's theology.

METAPHORICAL AND THEMATIC REFERENCES

Several common metaphors and themes between the Qumranic and Johannine writings are also worth noting. First, "living water" is associated in Qumran with spiritual blessing—a clear reflection of the need to have running water in contrast to stagnant pools if water is to be effective for drinking or cleansing. The importance of collecting running water is illustrated by the many cisterns in Qumran and their carefully engineered feeder streams. In 4Q504 4.1–21, the writer laments that people have abandoned "the fount of living water" and "have served a foreign god in their land." This lament is followed by the grateful prayer, "You have poured out your holy spirit upon us." The connection of "living water" and pouring out of the Holy Spirit found in John 7:38–39 reflects an intriguing Qumranic parallel. Second, parallel to the Matthean and Johannine references to "the light of the world" (Matt 5:14; John 8:12; 9:5), covenanters are encouraged in 4Q541 frag. 24 7 that "you will grow and understand and be glad in the light of the world; you will not be a disowned vessel." Third, references to "eternal life" are made in both sets of writings, and while eternal life is a prevalent theme in the Synoptics, its attainment is a central focus of the Johannine appeal to believe (John 3:15–16, 39; 20:31). Similarly, eternal life is presented in 1QS 4.6–8 as a "gracious visitation" through which "all who walk in this spirit will know healing, bountiful peace, long life, and multiple progeny, followed by eternal blessings, and perpetual joy through life everlasting." And, CD 3.20 describes eternal life as the result of remaining faithful to the religious (and priestly) house of Israel. Fourth, the "works of God" are described in CD 2.14–15 as what God commands, and this is indeed parallel to the request of the crowd in John 6:28, "What must we do to perform the works of God?"[65] Fifth, references to "idols" in 1QS 2.11–

---

65. Although one can also render ἐργαζώμεθα as "get" ("to *receive* a miraculous work") rather than "perform" (as in "work the works of God"), the conventional parallel to Qumran

12 and 4Q271 frag. 2 9 demonstrate interesting parallels with the last verse of the first Johannine Epistle (1 John 5:21): "Little children, keep yourselves from idols." While idolatry in 1 John was probably a direct reference to forbidding participation in cultic festivals in a Greco-Roman context, the reference in 1QS 2.11–12 guards against bringing idolatry into the community, and 4Q271 frag. 2 9 simply mentions the materials of which idols were made. In these metaphorical connections between the Qumranic and Johannine writings many parallels exist, both comparative and contrastive.

THE TEACHER OF RIGHTEOUSNESS VERSUS THE WICKED PRIEST AND OTHER VILLAINS

While impressive similarities exist between the Teacher of Righteousness and Jesus, parallels also extend to leaders within the Johannine situation. Likewise, the Johannine adversaries are presented in the Gospel and Epistles in ways parallel to the villainous Wicked Priest in the Qumranic literature. As a radical interpreter of the Law, the Righteous Teacher advocated a vision of following Moses and the Prophets; from a religious and political stance, he and his community must be considered the losers. He met opposition from more powerful priests in Jerusalem, and whoever "the Wicked Priest" might have been, this individual apparently asserted his influence against the Teacher. Likewise, the Johannine Jesus challenged the religious leaders in Jerusalem with a vision of adhering to the heart of the Law. The Fourth Gospel alone shows a sustained history of engagement between Jesus and Jerusalem leaders, involving at least four visits to Jerusalem, resulting in sustained challenges to Jesus' teachings and authority. While particular priests (Caiaphas, Annas) are portrayed with high esteem in John (even making prophecies about Jesus' atoning death, perhaps unwittingly, at John 11:47–53), it is some of the Jewish leaders in Jerusalem (not all of them) that sought to have Jesus put to death. That being the case, the Johannine narrative might actually inform the socio-religious situation in Jerusalem leading to the Qumranic secession.[66]

During the second period of the Johannine movement (70–85 C.E.), the challenges faced by the Beloved Disciple and other Johannine leaders in Asia Minor would have found parallels with the Qumranic leadership, especially as later

---

still stands. See Anderson, *Christology of the Fourth Gospel*, 200–202.

66. See Håkan Bengtsson, "Three Sobriquets, Their Meaning and Function: The Wicked Priest, Synagogue of Satan, and the Woman Jezebel," in Charlesworth, *Bible and the Dead Sea Scrolls*, 1:183–208; David Noel Freedman and Jeffrey C. Geoghegan, "Another Stab at the Wicked Priest," in Charlesworth, *Bible and the Dead Sea Scrolls*, 2:17–24; Martin G. Abegg Jr., "Who Ascended to Heaven? 4Q491, 4Q427, and the Teacher of Righteousness," in *Eschatology, Messianism, and the Dead Sea Scrolls*, ed. Craig A. Evans and Peter W. Flint (Grand Rapids MI: Eerdmans, 1997), 61–73.

generations of leaders sought to further the original vision and mission of the Teacher of Righteousness. Interesting parallels between the Johannine Epistles and the Qumranic writings include accusations of lying and deception. In the Johannine situation, such allegations are levied at false teachers who probably encouraged social and religious assimilation within their Greco-Roman civic setting, and yet Diotrephes as a local church leader is also accused of spreading untruths about Johannine believers (3 John 9–10). Parallel to the Qumranic leaders, the Johannine leaders elevate a primary value against a competing, false value, but we see it in two phases—a Palestinian phase and an Asia Minor phase. In Qumran the dichotomy was all Jewish: the Righteous Teacher versus the Wicked Priest. In the Johannine Gospel, Jesus the authentic prophet confronts the leading Judeans; in the Johannine Epistles, authentic Christ-followers confront the Antichrists (1 John 2:18–25; 4:1–3; 2 John 7) and also Diotrephes the primacy lover (3 John 1:9–10). In the Qumranic and Johannine writings, community heroes are similarly exalted, while familiar adversaries are countered with parallel pejorative rhetoric.

ASSOCIATIONS WITH JESUS AS THE CHRIST

In addition to the discussion of messianism noted above, some terms that appear in the scrolls are interesting simply because of their similarity to the presentation of Jesus as the Christ in the Gospel of John. First, "Son of God" also appears in the Qumran writings (see esp. 4Q246 frag. 2 1, "He will be called the Son of God, they will call him the son of the Most High"), apparently in reference to a false pretender whose reign will fall like a meteor.[67] Note the requirement of Jesus' death articulated by the Jerusalem leaders in John 19:7, where they accuse him of a capital offense in claiming to be the "Son of God." Therefore, "Son of God" can no longer be regarded as a purely Hellenistic messianic construct; it is in play here in sectarian Judaism a full century before Jesus' ministry. Second, clear criteria are presented for how to distinguish the authentic prophet from the false prophet. A collection of messianic proof texts anticipating the Prophet-like-Moses appears in 4Q175 1.1–4 (Deut 5:28–29) and 1.5–8 (Deut 18:18–19), and the test of a true prophet follows in 4Q375 (fulfilling Deut 18:18–22—the words of the authentic prophet must be heeded; the false prophet "must be put to death") and the Moses Apocryphon in 4Q377. Conversely, traits of false prophets

---

67. John J. Collins also notes the apocalyptic features of this title, "The Son of God Text from Qumran," in *From Jesus to John: Essays on Jesus and New Testament Christology in Honour of Marinus de Jonge*, ed. Martinus C. de Boer (JSNTSup 8; Sheffield: JSOT Press, 1993), 65–82. See also Joseph A. Fitzmyer, S.J., "The Aramaic 'Son of God' Text from Qumran Cave 4," in *Methods of Investigation of the Dead Sea Scrolls and the Khirbet Qumran Site: Present Realities and Future Prospects*, ed. Michael O. Wise et al. (New York: New York Academy of Sciences, 1994), 163–78.

in Israel are outlined in 4Q339. Similarly, debates over Jesus' authenticity in John 5–10 orbit around whether he is indeed the prophet predicted by Moses in Deut 18. Third, Elijah/Elisha typologies are developed in several passages, notably in the Apocryphon of Elijah (4Q382). As Jesus is portrayed as performing Elijah-type miracles in John (raising Lazarus from the dead, feeding the multitude with barley loaves), the Baptizer's denial of being either the Prophet or Elijah in John 1:19–27 serves the Evangelist's presentation of these two typologies being fulfilled in the ministry of Jesus. Fourth, the mention of the "eyes of the blind" (1QS 4.11) and the raising of the dead (4Q521) clearly resonate with Jesus' ministry in the Gospel of John (see John 9:39–41; 10:21; 11:1–52). Fifth, in a fascinating analysis of connections between the 153 days of Noah's flood in 4Q252 1.8–10 and the 153 fish mentioned at John 21:11, George Brooke suggests new insights for understanding this detail's meaning in the light of Jesus' mission.[68] Both in their similarity and dissimilarity, echoes with the scrolls abound in the Johannine presentation of Jesus as the Christ.

THE "TWO WAYS" AND THEIR IMPLICATIONS

Parallel to "the two ways" (the way of life and the way of death) in the *Didache*, a clear exposition on the two ways appears in 4Q473, inspired by Deut 11:26–28. In addition to parallels with "the narrow gate" and way leading to life versus the road to destruction in Matt 7:13–14, there are significant parallels in John 6:27–71, where Jesus invites his audience to choose the food that leads to life (which he gives) over food that leads to death. While 4Q473 frag. 2 2–7 promises blessing for following the way of life in contrast to the plight of those who follow the way of evil, John 6 calls for solidarity with Jesus and the way of his community instead of settling for lesser alternatives. In contrast to J. Louis Martyn's two-level, history-and-theology interpretation of John 9, the four sets of discussants in John 6 (the crowd, the Jews, the disciples, Peter) echo at least four challenges within the history of the Johannine situation during its second and third phases (70–100 C.E.).[69] Rather than exposing a singular crisis in the Johannine dialectical situation, the "challenge of the two ways" in John 6 addresses four largely-sequential-yet-somewhat-overlapping crises in the Johannine situation.[70]

---

68. George J. Brooke, "4Q252 and the 153 Fish of John 21.11," in his *Dead Sea Scrolls and the New Testament: Essays in Mutual Illumination* (Minneapolis: Fortress, 2005), 282–97.

69. See J. Louis Martyn, *History and Theology in the Fourth Gospel* (3d ed.; Louisville: Westminster John Knox, 2003).

70. See Paul N. Anderson, "The *Sitz im Leben* of the Johannine Bread of Life Discourse and its Evolving Context," in *Critical Readings of John 6*, ed. R. Alan Culpepper (BIS 22; Atlanta: Society of Biblical Literature, 2006), 1–59, for a description of these four alternative death-producing "ways"—a materialistic view of Jesus' works versus their signifying power, the "bread" that Moses gave versus that which the Father gives, the bread of the flesh of Jesus given for the

As John 6 was probably added to an earlier edition of the Gospel, the exhortation to chose the way of life—the life-producing food that Jesus offers versus its lesser alternatives—shows signs of being crafted for audience relevance as the Johannine narration developed. On this score, Qumranic and Johannine appeals to the way of life versus the way of death will be mutually informative.

QUESTION MARKS? SUGGESTIONS FOR FURTHER INQUIRY

In the light of the above history of research on Qumran and the Fourth Gospel, a number of questions follow. One cannot help but notice how the discussion has moved from discovery and grand hopes of promise, to a disparagement of the relationship, to a set of more nuanced approaches regarding the Johannine-Qumranic relationship. While direct contact need not be inferred to imply influence, and while even differences may provide important insights into Johannine faith and practice, finding the right tools and methods for ascertaining the Johannine ethos will be central to the success of one's investigation. That being the case, the following questions invite consideration, providing suggestions for further inquiry.

First, *What light do John the Baptizer's likely connections with Qumran shed on the Johannine perspective regarding his mission and the ministry of Jesus?* The Johannine presentation of John's baptizing across the Jordan (John 1:28; 3:26; 10:40) bears a good deal of topographical realism. Over the last decade or so, archaeological research in the vicinity of Wadi al-Kharrar has shown it to be the likely historical site of John's baptismal ministry.[71] This area is also associated with the ministries of Moses and Elijah, so one can understand how John would have been interpreted as following in the trajectories of Moses ("the Prophet") and Elijah (Mark 6:15; 8:28; John 1:21). What is odd, however, is that in the Fourth Gospel John claims that he is neither the Prophet nor Elijah, in contrast

---

life of the world on the cross, and Jesus' possession of the words of life versus emerging structural institutionalism.

71. The archaeological site at Wadi Kharrar is just east of the Jordan River (between Qumran and Jericho), showing a large natural pool in which Christian baptisms have been performed going back at least to the Byzantine area—even referred to by Origen as "Bethabara" after visiting the area on a personal investigation. This may be the site referred to as "Beth-bara" on the Jordan mentioned in Judg 7:25. See also Michele Piccirillo, "The Sanctuaries of the Baptism on the East Bank of the Jordan River," in *Jesus and Archaeology*, ed. James H. Charlesworth (Grand Rapids: Eerdmans, 2006), 433–43. Against a northern Jordan site, Batanaea, Matthew records the Jordan baptizing work of John as being in Judea—the south (Matt 3:1). Of course, John could have been baptizing in the north, as well; if he also baptized in Aenon near Salim (John 3:23) in Samaria, he could have baptized throughout Palestine, including the northern Jordan, which was near Bethsaida—the home of Philip, Peter, and Andrew (John 1:44).

with the presentations of the Baptizer in the Synoptics.[72] It seems that the Fourth Evangelist seeks to portray Jesus, not John, as fulfilling Moses and Elijah typologies. This is one case where the Johannine departure from Mark likely reflects theological rather than historical interests.

Second, *How does the multiplicity of messianic typologies in Qumran affect our understanding of Johannine Christology and its developments?* A striking fact about Qumran expectations of a priestly messiah (Aaron) and a royal messiah (Israel) is that it shows the diversity of messianic expectation in Israel leading up to the ministry of Jesus. While distinct from anticipated messianic typologies, the Teacher of Righteousness assumes a Prophet-like-Moses identity, therefore featuring anticipations of God's anointed agent as the Prophet, Priest, and King.[73] This makes it understandable how different messianic typologies are presented among the Gospel traditions; further, it helps to clarify why some of the Judean leaders refused to believe in Jesus. In John 7:42, this diversity of perspective is illustrated by the fact that the Judean religious leaders understand "the Prophet" to come from David's city, leading them to reject Galilean credentials out of hand. Conversely, the Galilean crowd in John 6:14–15 interprets Jesus as a prophet-king like Moses, although he rejects their attempts to rush him off for a hasty coronation.[74]

Third, *How do the distinctive dualisms of Qumran and the Johannine writings illumine experiential and ideological features of these communities' situations and histories?* Discussions regarding Johannine and Qumranic dualism have too often centered around cosmology and theology, when the primary occasion for dualistic thought was experiential disappointment and loss, accompanied by rhetorical and moral interests. The operative question, therefore, is how leaders in both of these Jewish communities interpreted community experiences and hopes in the light of dualistic constructs. The Qumranic sketch of cosmological warfare in the War Scroll, wherein Children of Light are presented as being at war with Children of Darkness, maintains two primary contentions: first, that those who reject the message and stance of the Qumran covenanters are wrong (and thus in the dark rather than in the light); second, that God will be the final judge,

---

72. It was from Mount Nebo that Moses glimpsed the Promised Land (Deut 34:1–5), and near this site that Elijah's mantle was transferred to Elisha (2 Kings 2:1–15) by striking the water with it, causing the parting of the Jordan. Another water reference is made to Elisha's legitimation as an authentic prophet, because he is remembered as pouring water over the hands of Elijah (2 Kings 3:11).

73. Richard A. Horsley, "The Dead Sea Scrolls and the Historical Jesus," in Charlesworth, *Bible and the Dead Sea Scrolls*, 3:37–60.

74. For an extensive analysis of prophet-king messianic expectations in first-century Palestine, see Wayne Meeks, *The Prophet-King: Moses Traditions and the Johannine Christology* (NovTSup 14; Leiden: Brill, 1967). See also the central role of Moses in Jewish messianic ideals, despite competing typologies, in Bowley, "Moses in the Dead Sea Scrolls," 159–81.

bringing the faithful to victory over their adversaries, who appear to have gotten the upper hand, at least for now. The Johannine dualism moves out of a similar structure, although the elements are different. In John, it is not the Children of Light who are rejected, but it is *Jesus as the light of the world* who is rejected by religious leaders, whose sin is that they claim to see (9:41). Further, the Evangelist explains this reality more as a reflection of their not having been rooted in God to begin with, or at least loving darkness rather than light (3:17–21). In that sense, both employ dualism as a means of explaining disappointment and the rejection of their communities' convictions. But the Qumranic interpretation sketches the outcome in terms of cosmological warfare, while the Johannine interpretation explains the reception on the basis of a dualism of decision. In presenting the truth-rejecting world as loving darkness rather than light, and the praise of men over the glory of God, the Johannine ethical dualism is structured more closely to Plato's "Allegory of the Cave" than Qumran's cosmic warfare.

Fourth, *What do the dialogical relationships between Qumran leaders and Jerusalem suggest about the Galilean Jesus and his Judean rejections in John?* Distinctive to the Johannine presentation of Jesus is his adversarial relationship with Jerusalem leaders—the Ἰουδαίοι—especially the priests and defenders of the Law and temple. Territoriality only exists between competing members of like species, and just as the Qumran leadership seems to have been in conflict with the priests of Jerusalem *as* a priestly tradition, the conflicts reported between the northern prophet and the Jerusalem leaders in the Fourth Gospel suggest some interesting parallels as well. Just as it would be wrong to accuse the Qumran covenanters of being anti-Semitic because they were at odds with Jerusalem priests, so it is wrong to see the Fourth Evangelist as anti-Semitic because the Jerusalem leaders are portrayed as rejecting the prophet from Galilee. If anything, the Johannine Jesus is presented as advocating a radical view of Judaism that fulfills the vision of Moses and the Prophets in a deeply spiritual way. Therefore, while some of the Ἰουδαίοι in John believe, the unbelieving Ἰουδαίοι should be seen as Judean leaders who reject the revealer and his revelation in the name of religious conventions.[75] Put otherwise, it is unlikely that the Qumran covenanters were the only devout and conservative Jewish group to have been alienated by Jerusalem's priestly establishment; Jesus and his followers likely experienced similar treatment and faced tensions with Jerusalocentric leaders. Therefore, sociological analyses of the Jerusalem-Qumran tensions and the Jerusalem-Jesus movement tensions would both benefit from comparative analysis. They show similar yet different experiences of Jewish religious movements that came to be at odds with

---

75. James Charlesworth puts this point well in "The Dead Sea Scrolls and the Gospel according to John," 65–97. The tensions with οἱ Ἰουδαίοι in the Fourth Gospel reflect not anti-Semitism, but rather north-south tensions between the Galilean prophet and Judean religious leaders.

religious leaders in Jerusalem, leading to similar yet different developments, one becoming a sectarian community in Qumran, and the other becoming a form of Jewish outreach to the nations in the Pauline and Johannine missions.

Fifth, *Are there parallels between the functions of the Teacher of Righteousness and the Beloved Disciple and what happened with leadership transitions following them?* While parallels between the Teacher of Righteousness and Jesus are telling, the relation between the Teacher of Righteousness and the Beloved Disciple may be even more significant within Johannine studies. Of particular interest is the way these leaders of their respective communities exercised their roles and how they conveyed their understandings of religious truth. Where the Teacher of Righteousness was working with his understanding of Torah and other Scriptures, the Beloved Disciple also sought to develop an understanding of how Jesus' ministry should be remembered, including how it fulfilled Scripture and continued to be relevant for later generations. That being the case, there may be value in analyzing approaches to Scripture in both the Qumran and Johannine writings and in noting how authoritative leadership is transferred from one generation to later ones within a religious community setting.

Sixth, *How do new understandings of the social situations of the Qumran community and Johannine Christianity impact our understandings of the contents of their respective writings?* If Kåre Fuglseth is correct to interpret John's Gospel as more cultic than sectarian, closer to the situation of Philo than Qumran, this could be highly significant. Both in its Palestinian experience (in my view, 30–70 c.e.) and in its Asia Minor settings (in my view, 70–100 c.e.),[76] a too-narrow view of the Johannine sociological situation as "sectarian" is flawed if conceived as a Qumranic sort of existence. In Palestine, Johannine Christianity would have reflected the north-south dialectic between Galilee and Judea, and it would have faced similar tensions with Jerusalem authorities as did the Qumranic leadership. However, rather than being a conservative appeal for stricter adherence to the Law and its implications, the Johannine appeal would have been more liberal—spiritualizing cultic and religious themes and challenging their literalistic interpretations. Taking the revelatory work of the Holy Spirit beyond the mere illumination of the biblical text, the Johannine identification of Jesus as fulfilling the agency role of the Prophet-like-Moses (Deut 18:15–22) would have challenged alternate approaches to Moses and the Prophets. In continuity with the original challenge posed by Jesus of Nazareth, this appeal to continuing revelation would have met resistance in Judea and beyond. Therefore, when the Johannine leadership translocated to the setting of one of the mission churches, plausibly

---

76. See Paul N. Anderson, *The Fourth Gospel and the Quest for Jesus: Modern Foundations Reconsidered* (LNTS 321; London: T&T Clark, 2006), 193–99, for a two-edition theory of Johannine composition and an outline of the history of the Johannine situation involving seven dialogical engagements over seven decades.

around 70 C.E. as a result of the Roman destruction of Jerusalem, dialogues with local Jewish communities expanded to engage local Gentile audiences with the news that Jesus was indeed the Messiah/Christ. Rather than fostering a sectarian existence within this Asia Minor setting (no other setting is more plausible than Ephesus and its environs), Johannine believers sought to draw Jewish and Gentile audiences alike into a believing relationship to Jesus as the Messiah/Christ. As the second and third phases of Johannine Christianity (70–85 and 85–100 C.E., respectively) saw the movement from a primary community to a multiplicity of communities as the Jesus movement continued to expand, this would have included more and more Gentile believers within the Johannine movement. Therefore, in their inclusion of Gentile believers into their worship life, it might be argued that, rather than being *between* the social settings of Qumran and Philo (with Fuglseth), the Johannine churches might be placed *on the other side of Philo* with regard to their Gentile outreach. Johannine audiences were exhorted to resist the world (John 17; 1 John 2) precisely because they were living in it.

Seventh, *What are the literary-rhetorical parallels between the Qumranic and Johannine writings?* In addition to sociological interests, a variety of new literary analyses of the Johannine and Qumranic writings are worth considering. Despite impressive differences between these two sets of writings, comparative analyses could still be highly suggestive. For instance, ways that both sets of writings approached Hebrew Scripture, articulated and motivated adherence to community values and standards, produced worship material, and recorded their history and aspirations will be relevant to such studies. As new literary approaches are applied to Qumranic writings, this will undoubtedly cast valuable light on the Johannine writings as well. In addition, the workings of the Johannine composition and editing processes will receive assistance from noting how the Qumran authors and editors worked.[77] At least one example is worth mentioning here. If indeed there appears to have been more than one beginning in the Temple Scroll, it is not unlikely that the Johannine Gospel was also composed with more than one beginning and more than one ending.[78]

These questions regarding future directions of Qumranic-Johannine research concern themselves more with the analysis of sociological parallels and their implications. In contrast to earlier interests seeking to establish direct or indirect influences, more recent studies have approached their analyses by noting the similarities and differences, making good use of contrastive features as well as comparative ones. In addition, as archaeological discoveries continue to be made

---

77. See Pilgaard, "The Qumran Scrolls," 126–42; Popkes, "About the Differing Approach," 281–317.

78. See George J. Brooke's analysis in "The *Temple Scroll* in the New Testament," in his *Dead Sea Scrolls and the New Testament: Essays in Mutual Illumination* (Minneapolis: Fortress, 2005), 97–114.

regarding the living conditions, sociology, economics, and character of the Qumranic situation, insights continue to emerge regarding what is known about this
Jewish movement.[79] That being the case, any solid knowledge about Qumran will
be applicable to biblical studies in general and Johannine studies in particular.

CONCLUSION

As the above survey suggests, similarities between the Qumran and Johannine
communities are no longer seen as requiring firsthand contact between these two
sectors of ancient Judaism, although some early contact likely existed. Further, as
much can be learned from the differences as the similarities, and more nuanced
analyses profit from contrasts as well as comparisons. As socio-religious analyses
of Qumran and Second Temple Judaism cast valuable light on the situation out
of which the Jesus and Johannine movements emerged, the Qumran writings will
continue to be a valuable source of information for conducting Johannine studies
as well.

As new discoveries lend themselves to additional insights, interpretation
will continue to grow in both Qumranic and Johannine fields of investigation.
Ironically, one of the unintended consequences of Qumranic-Johannine analyses
is that, as a result of learning more about contemporary Judaism, the Johannine writings are liberated from the need to be understood in the light of
contemporary Hellenistic literature alone.[80] They have now come to be interpreted
authentically as Jewish writings reflecting a movement in the process of indi-
viduating from its parent religious background, within a Hellenistic setting, and
thus undergoing the throes of reaching in several directions at once. If indeed
the Qumranic Yahad can claim, "When, united by all these precepts, such men as
these come to be a community in Israel, they shall establish eternal truth guided
by the instruction of His holy spirit" (1QS 9.3–4), the Johannine community was
by no means alone in its aspirations and ethos.

---

79. See especially here the important work of Eileen Schuller, *The Dead Sea Scrolls: What
Have We Learned?* (Louisville: Westminster John Knox, 2006).

80. While he does not do much with the Qumran writings in this setting, the famous
essay by James D. G. Dunn, "Let John Be John: A Gospel for Its Time" (in *The Gospel and the
Gospels*, ed. Peter Stuhlmacher [Grand Rapids: Eerdmans, 1991], 293–322), argues that John's
autonomy receives a boost from being considered in the light of contemporary Judaism, including the Dead Sea Scrolls.

PART 2
NEW APPROACHES AND APPLICATIONS

"MYSTERY" IN THE DEAD SEA SCROLLS AND THE
FOURTH GOSPEL

John Ashton

Twenty years ago I argued that although the actual words *mystery* and *revelation* are not found there, the Gospel of John is nonetheless related and indeed heavily indebted to Jewish apocalyptic, where the concept of a revealed mystery is all-important. In this essay I wish to return to this subject by emphasizing that certain ideas found in the Dead Sea Scrolls, especially in one key document that had not been published when I was engaged in the composition of *Understanding the Fourth Gospel*, are also important to John.[1]

In the first part of this essay, I want to focus on the phrase רז נהיה, asking (1) what, in this particular context, it *denotes* or refers to; and (2) what it *means*, and how it should be translated. The all-too-frequent confusion of these two questions is a major source of difficulty. The examination of this phrase will lead into a study of its association with the concept of *wisdom* and an inquiry concerning what this can add to our understanding of the Johannine notion of the Logos. The second part of the essay will address two related issues: (1) what is the relationship between Qumran's רז נהיה and Israel's revealed Law?, and (2) what is the understanding at Qumran and among the Johannine community of the new heavenly revelation ("truth") and of the special life that it confers?

MYSTERY

I begin with an overview and analysis of various contexts in which the term נהיה רז appears in the Qumran documents. The first appearance is in 1QMysteries:

The author wishes to acknowledge his indebtedness to the British Academy for funding that enabled him to present the paper on which this essay is based at the SBL meeting in San Diego, November 2007.

1. John Ashton, *Understanding the Fourth Gospel* (Oxford: Clarendon, 1991), ch. 10.

They know not *the mystery to come* (רז נהיה) nor do they understand the things of the past. They know not that which shall befall them, nor do they save their soul from *the mystery to come*.[2]

Ever since 1955, when Milik and Barthélemy published 1QMysteries in the first volume of *Discoveries in the Judaean Desert*, the term רז נהיה has been the occasion of some puzzlement. Milik's rendering, *le mystère future*,[3] is accepted by most translators and interpreters of this document (including, initially at any rate, García Martínez: "the future mystery").[4] One major problem with this passage is that elsewhere the term רז נהיה always has a positive connotation. Whether we render it as "the mystery to come" or "the future mystery" it remains decidedly opaque. If we accept Milik's transcription, then in this instance it must represent some dreadful fate or punishment awaiting the wicked, whereas the good, presumably, will be saved.[5] Yet such a negative denotation is not found anywhere else in the scrolls.

If we leave 1QMysteries on one side, there are two other important texts that must be taken into account if we want to get a clearer understanding of this expression: the Community Rule and 4QInstruction. Vermes translates the relevant sentence from the Rule as follows: "For my light has sprung from the source of His knowledge; my eyes have beheld His marvellous deeds, and the light of my heart, *the mystery to come*" (1QS 11.3).[6] For García Martínez the term has a future meaning in this context also (as well as in 1QMysteries): "the mystery of the future."[7] But it is hard to make any sense of this: neither the denotation nor the meaning is at all clear. In any case some commentators disagree about the meaning of the key term here. Alexander Rofé, for instance, understands it to refer to "the secrets of what has happened, i.e. the innermost significance of events" and

---

2. Translation Geza Vermes, *The Complete Dead Sea Scrolls in English* (London: Penguin Books, 1997), 389.

3. J. T. Milik and D. Barthélemy, *Discoveries in the Judaean Desert: Qumran Cave 1* (Oxford: Clarendon, 1955), 103.

4. Florentino García Martínez, *The Dead Sea Scrolls Translated: The Qumran Texts in English* (Leiden: Brill, 1994), 399. Yet on the very next page, the same phrase in another copy of the same document is translated as "the mystery of existence"!

5. Unless, like John Collins and Torleif Elgvin, we adopt the bold expedient of translating the Hebrew מן as "by": "they will not save themselves *by* the רז נהיה" (John Collins, "The Mysteries of God: Creation and Eschatology in 4QInstruction and the Wisdom of Solomon," in *Wisdom and Apocalypticism in the Dead Sea Scrolls and in the Biblical Tradition* [ed. Florentino García Martínez; Louvain: Louvain University Press, 2003], 289; Torleif Elgvin, "Wisdom at Qumran," in *Judaism in Late Antiquity, Part Five: The Judaisms of Qumran, a Systemic Reading of the Dead Sea Scrolls* [2 vols.; ed. Alan J. Avery-Peck, Bruce Chilton, and Jacob Neusner,; Leiden: Brill, 2001], 2.162).

6. Vermes, *Complete Dead Sea Scrolls*, 115.

7. García Martínez , *The Dead Sea Scrolls Translated*, 17.

notes (there being no past participle in Hebrew) that he "would construe *nihyeh* as a perfect, rather than as a participle."[8] He does not, however, attempt to explain the syntax required by this translation. Eduard Lohse in his selection of Qumran texts points נהיה with a *qamets* instead of a *tsere* and translates the whole phrase as "das Geheimnis des Gewordenen."[9] James Charlesworth, in the first volume of a major project involving a commentary and translation of all the scrolls, retains the future meaning but modifies it slightly: "the light of my heart beheld the mystery of what shall occur and is occurring forever."[10] In an even later publication, García Martínez translates it as "the mystery of existence."[11] Here, I suspect, he is transferring to the Community Rule a rendering that he uses for another, very different document, 4QInstruction.

The year 1999 saw the appearance of one of the last volumes in the splendid series *Discoveries in the Judaean Desert*, published by the Clarendon Press. Volume 34, edited by John Strugnell, Daniel Harrington, and Torleif Elgvin, contains a number of fragments (1Q26, 4Q415–418, 4Q423) of a document known originally as "Sapiential Text A" and subsequently as "4QInstruction." This document had been available to scholars since its preliminary publication by Ben-Zion Wacholder and Martin Abegg in 1991, and it forms the centerpiece of Harrington's study "Wisdom Texts from Qumran." The "understanding child" is enjoined to gaze and meditate day and night upon the רז נהיה:

> 6 *By* day and by night meditate upon the mystery that is to be/come and study it always. And then you will know truth and iniquity. . . . 7 . . . . Then you will discern between good and evil according to their works. For the God of knowledge is the foundation of truth, and by the mystery to be/come 9 He has laid out its foundation, and its deeds he has prepared with [. . .] wisdom, and with all cunning He has fashioned it. . . . 18 . . . And you, O understanding child, gaze on the mystery that is to be/come. And know the paths of everything that lives and the manner of his walking that is appointed over his deeds. (4Q417 frag. 2 6–19).[12]

Harrington comments that the רז נהיה

8. Alexandre Rofé, "Revealed Wisdom from the Bible to Qumran," in *Sapiential Perspectives: Wisdom Literature in Light of the Dead Sea Scrolls* (ed. John J. Collins, Gregory E. Sterling, and Ruth A. Clements; STDJ 51; Leiden: Brill, 2004), 2, 2 n. 3.

9. Eduard Lohse, *Die Texte aus Qumran: Hebräisch und deutsch; mit masoretischer Punktation, Übersetzung, Einführung und Anmerkungen* (Munich: Kosel, 1971), 41.

10. James H. Charlesworth, Frank M. Cross, and Jacob Milgrom, eds., *The Dead Sea Scrolls—Hebrew, Aramaic, and Greek Texts with English Translations.* Vol. 1: *Rule of the Community and Related Documents* (PTSDSSP; Louisville: Westminster John Knox, 1994), 47.

11. Florentino García Martínez and Eibert J. C. Tigchelaar, eds., *The Dead Sea Scrolls Study Edition* (2 vols.; Leiden: Brill, 1997), 1.97.

12. Daniel J. Harrington, *Wisdom Texts from Qumran* (London: Routledge, 1996), 52–53.

seems to be a body of teaching that concerns behavior and eschatology. It is probably an extrabiblical compendium, not the Torah. It may have been something like the "instruction on the Two Spirits" in 1QS iii 13–iv 26. Or it may have been the "Book of Meditation" (see 1QSa i 6–8) by which a prospective member of the movement was instructed (at home?) between the ages of ten and twenty. Or it may have been the "Book of Mysteries" (1Q27, 4Q299–301), which uses the term frequently in a cosmic context.[13]

But against this it should be said that the use of רז נהיה "in a cosmic context"— a use also evidenced in the line from the Community Rule cited above—makes it unlikely that the term refers to a written document, however prestigious and however prized. This is just possible if it was accorded the same authority as the Torah itself, identified with Wisdom in a famous passage in Sirach (24:23–24); but even this possibility vanishes if 1Q27 is taken into account. 4QInstruction (4Q416 frag. 2 3.18; 4Q418 frags. 10 a–b 1, frag. 123 2.4, frag. 184 2, frag. 190 2; 4Q423 frag. 5 2) speaks of "opening the ears (of the student or disciple) ברז נהיה." Harrington translates this in its first occurrence, "they [i.e., the student's parents] uncovered your ear *to* the mystery that is to be/come."[14] But "to" seems an improbable rendering of the preposition ב. (The difference in meaning between ב and ל is well illustrated in Job 36, where in v.10, "he opens their ear *to* instruction", the preposition is ל; whereas a little further on, in v. 15, "he opens their ear *by* adversity", the preposition is ב.) Elsewhere, it is true, in one of the songs of praise (1QH 9.23) we read, "Thou hast opened my ears *to* marvelous mysteries." But the Hebrew here, לרזי פלא, is unambiguous; whereas in yet another passage, where ב is used, Vermes (1997) translates, "thou hast given me knowledge *through* thy marvellous mysteries" (1QH 9.23; 15.30; 19.13). In the official edition of the text, DJD 34, Harrington allows an alternative rendering: "In this phrase, the preposition ב in ברז may indicate the subject matter of the revelation (i.e. 'about the mystery'), or the hermeneutic principle used for interpreting a revelation."[15] As a translation of the Hebrew ב, the latter suggestion ("by" rather than "to") seems much more likely to be right but raises once again the problem of how to determine the denotation of the term רז נהיה.

Fortunately, however, Harrington comes to our assistance here with another helpful suggestion. Rejecting the translation "mystery of existence" as "too metaphysical and static," he compares the term in its elusive indeterminacy to the phrase "kingdom of God" in the Synoptic Gospels.[16] (As Jesus uses this phrase, despite strenuous efforts by New Testament scholars to restrict its reference

---

13. Ibid., 49.
14. Ibid., 44.
15. See DJD 34, 537.
16. Daniel J. Harrington, "Two Early Jewish Approaches to Wisdom: Sirach and Qumran Sapiential Work A," in *The Wisdom Texts from Qumran and the Development of Sapiential*

either to the present or to the future, both references have to be retained.)[17] Harrington's suggestion occurs at the end of a paragraph in which he still favors the likelihood that the רז נהיה is a written document, but of course "kingdom of God" is not a text but a *concept* (a very powerful one), and the same is true, I believe, of the רז נהיה. This is not a new proposal. Elgvin thinks of רז נהיה as "a comprehensive word for God's mysterious plan for creation and history, His plan for man and for redemption of the elect," [18] a suggestion cited approvingly by Menahem Kister. [19] John Collins is also inclined to favor the idea that רז נהיה is "a comprehensive term for the entire divine plan, embracing past present and future;"[20] and elsewhere Elgvin nicely sums up his own suggestion as "the unfolding mystery of God."[21]

If we accept provisionally that this, or something very close, is what the term רז נהיה *denotes*, the question of what it *means*, how it should be translated, still has to be answered. Here too there have been many different proposals. The first word, *raz*, is in one sense unproblematic: it means, unquestionably, "mystery." Wacholder and Abegg, in their *Preliminary Edition*, rendered the Hebrew term רז נהיה by "the mystery of existence," [22] a rendering retained by Loren Stuckenbruck in an essay linking 4QInstruction with Enoch,[23] and by García Martínez in his translation of the whole corpus of the scrolls.[24] Along the same lines is an earlier modification of his original suggestion—"the secret of the way things are"—which has received the support of Philip Davies as "perhaps the most felici-

---

Thought (ed. Charlotte Hempel, Armin Lange, and Hermann Lichtenberger; Louvain: Louvain University Press, 2002), 272; idem, *Wisdom Texts*, 89–90.

17. See E. P. Sanders's excellent chapter "The Coming of the Kingdom" in *The Historical Figure of Jesus* (London: Penguin, 1993), 169–88.

18. Torleif Elgvin, "Wisdom and Apocalypticism in the Early Second Century BCE," in *The Dead Sea Scrolls Fifty Years after Their Discovery: Proceedings of the Jerusalem Congress, July 20–25, 1997* (ed. Lawrence H. Schiffman, Emanuel Tov, and James C. VanderKam; Jerusalem: Israel Exploration Society and the Shrine of the Book, 2000), 235.

19. Menahem Kister, "Wisdom Literature and its Relation to Other Genres," *Sapiential Perspectives: Wisdom Literature in Light of the Dead Sea Scrolls* (ed. John J. Collins, Gregory E. Sterling, and R. A. Clements; STDJ 51; Leiden: Brill, 2004), 31.

20. John J. Collins, "The Eschatologizing of Wisdom in the Dead Sea Scrolls," in *Sapiential Perspectives*, 55.

21. Torleif Elgvin, "The Mystery to Come: Early Essene Theology of Revelation," in *Qumran between the Old and New Testaments* (ed. Frederick H. Cryer and Thomas L. Thompson; Sheffield: Sheffield Academic, 1998), 133.

22. Ben-Zion Wacholder and Martin Abegg Jr., *A Preliminary Edition of the Unpublished Dead Sea Scrolls: The Hebrew and Aramaic Texts from Cave Four* (Washington, D.C.: Biblical Archaeology Society, 1991).

23. Loren T. Stuckenbruck, "4QInstruction and the Possible Influence of Early Enochic Traditions: An Evaluation," in *The Wisdom Texts from Qumran* [see n. 16], 263–75.

24. García Martínez, *Dead Sea Scrolls Translated*, 383–90.

tous" of all possible choices. Davies argues that the phrase "surely connotes the ultimate but hidden clue to the riddle of existence itself, and especially human existence."[25] But is this how the sectarians themselves conceived it? The rendering "mystery of existence" had already been dismissed as too philosophical by Harrington and Strugnell in their very critical review of the *Preliminary Edition*,[26] and indeed the term has an almost Heideggerian ring. Armin Lange's alternative proposal, "das Geheimnis des Werdens," [27] is interestingly different in its stress on "becoming" or "arising," but it too is scarcely satisfactory as a rendering of the Hebrew, for the word נהיה is not an abstract noun but a participle—that is to say, a verbal adjective.

Moreover, in the context of 4QInstruction, where "the understanding child" is invited to contemplate and meditate on the mystery day and night, it is even harder to admit a future meaning. The contemplation of a mystery, in principle unintelligible without a special revelation, is already paradoxical. To propel the mystery into the long grass of an indefinite future is to carry the paradox, in my view, to the point of incomprehensibility. The niph'al participle can bear a present meaning just as easily as a future, and accordingly I prefer to translate רז נהיה as "the mystery that is coming to pass." Following Harrington's imaginative comparison, I believe that the term implies the same sort of inaugurated eschatology as the gospel phrase "kingdom of God." [28]

Implicit also in the concept of the רז נהיה is an assurance of the *providence* of God. The universal Jewish belief in God as creator has broadened into an awareness of human history as the unfolding mystery of the divine plan. By means of the רז נהיה, the God who is the foundation of truth "has laid out its foundation [i.e., creation] and its works (מעשיה) [i.e., history]" (4Q417 frag. 1 1.9).

25. Philip R. Davies, "Death, Resurrection, and Life after Death in the Qumran Scrolls," in *Judaism in Late Antiquity, Part Four: Death, Life-after-Death, Resurrection, and the World-to-Come in the Judaisms of Antiquity* (ed. Alan J. Avery-Peck and Jacob Neusner; Leiden: Brill, 2000), 197, 197 n. 1.

26. Daniel J. Harrington and John Strugnell, "Qumran Cave 4 Texts: A New Publication," *JBL* 112 (1993): 491–99; see also Harrington, "Two Early Jewish Approaches," 272.

27. See Armin Lange, *Weisheit und Präedestination: Weisheitliche Urordnung und Präedestination in den Textfunden von Qumran* (STDJ 18; Leiden: Brill, 1995).

28. Some time after reaching this conclusion I consulted the more recent edition of 4QMysteries in DJD 20, *Qumran Cave 4.XV* (1997). On the term רז נהיה the editors remark simply: "This refers to the secret of that which is in the process of coming into being," adding that "this usage of Nip'al is common in Qumran Hebrew" and comparing the usage in 4QMysteries to Sir 42:19 and 48:25, "where נהיות is parallel to נסתרות, 'secrets'"(105).

WISDOM

4QInstruction combines the kind of paranetical instruction familiar from, say, Proverbs and Sirach with longer wisdom discourses built around the phrase רז נהיה. Torleif Elgvin, who has written extensively about the document (and indeed was responsible for the edition of one of the fragments included in DJD 34), proposed that it "represents a conflation of two literary layers."[29] Other scholars have rejected this proposal, but the very fact that it could be seriously entertained indicates the unusual nature of the document as a whole. Nevertheless, in this respect it resembles the book of Proverbs, which largely consists of dozens of (frequently platitudinous) aphorisms on how life is to be lived: "A cheerful heart is good medicine; but a downcast spirit dries up the bones" (17:22). But alongside these aphorisms, which may be grouped together under the heading of *accessible* wisdom, are ranged deep reflections upon a hidden, *remote* wisdom that can be accessed, if at all, only through a special revelation originating in God. In 4QInstruction *accessible* wisdom is represented largely by observations on how to cope with poverty: "Do not satiate yourself with bread when there is no clothing. Do not drink wine while there is no food. Do not seek luxury when you lack bread" (4Q416 frag. 2 2.19–20).[30] *Remote* wisdom has its own name in this document: רז נהיה, "the mystery that is coming to pass."

Any group that attaches special importance to an extra revelation above and beyond the Law, such as the רז נהיה, is properly speaking sectarian, because it thereby diverges from those whom we may call, with some hesitation, the representatives of mainstream Judaism. These, the direct ancestors of the writers of the Mishnah, thought of revelation very differently from the sectarian Jews of the Qumran community and the authors of some of their most cherished writings such as *1 Enoch*.

What looks like a party line is already discernible in Deuteronomy:

> For this commandment which I command you this day is not too hard for you
> (לא־נפלאת הוא ממך) neither is it far off. It is not in heaven, that you should say,
> "Who will go up for us to heaven, and bring it to us, that we may hear it and do
> it?" Neither is it beyond the sea, that you should say, "Who will go over the sea
> for us, and bring it to us, that we may hear it and do it?" But the word is very
> near you; it is in your mouth and in your heart, so that you can do it. (Deut
> 30:11–14)

Indeed, Deuteronomy *identifies* wisdom and understanding with the Law: "Keep [these statutes and ordinances] and do them; for that will be your wisdom and

---

29. Elgvin, "Wisdom and Apocalypticism," 226.
30. Translation from Vermes, *The Complete Dead Sea Scrolls*, 406.

understanding in the sight of the peoples" (4:6).[31] After reciting the ten commandments that God had dictated to him, Moses concludes, significantly, "and he
added no more" (5:22). In fact any subtraction from or addition to the Law had
been denounced in advance (4:2). What the author calls the "secret" or "hidden"
things (הנסתרות, LXX: τὰ κρυπτά) are reserved for God; "but the things that are
revealed (הנגלות, LXX: τὰ φανερά) belong to us and to our children for ever"
(29:28).

The famous passage in Job 28 that speaks of a wisdom that is in principle
inaccessible to mortal man, "concealed from the eyes of every living thing and
hidden (נסתרת) from the birds of the sky" (28:21), would have met with the
approval of the Deuteronomists. Not so the claim of the sage of Qumran to "have
gazed on that which is eternal (בהויא עולם) on sound insight (תושיה) hidden
(נסתרה) from men, on knowledge and wise design [hidden] from the sons of men"
(1QS 11.5–7). This claim, which surely concerns the רז נהיה, is properly speaking
apocalyptic, asserting as it does the revelation of hidden wisdom and rejecting
the tradition common to Job and Deuteronomy of a wisdom that remains permanently out of human reach. In fact the term apocalyptic is most appropriately
bestowed on works that highlight revelations over and above the Law, reserved for
the writer and his readers; and by analogy the community to which these belong
may reasonably be called apocalyptic also.[32]

---

31. The word translated "too hard for [i.e., *beyond*] you" in the passage from Deuteronomy
quoted above (30:11), the niph'al participle of פלא, reappears at Qumran in the hymnic conclusion to the Community Rule in a passage where it is parallel to the רז נהיה: "my eyes have
beheld his *marvelous deeds* (נפלאותיו) and the light of my heart the mystery of what is coming
to pass" (1QS 11.3). But this is simply a coincidence, for the term is a standard one, especially in
the Psalms (with the solitary exception of Ps 131), for the marvelous works that God has done
and will continue to do on behalf of his people. The meaning "too hard for" depends upon the
following מן, as in Deut 17:4; 2 Sam 13:2; Job 42:3; Ps 131:1; Prov 30:18; Jer 32:17, 27. The reflections of Menahem Kister on this verb, which include references to the Qumran material, are, to
say the least, tendentious ("Wisdom Literature," 21–22).

32. A classic example of apocalyptic is *1 Enoch*, on which George Nickelsburg observes
that "the text as a whole is presented in a self-conscious way as a document that is revealed
wisdom. . . . Thus, while the prophets claimed to reveal how God would work out the divine will
in the world's future, the function of revelation and the forms in which it is presented in 1 Enoch
justify using the term *apocalyptic* to distinguish the text's eschatology from that of its canonical
predecessors" (*1 Enoch 1: A Commentary on the Book of 1 Enoch* [Hermeneia; Minneapolis: Fortress, 2001], 55). It is something of an anachronism to speak of Enoch's "canonical predecessors"
in this context, and the term *apocalyptic* should not be confined to the sect's eschatology, but the
distinction is still valid. On the notable differences between the apocalypticists, most but not all
of whom embraced the tradition of hidden wisdom, see the seminal article of Michael Stone,
"Lists of Revealed Things in the Apocalyptic Literature" in *Magnalia Dei, the Mighty Acts of God:
Essays on the Bible and Archaeology in Memory of G. Ernest Wright* (ed. Frank M. Cross et al.;
Garden City, N.Y.: Doubleday, 1976), 414–52. *Accessible* wisdom, obviously, and *divine* wisdom
too can easily be accommodated by writers such as Baruch and also Ben Sira, who stands in

THE JOHANNINE LOGOS

Is there anything in these reflections on the concept of mystery in the scrolls that can further our understanding of the Gospel of John? Another few lines from the hymnic conclusion to the Community Rule may help us to answer this question.

All things come to pass by his knowledge (כול בדעתו נהיה); he establishes all things by his design (כול הווה במחשבותו יכינו); and without him nothing is done (יעשה). (1QS 11.11; cf. 1QH 9.9–12)[33]

The terms "come to pass" (נהיה) and "is done" (יעשה) both refer to human history and scarcely differ in meaning. They allude to divine providence, God's unremitting activity on behalf of his creation, which we have seen to be implicit in the concept of the רז נהיה. Rudolf Bultmann cites this passage without comment as a parallel to John 1:3 (πάντα δι᾽ αὐτοῦ ἐγένετο, καὶ χωρὶς αὐτοῦ ἐγένετο οὐδὲ ἕν ὃ γέγονεν), but I suspect that the parallel may be closer than he realized.[34] In the first place, the word πάντα corresponds very precisely to the Hebrew כול. That is to say, it refers not to the created universe (always τὰ πάντα in the New Testament and usually so in the Septuagint) but to the events of human history.[35] In the second place, the verb γίνεσθαι is used regularly in the sense of "happen" or "come to pass" and corresponds well to the niph'al of היה and the pe'al of hw'. This is also how this verse from the Prologue was understood by the Gnostic author of the Gospel of Truth, who, commenting on the revelation of the word ("the first to come forth"), asserts that "nothing happens without him, nor does anything happen without the will of the Father" (37:9–44). More significantly still, this is also how the verb γίνεσθαι was understood by the early Syriac translators (though the Sinaitic manuscript is deficient at this point). Unlike the vast majority of modern commentators, they were not misled by the parallel between the

---

the Deuteronomic tradition. Not so *hidden* wisdom: "hidden wisdom and unseen treasure, what advantage is there in either of them?" (Sir 20:30). Compare Sirach 18:4–6 and 3:21–23, which refers directly to Deuteronomy: "Seek not what is too hard for you, nor investigate what is beyond your power."

33. נהיה, the niph'al form of היה, is translated here by Vermes as a present, by García Martínez as a future ("By his knowledge everything *shall* come into being"), and by Lohse as a past ("durch sein Wissen *ist* alles enstanden"). The divergent translations are perhaps some indication of the temporal inclusiveness of the activity of God.

34. Rudolf Bultmann, *The Gospel of John: A Commentary* (trans. G. R. Beasley-Murray, R. W. N. Hoare, and J. K. Riches; Philadelphia: Westminster, 1971), 37 n. 5.

35. One of the rare instances in the LXX where πάντα refers to the created universe is Ps 8:7. This is quoted twice in the New Testament (1 Cor 15:7 and Heb 2:8), and in both of these passages the anarthrous πάντα is *corrected* into τὰ πάντα. Further evidence may be found in a long note (n. 37) in my article, "The Transformation of Wisdom: A Study of the Prologue of John's Gospel," *NTS* 32 (1986): 161–86.

first two words of the Prologue and the opening of Genesis into thinking that in what follows the writer is referring to the created universe. Thus, Burkitt's translation of the Curetonian version of John 1:3 reads, "Everything came to pass in Him, and apart from Him not even one thing came to pass in Him."[36] This is also the sense required in 4 Ezra 6:6: "But I planned these things and they came to pass [Syriac *hw'* plural] through me and not through another." See too Jdt 9:5: "the things thou didst intend came to pass (ἐγενήθησαν)."

Relevant here are two more texts from the scrolls. The first, from 4QInstruction, concerns the student of the רז נהיה, who "will know the hidden things of his [God's] thoughts (נסתרי מחשבת) when he walks in perfection in all his deeds. Seek them always, look at all their outcome. Then you will have knowledge of eternal glory with his marvelous mysteries and mighty deeds" (4Q417 frag. 2 1.11–13). The second is the passage already quoted above from the Community Rule (1QS 11.5–11) that refers to the thoughts of God and the wisdom concealed from men. The word מחשבות, literally "his thoughts," is often used of God's plans or designs (e.g., Jer 29:11; 51:29; Mic 4:12; Ps 33:11), above all in the famous epilogue to the prophecy of Second Isaiah, "For as the heavens are higher than the earth so are my ways higher than your ways and my thoughts than your thoughts" (Isa 55:8–9), an assertion directly followed by the affirmation of the universal fruitfulness of "every word that goes forth from my mouth" (v. 11), an affirmation that harks back to the same author's proclamation in the introduction to his work that "the word of the Lord abides for ever" (40:8). Thus the "thoughts" of God, his plan or design, are expressed in his "word." We could hardly be closer than this to the Fourth Evangelist's conception of the Logos. [37]

The Logos, moreover, like the רז נהיה for the Qumran Community, was an object of contemplation for the Johannine Christians. The verb θεᾶσθαι in John 1:14 is generally translated as "see" ("we have seen his glory"), but it really means "gaze at" and in some contexts—for example Plato, *Phaedo* 84b, where the object of the verb is "the true and the divine and what is above mere opinion"—it is best translated "contemplate." "We contemplated his glory" may not be far from what is meant here. And since John 1:3, as we have seen, probably does not refer to creation, as most scholars suppose, but to everything that happens or comes to pass, then what is being asserted might be exactly what the author of the hymnic conclusion to the Community Rule proclaimed in the passage that we have just looked at: "all things come to pass by his knowledge and he establishes all things

36. F. Crawford Burkitt, *Evangelion da-Mepharreshe: The Curetonian Version of the Four Gospels* (2 vols.; Cambridge: Cambridge University Press, 1904), 1:423.

37. This thesis was first set out a quarter of a century ago in the article cited above [n. 35], in which I modified and expanded the earlier work of T. E. Pollard, I. de la Potterie and P. Lamarche. To the best of my knowledge it has never been the object of any scholarly comment, either favorable or unfavorable. A slightly revised edition of the article was printed some years later in my *Studying John* (Oxford: Clarendon, 1994), 5–35.

by his design." If so (and I for one find this suggestion both plausible and attractive), the glory of the Logos is nothing less than the mystery of God's plan as, no longer hidden, it has finally been incarnated and revealed.

QUMRAN AND THE LAW

Given the importance attached by the Community to the רז נהיה, it remains to be asked how they could reconcile this with their abiding attachment to the Law, understood as God's revelation to Israel. Unlike those whom we might call the Enochic sectarians, who, as Nickelsburg puts it, "leapfrogged Moses and identified Enoch as the primordial recipient of all heavenly wisdom,"[38] they did not, apparently, subordinate the Law to their other source of revelation.

None of the writings composed by the Qumran sectarians themselves is strictly speaking an apocalypse, for visions and angelic interpreters are missing from them all. But the number of manuscripts of *1 Enoch* and *Jubilees*, plus a quantity of Aramaic texts found in their library, testifies to their appreciation of the genre, and their own work is suffused with their sense that they are the privileged recipients of a special revelation unavailable to ordinary mortals. This does not mean that they reject the Torah, and the presence among the scrolls of various halakhic texts, especially 4QMMT, shows how seriously they took its interpretation. But because of the value they attach to their own revealed mysteries the Torah may have been no more significant to them than this new truth. For Enoch, as we have just seen, the new revelation takes pride of place. In this regard both groups of writers differ widely from Ben Sira, who though respecting and indeed prizing the wisdom traditions he has inherited subsumes them all under the Law.

> Come to me, you who desire me, and eat your fill of my produce. For the remembrance of me is sweeter than honey, and my inheritance sweeter than the honeycomb. Those who eat me will hunger for more, and those who drink me will thirst for more. Whoever obeys me will not be put to shame and those who work with my help will not sin. All this is the book of the covenant of the Most High God, the law which Moses commanded us and an inheritance of the congregations of Jacob. (Sirach 24:19–23)

There are then two distinct attitudes toward revelation at Qumran, but even where the Law continues to occupy a central position there is still a need for interpretation. In the Rule of the Community everyone entering the community has to swear to revert to the Law of Moses; but this is "in compliance with all that has been revealed concerning it (לכול הנגלה ממנה) to the sons of Zadok, the priests who keep the covenant and seek [interpret?] his [God's] will (דורשי רצונו)"

---

38. Nickelsburg, *1 Enoch*, 52.

(1QS 5.9) through a revealed knowledge of the true interpretation of the law that is unavailable to outsiders. The Damascus Document interprets the well in Num 21:18 as the Law, "and those who dug it were the converts of Israel [שבי ישראל] who went out of the Land of Israel to sojourn in the land of Damascus." The staffs or staves with which the well was dug are envisaged as having been instructed to do so by "the staff," that is, the interpreter of the Law (המחוקק הוא דורש התוה; CD 6.2–11). The prophets too required interpretation, contrary to the opinion of Ben Sira, who says for instance of Isaiah that he revealed "hidden things before they came to pass" (Sir 48:25). Hence the prevalence at Qumran of the so-called *pesharim*, applications of prophetic texts to the present situation of the community. Thus it is said of the Teacher of Righteousness that God made known to him "all the mysteries of the words of his servants the prophets." But when the author of (one of) the Thanksgiving Hymns praises God for having instructed him in his wonderful mysteries (ברזי פלאכה; 1QH^a 12.27–28) this is something new: it was not enough for him to have the Law engraved on his heart (שננתה בלבבי; 1QH 12.10). And of course the נהיה (which I have already discussed at some length) was something other than the Law.

Unlike Enoch and the Qumran community, the Gospel of John abandons the Law completely. The Law is not just superseded but canceled: "for the law was given through Moses; grace and truth come through Jesus Christ" (John 1:17), and it is Jesus, so he himself asserts, to whom the scriptures bear witness (5:39). He has succeeded the Law and replaced it as the object of revelation.

Life in a Community of the Elect

Both the Qumran Yahad and the Johannine community saw themselves as the recipients of a special revelation. One word used in both their writings to underline this gratifying conviction is "truth." Before asking about their sense of the benefits this conveys, it is worth considering how they thought of the revelation itself.

The Community Rule speaks of "those in Israel who have freely pledged themselves to the House of Truth" (1QS 5.6) and goes on to speak of "the multitude of the men of the Covenant who together have freely pledged themselves to his truth" (5.10). Considering this truth to be a privileged possession bestowed on them by God (1QM 13.12), the covenanters saw it as something not lightly to be divulged to others, recommending instead "faithful concealment of the mysteries of truth" (1QS 4.6) in the well-known passage already mentioned that pits the spirit of light against the spirit of darkness and falsehood and claims for the community the title of "sons of truth in this world." The community is also often referred to in the Thanksgiving Hymns as "the sons of his/thy truth" (1QH 14.32; 15.32–33; 17.35; 18.29; 19.14) and elsewhere as "the community of truth" (1QS 2.24). "I know that no riches equal to thy truth," sings the poet (1QH 7.35–36).

A further point is this: *the knowledge of the truth is seen to depend upon the revelation of divine mysteries.* A passage from the Habakkuk *pesher* elucidating an instruction to the prophet to transcribe one of his visions (1QpHab 2.2) speaks of the Teacher of Righteousness, to whom God made known "all the mysteries (רזים) of the words of his servants the prophets" (1QpHab 7.1–5; cf. CD 1.11–13; 1QH 9.26). And the author of the Hodayot (possibly the very same Teacher of Righteousness) declares explicitly that he has been made "a discerning interpreter of marvelous mysteries (מליץ דעת ברזי פלא) on behalf of the elect of righteousness" (1QH 10.15). And again: "I [thank thee, O Lord] for thou has enlightened me through thy truth. In thy marvelous mysteries, and in thy loving kindness to a man [of vanity, and] in the greatness of thy mercy to a perverse heart Thou hast granted me knowledge" (1QH 15.29–30).

In another passage, having identified himself as the Instructor (משכיל) he says that he has known God through the spirit which he gave him and that through the same spirit "I have faithfully hearkened to thy marvelous counsel" (לסוד פלאכה; 1QH 20.15).

The term סוד, which also occurs in similar contexts elsewhere in the Hymns (1QH 12.28–29; 13.11; 19.7; cf. 4Q437 6.1; Job 15:8), suggests the same kind of privileged access to the most intimate secrets of God as the Jesus of the Fourth Gospel claims for himself (see John 10:15; 17:25), and in both cases it is this privileged communication that permits the two teachers to pass on what they know to others. But for the Fourth Evangelist the truth has an even greater significance than it has for the Qumran community: it belongs to the special vocabulary of the Johannine group, and its inner meaning is hidden from outsiders such as "the Jews," who fatally misunderstand the promise that "the truth will make you free" (John 8:32), and Pilate, who fails to recognize the truth when it is standing in front of him (18:38). For "the truth" in the Fourth Gospel is actually identified with the person of Jesus: "I am the way, the truth, and the life" (14:6).

In the Farewell Discourse in John 14–16, as often elsewhere in the Fourth Gospel, Jesus appears to be a second Moses. On this occasion, about to take leave of his disciples, he surveys what for them is the equivalent of the Promised Land. This is what he calls "the truth." Just as Moses in the book of Deuteronomy, who is to die before he can himself conduct his people into the "the whole land of Judah as far as the Western Sea, the Negeb and the Plain" (34:1–4), stands at the top of Pisgah, casts his eyes "westward and northward and southward and eastward" (3:27), and commissions his successor, Joshua, to carry out the task he is destined not to fulfill himself, so too Jesus, unable while alive to transmit his revelation to his disciples in a way that they can understand, but clearly foreseeing all that this revelation will come to mean to them, appoints the Paraclete, the spirit of truth, to guide them into the spiritual territory that he calls, simply, "all the truth" (John 16:12). As Hans Windisch observed long ago, the Paraclete is, among other things, Jesus' caliph or successor who will teach his disciples all things and bring to their remembrance all that he had said to them (John 14:26).[39]

We may now turn to a consideration of the benefits brought to both communities by the gift of the truth. Put very succinctly, the most important benefit is *life*. At Qumran, moreover, this involves sharing in the life of the angels.

> From the source of his righteousness is my justification and from his marvellous mysteries is the light of my heart. My eyes have gazed on what is eternal, on wisdom concealed from men, on knowledge and wise design (hidden) from the sons of men; on a fountain of righteousness and on a storehouse of power, on a spring of glory (hidden) from the assembly of flesh. God has given them to his chosen ones as an everlasting possession, and has caused them to inherit the lot of the Holy Ones. He has joined their assembly to the Sons of Heaven to be a Council of the Community, a foundation of the Building of Holiness, and eternal Plantation throughout all ages to come. (1QS 11.5–8)[40]

The sheer familiarity of this passage can blind us to the remarkable confidence with which the writer lays out his extraordinary claims. A list of rules and regulations astonishing in its overall severity is succeeded immediately by a solemn and insistent hymn of thanksgiving and then, without a break, by confident assertions concerning a privileged relationship with God based on a very special knowledge that marks out the writer and his community from the rest of mankind and justifies the assertion that they are not merely associated with "the sons of heaven," the angels, but virtually identified with them.

The present participation in the life of the angels is affirmed throughout the scrolls as a pledge of great peace "in a long life (כאורך ימים)," "eternal joy in life without end" (שמחת עולמים בחיי נצח)," and a "garment of majesty in unending light (באור עולמים)" (1QS 4.6–8). I used to believe that scholars such as Aune, Nickelsburg, and Collins were wrong to follow H.-W. Kuhn in finding in the scrolls, especially in the Hodayot, a belief in present participation in angelic life, coupled with the expectation of fulfillment in the future.[41] But I am now persuaded that my earlier reservations were mistaken. This view derives strong support from the sheer variety of the documents testifying to the community's sense that it was living among angels. Apart from the Hodayot (1QH 11.22–24; 14.15–17; 15.17–18; 19.14–17), the most important of these is the Songs of the

---

39. Hans Windisch, "Jesus und der Geist im Johannes-Evangelium," in *Amicitiae Corolla: Essays Presented to James Rendel Harris* (ed. H. G. Wood; London: University of London Press, 1933), 303–18.

40. Translation from Vermes, *Complete Dead Sea Scrolls in English*, 115.

41. See David E. Aune, *The Cultic Setting of Realized Eschatology in Early Christianity* (NovTSup 28; Leiden: Brill, 1972); George W. E. Nickelsburg, *Resurrection, Immortality, and Eternal Life in Intertestamental Judaism* (Cambridge: Harvard University Press, 1972); John J. Collins, "Apocalyptic Eschatology as the Transcendence of Death," *CBQ* 36 (1974): 21–43.

Sabbath Sacrifice (4Q 400–405; 11Q 17), which was unavailable to Kuhn and his first supporters. But there is other evidence besides.

First, there is the promise at the end of the Community Rule (quoted above) where "the chosen ones" are assured that God has "caused them to inherit the lot of the Holy Ones" and "joined their assembly to the Sons of Heaven to be a Council of the Community." Next there are the purity rules found both in the War Scroll (1QM 7.6) and in the Rule of the Congregation (1QSa 2.2–10) that exclude men suffering from pollution or any kind of physical blemish from belonging to the army ("for the holy angels are together with their armies") or from taking their place among "the men of renown" of the assembly ("for the holy angels are among their congregation"). To this we may add the evidence of 4QInstruction, which promises to the neophyte a place in the heavenly court: "among all the godly ones he has cast your lot" (4Q418 frag. 81 4–5), whether the Sons of Heaven, "whose lot is eternal life" (4Q418 frag. 69 2.13) are the human righteous, as is argued by Crispin Fletcher-Louis,[42] or the angelic host. Lastly, we may point to a short document in which the final destiny of the wicked is contrasted with a promise to the good that they will be counted "as a congregation of holiness in service for eternal life and [sharing] the lot of his holy ones . . . each man according to the lot which he has cast . . . for eternal life (לחיי עולם)" (4Q181; CD 3.20; 1QH 4.27; 7.29; frag. 23 2.10). Reminiscent though it may be of John's ζωὴ αἰώνιος, this promise is different from the immediate reward offered by Jesus to those who believe. There is certainly an analogy, to put it no more strongly, between the assurance of the Johannine community that they enjoyed a new kind of life, which might be characterized as the life of the new age, and the Qumran community's sense of having been admitted into the society of the angels. Yet perhaps one should not press the comparison too far. There is certainly no obvious resemblance between the Qumran and the Johannine communities, and nothing could be further from the calm sublimity of the discourses of Jesus in the Fourth Gospel than the curious mixture of self-loathing and exaltation that characterizes the Hodayot.

It should not be necessary to add that for the Fourth Evangelist all the large concepts I have discussed here—mystery, wisdom, Logos, truth, life—are summed up in the person of Jesus, who encapsulates in his own person the divine plan of God set out for the contemplation of the Johannine community, much as the רז נהיה was proposed for the contemplation of the "wise child" at Qumran. The actual term mystery is, of course, missing from the Fourth Gospel, but the concept of mystery is unquestionably present, an apocalypse in reverse, since it is played out not in heaven but on earth.

---

42. Crispin H. T. Fletcher-Louis, *All the Glory of Adam. Liturgical Anthropology in the Dead Sea Scrolls* (STDJ 42; Leiden: Brill, 2002), 119–20.

Conclusion

This essay was prompted by an exchange between Daniel Harrington and Joseph Fitzmyer in a volume dedicated to the memory of Raymond Brown. Responding to Fitzmyer's essay, Harrington raised the question whether the background shared by the Qumran literature and the Fourth Gospel was merely, as he put it, "apocalyptic Judaism," or something more concrete. To which Fitzmyer rather testily rejoined, "I should want to know what one means by 'apocalyptic' Judaism. That the Essenes were composing apocalyptic writings is clear, but when that adjective is applied to Judaism as such I do not know what that means."[43] Nevertheless, it is a word that has been used by other scholars, too, for example John Collins: "By an apocalyptic worldview I mean the view that human life is shaped to a significant extent by supernatural (angelic or demonic) powers and subject to a final judgment, not only on nations but also on the individual dead. . . . This view stands in sharp contrast to the worldview of the Mishnah and Talmud but is shared, broadly speaking, by the sectarian scrolls and most of the New Testament writings."[44] Similarly, Frank M. Cross, in one of the earliest general commentaries on the relevance of the scrolls to the Bible, had spoken of these as the literature of an "apocalyptic community," which Collins rightly took as a reference to "the belief of the Qumran community that it had already made the transition to a new form [of] life, while still in this life, in history."[45] Following Collins, I have tried in this essay to indicate reasons for believing that the Jewish sectarians at Qumran—and the Johannine community—were apocalyptic both in the sense in which earlier scholars understood that term and in the more specific sense of living lives shaped by a revealed mystery.

---

43. Joseph Fitzmyer, "Qumran Literature and the Johannine Writings," in *Life in Abundance: Studies of John's Gospel in Tribute to Raymond E. Brown* (ed. John R. Donahue; Collegeville, Minn.: Liturgical Press, 2005), 129.

44. John J. Collins, "Qumran, Apocalypticism, and the New Testament," in Schiffman, Tov, and VanderKam, *Dead Sea Scrolls Fifty Years after Their Discovery*, 133–38, quote 134.

45. Frank M. Cross, *The Ancient Library of Qumran and Modern Biblical Studies* (New York: Doubleday, 1958), 56; Collins, "Apocalyptic Eschatology," 26.

LUKE, JOHN, AND THE DEAD SEA SCROLLS

George J. Brooke

Since the general release of the unpublished Cave 4 and Cave 11 scrolls in 1991, the enormous task of sifting through the available information to see whether and how it might better inform various items of ongoing debate in New Testament scholarship has only just begun. As yet, there seems little sign that many New Testament scholars are returning to these Palestinian Jewish materials that may form the backdrop of some of the ideas of the New Testament.[1] The proposal that this essay investigates concerns some commonalities between, on the one hand, some of the traditions to be found in the Qumran scrolls and, on the other hand, some of the shared interests that exist between some parts of the special Lukan material (commonly designated "L," and possibly including parts or all of the infancy narrative) and some parts of the Fourth Gospel. There are thus three sets of preliminary issues that need clarification.

First, I take the view that the discoveries in the Qumran library are indeed significant for the better understanding of many aspects of the New Testament texts. Indeed, I have also espoused the view that by reading some of the New Testament texts correctly, suitable insights may be discovered that can lead to the clarification of some of the fragmentary remains of the Qumran library. There can be mutual illumination between these literary corpora. However, the relationship between the two bodies of texts is not a simple or straightforward one. It is difficult enough to discern what may have been the relationship between

---

1. The valuable study by Neil S. Fujita, *A Crack in the Jar: What Ancient Jewish Documents Tell Us about the New Testament* (Mahwah, N.J.: Paulist Press, 1986) predates the general release of the Cave 4 and Cave 11 scrolls in 1991. I have been surprised that since then there have been virtually no monographs that have tried to pick up the baton. Nevertheless, see Joseph A. Fitzmyer, *The Dead Sea Scrolls and Christian Origins* (SDSSRL; Grand Rapids: Eerdmans, 2000); James R. Davila, ed., *The Dead Sea Scrolls as Background to Postbiblical Judaism and Early Christianity: Papers from an International Conference at St. Andrews in 2001* (STDJ 46; Leiden: Brill, 2003); George J. Brooke, *The Dead Sea Scrolls and the New Testament: Essays in Mutual Illumination* (Minneapolis: Fortress, 2005).

John the Baptist and the Qumran community,[2] let alone how the life and deeds of Jesus, or the ways in which the remembrances of them were transmitted in early Christian circles, might have been influenced by some of the Jewish traditions preserved in the scrolls. Thus, I stand over against two approaches to all these materials: on the one hand, against those who too quickly equate John the Baptist and Jesus, or some of his relations, with the Qumran community and the wider movement of which it seems to have been a part; on the other, against those who deny any substantial relationship between the early layers of Christian tradition and the Second Temple literary sources now available to us through the remains of the Qumran library.[3]

Second, it is necessary to say something about the relationship between the scrolls and second- and third-generation Christianity. Here, from the outset, there has been a much more elaborate debate, and the Fourth Gospel in particular has often featured as part of that debate.[4] Put briefly, for the Fourth Gospel I am inclined to take note of two factors: (1) the NT never quotes the Qumran literature directly (or vice versa); and, (2) parallel concepts are often developed in different ways. The first factor has been noted emphatically by Raymond Brown: "The Johannine writings contain no clear quotation from a Qumran document and no reference to the Qumran community history. . . . Many suggested parallels are attractive but quite speculative."[5] The second factor has been argued by Richard Bauckham, using the example of light and darkness imagery in both corpora. Bauckham argues on the basis of the Hebrew Scriptures and other Jewish literature that in the Fourth Gospel there is "a development of Jewish light/darkness

---

2. See the subtle descriptions of this relationship by Robert L. Webb, *John the Baptizer and Prophet: A Socio-Historical Study* (JSNTSup 62; Sheffield: Sheffield Academic Press, 1991); also Joan E. Taylor, *The Immerser: John the Baptist within Second Temple Judaism* (Grand Rapids: Eerdmans, 1997).

3. A helpful attempt at providing examples of how this middle way might work is provided by Jörg Frey, "Zur Bedeutung der Qumran-Funde für das Verständnis des Neuen Testaments," in *Qumran–Bibelwissenschaften–Antike Judaistik* (ed. Ulrich Dahmen, Hartmut Stegemann, and Gunter Stemberger; Einblicke 9; Paderborn, Germany: Bonifatius, 2006), 33–65.

4. Cf. James M. Robinson, "Foreword" to Ernst Haenchen, *John: A Commentary on the Gospel of John* (Hermeneia; Philadelphia: Fortress Press, 1984), x: "Haenchen quoted Karl Georg Kuhn's enthusiastic statement of 1950, to the effect that in the Dead Sea Scrolls 'we reach the matrix of the Gospel of John,' but immediately pointed out its inappropriateness: 'The Gospel of John has nothing to do with this law piety. . . . Also nothing connects it with the apocalyptic piety of the Qumran congregation.'" See here Ernst Haenchen, "Aus der Literatur zum Johannesevangelium, 1929–1956," *TRu* 23 (1955): 323; Karl G. Kuhn, "Die in Palästina gefundenen hebräischen Texte und das Neue Testament," *ZTK* 47 (1950): 210.

5. Raymond E. Brown, "John, Gospel and Letters of," in *Encyclopedia of the Dead Sea Scrolls* (ed. Lawrence H. Schiffman and James C. VanderKam; 2 vols.; New York: Oxford University Press, 2000), 1.415.

imagery quite different from that which is distinctive to Qumran."[6] The evidence of the Qumran library has principally drawn attention to the Jewish background of much of the New Testament, including the Fourth Gospel, but it has not neatly provided the sole collection of literary sources from which the New Testament authors drew.[7] This means that the literary connection between the scrolls and the New Testament is likely to be indirect—at its closest through what some former Essene might have remembered after having joined a second- or third-generation Christian group of some sort, most probably after the fall of the Temple in 70 C.E.; at its most distant in a broadly shared cultural heritage. This applies to the Fourth Gospel as much as to other New Testament compositions.[8]

Third, in trying to perceive something of this indirect relationship between the scrolls and the Gospels in particular, it is necessary to consider briefly the relationship between the Synoptics and the Fourth Gospel. A century of scholarship on this matter has been neatly presented by D. Moody Smith, who has described the general swing of the scholarly pendulum from theories of dependence to a consensus on independence and back again to some kind of relationship.[9] Two scholars who wrote on the relationship between John and Luke seem to me to offer the most plausible theory. Pierson Parker proposed that a special, distinctly Judean, oral tradition peculiar to Luke and John was adequate for explaining the similarities.[10] Robert Maddox, like Parker (but apparently without awareness of Parker's conclusions), suggested that the common traditions, geographical

---

6. Richard J. Bauckham, "Qumran and the Fourth Gospel: Is There a Connection?" in *The Scrolls and the Scriptures: Qumran Fifty Years After* (ed. Stanley E. Porter and Craig A. Evans; JSPSup 26; Sheffield: Sheffield Academic Press, 1997), 278. Bauckham's approach has been followed in large measure by Jörg Frey, "Zur Bedeutung der Qumran-Funde," 56–63, but criticized by others.

7. This means, for example, that the enthusiastic position once held by John Ashton, that the author of the Fourth Gospel was a convert from Essenism, is not in the end sustainable; see John Ashton, *Understanding the Fourth Gospel* (Oxford: Clarendon, 1991), 199–204. See the comments on this in the contribution by James H. Charlesworth to this volume.

8. For references to other scholars who have generally been concerned with the character of the link between scrolls from Qumran and the Fourth Gospel, see the contribution by James H. Charlesworth to this collection and his essay, "A Study in Shared Symbolism and Language: The Qumran Community and the Johannine Community," in *The Bible and the Dead Sea Scrolls: The Princeton Symposium on the Dead Sea Scrolls* (ed. James H. Charlesworth, 3 vols.; Waco, Tex.: Baylor University Press, 2006), 3.97–152.

9. D. Moody Smith, *John among the Gospels: The Relationship in Twentieth-Century Research* (Minneapolis: Fortress Press, 1992).

10. Pierson Parker, "Luke and the Fourth Evangelist," *NTS* 9 (1962–63): 317–36. The Judean dimension of Parker's explanation was developed in subsequent studies that investigated the commonalities between John and Acts. Oral tradition lies at the basis of the more recent proposal of Tom Thatcher, that John attempted to combat antichrists through the writing down of oral history and eyewitness testimony (*Why John Wrote a Gospel: Jesus–Memory–History* [Louisville: Westminster John Knox, 2006]).

interests, and theological synergies shared by Luke and John arose from "the memories of Judaean disciples who followed Jesus in Judaea during his lifetime and who formed the core of the Judaean churches after his resurrection."[11] The Judean provenance of at least some of the traditions common to Luke and John seems to me probably to be correct; this is a topic to which I shall return as I suggest that some of the materials in these shared traditions have characteristics that are now discernible in some of the scrolls. Marie-Émile Boismard, who developed a four-stage compositional history of the Fourth Gospel, offered a third proposal that is relevant to this essay.[12] He argued that there was minor influence of pre-Matthean tradition in the second stage of the Fourth Gospel's composition, and influence of the Synoptics in their final form together with influence from Paul and Qumran as well as the *logia* of Jesus only at a third stage, once the author had left Palestine for Ephesus and his new situation required a reworking of the nascent Fourth Gospel.

In contrast to Boismard, Frans Neirynck and others have argued against the necessity for supposing earlier stages in the composition of the Fourth Gospel and proposed rather that the influence of the Synoptics should be acknowledged from the outset in the composition of the text.[13] But that is a moot point and goes against both the general trend of Johannine scholarship and some detailed studies, notably those by Anton Dauer and Hans-Peter Heerkerens, in which the existence of a Johannine *Grundschrift* independent of the Synoptics is reasserted.[14] Dauer supposes that the overlaps between John and Luke in the pericopae that he considers part of the pre-Johannine interaction with Lukan tradition rely possibly on oral, but more probably on some written, form of the early tradition. Furthermore, Dauer argues that each interaction between Johannine and Lukan traditions probably happened independently rather than by direct reliance on a written Gospel source. For Heerkerens, the final redactor of the Fourth Gospel

---

11. Robert Maddox, *The Purpose of Luke–Acts* (FRLANT 126; Göttingen: Vandenhoeck & Ruprecht, 1982), 174.

12. Marie-Émile Boismard, with Arnaud Lamouille and Gérard Rochais, *L'Evangile de Jean: Commentaire* (Paris: Editions du Cerf, 1977).

13. Frans Neirynck, *Jean et les Synoptiques: Examen critique de l'exégèse de M.-É. Boismard* (BETL 49; Louvain: Louvain University Press, 1979); see also idem, "John and the Synoptics: 1975–1990," in *John and the Synoptics* (ed. Adelbert Denaux; BETL 101; Louvain: Louvain University Press, 1992), 3–62, esp. 15. Neirynck's position has been adopted by Andrew T. Lincoln, *The Gospel according to St John* (BNTC 4; London: Continuum, 2005), 32: "[T]he Fourth Gospel provides evidence that its writer and editor not only knew Mark, to which it is most substantially indebted, but also knew and used both Matthew and Luke."

14. Anton Dauer, *Johannes und Lukas: Untersuchungen zu den johanneisch-lukanischen Parallelperikopen Joh 4,46–54/Lk 7,1–10–Joh 12,1–8/Lk 7,36–50; 10,38–42–Joh 20,19–29/Lk 24,36–39* (FB 50; Würzburg: Echter, 1984); Hans-Peter Heerkerens, *Die Zeichen-Quelle der johanneischen Redaktion: Ein Beitrag zur Entstehungsgeschichte des vierten Evangeliums* (SBS 113; Stuttgart: Verlag Katholisches Bibelwerk, 1984).

knew the Gospel of Luke but also knew three miracle stories (John 2:1–12; 4:46–54; 21:1–14) that came from a common source.[15]

The purpose of this study is to suggest that some of the parallels between Luke and John might possibly be illuminated further if considered against the background of the Jewish literature that is now available to us from the scrolls. That illumination might just be an accident of the way that the scrolls reflect ideas generally available in Judaism of the time,[16] but it might also be that specific traditions that emerged from Qumran were of more particular influence in the kinds of Palestinian Judaism that might have provided source materials for some parts of both L and John.[17] To explore this possibility, I will consider three specific instances in which the scrolls may shed light on John's use of material that he shares in common with Luke: the story of the miraculous catch of fish (John 21:1–14 // Luke 5:1–11); the use of "light and darkness" imagery; and the use of the messianic title "Son of God."

The Miraculous Draft of Fishes

The story of the miraculous draft of fish occurs variously in John 21:1–14 and Luke 5:1–11. A highly distinctive feature of the story in John, and an item that is not found in the Lukan counterpart, is the detail that there were 153 fish. Raymond Brown has summarized the five principal options that commentators over the ages have taken toward the 153 fish, given that the exactness of the number seems to demand some kind of interpretation.[18] First, in his commentary on Ezek 47:6–12, Jerome notes that the Greek zoologists had recorded 153 different kinds of fish; thus, by mentioning this number, the author of the Fourth Gospel may have been symbolizing the totality and range of the disciples' catch (cf. Matt 13:47). In fact, however, the form in which Jerome's own source for this theory, Oppian's *Halieutica*, has reached us mentions 157 kinds of fish, so it could well be that Jerome has interpreted Greek zoology by way of the Gospel. Second, Augustine and many subsequently have taken a mathematical approach to the number:

---

15. Recent German scholarship on the relation between John and the Synoptics is mentioned by Dietrich Rusam, "Das Johannesevangelium—eine 'Relecture' der synoptischen Evangelien? Intertextuelle Beobachtungen zu den 'Ich-bin-Worten' des Johannesevangeliums," in *Kontexte der Schrift. Band II, Kultur, Politik, Religion, Sprache–Text. Wolfgang Stegemann zum 60. Geburtstag* (ed. Christian Strecker; Stuttgart: W. Kohlhammer, 2005), 377–90, esp. 377–81.

16. This is the approach, e.g., of Rekha M. Chennattu, *Johannine Discipleship as a Covenant Relationship* (Peabody, Mass.: Hendrickson, 2006), 184–86, who sees nothing specific in the influence of the Qumran texts on covenantal ideas in the Johannine tradition.

17. It is also appropriate to remember that there are indeed distinct differences between Luke and John, such as in their treatment of wealth and poverty and of matters of apostolicity.

18. Raymond E. Brown, *The Gospel according to John* (2 vols.; AB; Garden City, N.Y.: Doubleday, 1966–70), 2.1074–76.

153 is the sum of all the numbers one to seventeen. As a triangular number based on the combination of seven and ten, both numbers representing completion, the number 153 itself would represent perfection.[19] Should this prove to be a reflection of Pythagorean understanding, then the links between some Essenes (*Ant.* 15.371), whom Josephus labels as like the Pythagoreans,[20] and the Lukan communities who similarly share goods could be relevant.[21] Third, there are the allegorical interpreters, such as Cyril of Alexandria (who has one hundred for Gentiles, fifty for Israel, and three for the Trinity), and Rupert of Deutz (who has one hundred for the married, fifty for the widows, and three for the virgins). A fourth avenue is that of gematria. Again several possibilities have been suggested, but the most persuasive proposal is that of John Emerton, who has argued that 153 is the value of *(En-)Eglaim* in Hebrew, and seventeen the value of *(En-) Gedi*.[22] Both these names occur in Ezek 47:10: "People will stand fishing beside the sea from En-gedi to En-Eglaim: it will be a place for the spreading of nets; its fish will be of a great many kinds, like the fish of the Great Sea." Brown, though taken somewhat with this fourth option since it is probable that both Rev 22:1–2 and John 7:37 refer to imagery from this text of Ezekiel, despairs of certainty and concludes that "we know of no speculation or established symbolism related to the number 153 in early thought." So Brown himself goes for a fifth option, that of eyewitness testimony: there actually were 153 fish caught that day as the eyewitness Beloved Disciple reports.[23]

I first became aware of the possibility that Palestinian Jewish traditions might illuminate the commonalities between Luke and the Fourth Gospel when I began to work on the traditions about the flood in the Commentary on Genesis

---

19. But compare Haenchen, who concludes that "it contributes nothing to our understanding to say that 153 is the triangular number of 17" (*John: A Commentary on the Gospel of John*, trans. Robert W. Funk, 2 vols. [Hermeneia; Philadelphia: Fortress, 1984], 2.224).

20. See the comments on the connections between the Essenes and the Pythagoreans by Philip S. Alexander, "Physiognomy, Initiation, and Rank in the Qumran Community," in *Geschichte–Tradition–Reflexion: Festschrift für Martin Hengel zum 70. Geburtstag* (ed. Hubert Cancik, Hermann Lichtenberger, and Peter Schäfer; 3 vols.; Tübingen: J. C. B. Mohr, 1996), 1.392; also Justin Taylor, *Pythagoreans and Essenes: Structural Parallels* (Collection de la Revue des Études juives 32; Louvain: Peeters, 2004).

21. See the studies of Pierson Parker, "When Acts Sides with John," in *Understanding the Sacred Text: Essays in Honor of Morton S. Enslin on the Hebrew Bible and Christian Beginnings* (ed. John Reumann; Valley Forge, Pa.: Judson Press, 1972), 210–15; "The Kinship of John and Acts," in *Christianity, Judaism, and Other Greco-Roman Cults: Studies for Morton Smith at Sixty* (ed. Jacob Neusner; 4 vols.; SJLA 12; Leiden: Brill, 1975), 1.187–205.

22. John A. Emerton, "The One Hundred and Fifty-Three Fishes in John xxi.11," *JTS* 9 (1958): 86–89.

23. Brown, *Gospel according to John*, 2.1076.

A (4Q252).[24] The Commentary in its final form is a sectarian compilation, but it seems to be made up from sources, some of which could be deemed to have been nonsectarian. The principal extant pericope of the Commentary is concerned with the precise chronology of the year of the flood. The narratives of Gen 6–8 are presented in a rewritten form with all extraneous material cut out.[25]

> And the waters of the flood burst over the [ ] earth in the year six hundred of Noah's life, in the second month, on the first [day] of the week, on its seventeenth [day]. On that day all the springs of the great abyss were split and the sluices of the sky opened and rain fell upon the earth forty days and forty nights, until the twenty-sixth day of the third month, the fifth day of the week. One hundred and fifty days did the waters hold sway over the earth, until the fourteenth day in the seventh month, the third [day] of the week. At the end of one hundred and fifty days, the waters decreased for two days, the fourth day and the fifth day, and the sixth day, the ark rested in the mountains of Hurarat, the seventeenth of the seventh month. (4Q252 1.4–10)[26]

The notice that the waters of the flood continued for 150 days is found in both Gen 7:24 and 8:3; the commentator cites the first occurrence and then moves directly to part of the precise dating formula found in 8:4 before repeating the 150 days from 8:3. In relation to the 364-day calendar that is being used, this takes Noah to the eve of Sukkoth and, because of the two quarter-days within the 150-day period, is two days short of the biblical date of the ark coming to rest on the seventeenth of the seventh month. The commentator copes with this problem by intercalating two days between the end of the 150 days and the ark coming to rest:[27] "and at the end of one hundred and fifty days the waters decreased for two days, the fourth day and the fifth day, and on the sixth day the ark came to rest

---

24. See my principal edition of this composition, George J. Brooke, "252. 4QCommentary on Genesis A," in *Qumran Cave 4.XVII: Parabiblical Texts Part 3* (ed. James C. VanderKam; DJD 22; Oxford: Clarendon, 1996), 185–207.

25. So, for example, there is no mention of the building of the ark, or, likewise, although Noah's age is mentioned in Gen 7:6 and 11, the commentator uses the second occurrence alone. The forty days mentioned in Gen 7:17 are redundant in the overall scheme of producing a flood that lasted for exactly one year, so they are omitted.

26. The translation here is based on the text in *The Dead Sea Scrolls: Electronic Reference Library 2* (ed. Emanuel Tov, trans. Florentino García Martínez; CD-ROM; Leiden: Brill, 1999).

27. Joseph M. Baumgarten argues that the author of *Jubilees* also knew of the problem concerning the two-day discrepancy and so studiously avoided the date on which the ark is said to have landed on the mountains of Ararat; see "The Calendars of the Book of Jubilees and the Temple Scroll," *VT* 37 (1987): 76. However, the context in *Jubilees* only concerns the quarter-days, the days of remembrance, which the author is concerned to associate with the flood narrative. The calendrical problems concerning the chronology of the flood with particular reference to *Jubilees* are highlighted by Baumgarten in *Studies in Qumran Law* (SJLA 24; Leiden: Brill, 1977), 108–9.

on the mountains of Hurarat; it was the seventeenth day in the seventh month" (4Q252 1.8–10). He is thus able to end the 150 days on the eve of Sukkoth and have the ark suitably come to rest on the eve of the Sabbath that falls within the octave of Sukkoth. For purposes of the present discussion, the point to note in all this calendrical calculation is that the ark comes to rest on Mount Ararat 153 days from the start of the flood. Although this number is not mentioned explicitly, to my mind this invests the number 153 with a significance not readily perceived previously and takes us to a reconsideration of the options for interpreting the 153 fish in John 21:11.[28]

In light of 4Q252, it now seems that an interpretation of John 21:11 involving some kind of symbolism by gematria is most appropriate, and this may go hand in hand with a calendrical interpretation based on the reworking of the flood narrative. Consideration of the purpose of the Johannine story is also important. All commentators agree that it concerns the character of the mission of the disciples: they are to be the fisherfolk. Since members are added to the Christian community through baptism, the water symbolism in the story is important, too. Furthermore, it is not a matter of baptism alone, but of an application of a particular typological understanding of baptism that gives the rite meaning through juxtaposition with the way in which Noah and his family are saved through water. This juxtaposition is clear in the Petrine traditions of 1 Peter 3: "God waited patiently in the days of Noah, during the building of the ark, in which a few, that is, eight persons were saved through water. And baptism which this prefigured now saves you . . . as an appeal to God for a good conscience, through the resurrection of Jesus Christ" (3:20–21). The context of both passages, John 21 and 1 Peter 3, with Peter as the lead swimmer in the former and the dispersed exiles in the latter, also hints at the persecution and suffering to be experienced by community members.

As is widely recognized, a similar miraculous catch story features in Luke 5:1–11. The call of Peter, together with James and John (also mentioned in John 21, together with some other disciples), takes place at the outset of Jesus' ministry as in the other Synoptics, but Luke uses the story perhaps to explain the psychology of the moment. "The whole episode is thus composed by Luke from transposed and redacted Markan material and other material from Luke's private source ('L')."[29] Given that it can be conjectured that the miraculous draft of fishes

---

28. Several of the following comments are derived from my study, "4Q252 and the 153 Fish of John 21:11," in *Antikes Judentum und Frühes Christentum: Festschrift für Hartmut Stegemann zum 65. Geburtstag* (ed. Bernd Kollmann, Wolfgang Reinbold, and Annette Steudel; BZNW 97; Berlin: Walter de Gruyter, 1999), 253–65; repr. in a slightly revised form in my *Dead Sea Scrolls and the New Testament: Essays in Mutual Illumination* (Minneapolis: Fortress, 2005), 282–97.

29. Joseph A. Fitzmyer, *The Gospel according to Luke*, 2 vols. (AB; Garden City, N.Y.: Doubleday, 1981–85), 1.560.

belonged to a miracle source used by John at some stage, it is likely that Luke's version of the tradition cannot be assigned to L in an unqualified way.[30] There seems to be enough evidence to suggest that a traditional resurrection story has somehow been mediated to Luke with most of the resurrection elements eliminated, whereas the Fourth Gospel preserved the narrative with an element that echoed a particular Jewish reading of the flood narrative now found in the scrolls from Qumran. Influenced by Mark, Luke adapted the tradition he found as a call to mission. The fish are not numbered in the Lukan version. The story is told so as to fit with the generally positive portrayal of Peter in Luke: Luke omits Jesus' rebuke of him (cf. Mark 8:32–33) and Jesus' reproach of him asleep (cf. Mark 14:37), but includes his running to the tomb to confirm the resurrection (24:12; cf. John 20:3–7).[31] Many other matters could be discussed, but the point for our immediate purposes is that a tradition common to Luke and the Fourth Gospel is, in the case of John, perhaps best understood once a text from Qumran is brought into the picture.[32]

SONS OF LIGHT

It has become almost tedious to say that, of the four canonical Gospels, John is most like the Qumran texts in its use of light and darkness motifs.[33] In fact, recent studies since the general release of the scrolls have led to two important qualifications of how such a parallel should be handled. First, from the side of the Qumran texts, the general availability of more scrolls has shown that the light and darkness imagery is not as pervasive as one might have thought. James Charlesworth has made the important suggestion that it is really only in the Rule of the Community 3.13–4.14 that one can see the imagery applied in depth. Charlesworth supposes that this section of the Rule had to be memorized by all aspiring

---

30. Heerkerens, *Zeichen-Quelle*, 45–94.

31. Haenchen also thinks John 21:11 indicates a positive view of Peter: with regard to the 153 fish, "the author does not intend to point to a physical tour de force on the part of Peter; rather, he is obliquely suggesting his spiritual proficiency in the administration of the church" (*John*, 2.224).

32. One should add the possibility here that the appearances to Peter in John 21 reflect a northern apocalyptic visionary tradition that had a long-standing hostility toward the Jerusalem priesthood. See here George W. E. Nickelsburg, "Enoch, Levi, and Peter: Recipients of Revelation in Upper Galilee," *JBL* 100 (1981): 575–600, whose suggestions about the Petrine trajectory seem to have survived the critique of Hanan and Esther Eshel, "Separating Levi from Enoch: Response to 'Enoch, Levi, and Peter: Recipients of Revelation in Upper Galilee,'" in *George W. E. Nickelsburg in Perspective: An Ongoing Dialogue of Learning* (ed. Jacob Neusner and Alan J. Avery-Peck; JSJSup 80; Leiden: Brill, 2003), 458–68.

33. The similarities between John and the Qumran texts outweigh the differences for Craig A. Evans, *Word and Glory: On the Exegetical and Theological Background of John's Prologue* (JSNTSup 89; Sheffield: JSOT Press, 1993), 146–50.

members and is the key passage for identifying what the term "sons of light" refers to in other scrolls.[34] Second, from the side of the Fourth Gospel, Richard Bauckham has argued that most, if not all, of the Johannine language of light and darkness is derived from scriptural passages, notably the creation story and various prophetic texts, rather than from the scrolls.[35] Bauckham notes cogently that the central meaning of the imagery in the Fourth Gospel is Christological and soteriological, whereas in Qumran texts it is conflictual. Furthermore, virtually none of the precise phraseology from the scrolls is used in the Fourth Gospel, and, conversely, key Johannine phrases—"true light," "to have the light," "to come to the light," "to remain in darkness," the contrast of day and night—are not to be found in the scrolls. Bauckham's argument puts a fresh perspective on the evidence for those who might be tempted to say that the author of the Fourth Gospel was an Essene.[36]

However, there is one passage to which Charlesworth rightly draws attention that Bauckham skates over: John 12:35–36, "Jesus said to them, 'The light is with you for a little longer. Walk while you have the light, so that the darkness may not overtake you. If you walk in the darkness, you do not know where you are going. While you have the light, believe in the light, so that you may become sons of light.'" This is the only passage in the Fourth Gospel that uses the term "sons of light," and it notably appears in a broader context that is concerned with the necessity of Jesus' death. In addition, if chapters 11–12 belong to the final stage in the redaction of the Gospel (along with chapter 21), then we might have here yet another hint that some aspects of the thought world of the redactor were influenced by Qumranic modes of thought. With regard to establishing John's relationship to the scrolls, caution is necessary: if the terms "sons of light" and "walking in darkness" occurred more frequently, one might be tempted to see a closer association of the Gospel and the scrolls, but one instance is not enough for the construction of elaborate theories of literary dependence.

For purposes of the present discussion, however, it is notable that Luke's is the only other Gospel that uses the phrase "sons of light" and, like John, uses it only once. In Luke 16:8, the "children of this age" are compared with the "sons of light" in the parable of the dishonest manager: "The master commended the dishonest steward for his shrewdness; for the sons of this world are shrewder in

---

34. James H. Charlesworth, "The Dead Sea Scrolls and the Gospel according to John," in *Exploring the Gospel of John: In Honor of D. Moody Smith* (ed. R. Alan Culpepper and C. Clifton Black; Louisville: Westminster John Knox, 1996), 70–71. Having largely rejected the possible influence of the Qumran texts on traditions used in the Fourth Gospel, it is not surprising that Haenchen makes no mention of the possible Jewish background of the label "sons of light" (see *John*, 2.98–99).

35. Bauckham, "Qumran and the Fourth Gospel," 269–79.

36. See especially John Ashton, *Understanding the Fourth Gospel* (Oxford: Clarendon, 1991), 235–37.

dealing with their own generation than the sons of light." This parable has been the subject of many diverse interpretations, since it almost seems to commend dishonesty. David Flusser, largely on the basis of the occurrence of the term "sons of light" in 16:8, has concluded that Jesus knew of, and here was criticizing, an Essene perspective.[37] That may be possible, but the parable should first be set within Luke's context, where it probably should be understood as of two parts (Luke 16:1–8a, 8b–13), the second of which is a Lucan "multiple conclusion."[38] Several Lucan scholars postulate that Luke–Acts is directed to a community that actively practiced common ownership of goods (Acts 4:32–5:12). While community of goods may be an ideal goal, such communism should not be at the expense of relations with the outside world, as Luke might have understood was the case with the "sons of light." Thus, in the overall context of Luke–Acts, the parable seems to suggest that, though an idea found in the sectarian scrolls at Qumran could be taken over, its means of being put into practice was to be questioned.

Of course, the Lukan context of the reference to the "sons of light" is a long way in subject matter from the context of its occurrence in the Fourth Gospel. The argument in John 12 is not about economics. However, there is something similar happening. Once the differences between the scrolls and the Fourth Gospel have been noticed, then it can be seen that the Johannine redactor has taken a sectarian idea and adapted it for his own purposes. According to the Rule of the Community, one is either a "son of light" or a "son of darkness," with no middle ground between the groups.

> He [God] created man to rule the world and placed within him two spirits so that he would walk with them until the moment of his visitation: they are the spirits of truth and of deceit. In the hand of the Prince of Lights is dominion over all the sons of justice; they walk on paths of light. And in the hand of the Angel of Darkness is total dominion over the sons of deceit; they walk on paths of darkness. (1QS 3.19–21)[39]

For the Johannine redactor, it is necessary to make the transition from darkness to light and Jesus is portrayed as the one who saves—who enables that transfer from darkness to light. Thus the language, which in its sectarian scrolls context

---

37. David Flusser, *Judaism and the Origins of Christianity* (Jerusalem: Magnes, 1988), 150–68.

38. Joseph A. Fitzmyer, "The Story of the Dishonest Manager (Lk 16:1–13)," in his *Essays on the Semitic Background of the New Testament* (London: G. Chapman, 1971), 166. Fitzmyer understands Luke 16:8 to be an independent saying of Jesus that has been joined to the parable (either by Luke or by his source). The Palestinian origin of part of the verse is clear—in this case, not just a general Palestinian background, but one that is reflected in the sectarian compositions from Qumran.

39. Cited from *The Dead Sea Scrolls: Electronic Reference Library 2*.

is unmistakably cliquish and sectarian, comes to designate what is the Johannine aspiration for all people. Thus, in an intriguing way, sectarian ideas are handled similarly by both Luke from L and by the Johannine redactor from his own store.

Here again, the evidence from the texts supports the basic thesis of this essay: it seems as if some elements in the final stages of the redaction of the Fourth Gospel are shared with Luke exclusively, and that some of those common elements are based on the worldview found in the sectarian (Essenic) Dead Sea Scrolls and possibly others preserved in the Qumran collection. Perhaps part of L was derived from a collection of stories told by an Essene Christian, and part of the outlook and material of the final redactor of the Fourth Gospel was derived from a similar source. All this is much more mildly stated than theories of Lukan dependence on the Fourth Gospel or vice versa (as Bailey), or than Boismard's proposal that Luke was the final redactor of the Fourth Gospel.[40] In a nuanced way, as suggested here, the Qumran scrolls may shed new light on questions raised about the provenance and sources of the Gospels.

Son of God and Son of the Most High

James Charlesworth has drawn attention to the way that 4Q246 shows how the designation "Son of God" featured as a title in a pre-Christian nonscriptural Jewish text, and he has discussed how this can reinforce the Jewish character of the Fourth Gospel.[41] In this section, I wish to discuss how Luke and John share, each very much in their own ways, the tradition reflected in 4Q246 of the combination of the titles "Son of God" and "Son of the Most High."[42]

4Q246, the so-called Son of God Text, is now well known and among the most discussed of the scrolls found at Qumran. In the principal extant fragment, a seer interprets a vision to a king. The first column is damaged on the right side, but the second column is more or less intact. The passage in question appears in column 2.

> He will be called son of God, and they will call him son of the Most High.... His kingdom will be an eternal kingdom, and all his paths in truth and uprightness. The earth will be in truth and all will make peace. (4Q246 2.1, 5–6)[43]

---

40. John Amedee Bailey, *The Traditions Common to the Gospels of Luke and John* (NovT-Sup 7; Leiden: Brill, 1963); Marie-Émile Boismard, "Saint Luc et la redaction du quatrième évangile (Jn iv, 46–54)," *RB* 69 (1962): 185–211. Boismard later came to recognize that this proposal was wide of the mark.

41. Charlesworth, "Dead Sea Scrolls and the Gospel," 72–73.

42. Both titles are also to be found in Mark, but the same kind of dependence on the tradition as now found in 4Q246 is not readily apparent.

43. Cited from *The Dead Sea Scrolls: Electronic Reference Library 2.*

Several theories about how this text should be understood have been in circulation, and none has yet decisively won the day. Before proceeding, these theories should be outlined briefly; they fall naturally under two major headings.

On one hand, some theorists, following the earliest editor of the composition, argue that the character designated "son of God" and "son of the Most High" is wicked. Józef Milik suggested in his public presentation of the text in 1972 that the "son of God" figure was a king, Alexander Balas, son of Antiochus Epiphanes.[44] He could be called "son of God" because he is identified on coins as *theopator* or *Deo patre natus*. Milik has found partial support in the official preliminary publication of the text by Émile Puech, who allows for the possibility that this is a reference to a Seleucid king, whether Alexander Balas or Antiochus Epiphanes himself.[45] Similarly, for David Flusser, the spaces in the text should control its proper interpretation: everything before the space in 4Q246 2.4 should be understood in terms of tribulations and afflictions, suggesting that the "son of God" should be viewed as evil. In Flusser's reading, however, the "son of God" figure is not an actual historical king, but the antichrist. Flusser's key argument is based on the oracle of Hystaspes (cited by Lactantius), which describes "a prophet of lies" who "will constitute and call himself God and will order himself to be worshipped as the Son of God."[46] Annette Steudel also aligns herself with those who see "the son of God" as a negative title, not least because of the way she understands the text to juxtapose "the son" and his negative attributes (4Q246 1.7–2.3) with those of the people of God, who have all the positive ones (4Q246 2.4–9).[47]

On the other hand, the majority of interpreters have identified the titles "son of God" and "son of the Most High" as referring to a positive character. Joseph Fitzmyer was the first to offer this proposal in print, though without using the terms "messiah" or "messianic" since they do not occur in the text. For him, the "king" addressed in the text is on the Jewish side, and the "son of God" is thus "a son of some enthroned king, possibly an heir to the throne of David"—a coming Jewish ruler, perhaps a member of the Hasmonean dynasty who will be a successor to the Davidic throne, but who is not envisaged as a messiah.[48] Florentino García Martínez is also convinced of the positive character of the "son of God" figure and seeks to interpret it in light of other Qumran texts. He draws

---

44. As reported by Joseph A. Fitzmyer, "The Contribution of Qumran Aramaic to the Study of the New Testament," *NTS* 20 (1973–74): 382–407; repr. in his *A Wandering Aramean: Collected Aramaic Essays* (SBLMS 25; Missoula, Mont.: Scholars Press).

45. Émile Puech, "Fragment d'une apocalypse en araméen (4Q246=pseudo-Dan^d) et le 'royaume de Dieu,'" *RB* 99 (1992): 98–131.

46. Flusser, *Judaism and the Origins*, 207–13.

47. Annette Steudel, "The Eternal Reign of the People of God—Collective Expectations in Qumran Texts (4Q246 and 1QM)," *RevQ* 17 (1996): 507–25.

48. Fitzmyer, *Wandering Aramean*, 102–7.

his parallels primarily from 11QMelchizedek and concludes that "son of God" is another designation for Melchizedek, Michael, or the Prince of Light.[49] Collins has argued more directly that the "son of God" of 4Q246 is a messiah; he sees 4Q246 as possibly the earliest interpretation of the Son of Man in Daniel 7 as an individual figure.[50]

What light can this rich variety of interpretations (or scholarly muddle) throw on Luke and John? I would suggest that there may be some truth in most of the interpretations just laid out—that is, that the text of 4Q246, or something very much like it, was known in the collection of Judean Essenic material which I am proposing was variously used by Luke and by the redactor of the Fourth Gospel, and was ambiguous even in antiquity.

Let us begin with the easy one. The correspondences between 4Q246 and the Lukan infancy narrative are striking.[51] In Luke 1:32–35, the same pair of titles occurs together with the phrase "he will be great." Collins comments that these correspondences are "astonishing" and that "it is difficult to avoid the conclusion that Luke is dependent in some way, whether directly or indirectly, on this long-lost text from Qumran."[52] Here, then, in Luke's infancy narrative we have an example of the messianic reading of the text and a reading that took the "son of God" figure as an individual. And so let us move on to how the Fourth Gospel may show some evidence of the material in 4Q246. In John 10:22–39, the narrative and its dialogues are presented against the backdrop of the Feast of Hanukkah, with Jesus walking in the temple itself.[53] The Jews demand that he tell them "plainly" whether he is the Messiah. Jesus' answer is eventually clear: "the father and I are one" (John 10:30). This causes an aggressive reaction as the Jews take up stones. They explain their position: it is not for good works that they react in such a way, but because they perceive that Jesus, though only a human being, is making himself God. Jesus disagrees that he makes himself anything, but tacitly affirms that he has a distinct status by using Ps 82:6 in his reply to show

---

49. Florentino García Martínez, *Qumran and Apocalyptic: Studies on the Aramaic Texts from Qumran* (STDJ 9; Leiden: Brill, 1992), 172–79.

50. John J. Collins, *The Scepter and the Star: The Messiahs of the Dead Sea Scrolls and Other Ancient Literature* (ABRL; New York: Doubleday, 1995), 163–69.

51. It is a moot point here whether the Lukan infancy narratives should be seen as part of L or as a separate source. Kim Paffenroth, *The Story of Jesus according to L* (JSNTSup 147; Sheffield: Sheffield Academic Press, 1997), 27–28, sides with those who distinguish Luke 1–2 from the rest of L. Nevertheless, the Palestinian Jewish character of much of Luke 1–2 cannot be denied.

52. Collins, *Scepter and the Star*, 155.

53. On the understanding of the Feast of Hanukkah as the inauguration of the altar, which explains the use of ἐγκαίνια in John 10:22, see Richard J. Bauckham, "The Holiness of Jesus and His Disciples in the Gospel of John," in *Holiness and Ecclesiology in the New Testament* (ed. Kent E. Brower and Andy Johnson; Grand Rapids: Eerdmans, 2007), 98–105.

that human beings can be called "god." He eventually describes himself as "Son of God" (John 10:36).

The wider context of Jesus' citation of the verse from Ps 82 needs to be considered. As Raymond Brown and many others have recognized, the whole verse (and sometimes the wider context of quotations) is important.[54] Psalm 82:6 reads, in full, "I say, 'You are Gods, sons of the Most High, all of you.'" Thus, as with Luke 1:32–35, John 10:36 uses a title "Son of God" with an allusion to "sons of the Most High" (Ps 82:6) within a heated debate about whether Jesus is making himself God (John 10:33). All these ingredients can be found in 4Q246. Furthermore, the difficult John 10:29, "My father, as to what he has given me, is greater than all," may be a reflection of the use of "great" at several points in 4Q246.

As an aside that may not be entirely irrelevant to our purposes, Brown notes that the question in John 10:24 concerning Jesus' messiahship is separated from questions about Jesus' sonship later in the pericope. Brown sees this as a reflection of the passion-narrative interrogations, but notes that parallels may be drawn especially with Luke. In Luke 22:67, alone among the Synoptics, the high priest asks Jesus if he is the Messiah in a way that is close to John 10:24: "if you are really the Messiah, tell us so." Jesus' answer in both Luke and John is virtually the same: in John 10:25, "I have told you and you do not believe"; in Luke 22:67, "If I tell you, you will not believe."[55] In Mark 14:61 and Matt 26:63 there is one question that mentions the Messiah, the son of God or the blessed, but Luke 22:67 mentions only the messiah in the first question; Luke 22:70 then has a second question asked by the high priest: "Are you the son of God?" Thus, Luke is closest to the Fourth Gospel, where the question of messiahship is followed later in the pericope by questions concerning Jesus making himself God or son of God.

Many and various have been the listing of the associations between Hanukkah and John 10.[56] Some have been content merely to note the particular details as authenticating the narrative: the timing in winter; the location in Solomon's portico, the only place to shield oneself from the winter wind; the discussion of messianism in the context of a nationalist celebration; and so on. Others point to some of the typology involved: for Jesus to be in Solomon's portico would recall the way in which he was to be viewed as the true Davidic son who in himself replaced—that is, consecrated—the Temple. In addition, Aileen Guilding has made several attractive proposals as to how various lectionary readings that may have belonged to the time of Hanukkah are reflected in the matters at issue in

---

54. Brown, *Gospel according to John*, 1.409–11.

55. Exclusive parallels between the passion narratives of Luke and John have long been noted; see D. Moody Smith, *John among the Gospels: The Relationship in Twentieth Century Research* (Columbia: University of South Carolina Press, 1992), 87.

56. See the literature cited by Bauckham, "Holiness of Jesus," 99 n. 16, 107 n. 35.

John 10.[57] However, to my mind, it is James VanderKam who has brought out the parallels between Hanukkah and John 10 most suitably for our purposes. He writes:

> It should be recalled that Antiochus IV not only banned the practice of Judaism and the temple cult but that he also imposed new forms of worship which included veneration of himself as a god in Jerusalem's temple. Jesus' strong assertions that he and the father are one (10:30), that he was the Son of God (10:36), and that the father was in him as he was in the father were uttered at a time when the blasphemous pretensions of Antiochus IV to be a god would have been particularly fresh in the minds of Jewish people.[58]

Antiochus's coins show that he advertised himself as a god, "God manifest" or "God manifest, the victorious." One also finds the shorter "of the king Antiochus God" on some of his coins. In Jewish texts, Antiochus's self-aggrandizement is apparent. In Daniel 7 (also 8:9–14, 23–24) the little horn variously makes war with the saints of the Most High and opposes God himself. Daniel 11:36–37 is more explicit about Antiochus's divine pretensions: "And the king shall do according to his will; he shall exalt himself and magnify himself above every god and shall speak astonishing things against the God of gods." Such blasphemy is also reflected in 1 Macc 1:59, which describes how sacrifices were offered on the altar that was on top of the altar of burnt offering on 25 Chislev (which later became the first day of Hanukkah). Likewise, in 2 Macc 9:29 Antiochus is described as a blasphemer; earlier in the chapter he had confessed that "it is right to be subject to God; mortals should not think that they are equal to god" (9:12). Thus, VanderKam concludes that the subject matter of Hanukkah should be considered as a thoroughly appropriate backdrop against which to view the debate about blasphemy as it is described in John 10.

4Q246 seems to confirm something of this. I have come to wonder whether, even if the text were whole, we would be any better off in being able to identify the figure referred to in 4Q246 2.1. Whichever way it should be read, it provides the language for making partial sense of what is at issue in John 10. The matters to be considered are whether Jesus is suitably "Son of God," one of the "Sons of the Most High," and whether he makes himself such or is consecrated and sent

57. Aileen Guilding, *The Fourth Gospel and Jewish Worship: A Study of the Relation of St. John's Gospel to the Ancient Jewish Lectionary System* (Oxford: Clarendon, 1960), 129–32.

58. James C. VanderKam, "John 10 and the Feast of Dedication," in *Of Scribes and Scrolls: Studies on the Hebrew Bible, Intertestamental Judaism, and Christian Origins Presented to John Strugnell on the Occasion of His Sixtieth Birthday* (ed. Harold W. Attridge, John J. Collins, and Thomas H. Tobin; CTSRR 5; Lanham, Md.: University Press of America, 1990), 211.

by the father.[59] The terms belong to both parties, whether truly or falsely. There is even the possibility of an angelic interpretation. For Brown, Ps 82 is cited in John because it speaks of Israel's judges, who have a quasi-divine function since judgment belongs to God (see Deut 1:17). However, the same Psalm is quoted in 11QMelchizedek to refer to the role of Melchizedek as judge.

In any case, both Luke in the infancy narrative, possibly part of L, and the Hanukkah debate of the Fourth Gospel seem to know of the Aramaic tradition that is present in 4Q246. Luke (or his source) plays it straight, so that all the terms are read messianically and individualistically of Jesus. The Fourth Gospel lets the ambiguity of the tradition set the tone for the debate in order to encourage the reader to make the right decision about Jesus. As is well known, this is a standard Johannine feature.

FURTHER POINTS OF CONTACT

Other possible common traditions between Luke and John involve the presentation of John the Baptist, the use of Jacob material, a particular temple focus, and the charge against Jesus of sedition. While these parallels can prove little about any direct relationship between the Fourth Gospel at some stage in its composition and some of Luke's special material, they indicate that both Gospels reflect Jewish traditions, probably Judean ones, and they may possibly indicate a common milieu in early Palestinian Jewish Christianity for the use of those traditions.

JOHN THE BAPTIST AND THE MESSIAH

Apart from some possible similarities between Luke's infancy narrative and the Fourth Gospel, the earliest similarity in the Lukan text between passages in the two Gospels is in connection with John the Baptist. Luke recounts how the crowd was wondering whether John might be the Messiah, to which John answers by referring to one who is coming whose sandal he is not worthy to untie (Luke 3:15–17). In the Fourth Gospel, priests and Levites are sent to make inquiry of the Baptizer,[60] to whom John eventually makes a very similar response concern-

---

59. On the relationship of this term in John 10:36 to Hanukkah, see Bauckham, "Holiness of Jesus," 98.

60. The appearance of priests and Levites together in John 1:19 is suggestive of a set of parallels between L and John that have resonance with Qumran traditions. The parable of the Good Samaritan (L) also features a priest and a Levite, together with a Samaritan. Despite the negative portrayal of the priest in Luke 10:31, Acts 6:7 suggests that a great many priests became "obedient to the faith," and Barnabas, a Levite, is the prime example of one who contributes to the common welfare (Acts 4:36–37), a motif commonly thought to echo Qumran or Essene practice; see, e.g., Brian Capper, "'With the Oldest Monks . . . ': Light from Essene History on

ing the one "the thong of whose sandal I am not worthy to untie" (John 1:27). Since the Baptizer's answer is in large measure also found in Mark (and partly even in Q), it is the combination of question and answer which is distinctively Lukan and somewhat parallel to John. In particular, Luke 3:15 is a Lukan construct (or L), used also in Acts 13:25. The similar material in the Fourth Gospel is too far removed from Luke to support any theory that its author depends on Luke explicitly, and there is nothing of this in the scrolls from Qumran.

However, the inquiry about John's status and function is turned around and represented as an inquiry from John concerning Jesus' status and function in the Q passage most often assessed through its form in Luke 7:18–35. At least part of this Q tradition reflects the influence of a Palestinian Jewish adaptation of Isa 61: "And he answered them, 'Go and tell John what you have seen and heard: the blind receive their sight, the lame walk, lepers are cleansed, and the deaf hear, the dead are raised up, the poor have good news preached to them'" (Luke 7:22). The juxtaposition of the resurrection of the dead and the preaching of good news to the poor also appears in 4Q521.

> For the Lord will observe the devout, and call the just by name, and upon the poor he will place his spirit, and the faithful he will renew with his strength. For he will honor the devout upon the throne of eternal royalty, freeing prisoners, giving sight to the blind, straightening out the twisted . . . for he will heal the badly wounded *and will make the dead live, he will proclaim good news to the meek*, give lavishly to the needy, lead the exiled and enrich the hungry. (4Q521 2.5–8, 12–13)[61]

As Frans Neirynck has neatly reminded us, the parallel is more a matter of similar *topoi* of descriptions of the time of salvation than any kind of literary dependence, such as proposed by John Collins.[62] Although the Q material in Luke 7:18–35 has gone through considerable editing, two brief comments seem appropriate. The first is the widespread acknowledgment that here Q preserves elements of a Palestinian Jewish use of Scripture which is developed independently by Matthew and Luke. The second is that Luke's adaptation involves the broader redactional

---

the Career of the Beloved Disciple," *JTS* 49 (1998): 42–47. The priests and Levites are separate groups also in the history of the sectarian movement reflected in the scrolls. The Damascus Document records a particular reading of Ezek 44:15: the "Levitical priests" of Ezekiel is read as "the Priests and the Levites" (see CD 3.21–4.2). These are two separate groups, the penitents or returnees of Judah and those who joined them. On Levi and Levites in the scrolls and the New Testament, see Brooke, *Dead Sea Scrolls and the New Testament*, 115–39.

61. Cited from *The Dead Sea Scrolls: Electronic Reference Library 2*, emphasis added.

62. Frans Neirynck, "Q 6, 20b–21; 7, 22 and Isaiah 61," in *The Scriptures in the Gospels* (ed. Christopher M. Tuckett; BETL 131; Louvain: Peeters, 1997), 62; cf. John J. Collins, "The Works of the Messiah," *DSD* 1 (1994): 107: "It is quite possible that the author of the Sayings source knew 4Q521; at the least he drew on a common tradition."

introduction of the story of the resuscitation of the widow of Nain's son (Luke 7:11–17) as a deliberate anticipation of Luke 7:22; commentators commonly draw parallels with the raising of Lazarus in John 11:1–44. Hints of an overlap between John and Luke in relation to John the Baptist have taken us directly to a separate pericope in which an interaction between John the Baptist and Jesus reflects Palestinian Jewish traditions that played a significant part in the editing of Luke, a part that is matched by similar concerns in the final editorial stages of the Fourth Gospel.

JACOB TRADITIONS

Luke 1:33 contains the intriguing comment that Jesus will reign over the house of Jacob for ever, and of his kingdom there will be no end. This comment falls within that section of the infancy narrative that bears some affinity to 4Q246, the "son of God" passage discussed above. Might Jacob be another element in that section of the narrative that can be related to Palestinian Jewish tradition, as can also be seen in the Qumran materials and some layers of the Fourth Gospel? There is little other mention of Jacob in Luke's Gospel. What there is can be found quite naturally in the genealogy (Luke 3:34) or in standard formulae in Q sayings.[63] However, Stephen's speech in Acts gives considerable prominence to Jacob, mentioning him seven times (Acts 7:8 [2x], 12, 14, 15, 32, 46). Though most of these mentions of Jacob are subordinate to the Joseph story or appear in the standard formula "God of Abraham, Isaac, and Jacob," one usage is noteworthy: the use of the expression "house of Jacob" in Acts 7:45–46 ("So it was until the days of David, who found favor in the sight of God and asked leave to find a habitation for the house of Jacob. But it was Solomon who built a house for him").[64] This same phrase occurs in Luke: "And he will reign over the house of Jacob forever" (1:33). There is a hint here of an alternative temple ideology which was linked with Jacob at Beth-el, literally "the house of God."

In the Fourth Gospel, Jacob is somewhat more prominent. The dream tradition lies behind the saying of Jesus in John 1:51, and the associations of the well with Jacob in John 4 are played with as the reader is encouraged to see Jesus as greater than Jacob and the woman at the well is instructed about the character of true worship (John 4:19–22). Though the mention of Jacob does not fall among the elements that are among exclusive overlaps between John and Acts, the limited interest in this figure seems to reflect particular southern tradi-

---

63. "There you will weep and gnash your teeth, when you see Abraham and Isaac and Jacob and all the prophets in the kingdom of God and you yourselves thrust out" (Luke 13:28; similarly 20:37).

64. The variant reading in Acts 7:46 of "God of Jacob" in A and other witnesses might reflect an assimilation to the concerns of Ps 132:5.

tions that have influenced both Luke–Acts and the Fourth Gospel.[65] Such Jacob
traditions are also to be found in the scrolls from Qumran. The almost ninety
references to Jacob in the nonscriptural scrolls have not yet been fully described
as a cluster. Naturally, there are mentions of Jacob in the quasi-scriptural *Jubilees*
and *Pseudo-Jubilees* texts, in which he plays a prominent role as founder of the
priesthood, and he features too, as expected, in the reworked Pentateuch manuscripts. Jacob is described as "beloved" in 4Q372 and, by implication, in 4Q462
(a fragmentary narrative that seems to allow the Gentiles a role in God's plan).
More significant, Jacob plays an important role in the Damascus Document (CD
3.3, 4; 4.15; 7.19; 20.17) and in the Temple Scroll. In 11QT 29.10, the divinely
created sanctuary is established according to the covenant that God made with
Jacob at Bethel, a remarkable statement since Genesis itself records no covenant
between God and Jacob.[66] The phrase "house of Jacob" occurs but twice, once in
a very fragmentary manuscript of *Jubilees* (3Q5 3.3) and once in the quotation of
Isa 10:20 in a Psalms Pesher: "On that day it will happen that the remainder of
the House of Israel and the survivors of the House of Jacob will not return to lean
on their aggressor but will lean on the Lord, the Holy One of Israel, in truth. A
remnant will return, a remnant of Jacob, to the warrior God" (4Q163 frags. 4–7
2.10–12). It is possible that there existed a set of distinctive traditions about Jacob
in Samaria and Judea, and that these have somehow come to influence some elements of the Lukan infancy narrative, Stephen's speech in Acts, and some parts of
the Fourth Gospel.

TEMPLE OUTLOOK

The mention of Jacob, especially the "house of Jacob," which might be con-
strued as either people or temple, takes us to the outlook on the temple that is a
distinctive feature in Luke and John. This hardly need be rehearsed in any detail
here. Luke's story begins and ends in the Jerusalem temple and frequently refers
in distinctive L material to groups such as women, Samaritans, and lepers who
are in some way marginalized from full participation in temple worship—Luke
seems concerned to put them back in the worship picture. The Fourth Gospel

---

65. As described by Parker, "When Acts Sides with John," and "The Kinship of John and
Acts." See the summary of the exclusive overlaps in Smith, *John among the Gospels*, 97–99. In
some of these overlaps it may be possible to discern a negative reaction against some elements
of tradition preserved in the Qumran library, such as the way both Acts and John closely align
the Spirit with Jesus, perhaps working to promote a view other than the juxtaposition of the
Spirit with Michael. See the discussion of the relevant literature in relation to John in Tricia
Gates Brown, *Spirit in the Writings of John: Johannine Pneumatology in Social-Scientific Perspective* (JSNTSup 253; London: T&T Clark, 2003), 183.

66. See Brooke, *Dead Sea Scrolls and the New Testament*, 106–12, for a discussion of the
parallels between the Jacob traditions in the Temple Scroll and the Fourth Gospel.

places the cleansing of the temple at the outset of Jesus' ministry, which is then portrayed as the replacement or fulfillment of the Sabbath and festivals that centered particularly in Jerusalem.

Both these concerns emerge variously in the scrolls.[67] On the one hand, several texts are concerned to define who is permitted within the congregation— that is, the community as temple—or the future divinely constructed temple: "no uncircumcised, no Ammonite, no Moabite, no half-breed, no foreigner, no stranger" shall ever enter the sanctuary (4Q174; cf. 1QM 7). On the other hand, elaborate purity regulations are put forward to ensure the sanctity of the sanctuary; this is the content of most of the rules in 4QMMT, and in the Temple Scroll columns 47–51, as well as in the purity documents themselves. Whereas Luke-Acts seems to be arguing for inclusivity and the Fourth Gospel for replacement, the sectarian scrolls from Qumran generally argue for an interim spiritualization of the temple until its purity can be established more thoroughly.

The persistence of the temple outlook in Luke–Acts and John can hardly be accounted for on the basis of the supposed audiences being Palestinian Jewish Christians who may even have still been attending the temple.[68] One suspects that the best way to acknowledge the temple ideology of Luke and the Fourth Gospel is to recognize that there was a set of traditions, even a group of traditors of such traditions, who had the status of the temple at the center of their concerns. Such a concern is certainly to be found in the Qumran community texts, though not exclusively so.

The Charge of Sedition

There are several distinctive overlaps in the passion narratives of Luke and John.[69] One of these concerns the charges against Jesus: only in Luke 23:2 and John 19:12–15 is Jesus charged with sedition by the Jewish authorities.[70] Though expressed somewhat differently, both Gospels know of a similar charge. The basis for such a charge is now plain to read in the Temple Scroll: "If a man passes on information against his people or betrays his people to a foreign nation, or does evil against his people, you shall hang him on a tree and he will die. On the evidence of two witnesses or on the evidence of three witnesses he shall be put to

---

67. The way that socially driven views may account for some of these similarities and differences, at least as far as the Fourth Gospel is concerned, is set out by Kåre S. Fuglseth, *Johannine Sectarianism in Perspective: A Sociological, Historical, and Comparative Analysis of Temple and Social Relationships in the Gospel of John, Philo, and Qumran* (NovTSup 119; Leiden: Brill, 2005).

68. See Brooke, *Dead Sea Scrolls and the New Testament*, 169–71, on the shared concerns of 4QMMT and Luke–Acts in relation to Jerusalem and the temple.

69. See Smith, *John among the Gospels*, 87, for a brief summary of the principal overlaps.

70. Smith points to the discussion of this parallel in Maddox, *Purpose of Luke–Acts*, 164.

death and they shall hang him on the tree" (64.6–9). The charge here is partly based on Lev 19:16, but that text has been given a political edge in its adaptation in the Temple Scroll, where the punishment is adapted from Deut 21:22–23. As has become well known, the Temple Scroll inverts the verbs so that the hanging on the tree precedes death, whereas Deut 21:22 implies that execution precedes exposure. In this way, the text of the Temple Scroll appears to legitimize crucifixion. The significance of this text for the better understanding of the New Testament has been widely discussed.[71] Beyond the likely recognition of such a tradition by both Luke (also in Acts 5:30) and John as they rehearse the passion of Jesus, Paul also seems to know of this tradition, which makes sense of his use of Deut 21 in Gal 3.[72]

---

71. Joseph M. Baumgarten, "Does *TLH* in the Temple Scroll Refer to Crucifixion?" *JBL* 91 (1972): 472–81; repr. in his *Studies in Qumran Law* (SJLA 24; Leiden: Brill, 1977), 172–82; also idem, "Hanging and Treason in Qumran and Roman Law," *ErIsr* 16 (1982): 7–16; André Dupont-Sommer, "Observations nouvelles sur l'expression 'suspendu vivant sur le bois' dans le Commentaire de Nahum (4QpNah II 8) à la lumière du Rouleau du Temple (11Q Temple Scroll LXIV 6–13)," *CRAI* (1972): 709–20; Joseph A. Fitzmyer, "Crucifixion in Ancient Palestine, Qumran Literature, and the New Testament," *CBQ* 40 (1978): 493–513; Josephine Massyng-berde Ford, "'Crucify Him, Crucify Him' and the Temple Scroll," *ExpTim* 87 (1975–76): 275–78; David J. Halperin, "Crucifixion, the Nahum Pesher, and the Rabbinic Penalty of Strangulation," *JJS* 32 (1981): 32–46; Luis Merino Díez, "La crucifixíon en la antigua literatura judía (Período Intertestamental)," *EstEcl* 51 (1976): 5–27; also idem, "El suplicion de la cruz en la litertura judía intertestamental," *SBFLA* 26 (1976): 31–120; Liliana Rosso-Ubigli, "Deuteronomio 21, 22: Contributo del Rotolo del Tempio alla valutazione di una variante medievale dei Settanta," *RevQ* 9 (1977–78): 231–36; Rafael Vicent Saera, "La halaká de Dt 21, 22–23 y su interpretación en Qumrán y en Jn 19, 31–42," in *Salvación en la palabra: Targum–derash–berith. Homenaje al prof. A. Díez Macho* (ed. Domingo Munoz Léon; Madrid: Ediciones Cristianidad, 1986), 699–709; Max Wilcox, "'Upon the Tree'—Deut 21:22–23 in the New Testament," *JBL* 96 (1977): 85–99.

72. Ernst Haenchen contends that Acts 5:30 and 10:39 allude to LXX Deut 21:22–23, suggesting that this text belongs to early Christian scriptural proof (*The Acts of the Apostles: A Commentary*, trans. Bernard Noble, Gerald Shinn, and Robert McLean Wilson [Philadelphia: Westminster, 1971], 251, 353). Hans Conzelmann does not mention the LXX and more aptly asks whether Deut 21:22–23 in Acts 5:30; 10:39, and Gal 3:13 belongs to a traditional Christian apologetic tradition (*Acts of the Apostles*, trans. James Limburg, A. Thomas Kraabel, and Donald H. Juel [Hermeneia; Philadelphia: Fortress, 1987], 42). More recently, Rudolf Pesch refers not to the LXX but to the interpretation of Deut 21:22–23 in 11QT^a for understanding the text of Acts (*Die Apostelgeschichte* [EKKNT 5/1; Neukirchen-Vluyn: Neukirchener Verlag, 1986], 217 n. 31). Yigael Yadin himself drew attention to the significance of 11QT^a for a better understanding of Gal 3:13 (*The Temple Scroll*, 3 vols. [Jerusalem: Israel Exploration Society, 1977–83], 1.379). Hans-Dieter Betz allows that Paul's use of Deut 21:22–23 may have been based on a *Vorlage* like that of 11QT^a (*Galatians: A Commentary on Paul's Letter to the Churches in Galatia* [Hermeneia; Philadelphia: Fortress, 1979], 151–52 n. 133). The version of Deut 21:22–23 in the Temple Scroll eases the difficulties in all these New Testament passages. Of the four passion narratives, those of Luke and John come closest to representing the concerns of the Temple Scroll in their descriptions of the charges against Jesus. John also reflects these concerns by having the soldiers

Conclusion

I have suggested here, somewhat tentatively and briefly, that part of what is common to some of Luke's special material and some of the later redactional sections of the Fourth Gospel are grounded in a collection of Judean traditions now known to us in various ways from the manuscripts of the Qumran library. This conclusion is not altogether surprising, but the possibility that some common Jewish background with a resonance of the Qumran library may lie behind some of the elements common to Luke and John is intriguing. Some of this resonance seems to be exclusive to the three traditions; others are now only known in contemporary Judaism in the Qumran scrolls but might have been more widely known, such as the particular form of the charge of sedition in the Temple Scroll.

Several other concluding points should be offered. First, my suggestion here does not explain all the similarities between Luke's special material and the Fourth Gospel. Second, my suggestion cannot account for everything in the special Lukan material, but it does seem to account for some of it. As such, it would suggest that L was not a single uniform written collection of materials. Rather, as is widely recognized, L was more probably made up of a number of different sets of material, some of which may also have been known in Johannine circles. Third, my suggestion does not account for everything in the final redactional stages of the Fourth Gospel, but it opens up a way of allowing for some Qumranic influence in the Gospel without forcing us to subscribe to wholehearted theories of direct Essene influence or authorship. It thus allows us to account for the differences between John and the scrolls while also stressing the similarities. Fourth, some of the sources that we have looked at are in Aramaic, and some in Hebrew. Thus, we have some clue that it is not good to be either a pan-Aramaist or a pan-Hebraist when it comes to looking for Semitic sources behind the Gospel texts. Fifth, perhaps the strongest argument in favor of the approach of this essay comes from the way in which the same motifs recur in several places in the selected L material and the redactional sections of the Fourth Gospel. At the most, this may suggest that there was some kind of coherent set of traditions that has been variously used by Luke and the redactors of the Fourth Gospel; at the least, this essay has shown the Judean character of the Jewish traditions behind parts of Luke and John.

---

break the legs of those crucified with Jesus so that the Law might be kept (John 19:31–33). This is similar to Mark's emphasis on the need to take Jesus from the cross because evening had come (Mark 15:42–44).

John, Qumran, and Virtuoso Religion

Brian J. Capper

Discussions about the Gospel of John, Essenism, and the Dead Sea Scrolls commonly employ the sociological category *sect*. The "sectarian thesis" concerning Johannine Christianity is widely accepted among scholars who find in the Johannine literature typical social characteristics of sectarianism, including self-legitimating strategies and exclusivity. Wayne Meeks and J. Louis Martyn were the principal proponents of this view.[1] For Meeks and Martyn, the Gospel narrative expresses a sense of alienation from the "world." This sense is understood to have derived from the social situation of the Johannine community, which had recently undergone a process of exclusion from the synagogue and found itself, like the Johannine Jesus, estranged from its former world of Judaism.

The sectarian thesis concerning the Gospel of John, however, is not without difficulties. In applying the category of *sect* to the Gospel, perceptions often merge between seeing the Fourth Gospel as sectarian vis-à-vis its matrix of Judaism and seeing an exclusivist relationship of the Johannine community vis-à-vis the emerging "Great Church" of early Christianity. Against the latter view, Raymond Brown and Martin Hengel sought to emphasize the mainstream character of Johannine Christianity.[2] In a recent survey on the question of the "sectarian" identity of Johannine Christianity, Craig Keener has concluded that the Fourth Gospel "differentiates Jesus' followers from the outside 'world' no less clearly than did the Essenes," but notes that interpreters have found this distinction from the outside world to be common to all of early Christianity.[3] One such interpreter was Robin Scroggs, who characterized the early Christian communities together

---

1. Wayne A. Meeks, "The Man from Heaven in Johannine Sectarianism," *JBL* 91 (1972): 44–72; J. Louis Martyn, *History and Theology in the Fourth Gospel* (New York: Harper & Row, 1968).

2. Raymond E. Brown, *The Community of the Beloved Disciple: The Life, Loves, and Hates of an Individual Church in New Testament Times* (New York: Paulist, 1979), 16–17; Martin Hengel, *The Johannine Question*, trans. John Bowden (London: SCM, 1989).

3. Craig S. Keener, *The Gospel of John: A Commentary*, 2 vols. (Peabody, Mass.: Hendrickson), 1.150.

as a "sectarian movement."[4] Similarly, Philip Esler has found that Luke–Acts represents a "sectarian" perspective in early Christianity, and Graham Stanton has argued that Matthew reflects a "sectarian" form of early Christianity, drawing parallels between "sectarian" features in Matthew and Qumran.[5] The perception of all of early Christianity as "sectarian" raises questions concerning the heuristic value of the sociological category of *sect* for understanding the distinctiveness of the Johannine literature and community.

In the quest for a sociological tool of greater refinement, Bryan Wilson's typology of sectarianism has been applied to both John's Gospel and the Qumran literature. Wilson classifies religious groups according to how their soteriological strategy responds to the "world," identifying seven ideal types: conversionist, manipulationist, thaumaturgical, reformist, revolutionist, utopian, and introversionist.[6] In this framework, "sectarian" religious movements are those which demonstrate a different soteriological strategy from their surrounding, wider society. Philip Esler has sought to use Wilson's category "introversionist" to define what was uniquely Johannine.[7] However, despite his attempt to depict the Johannine community as withdrawn and inwardly directed, John's Gospel is not uniformly negative regarding the "world." The Gospel is interested in the world's salvation: the Father loves the world and sends the Son (3:16–17), who is the "Savior of the world" (John 4:42) and the bread which gives life to the world (6:33, 51). The disciples, too, are sent into the world (17:18). It is hoped that all people will be drawn to the Son (12:32) and that the world will believe (17:21). Moreover, the Gospel also shows affinities with Wilson's "conversionist" sect type: it does not advocate leaving or renouncing the world and does not offer a soteriology based upon a separated community, but rather includes an individualistic dimension.[8] Overall, the application of Bryan Wilson's typology does not yield an unambiguous explanation of Johannine Christianity as "sectarian."

This study will argue that the forms of religion reflected in the Johannine and Qumran texts, as well as in the classical sources for the Essenes, are, at least

---

4. Robin Scroggs, "The Earliest Christian Communities as Sectarian Movement," in *Social-Scientific Approaches to New Testament Interpretation* (ed. David G. Horrell; Edinburgh: T&T Clark, 1999), 69–91; cf. Brown, *Community of the Beloved Disciple*, 14–15.

5. Philip F. Esler, *Community and Gospel in Luke-Acts: The Social and Political Motivations of Lucan Theology* (Cambridge: Cambridge University Press, 1987); cf. Timothy Ling, *The Judaean Poor and the Fourth Gospel* (SNTSMS 136; Cambridge: Cambridge University Press, 2006), 165; Graham N. Stanton, *A Gospel for a New People: Studies in Matthew* (Edinburgh: T&T Clark, 1992), 85–107.

6. Bryan Wilson, *Magic and the Millenium: A Sociological Study of Religious Movements of Protest among Tribal and Third-World Peoples* (New York: Harper & Row, 1973), 22–26.

7. Philip F. Esler, *The First Christians in Their Social Worlds: Social-Scientific Approaches to New Testament Interpretation* (London: Routledge, 1994), 70–91.

8. Cf. Ling, *Judaean Poor and the Fourth Gospel*, 157–60.

in certain phases of these communities' histories, best classified as "religious orders" rather than "sects." For the purposes of this essay, the social type of the religious order will be characterized as a form of "religious virtuosity" or "virtuoso religion," a category originated by Max Weber. When Weber coined the term "virtuoso religion" he applied it to both the sect and the religious order, noting close similarities between these social types. These similarities are key to the present argument and will be explored in detail below.[9] However, here I will apply the terminology of "religious virtuosity" and "virtuoso religion" only to the activity of the individual ascetic and aggregations of such persons in religious orders, and *not* to the social type of the sect. I will argue that, around the turn of the eras, Essenism generally functioned within the wider, temple-worshiping Jewish religious community as a *religious order*. I will argue that most Essenes were not at this time sectarian, detached from central temple authority and disengaged from surrounding society. I will also argue that there are a good number of indicators that the Johannine tradition had its origins with this form of "virtuoso religion" in Judea, especially in the Jerusalem area.

To explore these possibilities, this study will first examine the sociological models used in most discussions of the Essenes and introduce another model, the "religious order." In this discussion, I will distinguish between Essenism in general and the particular form of Essenism known through the Dead Sea Scrolls. This section will situate Essenism within mainstream Judaism around the turn of the eras. Following the analysis of Essenism as a distinct form of piety *within* Second Temple Judaism, I will argue that this form of religious piety was particularly associated with the region of Judea, and was found in Jerusalem and at an Essene settlement close to Jerusalem, in Bethany. This will lead into a discussion of Jesus' contacts in Jerusalem and Bethany as recorded in the Gospels, leading to the conclusion that Jerusalem and its environs, especially Bethany, may have provided the geographical and social context where Essene ideas influenced the nascent Johannine tradition.

Sects/Sectarianism or Religious Orders/Virtuoso Religion

Philip Esler has sought to characterize the authors of the Damascus Rule not as a "sect" but as a "reform movement," still a part of the wider Jewish religious community. Similarly, Kåre Fuglseth finds the Johannine community to have been "cult-like," manifesting tension with the group's Jewish parent body but not dem-

---

9. See Weber's essay "The Social Psychology of the World's Religions," in *From Max Weber: Essays in Sociology* (ed. H. H. Gerth and C. Wright Mills; London: Routledge & Kegan Paul, 1948), 267–301, esp. 287–91.

onstrating the complete segregation of the "sect."[10] Yet the "reform movement" and Fuglseth's "cult-like" model, both drawn from the study of modern groups, are not the only social forms that share exclusivist features with the "sect." The religious order, too, exists in a liminal social position but falls short of breaking all ties with its wider religious community.[11] As will be shown below, the social feature which distinguishes the "religious order" from the "sect" is precisely the religious order's abiding connection with the wider religious community; the sect, by contrast, shuns any "external authority." Ilana F. Silber employs the terms "virtuoso religion" and "religious virtuosity" to describe the piety of both the individual ascetic, who exists as part of a wider religious community, albeit in a liminal position, and the practice of the religious order, which exists, also liminally, as an accepted, legitimate part of a larger religious community while expressing a whole-of-life focus on religious concerns and discipline.[12] Silber offers a typology defining religious "virtuosity" across different cultural contexts and historical periods which may be summarized as follows. Religious virtuosity:

1. Is a matter of individual choice;
2. Involves an intensification of personal commitment over normal compulsory religious routine, norms, and behavior;
3. Involves the seeking of perfection, an extreme urge to go beyond everyday life and average religious achievement;
4. Sustains the seeking of perfection in a disciplined, systematic fashion, a defined rule or method;
5. Implies a normative double standard—its rigor is not only not necessary for all, but also impossible for all;
6. Is based in achievement and non-ascriptive criteria and is in principle an option for all, although in practice only achieved by a "heroic" minority.[13]

10. Esler, *First Christians in Their Social Worlds*, 70–91. Esler sees the Johannine community as a "sect." This categorization has been strongly contested by Kåre Sigvald Fuglseth, *Johannine Sectarianism in Perspective: A Sociological, Historical, and Comparative Analysis of Temple and Social Relationships in the Gospel of John, Philo, and Qumran* (NovTSup 119; Leiden: Brill, 2005), see esp. 373–74.

11. "Cult-like" groups may, like the religious order, accept the essential legitimacy of other churches but hold that not all are called to the special practices of the group—for example, a pronounced focus on mission. In such cases, "cult-like" groups are, in effect, religious orders.

12. Ilana F. Silber, *Virtuosity, Charisma, and Social Order: A Comparative Sociological Study of Monasticism in Theravada Buddhism and Medieval Catholicism* (Cambridge: Cambridge University Press, 1995).

13. Ibid., 191–92.

As has been noted, the sociological description of the "sect" may be very similar to that of the religious order. Martin observed that the religious order is "an analogue, within the inclusive church, of the spiritual elitism which finds expression in the sect."[14] Hill called the religious order a "sect within the church" and a "quasi-sect,"[15] noting many similarities between the sect and the religious order.[16] Both sect and religious order:

1. Are voluntary associations;
2. Accept members on the basis of achievement (proof of merit);
3. Demand an unusually high level of personal commitment;
4. Emphasize exclusivity and expel deviants;
5. Carry the self-conception of an elect;
6. Have personal perfection as their goal;
7. Exercise totalitarian control over their members;
8. Characteristically tend, in different ways, to keep away from the world.

Given this extensive correlation, it is significant that the set of features distinguishing the religious order from the sect is very limited. Hill finds, at most, only two:

1. *Religious orders*, as part of the wider church, acknowledge a source of authority which is ultimately external to the group, although they are in practice allowed a very considerable degree of autonomy in their internal arrangements, while *sects* are, by contrast, are self-legitimating and acknowledge no external sanctions in regulating their beliefs and structures;
2. While *religious orders* are typically celibate, *sects* are only rarely celibate.

Hill expressed his first distinguishing criterion, unlike his second, without qualification. It is therefore the only firm guide he gives for distinguishing between the sect and the religious order: the religious order is "distinguished from the sect proper by its acceptance of an external, ecclesiastical source of authority."[17] Only the religious order's acknowledgment of a source of authority outside its own ranks clearly distinguishes it from the sect.

---

14. D. A. Martin, *Pacifism* (London: Routledge and Kegan Paul, 1965), 4, cited in Michael Hill, *The Religious Order: A Study of Virtuoso Religion and Its Legitimation in the Nineteenth-Century Church of England* (London: Heinemann, 1973), 15.

15. Hill, *Religious Order*, 12.

16. Michael Hill, "Typologie sociologique de l'ordre religieux," *Social Compass* 17 (1971): 45–64; idem, *A Sociology of Religion* (London: Heinemann, 1973), 84–87; idem, *Religious Order*, 61–71.

17. Silber, *Virtuosity, Charisma, and Social Order*, 40.

The close proximity between the categories of "sect" and "religious order" is shown by overlaps among the terms "virtuoso religion," "sect," and "religious order" in the early sociology of religion, and by observations of historical transitions between the social forms so termed. Max Weber distinguished "virtuoso religion" from other forms of religious expression such as "charismatic religion" and "mass religion." As noted above, he included both "sects" and "religious orders" within the category "virtuoso religion," observing affinity between the sect and the religious order.[18] Ernst Troeltsch regarded both the voluntary association and the religious order as expressions of "sect-type" religion. He found that the sect-type religion of the voluntary association could be transformed from sect into "religious order" by becoming subject to legitimating lines of control from the church of mass religion. Troeltsch argued, for example, that "the Franciscan movement belonged originally to the sect-type of lay religion."[19] Early sociology of religion observed not only the close proximity between "sect" and "religious order," but also the possibility of transitions between these social forms in either direction. Hence, caution must be exercised in classifying a particular religious group as a sect rather than a "religious order" in all phases of its history.

This caution necessarily applies to the choice between the categories of "sect" and "religious order" when seeking to characterize the hypothetical communities behind the Gospel of John and the Dead Sea Scrolls and Essenism (if this grouping is to be distinguished from the authors of the Dead Sea Scrolls). Many characteristics that appear to justify a sociological classification as sect also figure in typologies of the religious order, and may therefore constitute evidence that the group under consideration is a religious order. Focus on what *distinguishes* the sect from the religious order is necessary to justify choice of either category. Furthermore, since historical examples show that social transitions are possible both *from* sect *to* religious order and *to* sect *from* religious order, a firm grasp of developments *over time* is required for a legitimate classification of a particular group at a particular time. Where certainty about the chronological and historical relationships between diverse and partial sets of evidence is difficult to establish, classification may easily err. The possibly diverse, multiform, or fragmented character of Essenism gives cause for caution in pronouncing upon the true state of affairs in a particular era of Essene history, or in the case of a particular sector of Essenism. The historian, who is expected to synthesize all available evidence into an overall portrayal, must have regard for the dangers of homogenizing or harmonizing the available materials. This note is now often sounded in Dead Sea Scrolls studies, since the range of clearly interrelated evidence emerges in sources

---

18. Weber, "Social Psychology of the World's Religions," 287–88; cf. Hill, *Religious Order*, 12.

19. Ernst Troeltsch, *The Social Teaching of the Christian Churches* (2 vols.; trans. Olive Wyon; London: Allen and Unwin, 1931), 1.355; cf. 2.723. Subsequent citations of Troeltsch will appear in parenthesis in the main body of text here.

that are of different types and sometimes uncertain provenance, and which are the possibly chance remains of a complex social development that occurred over a long time period.

Transitions between "Sects" and "Religious Orders"

The studies of Ernst Troeltsch show the value of extending the range of heuristic sociological categories in the investigation of Essenism to include the "religious order" as well as the "movement" and the "sect." Troeltsch's work concludes that the sect may, through a process of ecclesiastical inspection, approval, and incorporation, become a religious order of the wider religious community. Conversely, the religious order may become intolerable within the host religious body (1.349–69; 2.723). Troeltsch found that transitions between "movement," "sect," and "religious order" proceeded in various directions in mediaeval Catholic religion in southern Europe in the fourteenth and fifteenth centuries. At times, the late medieval groups he surveyed achieved accommodations with the wider ecclesiastical establishment; at other times, they did not. Troeltsch pointed to transitions in the case of particular groups from movement to sect, from sect to religious order, and also to the emergence of sects *out of* dissatisfied sectors of religious orders. To note but one major example, Troeltsch observed that the Waldensians originated as what he termed a "home mission movement"; its popular preachers lived in poverty, in literal obedience to the Gospel mission charge (Matt 10:1–16; Mark 6:7–13; Luke 9:1–6; 10:1–11). By this means, they identified with the poorest of the population, who were their principal audience. Later, "when they were prohibited by the Church they became a sect," characterized by an egalitarian ideal (1.354). Troeltsch noted the connections between the Waldensian Poor Men of Lombardy and Poor Men of Lyons and the movement of St. Francis of Assisi. In the case of the latter, "however, the Church understood the situation, incorporated the new movement into her system" as a religious order "and made use of it precisely for winning back the endangered city elements of the population to the Church" (1.355). Early on, the Franciscans encouraged an anti-ecclesiastical mysticism amongst the laity, especially through their associate members. Later, tensions arose between the church hierarchy and the religious orders of "Spiritual" Franciscans, with their ideals of "the Primitive Church," of "the poor church," and of the apostolic life lived in service to the poor. The "Spiritual" Franciscans finally splintered into a variety of "sects" and "heresies" enthusiastic for a rekindling of the perceived fervor and poverty of primitive Christianity but condemned by the church. Later came the Flagellants, the Soccati, the Apostolic Brethren, and other sects that expressed fervor similar to that of the Franciscan order but which could not be similarly accommodated within the ecclesiastical structure and which drew converts from the pool of enthusiasts that also supplied recruits to the religious orders (1.354–56).

Troeltsch's survey of the religious ferment of southern Europe prior to the Reformation gives food for thought when considering the complex of Jewish groups and movements over the periods before and during the emergence of Christianity as a religion distinct from Judaism. The late medieval groups considered by Troeltsch were characterized by a desire for a return to a pristine, supposedly original form of religion. They manifested mystical, enthusiastic, apocalyptic, and egalitarian tendencies. They expressed their search for religious authenticity in new social forms, which sometimes included the communalizing of property. All of these features characterize the so-called sectarian documents of the Dead Sea Scrolls and the Essenes as portrayed in the classical sources; all these features are also attested in the New Testament sources for early Christianity.

QUMRAN IN RELATION TO THE JUDEAN ESSENE MOVEMENT

Manifest similarities between the Dead Sea Scrolls and the classical writings on the Essenes allow most interpreters to designate the Qumran community as a form of Essenism. Analysis of the Dead Sea Scrolls corpus now commonly distinguishes "pre-sectarian" from "sectarian" documents. Current views on the relationship of the Qumran community to the broader Essene movement include proposals that see the Qumran group as a sectarian breakaway from the wider Essene movement. Gabrielle Boccaccini, building upon this thesis, has termed the broader Essene movement "Enochic" Judaism. This type of Judaism generated the pattern of thought found in the Enoch literature, from which the Qumran community diverged. According to Boccaccini, the movements led by John the Baptist and Jesus grew out of later "Enochic Judaism," that is, out of Essenism.[20] Such analyses suggest the possibility that the term "sect" is only appropriate for the community at Qumran, but not for the whole Essene movement. I would argue that there are three strong indicators that, at least from a point during, and for some time after, the reign of Herod the Great, many Essenes were not sectarians but *virtuosi* gathered in a religious order which maintained a connection with Judaism's central temple authority.

First, *the Essenes sent offerings to the temple, and thus enjoyed a legitimating relationship with Jewish "ecclesiastical authority."* Josephus wrote concerning the Essenes' sacrificial practices that "they send offerings to the Temple, but perform their sacrifices using different customary purifications. For this reason, they are barred from entering the common enclosure, but offer sacrifice privately" (*Ant.*

20. Gabrielle Boccaccini, *Beyond the Essene Hypothesis: The Parting of the Ways between Qumran and Enochic Judaism* (Grand Rapids: Eerdmans, 1998); note especially Boccaccini's chart on p. xxii. Cf. Jonathan Campbell, *Deciphering the Dead Sea Scrolls* (Oxford: Blackwell, 2002), 46–77.

18.1.5 §19). Josephus gives no indication that temple officials looked askance at Essene offerings, as if from a group known to be antipathetic to the status quo in Jerusalem. We must accept therefore that in the era to which his account refers, fellow Jews apparently saw all Essenes, or the vast majority, as part of the temple-worshiping community, submitted to the high priest. Differences of opinion concerning procedure and purity justified neither complete Essene separation from the temple nor withholding of offerings. It is very unlikely indeed that Josephus would find cause to mention the surrender of Essene material wealth if most Essenes challenged temple authority. The harsh attitude of sections of the Rule of the Community, with its explicit prohibitions of forming any fellowship of property with the "men of the pit," the "men of injustice" under the dominion of Belial (1QS 2.4–9; 3.20–24; 9.8–9, 21–23) cannot, for the Essenes Josephus described, have applied to the temple hierarchy.

Second, *Herod the Great's friendliness toward the Essenes suggests that they played a role in his political establishment and temple.* Herod the Great appears to have exploited inner-Jewish rivalries to assert himself against the Hasmonean dynasty, which he had deposed. It is frequently hypothesized that a key impulse toward the formation of Essenism was the Maccabean seizure of the high priesthood from the "Teacher of Righteousness." Herod appears to have turned to the prestigious Essenes, who early in their history had experienced tensions with the Hasmoneans, to bolster his establishment against popular support for the Hasmoneans.[21] According to Josephus, Herod "held the Essenes in great honor, and thought more highly of them than their mortal nature required." Herod's reason was his supposed boyhood receipt, from the Essene Menahem, of a prophecy of his future rise. "At the height of his power" Herod thanked Menahem, an apparently political maneuver (*Ant.* 15.10.4–5 §372–79). Many Essenes may have found the possibility of gaining influence on Herod's reconstruction of the temple very attractive. The Temple Scroll, discovered at Qumran, offers a plan for an ideal temple and Holy City; Delcor has argued that this plan influenced the design of Herod's temple.[22] Many Essenes may have considered Herod's temple at least a step toward the realization of the Essene plan for an ideal temple in Jerusalem. Prior to the turn of the eras, Essenism appears to have gained a privileged position connecting it with supreme power in Jerusalem. In my view, Herod's patronage probably both increased the general popularity and attraction of the Essene way and led to substantial and influential settlement of Essenes in and around Jerusalem. Many Essenes, enjoying a reputation for scrupulous Levitical

---

21. Cf. Ernst Bammel, "Sadduzäer und Sadokiden," *ETL* 55 (1979): 107–15; Brian J. Capper, "'With the Oldest Monks . . . ': Light from Essene History on the Career of the Beloved Disciple?" *JTS* 49 (1998): 26–36.

22. Mathias Delcor, "Is the Temple Scroll a Source of the Herodian Temple?" in *Temple Scroll Studies* (ed. George J. Brooke; JSPSup 7; Sheffield: JSOT Press, 1989), 67–90.

purity, may have worked cutting stones for the temple, which were finished off-site. Herod's accommodation of the Essenes may have led to their dispatch of offerings to his temple.

Third, *celibate Essene males gave alms and assistance to the needy deemed worthy among the general Judean populace.* The consistently "sectarian" interpretation of Essenism overlooks a further statement of Josephus, who, after explaining the apportionment of food by officers at Essene common meals, writes: "On the whole, therefore, they do nothing unless ordered by the superiors. Two things only are left to individual discretion, the rendering of assistance and compassion. Members may of their own accord help the deserving, when they ask for alms, and supply food to the needy, but they have no right to subsidize members of their own families without the authority of the officers" (*J. W.* 2.8.6 §128–134). Essene celibate males supplied food to outsiders of their immediate community. Josephus has just emphasized that all within the community ate well, though not to excess, at common meals (*J. W.* 2.8.6 §133). The "needy" to whom food was supplied at individual discretion cannot have been members of the community, who were allotted exact, appropriate portions. The judicious regulation prohibiting donations to family members indicates the same. Anyone received into the community, perhaps as an adoptee from a needy local family unable to feed all its children, might experience a clash of loyalties. Illegitimate and unregulated requests from kin external to the community might waste precious resources. Hence, while the Essenes thought it appropriate to feed deserving outsiders, they insisted that officials always be consulted in the case of members of the individual Essene's (former) family, lest kinship ties siphon off resources.[23]

The social import of this text is clear. The Essenes described by Josephus did not regard all outside their communities as "sons of darkness" to be hated as "men of injustice" whose needs were of no consequence (4Q496; 1 QM 1.1; 13.1–6, 9–12; 1QS 1.9–11; 3.13; 8.12–15). While such an attitude toward all outsiders would be rightly labeled "sectarian," Josephus's male Essene celibates, who consumed communally and modestly and offered succor to deserving outsiders, were not sectarians but a religious order. They served the wider temple-worshiping Judean community from a liminal social position. Yet while the many communities of celibate Essenes across Judea pursued a distinctively regulated social life, perhaps preserving secret teachings (see *J. W.* 2.8.7 §141–42), they nonetheless regarded the poor whom they assisted as legitimate co-members in the wider, temple-loyal Jewish religious community. They understood both themselves and the beneficiaries of their charitable activities to belong to the same faith community, while seeing themselves as serving a special vocation within that community.

---

23. Cf. Jesus' insistence that allegiance to his disciple group, as a new family, had priority over links to the disciple's blood family (Mark 3:31–35).

From before the turn of the eras, then, while some Essene groupings may have functioned antagonistically toward temple authority, at least the great majority of Essenes accepted the authority of the temple and aided the deserving poor. By the time of Jesus' birth, most Essene male celibates belonged to a religious order of *virtuosi* legitimated by the authority of temple, high priest, and ruler. It is fair to speak of the majority of Essenes of the early first century as belonging to a "movement" that included a celibate male "religious order" alongside further orders for married members and perhaps for celibate females and widows, too; it would be incorrect to speak of the broad sweep of Essenism as "sectarian."[24]

It is against this background of the Essenes as a widespread Judean movement of "virtuoso religion" that I now turn to discuss how this movement may inform our understanding of Jesus and his disciples.

JESUS' TRAVELING DISCIPLESHIP GROUP AND JUDEAN VIRTUOSO RELIGION

Jesus selected the twelve from his larger circle of disciples to travel with him in a common life of meal fellowship, regular teaching, and witness (Mark 3:13–19; cf. Luke 6:12–16 and perhaps John 7:1–2). The group's property was held in a common purse (John 12:6; 13:29) into which were placed, we may rightly assume, the supporting contributions of its wealthy women patrons (Luke 8:1–3). While some meals of Jesus' traveling party were for private instruction (Mark 7:17, 24; 10:10, 30–31, 33), it appears that on other occasions needy hearers ate well as they listened to Jesus (Mark 2:15; 3:20 [by implication]; 6:10; 7:17, 24; 14:3). Since Jesus urged the rich to give generously to the poor (Matt 6:24; Mark 10:17–27; Luke 12:16–21 [cf. *Gospel of Thomas* 63], 33; 14:7–33; 16:1–15, 19–21; 19:1–10), it is likely that his party also offered assistance from their perhaps substantial pooled resources. Several texts suggest that alms were given from the common purse (John 12:4–6; Mark 14:4–5; cf. Matt 26:8–9). When Jesus asked Philip where bread might be purchased to feed a vast crowd near Passover, Philip exclaimed that two hundred *denarii* would not suffice. Jesus' question was

---

24. Celibacy dominates the ancient reporting about the Essenes because it was newsworthy, something unusual and intriguing. However, historical analogies, for example from Christianity or Buddhism, show that celibacy is usually undertaken by only a small minority within a religious community. Celibate males may have formed only a minority within Essenism, perhaps indeed a small minority. Entirely disproportionate space may be taken up in the ancient reports of Essenism with attention to the distinctive lifestyle of the perhaps only slightly more than four thousand Essene male celibates (*Ant.* 18.1.5 §20–21). Josephus gives only a passing reference to married Essenes who most likely outnumbered the celibate: "Moreover, there is another order of Essenes, who agree with the rest as to their way of living, and customs, and laws, but differ from them in the point of marriage, as thinking that by not marrying they cut off the principal part of the human life, which is the prospect of succession; nay rather, that if all men should be of the same opinion, the whole race of mankind would fail" (*J.W.* 2.8.13 §160).

intended to test Philip (John 6:5–7), presumably because the generous donations of elite patrons meant that it was not usually beyond the means of Jesus' traveling party to aid the needy in his audience from the financial resources of the common purse. Jesus' form of educative, communal life and service in frequent, intimate contact with the poor was a form of "religious virtuosity" or "virtuoso religion." Jesus called some who believed in him to this common life; he did not require it of all.

The common life of Jesus' traveling party, as described above, appears to have derived from *Judea*, where virtuoso religious practice was prominent. Jesus was linked to the Judean group of John the Baptist immediately before entering upon a public ministry in Galilee (cf. Mark 1:1–20 and parallels; John 1:19–43). He appears to have "taken north" the Judean concept of an intensely integrated, common religious life, perhaps developed by John the Baptist into a peripatetic, prophetic form, partly in imitation of the Elijah and Elisha narratives. He gathered chosen disciples into a traveling party that shared daily meals and received special instruction. Such common life appears not to have been a common Galilean practice; there are no other attested contemporary examples. By contrast, the practice of common life is very well attested amongst the Essenes in Judea, the region to which Philo limited the Essene movement (see *Apology for the Jews* §1).[25] The community of property of the earliest Jerusalem church (Acts 2:42–47; 4:32–5:11; 6:1–6) seems also to reflect specifically Judean social practice.[26] This practice of communal property seems to have developed in Judea in response to the economic problems of the age.

Close communitarian forms of living had developed in Judea because its social and religious world was somewhat different from the Galilean milieu. Galilee was more fertile than Judea. It lay on major trade routes and was well connected to the coast, making it more outward-looking and affording different economic opportunities. By contrast, the Judean heartland was a land-locked, rugged, semi-arid inland region off the major trade routes. Judea had a long history as a temple state, ruled by its clergy; its religious, social, and economic world was dominated by its massive temple. I would deduce that ideals of holiness and consecration dominated the Judean religious and social world in an almost totalitarian fashion, far more comprehensively than they did the Galilean milieu.

---

25. On the essential limitation of Essenism to Judaea, see Brian J. Capper, "Essene Community Houses and Jesus' Early Community," in *Jesus and Archaeology* (ed. James H. Charlesworth; Grand Rapids: Eerdmans, 2006), 473–79.

26. Cf. Brian J. Capper, "The Palestinian Cultural Context of Earliest Christian Community of Goods," in *The Book of Acts in Its Palestinian Setting* (ed. Richard J. Bauckham; BAFCS 4; Grand Rapids: Eerdmans, 1995), 323–56; idem, "Community of Goods in the Early Jerusalem Church," in *ANRW* II, 26.2 (1995): 1730–74; idem, "Two Types of Discipleship in Early Christianity," *JTS* 52 (2001): 105–23; idem, "Holy Community of Life and Property and Amongst the Poor: A Response to Steve Walton," *EvQ* 80, no. 2 (2008): 113–27.

Judea's lower rainfall and more rugged terrain posed the problems of survival in a subsistence economy somewhat more sharply than the more "open" economy of Galilee, especially for Judeans who sought to remain in their beloved ancestral land, close to their temple and holy city.[27]

In these unusual circumstances, the particular Judean response to the problems of subsistence in the ancient agrarian world took an unusual form. In Judea, the Essene movement developed widespread, well-understood, and judiciously regulated forms of economic sharing. The Essene pattern of social organization was long established in Judea by the first century C.E. Philo and Josephus describe a prestigious "upper echelon" of more than four thousand celibate male Essenes, whose many communities fully shared property.

> This is demonstrated by that institution of theirs which will not suffer anything to hinder them from having all things in common; so that a rich man enjoys no more of his own wealth than he who has nothing at all. There are about four thousand men that live in this way, and neither marry wives, nor are desirous to keep servants; as thinking the latter tempts men to be unjust, and the former gives the handle to domestic quarrels; but as they live by themselves, they minister one to another. They also appoint certain stewards to receive the incomes of their revenues, and of the fruits of the ground; such as are good men and priests, who are to get their corn and their food ready for them. They none of them differ from others of the Essenes in their way of living, but do the most resemble those Dacae who are called Polistae ["dwellers in cities"]. (*Ant.*18.1.5 §20–22)

Although the figure "over 4000" clearly enumerates only *male celibate* Essenes, Philo and Josephus are often wrongly taken to number the *whole* Essene movement at four thousand (see *Ant.* 18.1.5 §20–21; *Every Good Man Is Free* §75). This misreading diminishes appreciation of the scale and importance of Essenism in the Judean social and religious world. On most days, Essene celibate males worked as artisans and labored in the fields of local estate owners (Philo, *Apology for the Jews* §4–9).[28] In the evenings they shared common meals, open-handedly entertaining members of the order from elsewhere, who probably traveled to find work, disseminate news, and socialize (*Apology for the Jews* §10–11; *J.W.* 2.8.4 §124–25). This cadre of Essene male celibates was distributed through the perhaps two hundred villages and towns of the Judean landscape in small communities of ten or more, and occupied an important center on the southwest hill of Jerusalem, where Josephus locates the "Gate of the Essenes" (see 1QS 6.3–4;

---

27. On the relationship between this socio-geographic differentiation and Judea's different social world, see Ling, *Judaean Poor and the Fourth Gospel*, esp. 78–97.
28. Cf. Brian J. Capper, "The New Covenant in Southern Palestine at the Arrest of Jesus," in *The Dead Sea Scrolls as Background to Postbiblical Judaism and Early Christianity* (ed. James R. Davila; STDJ 46; Leiden: Brill, 2003), 95–98.

J.W. 2.8.9 §146; 5.4.2 §145; *Ant.* 18.1.5 §20–21; *Every Good Man Is Free* §75).[29] The celibate male order was associated with a second order of marrying Essenes, as noted above, which was probably much larger. The ancient sources give us no figures for this group, but since celibacy is always a less popular option than marriage, I would suggest it probably numbered at least several tens of thousands.

Hartmut Stegemann, one of the principal early researchers of the Dead Sea Scrolls, came to conclude that the Essene movement was the "main Jewish union of the second Temple period."[30] I have argued, by a statistical method, that Essenism was economically capable of relieving destitution amongst the lowest classes of Judea and may have been a powerful social and religious force amongst the laborers, artisans, and needy of its villages and towns.[31] I would also suggest that the Essenes were well represented among the poor urban population of Jerusalem.

Overpopulation and scarcity of resources characterized the ancient agrarian economy. The needy were frequently compelled to work on large estates as servants or slaves, forced into soldiering, or compelled to migrate to the large coastal cities to find work as sailors or in trading. Women were frequently forced into prostitution. Essenism offered different options for the needy of Judea. Children who could not be fed in poor local families could be adopted into Essene communities, where they received training in work, economic security, and education in holy tradition (*J.W.* 2.8.2 §120). By this route, many male children of the poor came as adults to renounce the pleasures and social standing of normal family life, enjoying instead highly honored status as Essene celibates and a replacement form of fictive kinship in an extensive and loving religious order. There may also have been honored Essene orders for widows or life-long celibate women—note here the "mothers" of the community in 2Q270 frag. 7 1.13–14 and CD 14.15–16. The Essenes labored among the mass of the Judean population, who found it hard to garner sufficient means to support themselves and their families—as Essene

---

29. Cf. Bargil Pixner, "Mount Zion, Jesus, and Archaeology," in *Jesus and Archaeology* (ed. James H. Charlesworth; Grand Rapids: Eerdmans, 2006), 309–22; Rainer Riesner, "Essener und Urkirche auf dem Südwesthügel Jerusalems (Zion III)," in *Laetare Jerusalem* (ed. Nikodemus C. Schnabel; Münster, Germany: Aschendorf, 2006), 200–234; Capper, "Palestinian Cultural Context," 341–50; Capper, "'With the Oldest Monks . . . ,'" 19–36.

30. Hartmut Stegemann, *The Library of Qumran: On the Essenes, Qumran, John the Baptist, and Jesus* (Grand Rapids: Eerdmans, 1998), 140–53; see also idem, "The Qumran Essenes: Local Members of the Main Jewish Union in Late Second Temple Times," in *The Madrid Qumran Congress* (ed. Julio Trebolle Barrera and Luis Vegas Montaner, 2 vols.; STDJ 11; Leiden: Brill, 1992), 1.83–166.

31. See Capper, "Essene Community Houses," 472–502; idem, "The New Covenant in Southern Palestine" 90–116; idem, "The Church as the New Covenant of Effective Economics," *IJSCC* 2 (2002): 83–102; idem, "Two Types of Discipleship," 105–23.

frugality, sharing of possessions, and adoption of the children of poor families all show.[32]

Josephus tells us that the Essenes were "lovers of each other" (*philalleloi*), more than other Jewish groups (*J. W.* 2.8.2 §119). Philo emphasizes their mutual service in menial tasks, care of the sick, and care of the old by the young (*Every Good Man Is Free* §79, 87–88). Since numerous males did not father children, but cared for those of others, Essene celibacy came to function, in the Judean heartland, as an important rectifying mechanism against overpopulation and inadequate nourishment. Josephus notes that Essenes studied the treatment of disease and medicinal roots. Both Essene houses and traveling Essene celibates probably offered care for the sick; Josephus's understanding may have included this when he wrote that male celibate Essenes offered assistance to outsiders (*J. W.* 2.8.6 §134, 136).[33]

The population of Jerusalem in the first century C.E. numbered roughly sixty thousand to eighty thousand.[34] The population of rural Judea was of a similar size, the two hundred or so villages and towns averaging a few hundred souls each, including children.[35] The more than four thousand celibate male Essenes, about 3 percent of the total Judean population, were sufficient in number to form core communities of ten to twenty monks in most, if not all, of the towns and villages in the region. This powerful, firmly united core of more than four thousand skilled, educated, and highly disciplined male celibates was supported by, I would suggest, at least several thousand families of the second Essene order. The Essene "house of the community" in each village and town, staffed and funded by Essene celibate males, most of whom worked in the local economy, was also supported by regular contributions from local families of the second order. This collective support meant that children unsupported by local kinship structures could be adopted into the Essene community houses (see CD 14.12–17; cf. *J.W.* 2.8.2 §120). Such adoptions probably led, over time, to the loyalty of a large proportion of the smallholders, small tenant farmers, laborers, and artisans of the Judean population to the extensive network of Essene poorhouses. Indeed, for every child adopted by the Essenes, a reciprocally grateful family of limited

---

32. Full analysis of the social location of the Essenes as laborers and artisans and their work with the destitute is given in Capper, "Essene Community Houses," 480–98, and idem, "New Covenant in Southern Palestine," 95–113.

33. Some scholars have argued that the name "Essene" derives from the Aramaic *'sy'*, "healers." See Geza Vermes, "The Etymology of Essenes," in his *Post-biblical Jewish Studies* (SJLA 8; Leiden: Brill, 1975), 8–29.

34. Cf. Wolfgang Reinhardt, "The Population Size of Jerusalem and the Numerical Growth of the Jerusalem Church," in *The Book of Acts in Its Palestinian Setting* (ed. Richard J. Bauckham; BAFCS 4; Grand Rapids: Eerdmans, 2005), 237–65.

35. See Capper, "Essene Community Houses," 473–76, 492–93; idem, "New Covenant in Southern Palestine," 91–95, 104–8.

means may have joined the married Essene order. It would not be surprising if over time most rural clans and families had expressed gratitude to the Essene movement by such secondary association. Many wealthy of Judea, seeing such good works, may have become patrons of the Essene community houses. These two orders, acting in concert, probably exercised great influence upon the social, political, and religious world of Judea's rural villages. The long-standing, honored presence of the celibate male Essene order throughout Judea, its intimate connections through adoption with the local population, and its willingness to assist rural families facing economic crisis when there were too many mouths to feed (see *J.W.* 2.8.2 §120; 2.8.6 §134), may indeed mean that virtually all the families of Judea's villages, and many laborers and artisans in Jerusalem, had been absorbed into the second Essene order by the time of Jesus.

JOHN AND ESSENE LOCATIONS IN AND NEAR JERUSALEM

Having located the ancient Essenes as a form of virtuoso religion on both the schema of modern sociological analysis and the ancient Judean cultural landscape, I now turn to more specific points where the Essenes and their outlook may have intersected more particularly with the ministry of Jesus and the roots of the Johannine tradition.

HOSPITALITY AT BETHANY

There is some evidence of Essene settlement in the two locations where Jesus had personal connections in the Jerusalem area, especially according to John's Gospel. All the Gospels show that Jesus made his lodging in Bethany during the final days of his life, where his commands concerning the collection of the colt for his triumphal entry into Jerusalem show that he had long-standing personal acquaintances (Matt 21:1–19; Mark 11:1–11; Luke 19:28–38; John 12:1–19). Since Jerusalem raised special issues of ritual purity, it is likely that the Essenes would care for the sick outside the holy city. A passage in the Temple Scroll prescribes the establishment of three places to the east of Jerusalem, one of which was to be for the care of lepers. The passage also defines a radius of three thousand cubits around the city within which nothing unclean should be visible (11Q19 46.13–18). The three villages east of Jerusalem, Bethany, Bethphage, and En-shemesh, correspond well with the prescription of the Temple Scroll. It is striking that Jesus is found, at Mark 14:3–10, dining in the house of Simon the leper at Bethany. The correspondence suggests that the story of an Essene care center at Bethany is continued in the Christian Gospels, and that the healer Jesus was welcomed there. Lazarus, a close friend of Jesus, also received care at Bethany when ill (John 11:1–12:11).

The name "Bethany" (Greek Βηθανία) suggests a wordplay on the village's function as a center for care of the poor and sick. Jerome's *Onomasticon* defines its meaning as *domus adflictionis*, "house of affliction," a conclusion he deduced from the Hebrew *beth 'anî* or Aramaic *beth 'anyâ*, "house of the poor [man]." The Christian Palestinian and Syriac versions of the New Testament both give the Aramaic version of this name and confirm Jerome's understanding.[36] It is sometimes suggested that the form Βηθανία represents a contraction from "Beth Ananiah"; Ananiah appears as a place name at Neh 11:32. This contraction is unattested but is fairly close to a known pattern (cf. the common shortening of Hananiah to Honi in Hebrew). Both of these connections may be valid. *Beth Ananiah* may have been shortened in common parlance to *Beth-'anyâ*, the abbreviation becoming universal since it conveniently alluded, by a typical Semitic wordplay, to Bethany as the "house of affliction" or "house of the poor," alluding to the situation and work of a major Essene center for care of the poor and sick.

John notes that Bethany was fifteen stadia (about two miles) from the holy city (11:18), a distance which placed Bethany comfortably beyond the purity perimeter defined in the Temple Scroll. The village was invisible from the city and temple since it lay on the further slope of the Mount of Olives, fulfilling Essene purity requirements. As the last station on the pilgrim route up from the Jordan Valley to Jerusalem, the Essene hospice of Bethany was apparently where pilgrims who arrived by this route could receive assistance near the end of their journey, find lodging, bathe, and set their dress in order before entering the holy city. Hence, Jesus billets in Bethany his Passover pilgrim party from Galilee in the Gospels.[37] When Jesus washes his disciples' feet in John's Gospel, he speaks of Peter's recent bath: only Peter's feet needed to be washed, since after preparation at Bethany he had walked the dusty path to the room of the last meal in Jerusalem (13:10). Among the Evangelists, John appears to be uniquely acquainted with Jesus' associates in the Essene environment of Bethany and activities there.

HOSPITALITY IN JERUSALEM

It is striking that John offers a much longer account of Jesus' last meal with his disciples (John 13–17) than do the Synoptic Gospels. This major narrative section, distinctive of this Gospel, may suggest an interest in the meal's location and its function as a place of private instruction. Yet John omits the peculiar story of how Jesus directed his disciples to seek out this room (Mark 14:12–16). Perhaps he preferred not to explain its location, keeping it secret; or, he may simply give the perspective of an insider who was the host who welcomed Jesus and

---

36. As a resident of Bethlehem, about six miles south of Bethany, Jerome knew Hebrew and local tradition. His explanation trumps the modern derivation of "Bethany" from *Beth hini*, "house of figs." Although nearby Bethphage was the "house of *unripe figs*" (*phagîm*), the a in the second syllable of βηθανία cannot be accounted for from *hini*.

37. Cf. Capper, "New Covenant in Southern Palestine," esp. 109–16.

his disciples into this place. Certainly the "Beloved Disciple" was present at the meal, for it is here that his intimate connection with Jesus is emphasized. Guests at a formal meal reclined on their left elbow and ate with their right hand. The Beloved Disciple "lay in the breast of Jesus" at the meal (13:21–28), indicating that he reclined on Jesus' right. Jesus, as the guest of honor, took the place to the left of the Beloved Disciple, the host. Peter, the principal disciple, seems to have been seated in the second place of honor, to his host's right. Hence, when Peter did not understand Jesus' words, he could lean discreetly back toward his host, asking him quietly to inquire of Jesus. The Beloved Disciple was able to do this discreetly because he reclined at Jesus' chest. Jesus obliged, whispering his explanation about the sop he then distributed.[38]

As Jesus' host, the Beloved Disciple seems to have had charge of the premises in Jerusalem where Jesus ate with his disciples, and was thus either the *oikodespotes* mentioned in the "external" perspective of the Synoptics or a close associate of this figure (Mark 14:14–15; cf. Matt 26:18). Only John may know that, on account of his local premises, Jesus was able from the cross to entrust his mother into the Beloved Disciple's care (John 19:25–27). The event suggests that a form of "fictive kinship" involving mutual support existed between Jesus and the Beloved Disciple, and perhaps also that the Beloved Disciple's premises may have accommodated a community of coreligionists with whom a member's elderly dependents might by arrangement find lodging, food, and care. The Beloved Disciple's premises appear to have been substantial and oriented toward hospitality: he was able to accommodate Jesus' large traveling party at Passover; he could instantly accommodate Jesus' mother; his "upper room" became the regular meeting place of the earliest post-Easter community of Jesus' followers, who numbered 120 (Acts 1:13, 15; 2:1). Members of this community soon engaged in major events of property surrender and common meals, suggestive of a common life akin to Essene community living (Acts 2:42–47; 4:32–5:11; 6:1–6). Their communal way of life appears to have followed the pattern of a local Essene group, for while Josephus locates the "Gate of the Essenes" on the southwest hill of Jerusalem (*Ant.* 5.4.2 §145), later church tradition[39] locates the "upper room" also on the southwest hill, some 150 yards to the north of the remains of this gate.[40] On this part of the southwest hill, an Essene "holy congregation" probably pursued the highest Essene ideals of property sharing and mutual service in a community respected by all Jerusalem. The social form of this community necessarily

38. See D. E. H. Whiteley, "Was John Written by a Sadducee?" *ANRW* II, 25.3 (1985): 2494.

39. Beginning with Epiphanius, *On Weights and Measures* 14.

40. Capper, "'With the Oldest Monks . . . ,'" 26–29, 36–47; "Two Types of Discipleship," 117–18; idem, "Community of Goods in the Early Jerusalem Church," 1752–60; idem, "Palestinian Cultural Context," 341–50; Rainer Riesner, *Essener und Urgemeinde in Jerusalem: Neue Funde und Quellen* (BAZ 6; Giessen: Brunnen, 1998), 2–55.

involved a degree of segregation from the outside world as it pursued its mysticism and high standards of purity. However, it entertained good relations with the high priesthood and the temple.[41]

Thus, both of the places of Jesus' intimate personal connections in John's Gospel in the Jerusalem area—Bethany and this part of Jerusalem's southwest hill—are linked by tantalizing strands of evidence to Essenism. The Essene almshouse of Bethany and the Essene congregation on Jerusalem's prestigious, highest hill were probably the most important Essene centers in the Jerusalem area. It appears that, since John knows most about Jesus' activities in these places, the origins of this Gospel's tradition bear a unique relationship with Jerusalem Essenism and these two important Essene communities.

BETHANY/JERUSALEM AND THE COMMON PURSE

The sharing of Jesus' post-Easter disciples described early in Acts appears to have been a natural continuation of the practice of Jesus' party of traveling disciples. However, the very rapid expansion, to which Acts bears witness, of this economic form suggests that it was a pattern of economic and social life well understood by many early Judean adherents of Jesus' movement—and, indeed, that many of these adherents derived from Essene or Essene-like groups in Jerusalem and Judea. Jesus had formed his largely Galilean traveling group after the model of the *Judean* practice of communal sharing. He now returned with the group he had assembled and trained largely in the north and may have incorporated it into an already existing Essene congregation in Jerusalem, which shared all its property and life and with which he had long-standing associations.

We have no reason to doubt the existence of the common purse of Jesus' traveling party. However, it is striking that only John's Gospel makes explicit reference to this common purse and that John's Gospel mentions the common purse only at the locations of Bethany (12:6) and the room of the Last Supper (13:29). We see in these two incidents and locations an insider perspective on common Judean virtuoso religious practice. Many Judean communities of coreligionists collected their wealth into a common purse and lived frugally together from this fund, also making disbursements to relieve the poor and support other charitable works. Aid for the destitute and close identification with them through frugality and voluntary renunciation of personal property was intrinsic to the life of the Judean religious "virtuoso." Jesus' anointing at Bethany is the only account in the Gospels in which we find mention of care for the poor on the lips of Jesus' disciples. Their embarrassment suggests that Bethany had an unusual function as a place of care for the poor. In view of the strands of evidence noted above, which suggest that both Bethany and the southwest hill of Jerusalem were locations of

---

41. Capper, "'With the Oldest Monks . . . ,'" 13–15, 29–36.

Essene communities, it may be correct to deduce that John understood that the practice of Jesus' disciple group mirrored the Essene property-sharing practices in these locations. The generous, self-denying economic practice of Jesus and his disciple group was one with the Essene economic practice of their hosts and did not fall behind it in virtue.

Ling has observed that, while the poor feature rarely in John's Gospel compared with Jesus' frequent references to poverty and wealth in the Synoptic Gospels, it is precisely in Bethany and in the room of the Last Supper on Jerusalem's southwest hill that we find John's only two references to the poor. John only mentions the poor at the dispute over the apparent waste of expensive perfumed oil at Jesus' anointing at Bethany (12:5–8) and again when the disciples conjecture that Judas departed from Jesus' Last Supper to give alms to the poor from the common purse (13:29). This reflects John's "social witness" to local, indigenously Judean virtuoso religion.[42]

The Virtuoso Group's Influence upon the Wider Religious Community

Michael Hill emphasizes a basic distinction between the "charismatic" and the "virtuoso." The virtuoso aims, through rigorous reenactment of religious tradition, at "revolution by tradition," while the charismatic opposes tradition. The charismatic devises a new basis for normative obligation, but the virtuoso forcefully restates tradition and emphasizes *practice*. Virtuosity is disciplined and sustained in character, while charisma is intrinsically volatile. "Charismatics proclaim a message; virtuosi proclaim a method."[43] The virtuoso group, because of its emphasis on discipline, method, and practice, is able to maintain a distinctive social form and identity while remaining connected with its wider social world. The virtuoso religious group thus forms "an alternative structure within society at large," rather than *apart from* wider society.[44] Moreover, although liminal to society, religious virtuosi have a disproportionately large influence upon their surrounding social world because their practice commands wide respect. The high *honor* in which the practice of religious virtuosi is held affords their exhortation of the outside world considerable leverage. The emphasis of religious virtuosi on practice and their marked wider social effect may be compared with the love commandment of Jesus, which is unique to John's Gospel and understood to be the principal mode of witness. It is by the visible love of Jesus' disciples for one another that all will know they are his (John 13:34–35). Similarly, the only maca-

42. Cf. Ling, *Judaean Poor and the Fourth Gospel*, 170–81.
43. Hill, *Religious Order*, 2
44. Silber, *Virtuosity, Charisma, and Social Order*, 40.

rism (i.e., beatitude) of John's Gospel is upon mutual service, also a part of Jesus' instruction following his washing of his disciples' feet (13:17).[45]

When I began preparing this essay in the fall of 2007, an example of the high social impact and worldly involvement of religious virtuosi was being played out on news screens across the world. In Myanmar, thousands of Buddhist monks and nuns were leading demonstrations against the military government, supporting the Burmese people in their protests against sharply rising food prices and demands for democracy. The monks' distinctive maroon robes and saffron sashes made them easy targets; the nuns' saffron sashes and white or pink overgarments over red tunics equally so. Yet government troops were initially cautious in their response to the Saffron Revolution, since all shared a common respect for the learning, religious devotion, and self-deprecation of the nuns and monks.[46] Respected religious virtuosi are not lightly attacked. As I conclude this piece, Buddhist monks in Tibet have been involved in protests against China; an early incident is a nonviolent sit-down protest by the monks. In the words of Peter Firstbrook, producer of the BBC series *A Year in Tibet*, "China's crackdown on monk-led rallies in Lhasa is part of a long history of state control of monasteries. . . . Buddhist monasteries are among the few institutions in China which have the potential to organize resistance and opposition to the government—so the Chinese Communist Party constantly worries about them."[47]

The four thousand white-robed (*J. W.* 2.8.3 §123) Essene celibate males of the small temple state of ancient Judea probably exercised similarly disproportionate influence, which the Herodian establishment successfully harnessed. Religious virtuosi can, paradoxically, speak loudly to the world from their liminal social position. It would be equally erroneous to caricature the present-day Buddhist monks of Myanmar, the male celibate Essenes of Judea in the Herodian period, or the Gospel of John, as commending disinterest in the wider world and complete withdrawal from it.

CONCLUDING OBSERVATIONS

In 2005, a front-page article in the *Wall Street Journal* pointed to the leverage exercised by religious virtuosi. The article highlights two white-robed Catholic Sisters of the Poor, who regularly and successfully cajole generous donations of food from market traders and warehouse owners. They do this because the

---

45. Cf. Ling, *Judaean Poor and the Fourth Gospel*, 114–44 and 207–9.

46. See "100,000 Protestors Flood Streets of Rangoon in 'Saffron Revolution,'" n.p. (cited 24 September 2007), online: http://www.novinite.com/view_news.php?id=85644; also Richard Lloyd Parry, "Nuns Join Monks in Burma's Saffron Revolution," n.p. (cited 24 September 2007), online: http://www.timesonline.co.uk/tol/news/world/asia/article2516773.ece.

47. See "Tibetan Monks: A Controlled Life," n.p. (cited 20 March 2008), online: http://news.bbc.co.uk/1/hi/world/asia-pacific/7307495.stm.

elderly for whom they care in nursing homes cannot fund their own meals. Respected nuns, who do not even own the clothes they themselves wear and who care for the elderly, cannot be accused of seeking material resources for themselves. Voluntary personal poverty *enables* these nuns to be a trustworthy channel of material resources from the well-off to those who have too little.[48] I would argue that Jesus' disciple group functioned in a similar fashion, effectively stimulating care of the wealthy for the poor, as it traveled with only a common purse, renounced personal wealth, and exhorted those with more than enough to give generously. The celibate Essenes of Judea also functioned as conduits of economic redistribution, perhaps even of supplies cajoled from local wealthy patrons or received by royal patronage from Herodian granaries (at least until the time of Archelaus's demise). What later probably became an inner core within the Jerusalem congregation of believers in Jesus acted similarly, renouncing personal property (Acts 2:44-45; 4:32-5:11) but administering meals at which many were fed (cf. 2:46; 6:1-6), perhaps supported by wealthy patrons. Such was the highly effective practice of Judean religious virtuosi.

The preceding discussion has shown that, from a point in Herod the Great's reign, most celibate male Essenes were not "sectarian" but belonged to a Judean *religious order*, part of a broader nonsectarian "movement" that also included an order for married members and perhaps also an order for celibate females and widows. Moreover, there is evidence of Essene settlement in the two locations where John locates Jesus' most intimate connections in the Jerusalem area, Bethany and some premises on the southwest hill of Jerusalem. Since the Johannine tradition bears particular witness to Jesus' connections in these locations, we may discern in these connections, especially through the Beloved Disciple, the historical and geographical conduit through which Essene concepts attested in the Dead Sea Scrolls first exerted influence on the Johannine presentation of the story of Jesus. The examples given in the preceding section show the exegetical usefulness of a model of "virtuoso religion" for approaching John.

I raise in closing two further possibilities. The first concerns the appearance in John of a disciple uniquely loved by Jesus. As noted above, Josephus characterizes the Essenes as "lovers of one another," more than other Jewish groups (*J. W.* 2.8.2 §119). In this expression he encapsulates, particularly, the familial character of the Essene celibate male communities, their mutual service, and their sharing of all possessions. Does this use of "love" explain why a particular Jerusalem disciple of Jesus, of whom Jesus can demand accommodation when he requires it (Mark 14:12-16), could be designated "the disciple whom Jesus loved"? Might the claim of the unique witness behind John's Gospel be that of one with whom Jesus shared an especially committed relationship as a fellow member of a Jerusa-

---

48. Clare Ansberry, "Sister Rosemarie Wants You," *The Wall Street Journal*, December 17-18, 2005, pp. A1, A6.

lem *religious order*, a relationship that pre-dated Jesus' formation of his group of twelve traveling disciples? Were Jesus and the Beloved Disciple "brothers" within a Jerusalem religious order? Did this mutually committed relationship provide a fictive kinship basis for Jesus' transferal of his filial relationship with Mary to the Beloved Disciple (John 19:26–27)? Were Mary, Martha, and Lazarus, Jesus' acquaintances in Bethany whom he also "loved" (John 11:3, 5, 36), also his companions in this religious order? At Bethany, Jesus could take property for his own use if needed. Jesus' assumption that he may take the colt when he needed it for his triumphal entry and return it later (Matt 21:1–3; Mark 11:1–6; Luke 19:29–34), bears comparison with Josephus's description of the common use of possessions amongst the Essenes: "There is no buying or selling among themselves, but each gives what he has and receives in exchange something useful to himself; they are, moreover, freely permitted to take anything from their brothers without making any return" (*J. W.* 2.8.4 §127). In Jerusalem, "need," the only justification for use of resources within a communal economy, would soon become the criterion of consumption within the community of Jesus' post-Easter followers (Acts 2:45; 4:35).

The second possibility to be mentioned here concerns Jesus' washing of his disciples' feet, also uniquely recorded in John's Gospel. Jesus' action shocked his disciples; clearly, he had not done this before. Jesus had apparently traveled with the twelve for more than two years by this time, as we know from the three Passovers mentioned in John's Gospel. Does John, therefore, depict Jesus training these special disciples over a period of two to three years, a training of similar duration to that of the Essene novice (see 1QS 6.13–23; *J. W.* 2.8.7 §137–42), after which Jesus initiated them into a permanent life of complete mutual service and community of property?

Jesus washes his disciples' feet in the upper room of the Beloved Disciple; soon after, this location becomes the venue for the first post-Easter fellowship of Jesus' disciples (Acts 1:12–14), within which property was notably shared (Acts 2:42–47; 4:32–5:11; 6:1–6). As noted earlier, this property sharing seems to bear some relationship with the sharing of Essenes already resident on the southwest hill of Jerusalem. Was Jesus, in washing the disciples' feet, initiating them into the life of complete mutual service in a community of which the Beloved Disciple, his host, was already a part? At the Last Supper, Jesus promotes his disciples to the status of "friends," with profound emphasis on the total commitment demanded by the new covenant of mutual love (John 13:33–34; 15:12–15). Jesus becomes what they are no longer to him: their servant. Yet he exhorts them to profound mutual service (13:14), symbolized by washing each other's feet.

We may in this event be witnessing the disciples' incorporation into an established virtuoso social form that included mutual service and the full sharing of property. Philo reports that there were no slaves amongst the Essenes, "but all being free perform menial services for each other" (*Every Good Man Is Free* §79). Philo's report of Essene mutual service is directly comparable with Jesus' action and instruction. Jesus would apparently have his disciples form a society of friends in which there are no slaves, yet one in which all are to act as slaves of one another. Moreover, the establishment of a mutual slave relationship implies the complete sharing of property, since a slave cannot own property independently of his master.[49] As Jesus commanded his disciples to serve each other as slaves after the model of the Essene property-sharing communities, he may have been constituting them as a new, local, abiding property-sharing community of religious *virtuosi*, who were to share life and property completely. Or, he may have incorporated them into an existing community, which fully shared all life and property on the southwest hill of Jerusalem. Their obviously symbolic number, twelve, parallels both the number of the phylarchs and of the early Essene founding group of twelve (see 1QS 8.7–12). Jesus may have been installing his freshly graduated group of twelve traveling disciples as the leadership of an already established virtuoso community in Jerusalem no longer allegiant to such a council, or as a group around which he hoped local communitarians would coalesce. The Essenes of Jerusalem may have long rescinded allegiance to a council of twelve at Qumran, perhaps during the reign of Herod the Great. Were many now drawn into the movement of Jesus?

As the community of Jesus' disciples expanded after Pentecost, they were at the heart of a property-sharing community (Acts 2:42–47; 4:32–5:11). Their early converts joined them in a life of intense social and religious fellowship and mutual service, a virtuoso religious life. In the perspective of Christian history this group stands as the first church of Jerusalem, but it may first have functioned as a *religious order* rather than as a fully distinct religious congregation. The Johannine tradition bears witness to its virtuoso social form.

---

49. Cf. the discussion in *b. Kiddushin* 23a concerning how a slave, who has no independent power to acquire property, can legally acquire a document from his master giving him his freedom.

PURIFICATION IN THE FOURTH GOSPEL IN LIGHT OF QUMRAN

Hannah K. Harrington

In studies on purification in Christianity and early Judaism, the belief persists that Jewish rituals of water purification are part of an ancient past in Hebrew religion that has now been superseded by the work of the Spirit through the person of Jesus. The Fourth Gospel has often been offered as a prime example of the use of water symbolism to represent Israel's "obsolete" heritage. However, recently, it has been suggested that the author of this text uses water to convey "anticipation and fulfillment rather than renouncement and replacement."[1] The following essay will develop Ng's suggestion of water as "anticipation and fulfillment" to illuminate the use of ablutions in the Fourth Gospel by examining their function in contemporary Jewish thought, especially as reflected in the Dead Sea Scrolls.

It seems, at first glance, that water rituals are "out" in the Fourth Gospel and Jesus offers instead something new, namely, the power of the Spirit.[2] In the opening chapter, John's water baptism is decidedly inferior to Jesus' spirit baptism (John 1:33; cf. 3:34). Jesus' first miracle transforms water, stored in traditional Jewish purification jars, into wine (John 2:1–11). Similarly, the water jar of the

---

1. Wai-Yee Ng, *Water Symbolism in John: An Eschatological Interpretation* (StBibL 5; New York: Peter Lang, 2001), 69; cf. also Rudolf Schnackenburg, who points out that the Fourth Gospel mentions various Jewish ritual customs without disparagement (cf. John 7:22; 11:55; 18:28; 19:40; Rudolf Schnackenburg, *The Gospel according to St. John*, trans. Kevin Smyth, 3 vols. [HTKNT; New York: Crossroad, 1980–82], 1.339).

2. Raymond Brown regards one of the principal themes of the Fourth Gospel to be "replacing Jewish institutions and religious views" and mentions, in particular, "the replacement of the water for Jewish purifications" (*An Introduction to the Gospel of John* [ed. Francis J. Moloney; ABRL; New York: Doubleday, 2003], 305). Larry Paul Jones traces the early appearances of water in the Fourth Gospel and links them to issues of baptism and purification (*The Symbol of Water in the Gospel of John* [JSNTSup 145; Sheffield: Sheffield Academic Press, 1997], 37). C. H. Dodd suggests that the water symbolizes the Mosaic Law, which is "powerless to create the will to live," as opposed to the life-giving words of Jesus (*The Interpretation of the Fourth Gospel* [Cambridge: Cambridge University Press, 1953], 319–20).

Samaritan woman may symbolize her past expectation of water from Jacob's well in contrast to Jesus' living water, which brings eternal life (John 4:4–52). On the other hand, the Johannine Jesus does not explicitly argue against the use of water purification. In fact, he baptizes disciples himself (John 3:22, 26), and the Jewish ritual continues in Christian baptism. The people at large appear to know the significance of ritual immersion in water within Judaism, and from this general religious awareness many respond to John's baptism.[3] John's arguments with the Pharisees (John 3:25) demonstrate that purification rites were significant to all of them. So, the question at issue here is: What was that common understanding of ritual ablutions that the Fourth Gospel utilized to make certain claims about Jesus?

The scrolls found at Qumran provide information on Jewish ideas in the first century and therefore may shed new light on the common understanding of Jewish ablutions, thus assisting our understanding of John's use of water in the Fourth Gospel. The affinity between John and the scrolls is probably not due to direct influence from the Qumran Community on the Fourth Gospel but represents a general attitude among many Jewish groups.[4] Like the Fourth Gospel, several scrolls emphasize a sort of ethical and eschatological (not Gnostic) dualism, with forces of light and truth struggling against forces of darkness and perversion. But the similarities do not end there. In certain Qumran texts, there also exists an ideology regarding the use and symbolism of water which is similar to that reflected in John's Gospel. This parallel will be the focus of this chapter.[5]

In the Fourth Gospel, the terms for "purity" and "purification" are καθαρισμός ("purification"), used of the purification jars at Cana (John 2:6) and in a question about baptism (3:25); καθαρός ("pure"), used in the foot-washing

---

3. John A. T. Robinson, "The Baptism of John and the Qumran Community: Testing a Hypothesis," in his *Twelve New Testament Studies* (SBT 34; London: SCM, 1962), 15–17; Ng, *Water Symbolism in John*, 31, 69.

4. Aage Pilgaard points out that John used to be considered the most Greek of the Gospels but now appears to be the most Jewish ("The Qumran Scrolls and John's Gospel," in *New Readings in John: Literary and Theological Perspectives* [ed. Johannes Nissen and Sigfred Pedersen; JSNTSup 182; Sheffield: Sheffield Academic Press, 1999], 126–27). Cf. also Raymond E. Brown, "The Scrolls and the New Testament," in *John and the Dead Sea Scrolls* (ed. James H. Charlesworth; New York: Crossroad, 1990), 3, 7–8; Robinson, "Baptism of John and the Qumran Community," 26.

5. Scholars disagree on the possible influence of the Qumran Community on John the Baptist. John C. Hutchinson outlines differences and similarities between the messages of these two groups and concludes that the differences are too striking for the Baptist to have been influenced by Qumran (see "Was John the Baptist an Essene from Qumran?" *BSac* 159 [2002]: 187–200). But cf. Joseph A. Fitzmyer, who thinks John may have been influenced by the sect in his younger years ("The Dead Sea Scrolls and Early Christianity," in his *The Dead Sea Scrolls and Christian Origins* [Grand Rapids: Eerdmans, 2000], 17–40). Much of the commonality between their views is certainly due to the shared foundation of the Hebrew Bible.

episode in both the literal meaning of clean feet and the figurative meaning of moral purity (13:10–11), as well as in the claim that Jesus' words make the disciples pure (15:3); ἁγνίζω ("to purify"), used to describe preparations for the feast (11:55); and, ἁγιάζω, ("to sanctify") in the sense of inner purification by means of God's word/truth (17:17–19). More frequently than all of these instances combined, however, is the use of the term βαπτίζω (twelve times), all in the context of John's and Jesus' activity of immersing Jews in water. This latter process of ritual immersion will be the main focus of the present study.

It appears that the use of ritual ablutions and the symbol of water in the Fourth Gospel are not as innovative as generally believed, but rather are predated in Jewish tradition. Like the Fourth Gospel, several Qumran authors imply that Jewish purification rituals anticipated the work of the Holy Spirit. The bather expected the intervention of the Spirit to follow the ritual. It is my claim that, for many Jews in the late Second Temple era, purification in water preceded and anticipated the work of the Spirit to generate life, provide atonement, bring divine revelation, and usher in the eschaton. This concept is subtle already in the Hebrew Bible, but a study of the scrolls on the topic brings it into sharp relief.

WATER ANTICIPATES NEW LIFE

The notion that water is needed for generating life is organic and cross-cultural. Just as water brings life to plants and creatures in the physical realm, so it is associated with life in a metaphysical way. Water beads in the shape of the Egyptian *ankh*, symbol of life, were used for Egyptian ritual purification and, as in certain other cultures, the dead were baptized to resuscitate them for the afterlife. In fact, for many, water itself is a life-giving deity.[6] According to the Hebrew Bible, however, only God, through the agency of the Spirit, gives life. In the biblical creation story, the Spirit hovers over water to create the world (Gen 1:2). The notion of water bringing new life is used metaphorically by the prophets to illustrate God's renewal of Israel: "For I will pour water upon the thirsty, and floods upon the dry ground: I will pour my Spirit upon your seed, and my blessing on your offspring; and they shall spring up as among the grass, as willows by the water courses" (Isa 44:3–4). Again, God's Spirit is poured out like water to bring forth fruit (Isa 32:15). The river of the eschatological sanctuary brings healing and new life in the desert (Ezek 47:8–9).

---

6. As, for example, Hapi, the Nile River god, in ancient Egypt, and Apsu and Tiamat, principal water gods of Mesopotamia. According to James Preston, "It [water] is the 'mother of being' in opposition to the accumulation of filth, evil, defilement, and decay associated with death" ("Purification," in *Encyclopedia of Religion, Volume 11* [ed. Lindsay Jones; New York: Macmillan, 2005], 7507).

Jacob Milgrom has demonstrated that the death/life dynamic undergirds the entire biblical purity system. The most impure item in the system is the corpse, and its contagion reaches all who touch it or share a room with it. Other impurity bearers are in some way related to the loss of life, including the deteriorating scale-diseased person, the loss of life-giving sexual discharges, and various animals that are considered impure only when dead. Purification, usually by water, transfers an unclean individual from the realm of death, where he is forbidden to worship God, to the realm of life, in which he regains access to the deity.[7] This ritual of purification in water dramatizes the passage from exclusion and death to participation and life in the holy community every time an individual becomes impure.

The Dead Sea Scrolls reveal a synthesis of biblical thought on the subject of purification. Like the Pentateuch, the scrolls reveal an emphasis on the habitual practice of ritual purification in order to engage in the religious life of the community. Like the prophets, the scrolls' authors recognize the participation of the Spirit of God in this religious endeavor. Both purifying waters and the Spirit of God are necessary to initiate each individual into the new life of the community.

> But by the holy spirit of the community, in its truth, he can be purified from all of his sins and through an upright and humble attitude his sin may be atoned, and by humbling himself before all God's laws his flesh can be made clean by sprinkling with waters of purgation and sanctified by purifying waters. (1QS 3.4–9; cf. 4Q255 2.1–4)

At the same time, the Community Rule forbids any wicked person (i.e., nonmember) from water purification: "None of the perverse men is to enter the purifying waters used by the men of holiness and so contact their purity" (1QS 5.13). "Enter the purifying waters" may refer to a ritual bath before eating the communal meal, since "purity" often refers to the pure meals and property of the community, or it may even refer to an initiatory bath that inducts a new member into the community, as is suggested by the phrase "enter the covenant" in line 8

---

7. New life undergirds the biblical system of purity/impurity as well as that of other ancient cultures; see Jacob Milgrom, *Leviticus 1–16* (AB; New York: Doubleday, 1991), for a survey. See also Robert Parker, *Miasma: Pollution and Purification in Early Greek Religion* (Oxford: Clarendon, 1983), 64, for purification from corpse impurity in Greek culture. Parker explains that the mourner is participating metaphysically in the physical pollution of the dead person, and his subsequent purification reinstates him into the world of the living. This is also apparent in the Hebrew Bible, where a weeklong purification, including bathing and other rituals, is required after mourning the dead (Num 19).

(cf. 3.4–12).[8] Even if this washing was not initiatory per se, it was still significant as the first purification of a new member of the sect.[9]

The initiation into the sect began with a series of tests of the novice's character ("spirit and deeds"), each of which were demarcated by restrictions from pure food and drink. According to the Community Rule,

> he must not touch the pure food of the Many while they examine him regarding his spirit and his deeds until he has completed a full year. . . . he must not touch the drink of the Many until he has completed a second year among the men of the Community. . . . they shall enter him in the Rule according to his rank . . . for purity and for intermingling his possessions. (1QS 6.16–22; cf. also CD 15.15; 4Q265 frag. 1 2.3–9)

In Josephus's description of Essene initiation (*J. W.* 2.138), "waters of purification" mark stages in the novitiate process, admitting candidates to the "purity" (i.e., the pure food and drink of the sect), and they probably also apply in the Qumran version. Lawrence Schiffman puts it this way: "The new member gradually became less and less impure through the initiation process."[10] Conversely, each ablution allowed the candidate greater access to the purity of the holy community.

In fact, the notion of the initiation of Israel to a holier status by means of water purification is found in the Hebrew Bible. Leviticus 8 describes an induction ceremony for the priests that includes ablutions: Moses, in this case, is said to have washed Aaron and his sons in water (8:6). Also, the induction ceremony for the Levites requires water purification (Num 8:6–7). Thus, the notion of immersion as initiating a new and more holy phase of life was not unknown to Judaism of this period. This was not a mindless ritual but the gateway through which one's "spirit and deeds" were tested for acceptance into a new life of service to God.

The scrolls' authors, too, emphasize that a person must be ritually purified in order to perform special acts of service to God. For example, "no man suffering from impurity in his flesh" may join the troops in holy war on account of the holy angels present among them (1QM 7.4–6), join the messianic assembly (1Q28a 2.3), or enter the temple city (11Q19 45.11–18). Similarly, 4QSongs of the Sage[b] promises, "Among the holy ones, God will consecrate for Himself an eternal sanctuary and there will be purity among those who are purified. And they

---

8. Robinson, "Baptism of John," 18. Joseph Baumgarten infers from the context of 1QS 3.4–5 that "entrance into the Qumran community was marked by some rite of baptismal purification" ("The Purification Rituals in DJD 7," in *The Dead Sea Scrolls: Forty Years of Research* [ed. Devorah Dimant and Uriel Rappaport; STDJ 10; Leiden: Brill, 1992], 200).

9. Edmund F. Sutcliffe, "Baptism and Baptismal Rites at Qumran?" *HeyJ* 1 (1960): 188.

10. Lawrence H. Schiffman, *Sectarian Law in the Dead Sea Scrolls: Courts, Testimony, and the Penal Code* (BJS 33; Chico, Calif.: Scholars Press, 1983), 216.

shall be priests, His righteous people, His army, and servants, the angels of His glory. They shall praise Him" (4Q511 35.2–5).

The Qumran sect provides a close parallel to John's baptism because ritual purity separated Jews who were "elect" from those who were outsiders.[11] John's baptism and the repentance it required was, at the very least, an initiation into the elect who would escape the judgment of God.[12] There is a change of status in the one whom John has baptized. That person becomes an insider by making the transition from sinner to elect and is now ready for God's eschatological plan because he has been purified. According to more than one Gospel, John emphasized that just being of the seed of Abraham did not make one a righteous Jew (Matt 3:9; Luke 3:8). Josephus says John's followers were "joined together by means of baptism" (*Ant* 18.116–17).[13] Water purification was the key to unlock the process of acceptance.

Among the rabbis, too, immersion was viewed as a ritual of initiation into the people of God; ritual immersion was necessary as part of the proselyte's conversion to Judaism. In fact, the Mishnah compares the convert to a mourner and a corpse-contaminated individual (*m. Pes.* 8:8). This cannot mean that the convert was required to undergo a week-long purification, because the text states that if he performs the ritual on the day before Passover he is allowed to eat the Passover meal on the next day. Furthermore, in other places, the rabbis compare the convert's impurity to other types of impurity bearers. It seems that the ritual is more of an initiation than a medium to remove impurity.[14] Apparently, the full

---

11. William H. Brownlee, "John the Baptist in the New Light of Ancient Scrolls," in *The Scrolls and the New Testament* (ed. Krister Stendahl and James H. Charlesworth; New York: Crossroad, 1992), 39.

12. Scholars continue to argue as to whether or not John's baptism was an initiation rite into a new group; cf. Adele Yarbro Collins, "The Origin of Christian Baptism," *SL* 19 (1989): 28–46. Certainly neither John's nor Qumran's definition of baptism contains the Hellenistic notion that the immerser joined the body of a deity; see Joan E. Taylor, *The Immerser: John the Baptist within Second Temple Judaism* (SHJ; Grand Rapids: Eerdmans, 1997), 76–81.

13. Robert L. Webb, "John the Baptist and His Relationship to Jesus," in *Studying the Historical Jesus: Evaluations of the State of Current Research* (ed. Bruce Chilton and Craig A. Evans; NTTS 19; Leiden: Brill, 1994), 196.

14. Brownlee thinks that converts to Judaism washed away the ritual defilement accrued by not observing Jewish ritual purity; similarly, Robinson sees the rite as cleansing ritual impurity only (Brownlee, "John the Baptist," 36; Robinson, "Baptism of John," 16). Against these views, Christine Hayes and Shaye Cohen argue that the water ritual was an initiation rather than an impurity rite. See Christine E. Hayes, *Gentile Impurities and Jewish Identities: Intermarriage and Conversion from the Bible to the Talmud* (Oxford: Oxford University Press, 2002), 120–22; Shaye Cohen, "Is 'Proselyte Baptism' Mentioned in the Mishnah? The Interpretation of *m. Pesahim* 8:8 (= *m. Eduyot* 5:2)," in *Pursuing the Text* (ed. John C. Reeves and John Kampen; JSOTSup 184; Sheffield: Sheffield Academic Press), 278–92.

significance of the conversion ritual was not just to symbolically wash off Gentile impurity, but also to obtain a new life as a Jew.[15]

In addition to the general association of water and life, there is a technical term, מים חיים ("living water"), which refers to running or fresh water as explicitly required in the Torah for the purification of certain severe ritual impurities (e.g., gonorrhea, Lev 15:13). The prophets associated מים חיים with God (Jer 2:13; 17:13) and God's Spirit (Isa 44:2–3). The scroll writers continue this concept and especially associate "living water" with God's revelatory word as interpreted by the community. However, the technical use of "living water" as a remedy for severe ritual impurity also continues among the scrolls, in fact, even more extensively than its usage in Scripture, prompting Joseph Baumgarten to assume its usage for all impurity bearers (cf. 11Q19 16.15–17; 4Q512; 4Q277 2.2).[16] Indeed, the rabbis view only water that has issued directly from God—that is, from rain, a natural pool, or a stream—as effective for ritual purification (Sifra *shemini sheratzim* 9.1; 11.7).[17]

The writer of the Fourth Gospel also developed the OT use of the symbol "living water." He associates "living water" with Jesus himself, as the giver of life. Just as fresh, running water from a natural source was the most effective water purgation agent in the Hebrew Bible, so Jesus offers his followers "a fountain of water, springing up into life everlasting" (John 4:14). According to John, on the last day of the feast of Sukkot, the great "water" festival, Jesus promised "rivers of living water" to those who would believe in him (John 7:37–39; cf. Rev 7:17; 21:6). Sukkot not only celebrates God's provision and protection of the early Israelites, but with daily water libations also anticipates the gift of the coming rains

---

15. It is not clear when proselyte immersion as a form of initiation came into Jewish circles. There is no evidence for it until the end of the first century c.e., and so scholars are reluctant to use it to clarify John's baptism. Nevertheless, it is hard to see Jews developing this rite after it had become a sacrament in Christianity. More likely, it existed in some form in Judaism as early as John's time. John Pryke suggests that proselyte baptism may have come into Christian circles through John (see "John the Baptist and the Qumran Community," *RevQ* 16 [1964]: 490). Brownlee and Pfann agree with an early date for proselyte baptism (Brownlee, "John the Baptist," 36; Stephen J. Pfann, "The Essene Yearly Renewal Ceremony and the Baptism of Repentance," in *The Provo International Conference on the DSS: Technological Innovations, New Texts, and Reformulated Issues* [ed. Donald W. Parry and Eugene Ulrich; STDJ 30; Leiden: Brill, 1999], 347ff.). Still, there is no hard evidence for proselyte baptism until Epictetus (108 c.e.) and the mishnaic discussions of the Schools of Shammai and Hillel. See here Joseph Thomas, *Le mouvement baptiste en Palestine et en Syrie* (Gembloux, Belgium: Duculot, 1935), 356ff.; cf. the discussion in Taylor, *Immerser*, 64–69.

16. Joseph M. Baumgarten, ed., *Qumran Cave 4 XXV: Halakhic Texts* (DJD 35; Oxford: Clarendon, 1999), 83–87; cf. discussion in Hannah K. Harrington, *The Purity Texts* (CQS 5; London: T&T Clark, 2004), 22.

17. For full discussion, cf. Hannah K. Harrington, *The Impurity Systems of Qumran and the Rabbis: Biblical Foundations* (SBLDS 143; Atlanta: Scholars Press, 1993), 134–35.

and, metaphorically, the eschatological blessing of the Spirit.[18] Thus, water is used to illustrate rejuvenation and renewal, not as an innovation on the part of the Fourth Gospel but because that association was already embedded in the water rituals of Judaism. To be sure, only the Spirit of God can bring true renewal, but the water ritual anticipates and illustrates that gift (cf. John 7:37–39).[19]

Furthermore, Jesus himself is revealed via his baptism, which inducts him into a life of ministry, as it did the biblical priests and Levites. It is while he is in the purifying water of the Jordan River that the Spirit of God rests upon him. The Fourth Gospel depicts the Spirit as a dove hovering over Jesus at his baptism, a symbol that was no doubt included to trigger thoughts of Gen 1:2 and to make an implicit point that "Jesus was the bringer of a new creation."[20] The Spirit of God then consecrates him for ministry. As John Robinson points out, water baptism points to the Spirit, "which was to consecrate the coming one for his mission (John 1:31), the ultimate divine mission of taking away the sin of the world (John 1:29) and of pouring out upon believers the holy spirit of God (John 1:33)."[21] Jesus' baptism became the occasion and catalyst for the Spirit to rest on him and inaugurate his ministry. The Fourth Gospel's notion that new life follows baptism is not unusual in light of biblical and Qumran precedents.[22]

In the Fourth Gospel, water is not used to symbolize the old method of purification but rather functions as expected in Judaism: to dramatize the transfer from death to life. In this transition, water baptism anticipates and works in conjunction with the Spirit. John the Baptist's ablutions point to the one who will baptize with the Spirit (John 1:33). Water also works in anticipation of the Spirit to bring about the "new birth" that Jesus requires (John 3:5). Raymond Brown recognizes this connection as a unique contribution of the Fourth Gospel: "It is John who tells us that through baptismal water God begets children unto himself and pours forth upon them his Spirit (3:5; 7:37–39)."[23] Perhaps "water" here refers to both a ritual and moral cleansing that anticipates the entry of the "Spirit."

---

18. See discussion in Ng, *Water Symbolism in John*, 77–81.

19. As Morna Hooker puts it, in John 7:37–39 water is used as "an analogy for the future gift of the Spirit" ("John's Baptism: A Prophetic Sign," in *The Holy Spirit and Christian Origins* [ed. Graham N. Stanton, Bruce W. Longenecker, and Stephen C. Barton; Grand Rapids: Eerdmans, 2004], 37). The spring of water provided by Jesus (John 4:14; 7:38) brings renewal and life.

20. Dale C. Allison, *Scriptural Allusions in the New Testament: Light from the Dead Sea Scrolls* (DSSCOL 5; North Richland Hills, Tex.: Bibal Press, 2000), 11.

21. Robinson, "Baptism of John," 24.

22. Cf. Herman Lichtenberger, "The Dead Sea Scrolls and John the Baptist: Reflections on Josephus' Account of John the Baptist," in *The Dead Sea Scrolls: Forty Years of Research* (ed. Divorah Dimant and Uriel Rappaport; STDJ 10; Leiden: Brill, 1992), 81.

23. Brown, *Introduction to the Gospel of John*, 234. Larry Jones translates this phrase epexegetically, so that both elements are used to fulfill a single objective (*Symbol of Water*, 70). Ng sees both a ritualistic and figurative usage of the water symbol (*Water Symbolism in John*, 66).

Water Anticipates Atonement

The significance of a water ritual before asking forgiveness almost goes without saying. Water is the universal cleanser, and despite cultural diversity ritual immersion in water carries its own organic message that it can absorb pollution and carry it away. Thus, washing is the means par excellence of expressing a desire for cleaning on a metaphysical level as well.[24]

The association of ritual ablutions with atonement, although not explicitly part of the priestly system, is already mentioned in the Hebrew Bible. Indeed, it is a Levitical principle that ritual impurity bars a person from God's presence, while purification in water invites God's presence and restoration (Num 19:20).[25] Purity was necessary before any contact with holy things (Lev 7:20–21). According to the Mishnah, on the Day of Atonement the high priest immersed himself five times (once before each of the holy rituals) and washed his hands and feet ten times (*m. Yom.* 3.3).[26] Before holy events, too, such as the Sinaitic revelation, all Israel were required to purify themselves (cf. Exod 19:10–11).[27] Thus, water purification was performed before access to God and holy things.[28]

Occasionally in the biblical narratives, washing is explicitly performed before approaching God for atonement. For example, both Job and Jacob order their families to wash themselves before attending expiatory sacrifices; as Job explains, "It may be that my sons have sinned" (Job 1:6). In Jacob's case the idolatry is evi-

---

24. In religious contexts, this cleansing has to do with the person's sense of dirtiness when approaching the deity. Even today, "Muslims clean their mouths and ears with water to sanctify their prayers and open their hearing to the will of God." In some cases, the impurity may represent the individual's domination by an impure spirit. In a Mesopotamian text, the bewitched performs ablutions and cries out, "As I purify, so purify me!" (Preston, "Purification," 7507).

25. Cf. Milgrom's argument that in the biblical priestly system bathing and laundering are performed on the day before one's admission to the presence of God (*Leviticus 1–16*, 966). See also his cross-cultural survey of ritual purity requirements before encounter with the sacred (957–63).

26. Milgrom states that this was probably the actual practice in the Herodian temple (*Leviticus 1–16*, 1047).

27. Jonathan Lawrence sees ritual purity as originally a preparation for a single encounter with God, which was later institutionalized into cultic systems that preserved purity for the community's encounters with God (*Washing in Water: Trajectories of Ritual Bathing in the Hebrew Bible and Second Temple Literature* [SBLAcB 23; Atlanta: Society of Biblical Literature, 2006], 196).

28. Israel must immerse before handling holy things of any kind (e.g., tithes, dedicated items; see 2 Sam 8:7–11; 1 Kings 7:51; 14:26–27; 15:15). This is documented cross-culturally; cf. the survey in Milgrom, *Leviticus 1–16*, 968–75. See also Milgrom's argument that in the biblical examples both bathing and laundering are performed on the day before one's admission to the presence of God (966).

dent, as he orders his household, "Put away the strange gods that are among you, and be clean, and change your garments" (Gen 35:1–3). Similarly, humility and repentance played a large role in Naaman's healing and conversion, which were preceded by bathing in the Jordan River (2 Kings 5:14).

The association of ritual ablutions with atonement becomes more pronounced in Second Temple Judaism, especially in the Dead Sea Scrolls.[29] Ablutions were not just a technical duty or a symbol but a means of invitation to the atoning work of God. The Community Rule states that new members are cleansed by their humble repentance as well as the sprinkling of cleansing waters (1QS 3.6–9). Conversely, no ablutions will be effective in removing the impurity of one who rejects the community's laws.

> He [who refuses to repent] cannot become innocent by acts of atonement, neither can he be purified by waters of purgation. He cannot be purified in oceans and rivers, nor purified by any water of ablution. . . . But by the holy spirit of the community, in its truth, he can be purified from all of his sins and through an upright and humble attitude his sin may be atoned, and by humbling himself before all God's laws his flesh can be made clean by sprinkling with waters of purgation and sanctified by purifying waters. (1QS 3.4–9; cf. 4Q255 2.1–4)

The synonymous interchanging of the terms "purify" and "sanctify" reveals the interconnectedness of ritual and moral purification here. The author does not accept one without the other; the two are inextricably linked in the repentance process.[30] The same holds true for the Damascus Document, in which the word of a transgressor is only believed after he has been ritually purified (CD 10.2).[31] Thus, ablutions fulfill a vital role in the restoration of an offender to the community.

---

29. Lawrence points to various uses of immersion in Second Temple Judaism (initiation, before prayer, before eating, before Sabbath and festivals) and gives various Second Temple explanations for washing (innocence, humility). He concludes that washing was not just a ritual but carried a spiritual quality (*Washing in Water*, 201). The opposite position, however, is taken by Hartmut Stegemann: "Nor did the bath have any sacramental meaning such as forgiveness of sins, but provided only ritual purity" ("The Qumran Essenes: Local Members of the Main Jewish Union in Late Second Temple Times," in *The Madrid Qumran Congress* [ed. Julio Trebolle Barrera and Luis Vegas Montaner; 2 vols.; STDJ 11; Leiden: Brill, 1992], 1.110).

30. According to 1QS 5.14–20, ritual impurity adheres to a sinner's possessions; cf. Josephus's comment that the elders of the Essene community (i.e., those at the top of the ladder of moral integrity) become ritually impure if they touch those of lower rank (*J.W.* 2.150). Apparently, as one matures in moral character, sensitivity to impurity increases.

31. The impurity of leprosy is referred to as the work of a malevolent spirit, not just a condition in need of the prescribed purifications of Lev 14 (4Q272 1.1–16). The *zab* (i.e., gonorrheic), like the leper, is considered a sinner because his condition is brought on by lustful thoughts. This stands in contrast to the rabbinic insistence that the *zab*'s condition did not result from sexual stimuli. See DJD 35, 88.

The linkage of moral and ritual purification is apparent as well in several columns of text from Cave 4. Although fragmentary, 4QRitual of Purification A and B (4Q414 and 4Q512) contain a serious note of contrition, as ritually impure individuals perform ablutions and give thanks to God for purifying them and making them holy.[32] The impurities involved are clearly of a ritual nature, as evidenced by specific terms—including "impure flux" (4Q512 frags. 10–11), "holy ash," and "third day"—which were important for purification from a corpse (4Q512 frags. 1–3). Nevertheless, the individual seeking purification confesses sin and asks for forgiveness (4Q512 frags. 29–32 7.18; frag. 28 4; frag. 99 2; frag. 34 5.15). The following passage from 4Q414 illustrates the mixture of the language of atonement and ritual purification in these documents.

> For You made me [. . .] your will that we purify ourselves befo[re . . .] and He established for himself a law of atonement [. . .] and to be in rig[hteous] purity and he shall ba[t]he in water and sprinkle up[on . . .] [. . .] And then he will return from the w[ater . . .] cleansing his people in the waters of Bathing (רוח במימי) [. . .] second time upon his station. And he shall [say] in re[sponse, 'Blessed are You, ...] [. . .] You purified (טה[ר]ת[ה]) in your glory [. . .] [. . .] eternally." (4Q414 13.1–10)

"Rig[hteous] purity" and "atonement" are accomplished here by the combination of ritual bathing and humility before God. In fact, the combined purity of body and spirit is seen as a "primary duty" by the Damascus Document—"to separate from all impurities according to the law and to let no man defile his holy spirit" (CD 7.3–4).

This conjunction of baptism and repentance, while prominent in the Qumran texts, is also present elsewhere in Second Temple Judaism. In some apocryphal texts, the penitent immerses in water before he pleads for forgiveness. In Life of Adam and Eve, Adam says to Eve, "Stand clothed in the water up to [your] neck, and let no speech come out of your mouth, because we are unworthy to entreat the Lord since our lips are unclean" (6–7). Similarly, Sibylline Oracle 4.165–68 calls for immersion of the whole body in rivers followed by prayer for forgiveness. Furthermore, Testament of Levi 18.7 explains that divine cleansing takes place in the water: "And the spirit of understanding and sanctification shall rest upon him in the water."[33] Levi is obligated to bathe before he prays that the Lord make known to him the "spirit of holiness" (T. Levi 2.3; cf. Jdt 12:7–8).

---

32. See full discussion in Baumgarten, "Purification Rituals in DJD 7," 199–209, and Esther Eshel, "4Q414 Fragment 2: Purification of a Corpse-Contaminated Person," in Legal Texts and Legal Issues: Proceedings of the Second Meeting of the International Organization for Qumran Studies, Cambridge 1995 (ed. Moshe Bernstein, Florentino García Martínez, and John Kampen; STDJ 23; Leiden: Brill, 1997), 3–10.

33. Trans. by Brownlee, "John the Baptist," 43.

For these forms of Second Temple Judaism, water purification was not just a neutral experience that symbolized one's inner penitence, but rather was a catalyst for spiritual renewal. The *Hodayot*, or Thanksgiving Hymns, read:

> And because I know that You have recorded the spirit of the righteous, I myself have chosen to purify my hands in accordance with your wil[l]. The soul of your servant a[bho]rs every work of injustice. I know that no one can be righteous apart from You. And I entreat your favor by that spirit which You have placed within [me], to fulfill your [mer]cy with [your] servant for[ever], to purify me by your holy spirit, and to bring me near by your will according to the greatness of your mercy. (1QH 8.28–30)

Here, the sinner washes his hands before he entreats God for mercy; ritual purification anticipates spiritual purification (cf. also 11Q5 19.13–14). In 4Q texts, too, the blessing comes after washing while the cleansed person is standing in the water (4Q512; 4Q414 frags. 2–3 2.3–5; "And then he shall enter the water . . . And he shall say in response, 'Blessed are Y[ou . . .] . . .'").

Thus, the act of immersion dramatizes and expresses the need of divine grace and intervention by the community, and thus precedes prayer, whether entering the temple or not (4Q414 frag. 2 2.5–6; 4Q512 frags. 42–44 2). So also, at Jesus' baptism, blessing comes after washing while standing in water (cf. Matt 3:16–17). Rabbinic blessings come after immersion, too, although not while still standing in the water (*b. Ber.* 51a and *b. Pes.* 7b).

Although ablutions could not force God to forgive, they facilitated the repentance process. Indeed, God is described as the one who wills "to purify his people in cleansing water" (4Q414 frag. 10 7).[34] The blessing recited by the purifying person in the Community Rule reveals that the individual is keenly aware of his sinful condition but trusts in God's ultimate goodness to show him mercy: "In his great goodness he atones for all my iniquities. In his righteousness he cleanses me of the impurity of the human and [of] the sin of the human being, in order [that I might] praise God [for] his righteousness, and the Most High [for] his glory" (1QS 11.14; cf. also 4Q512 frag. 39 2, 8). As Joseph Baumgarten puts it, "Far from being merely external acts . . . these purifications were viewed as the means by which the holy spirit restores the corporate purity of Israel."[35]

With the perceived lack of a proper temple cult at Jerusalem, water rituals at Qumran began to take on greater significance. With the sanctuary and its feasts on hold, ritual ablutions apparently helped to make up for this spiritual gap. Their function, just as in the Hebrew Bible, seems to be to invite the presence of the

---

34. See the discussion in Baumgarten, who notes the connection here of spiritual and ritual cleansing and points as well to the use of the ritual purity verb יצק, "to pour out like water," in 4Q504 frags. 1–2 5 ("Purification Liturgies," 208).

35. Ibid., 211.

spirit and action of God into the community (e.g., sanctification before the acts of divine power at Sinai and the opening of the Jordan River, etc).[36]

Like the Qumran texts, water purification in the Fourth Gospel prepares the hearts of penitents for the activity of the Spirit. The critical moment in John 1, for example, is the identification of the sacrificial lamb that would be able to atone for sin. This epiphany occurs during Jesus' baptism when John proclaims, "Behold the lamb of God who takes away the sin of the world" (John 1:28–29; cf. 11:45–53). Nowhere in Judaism in the texts discussed above was water used as the sole means of atonement,[37] and this also seems to be the understanding of the Fourth Gospel.[38] In fact, in the Fourth Gospel, John the Baptist's ministry points to the lamb (Jesus) who was expected to take sins away (John 1:29, 36), indicating that atonement is not the function of John's immersion. Water did not by itself effect atonement, but it did contribute to a person's experience of repentance by expressing his/her desire for cleaning and dependence on God's grace.[39]

Although John's baptism is not specifically termed *baptisma metanoias* in the Fourth Gospel, the notion of atonement surfaces in the identification of Jesus as

---

36. Hyam Maccoby, *Ritual and Morality: The Ritual Purity System and Its Place in Judaism* (Cambridge: Cambridge University Press, 1999), 212.

37. Catherine Murphy proposes that Josephus's statement "only then [after acts of justice, etc.] would the baptism be acceptable" suggests that "baptism is presented as a kind of sacrifice; notice the concern that the baptism be acceptable to God" (see *John the Baptist: Prophet of Purity for a New Age* [Collegeville, Minn.: Liturgical Press, 2003], 5). This is an unnecessary assumption. All of the rituals of the Hebrew Bible must be done properly or they will not be acceptable to God, but not all concern atonement.

38. Much debate centers on the question of whether the Fourth Gospel abrogates the atonement of the sacrifices at the temple. John 4:21–23, for example, envisions a time when the temple will be obsolete. Pilgaard regards Jesus as the only true temple in the Fourth Gospel: "Jesus is the one on whom the Spirit came down and remained (1.33). He is therefore the place for the revelation of God's glory, God's true temple (2.21-22)" ("Qumran Scrolls," 141). Alternatively, Fuglseth sees the Johannine community as accepting the temple because it was a scripturally ordained institution (cf. 1:45; 5:46) but with a critical stance, in principle like Philo and some Qumran authors. "The temple, festivals, and other institutions mentioned in the [Fourth] Gospel are reinterpreted in a way that may have prepared for a replacement at a later stage and they were easily at hand when the temple was destroyed. . . . [W]e can infer a practice of abrogation neither of the temple institution nor of other traditional Jewish institutions" (see Kåre Sigvald Fuglseth, *Johannine Sectarianism in Perspective: A Sociological, Historical, and Comparative Analysis of Temple and Social Relationships in the Gospel of John, Philo, and Qumran* [NovTSup 119; Leiden: Brill, 2005], 283).

39. Walter Wink suggests that John's baptism is "solely for the purpose of manifesting to the world its need for the purification which Christ alone brings (1:31). . . . If Jesus is the Lamb of God who takes away the sins of the world (1:29, 36), then clearly John's baptism can no longer be for the forgiveness of sins. We see him baptize no one, nor is he once called 'the Baptist' in this Gospel" (see *John the Baptist in the Gospel Tradition* [SNTSMS 7; Cambridge: Cambridge University Press, 1968], 90).

the "lamb" (John 1:29) who would atone for sin by his death and offer life to his followers (John 4:14).[40] Johannine scholars have made further connections in the Fourth Gospel between water rituals and atonement. B. H. Grigsby suggested that the water-pouring rituals of the feast of Sukkot may anticipate the salvific work of Jesus (John 7:2): the pool from which the water was taken, Siloam ("sent one"), may refer to the Messiah and the "salvific bath" he provides—sinners are washed in the fountain of cleansing water at Calvary.[41] Rudolf Schnackenburg suggested that the humble foot-washing episode may also foreshadow the sacrificial atonement on the cross (John 19:31–37), where water and blood join in a flow from Jesus' side.[42] The point here is that John the Baptist in the Fourth Gospel was not the first to use water purification in the process of repentance. As demonstrated by Qumran and other Second Temple texts, many Jews purified themselves in water when asking God for purity, both moral and ritual.

WATER ANTICIPATES REVELATION

Water purification among the sectarians anticipated the activity of the Spirit not only for a new way of life and atonement for sin, but also for the experience of divine revelation. While there is no explicit command in the scrolls to bathe before studying the Torah or seeking divine wisdom, it is a logical assumption. Two points should be noted even before turning to the Qumran texts. First, the rabbis, who shared with the scroll writers an interest in ritual purification, were explicit that ritual purification must precede the study of the Bible.[43] Since the sectarians required even more purification, as well as more study of the Torah,

---

40. As Charlesworth points out, the Gospels of Mark and Luke particularly note that John's baptism was "a baptism of repentance for the forgiveness of sins"—that is, part of the repentance process (see "John the Baptizer and Qumran Barriers in Light of the Rule of the Community," in *The Provo International Conference on the DSS: Technological Innovations, New Texts, and Reformulated Issues* [ed. Donald W. Parry and Eugene Ulrich; STDJ 30; Leiden: Brill, 1999], 357–58).

41. B. H. Grigsby, "Washing in the Pool of Siloam: A Thematic Anticipation of the Johannine Cross," *NovT* 27 (1985): 227–35.

42. "The blood is, presumably, a sign of Jesus' saving death (cf. 1 Jn 1:7) and the water is symbolic of Spirit and life (cf. Jn 4:14; 7:38)" (see Schnackenburg, *Gospel according to St. John*, 3.294).

43. Although the Qumran texts do not explicitly require purification before study, it is logical to assume that they did (see Joseph Baumgarten, "Qumran/Essene Restraints on Marriage," in *Archaeology and History in the Dead Sea Scrolls* [ed. Lawrence H. Schiffman; JSPSup 8; Sheffield: JSOT Press, 1990], 19). The sect spent one-third of every night studying Scripture in order to illuminate its hidden meaning (1QS 6.6–8; cf. CD 3.13–16; 5.2–5; 1QS 9.17). Some rabbis considered ritual immersion before Torah study to be a Scriptural injunction (e.g., R. Joshua ben Levi and R. Eleazar [cf. *b. Ber* 22b; *y. Ber.* 3, 6c]). This purification is primarily for seminal impurity, but other reasons are mentioned, too. See Baumgarten, "Qumran/Essene

than the rabbis, they probably required ritual washing before study. Second, according to Josephus, the Essenes, whom the majority of scholars link with the Qumran community in some way, did require ritual purification as a prerequisite for the reception of prophecy: they utilized the books of the prophets and also "various forms of purification" (*J.W.* 2.159).[44]

One fragmentary text from Qumran does support the practice of ritual washing as a preparation for divine revelation. 4QAramaic Levi[b] (4Q213a) corroborates the existence of the *Testament of Levi* at Qumran, which when combined gives an account of purification before divine revelation.

> [Then] I [washed my clothing and purified them with pure water,] [and] I bath[ed all over in living water, so making] all [my ways correct. Then] I raised my eyes [and face] to heaven, [I opened my mouth and spoke,] and my fingers and hands [I spread out properly in front of the holy angels. So I prayed and] said . . ." (4Q213a 1 1.6–10, with the *Testament of Levi*, Mt. Athos MS, in brackets)

In this passage, Levi's entreaty before the holy angels is preceded by bathing. In the next column his purification and supplication are rewarded with a supernatural vision in which he is ushered into heaven.

> Then I saw visions [. . .] in the appearance of this vision, I saw [the] [heav]en opened, and I saw a mountain] underneath me, high, reaching up to heaven [. . .] to me the gates of heaven, and an angel [said to me: Enter Levi . . .].[45]

Of course, the model for expectation of divine revelation after purification is the quintessential revelation at Sinai. Here all Israel is told to "sanctify" themselves in the sense of ritual purification, even laundering and abstinence from sexual intercourse, as the necessary preparation to stand in the presence of God and receive the law.[46] Although Scripture is not explicit about immersions being required,

Restraints," 3, 33, 17; Gedalia Alon, *Jews, Judaism, and the Classical World: Studies in Jewish History in the Times of the Second Temple and Talmud* (Jerusalem: Magnes, 1977), 192.

44. Baumgarten, "Purification Liturgies," 207.

45. Lawrence (*Washing in Water*, 110), suggests that this passage could describe a preparation for theophany.

46. The term *mitqadesh* is often translated "sanctify," but it is clear that this term indicates washing with water. For example, Bathsheba's *mitqadeshet* after menstruation (2 Sam 11) is clearly not a moral issue but one of washing. Although some may argue that the menstruant need not bathe according to the priestly laws, this is controverted not only by the example of Bathsheba but also by the fact that Leviticus is explicit that the person who touches even the menstruant's bed or seat must bathe; *a fortiori*, the menstruant herself must bathe. See Milgrom, *Leviticus 1–16*, 965.

ancient Jewish interpreters understood it this way.[47] Other acts of divine revelation and power in the Hebrew Bible are preceded by sanctification as well. The miracles of the quail (Num 11:18), crossing the Jordan (Josh 3:5), and the divine revelation of the results of the lot-casting (Josh 7:13–14) are all preceded by sanctification—that is, a required immersion of all Israel.[48] Holy war is only victorious if the troops maintain ritual purity (Deut 23:9–14). In Second Temple Judaism, sacred days also are preceded by immersion, anticipating some encounter with God.[49]

The strength of the tradition of ritual purification before divine revelation is evident in the fact that many later rabbis believed ritual immersion could facilitate divine insight and power. The rabbinic mystics of the Hekhalot texts form a close parallel to the Qumran sectarians since both were trying to influence or contact the angels. In these texts immersions play an important role in facilitating various adjurations.[50] The ritual for drawing down the *Sar ha-Torah* demands twenty-four immersions daily. Another *Sar ha-Torah* ritual requires immersions in a river every morning and evening for nine days. According to rabbinic legend, even Moses immersed before the revelation and finally had to separate permanently from his wife so that he could be pure and ready constantly for additional revelation (*b. Shab.* 87a, 88b; *Abot de Rabbi Nathan* 2).

On another level, the divine revelation, whether commandments or visions, can purify individuals in a metaphysical way. "But You, O my God, have placed your words in my mouth, as showers of early rain, for all [who thirst] and as a spring of living waters" (1QH 16.17)—metaphorically, God's words are purifying waters to the dry soul. Other Qumran texts agree:

> They tolerate none who trans[gress] the true way, nor is t[here] any impure among their holy ones. [The laws of the ho]ly ones He has inscribed for them, that all the eternally holy ones might thereby be sanctified and He purifies those of pure light. (4Q400 1.14–15)

> Then God will purify by his truth all the works of man and purge for himself the structure of man to utterly destroy the spirit of deceit from the innermost part of

---

47. *Mekh. Yitro* 3: "In the Torah there is no laundering that does not require [bodily] immersion" (trans. Milgrom, *Leviticus 1–16*, 682). Cf. also *Mekh. RS* 96–97; *b. Ker.* 9a; *b. Ger.* 2; *Mekh. baHiodesh* 6, 63b–64a; Philo, *Decalogue* 11; *b. Yeb.* 46a; *y. Shab.* 9, 12a. A contrary view is taken by Lawrence (*Washing in Water*, 35–41), who sees ritual washing as a rare occasion in the Hebrew Bible, limited primarily to the priesthood.

48. Milgrom, *Leviticus 1–16*, 965–66.

49. Lawrence, *Washing in Water*, 62–63.

50. Rebecca Macy Lesses, *Ritual Practices to Gain Power: Angels, Incantations, and Revelation in Early Jewish Mysticism* (HTS 44; Harrisburg, Pa.: Trinity Press International, 1998), 132–33, 155. According to Lesses, Hekhalot texts can be dated as early as the first century C.E. in Palestine (10).

his flesh and to purify him by the holy spirit from all wicked deeds and sprinkle upon him the spirit of truth as waters of purification from all the abominations of falsehood and from being polluted by a spirit of impurity. (1QS 4.20–22)[51]

Alexander and Vermes explain that, in the Community Rule, "by his truth" refers to the "instrument by which the 'holy spirit' has come to inhere in the Community—the special revelation of God's truth to the Teacher of Righteousness. There is a link in S [all versions of the Community Rule] between 'truth' and the 'holy spirit,' seen as the spirit which inspired the prophets" (citing 1QS 9.3–4; 8.16; 2.26).[52] For the sectarians, God's word was like a purifying stream that could purge misinformation and deception from the human mind via the Spirit of God, and fill it instead with refreshing truth.

Revelation for the Qumran community meant its own understanding of Scripture. Even in order to join the community and begin its restricted life, one had to become pure. Those who reject the community's interpretation reject divine truth: "So are all the men who entered into the New Covenant in the land of Damascus and turned backward and acted treacherously and departed from the well of living water" (CD 19.33–34).[53] Furthermore, these rebels also become impure. The writer applies the call of the leper, "impure, impure," to the person who "rejects the decrees of God, refusing to be disciplined by the community of his counsel" (1QS 3.4–6). Thus, the immersion of an individual seeking divine revelation mirrors and anticipates the purging of the revelation itself, but those who do not accept this process are still impure.

With this conceptual background in place, the ideas that ritual ablutions are preparatory to divine revelation and that spiritual truth purifies are clearly not original to the writer of the Fourth Gospel; both notions pre-date Christianity. The Fourth Gospel is not relegating water purification to an obsolete past but is utilizing it to point to the next work of the Spirit. The Evangelist presents John the Baptist performing ritual ablutions in preparation for the revelation of the word incarnate, Jesus. It is while John is baptizing penitent Jews that the identification of Jesus as the Messiah and giver of the Spirit is revealed. What *is* unique in the Fourth Gospel with regard to purification by divine truth is that "Word," "Truth," and "Living Water" are all personified by Jesus himself, who is expected to purify believers. Jesus is presented as the embodiment of the preexistent Word of God (John 1:1) and a living representation of divine truth (John 14:6), as well as the giver of the "living water" (John 4:10, 14). It is a basic thesis of the Fourth Gospel

---

51. Cf. also 1.11–13, where one's knowledge can be purified by the truth of the laws of God.

52. Philip S. Alexander and Geza Vermes, *Qumran Cave 4 XIX: Serekh ha-Yahad and Two Related Texts*, DJD 26 (Oxford: Clarendon, 1998), 35.

53. Cf. also CD 3.16: "They dug a well of much water"; CD 6.4–5: "The well is the Torah, and they who dug it are the penitents of Israel. . . ."

that the disciples of Jesus are pure because of their acceptance of Jesus' teaching: "Now you are pure through the word which I have spoken to you" (15:3). Jesus' word purges the disciples because it is divine—for example, in John 17:17, "Sanctify them in truth. Your word is truth." The Qumran sectarians and the writer of the Fourth Gospel would disagree on the role of Jesus, but they would share common ground in performing ritual purification for the reception of divine revelation.

WATER ANTICIPATES THE ESCHATON

The connection of water purification and the eschaton is a biblical principle. Just as the Spirit worked in conjunction with water to effect the first creation (Gen 1:2), so also at the eschatological rejuvenation. In fact, the prophet Zechariah promises the outpouring of the Spirit at the opening of the eschaton, culminating in a divine fountain that will purify Israel (Zech 12:10; 13:1). Ezekiel, too, predicts divine sprinkling of pure water on wayward Israel to purify the people of sin, giving them a new heart and a new spirit (Ezek 36:25). As Bruce Chilton says, "The close and causal connection between water and spirit here has led to the suggestion that we have an important scriptural precedent of Yohanan's immersion."[54] This connection was not only important to John the Baptist but was adopted by other Jews as well, including the Qumran community (cf. 1QS 4.19–23; *Jub.* 1.22–25).

The idea that purification precedes the eschaton is not just a spiritual and symbolic notion of the prophets. With the emphasis on ritual purification in water prevalent in so many forms of Second Temple Judaism, the first association Jews would have made when hearing purity terms would have been a physical cleansing in water. From the Pharisees to the Essenes, purification by washing was a habitual religious practice. The Qumran community especially is known for its ritual purification, and the Dead Sea Scrolls clearly portray ritual purification as preparation for the eschaton. According to the War Scroll, a great war in the messianic era will be fought on heaven and earth engaging both natural and supernatural forces. Because angels will be present in this battle, those impure from a sexual discharge are not allowed to participate (1QM 7.3–6). Also, the Rule of the Congregation prohibits any impure person (i.e., anyone afflicted with ritual impurities) from serving on the eschatological council (1Q28a 2.2–4; cf. Lev 5:3; 7:21). As Lawrence Schiffman has argued, the Qumranites lived in

---

54. Bruce Chilton sees John's baptism as a purification ritual with eschatological overtones (see "Yohanan the Purifier and His Immersion," *TJT* 14, no. 2 [1998]: 211 n. 45); cf. Otto Böcher, "Johannes der Täufer," *TRE* 17 (1988): 172–81, esp. 175.

expectation of this messianic era in the present, and so required the constant purification of all impurity in their ranks.[55]

Purification during the eschaton can even facilitate the resurrection of the dead. According to the writer of *Hodayot*,

> For your glory's sake You have purified man from transgression, so that he can purify himself for You from all impure abominations and the guilt of unfaithfulness, so as to be joined wi[th] the children of your truth; in the lot with your holy ones, that bodies, covered with worms of the dead, might rise up from the dust to an et[ernal] council; from a perverse spirit to your understanding. That he might take his position before You with the eternal hosts and spirits . . . , to be renewed with all that shall be and to rejoice together with those who know. (1QH 19.13–17)

According to this text, God has granted atonement from sin so that the individual is now able to purify himself. The language used here seems to indicate both ritual and moral impurity. God's Spirit is then able to resuscitate the individual and change his "perverse spirit," granting him a place among the righteous forever. This passage foreshadows the later rabbinic dictum that ritual purity leads to separation, then to holiness, and eventually to the Holy Spirit and the resurrection of the dead (*m. Sotah* 9.15).

We even have among the scrolls the innovative notion that a messianic figure will introduce the Spirit. In 4Q521 Messianic Apocalypse, a figure is expected who will be endowed with the divine spirit and be able to renew the faithful.

> [For the heav]ens and the earth will obey his messiah . . . for the Lord will consider the pious, and call the righteous by name, and his spirit will hover upon the poor, and he will renew the faithful with his strength . . . freeing prisoners, giving sight to the blind . . . heal the badly wounded and will make the dead live, he will proclaim good news to the poor.[56]

The messianic usage of Isa 61:1 was apparently a popular Jewish interpretation in Second Temple times (cf. Luke 4:18). The author of 4Q521 makes a further connection between the Spirit and the Messiah by alluding to Gen 1:2 as well. As at the first creation where the Spirit "hovered" over water, so also in the eschaton the Spirit will "hover" over the righteous (those who are pure) to renew them. The Damascus Document also indicates that the Messiah will introduce the Spirit: "He made known to them his holy spirit through his messiah(s)" (CD

55. Lawrence H. Schiffman, "Purity and Perfection: Exclusion from the Council of the Community in the *Serekh ha-'Edah*," in *Biblical Archaeology Today* (ed. J. Amitai; Jerusalem: Israel Exploration Society, 1985), 374, 383–85.

56. Cited by Allison, *Scriptural Allusions*, 12.

2.12). These texts show a mutual context in Palestinian Judaism for the Fourth Gospel's notion that the Messiah was the giver of the Spirit.[57]

The eschatological dimension of purification by water in the Fourth Gospel has been debated.[58] According to one view, the eschatological angle is an innovation by the church,[59] but this theory is clearly refuted by the examples from the scrolls presented above. Most scholars do recognize an eschatological dimension to John's baptism, especially in the Fourth Gospel. His message is both a warning of divine judgment about to occur as well as hope that a messianic figure will bring rescue to the Jews. Indeed, the notion of baptism preceding deliverance is taken up by other Jews of this period (cf. 1 Cor 10:1–5). As Robert Webb explains, "John's baptism is the final opportunity to prepare for the eschatological judgment and restoration to be brought by the expected figure."[60] In the Fourth Gospel, baptism is the prerequisite for identifying the Messiah and receiving his blessings, in particular, the baptism of the Spirit. According to Wai-Yee Ng, John's identification of Jesus during baptism is the fountainhead to the "subsequent and successive use of water symbolism" throughout the Fourth Gospel, where water often symbolizes eschatological blessing. For example, "When John the Baptist says ἐκεῖνον δεῖ αὐξάνειν, ἐμὲ δὲ ἐλαττοῦσθαι (3:30) he implies that ceremonial washing is preparatory to eschatological salvation and that eschatological salvation is symbolized by the joyful event of the bridegroom's wedding."[61]

57. Fitzmyer, "Dead Sea Scrolls and Early Christianity," 17–40.

58. Craig A. Evans, "Jesus, John, and the Dead Sea Scrolls: Assessing Typologies of Restoration," in *Christian Beginnings and the Dead Sea Scrolls* (ed. John J. Collins and Craig A. Evans; ASBT; Grand Rapids: Baker Books, 2006), 61; cf. Jonathan Klawans, *Impurity and Sin in Ancient Judaism* (Oxford: Oxford University Press, 2000), 139.

59. "Nowhere in Jewish tradition was baptism associated with the messiah or the end times, notwithstanding the interrogation of John by priests and Levites in the Fourth Gospel (John 1:19–28). This is discontinuous with Jewish tradition and therefore more likely to be a historical innovation, at least of the evangelists' and perhaps of John's" (Murphy, *John the Baptist*, 60; see also Taylor, *The Immerser*, 9). Against this position, Chilton claims that, while John's baptism was definitely ritual bathing and did not bring atonement, it "was driven by an eschatological expectation; not necessarily of a messiah but of divine judgment. Of all the statements attributed to Yohanan, the claim that after him a baptism of spirit was to come stands out as possibly authentic" ("Yohanan the Purifier," 207–11).

60. Webb, "John the Baptist," 194; cf. Sutcliffe, "Baptism and Baptismal Rites at Qumran?" 180. Ian MacDonald notes that the Gospels speak of John the Baptist's eschatological urgency, although it is absent in Josephus's account of both the Baptist and the Essenes probably due to political reasons: "We can relate him to those circles of piety that emphasized purity, cleansing and the practice of righteousness within an ethos of eschatological intensity" ("What Did You Go Out to See? John the Baptist, the Scrolls, and Late Second Temple Judaism," in *The Dead Sea Scrolls in Their Historical Context* [ed. Timothy H. Lim; Edinburgh: T&T Clark, 2000], 63–64).

61. Ng, *Water Symbolism in the Fourth Gospel*, 60. For Ng, the question at stake in the first chapter of the Fourth Gospel is, Who is the eschatological figure who will bring in the salvation that John's baptism anticipates? In Ng's view, the juxtaposition of water baptism and

Thus, purification, both moral and ritual, prepares the way for the Spirit even in the role of inaugurating the new age. The Fourth Gospel begins with a special interest in the imminent arrival of the Messiah, and John the Baptist urges Jews to prepare for this event by repentance and purification in water. Only then will they be able to participate in the coming kingdom of God and receive the Messiah's gift of the spirit.[62] Perhaps, as Robinson suggests, John was baptizing "precisely to force the eschatological issue," since he too was unaware of the Messiah's identity (John 1:26, 31, 33). "What distinguished John was his certainty that this figure now stood waiting only to be revealed (John 1:26). And so he emerges, at the prompting of God (John 1:33), to set the last things in motion by his baptism of water."[63] Thus, at least one purpose of John's baptism in the Fourth Gospel was so that both John and those he baptized could identify the Messiah who would bring the Spirit (John 1:31–33). The Qumran authors would have understood John's reasoning; ritual purification in water prepared for eschatological blessing.

CONCLUSION

In light of the foregoing analysis, the use of water for purification in the Fourth Gospel does not seem unusual or innovative in Second Temple Judaism. It is simply inaccurate to say that the author is only using water as a symbol to renounce the past, which will be replaced by Jesus. Rather, the writer uses water ablutions as they would have been understood in contemporary Judaism—not just a doing away with impurity and the past, but a way in which the purifier was asked to prepare for and focus on the activity of the Spirit of God.

As discussed above, several Second Temple Jewish texts, and especially the Qumran scrolls, corroborate the notion in the Fourth Gospel that purification in water anticipated the work of the Spirit. First, the Spirit was expected to renew life, whether it meant the restoration of a ritually impure individual back into the community, or an individual's embarkation on a life of service to God. Second, the Spirit was essential in the process of atonement, and this was both illustrated and anticipated by purification in water. By submitting to ritual ablutions,

---

the emergence of the Messiah who gives the spirit is intentional: "Juxtaposition symbolizes an eschatological expectation and its corresponding fulfillment brought about by Jesus, and the former anticipates or prepares for the latter" (68).

62. Lawrence agrees that John's baptism could be seen as a preparation for theophany, as often was the case in the Hebrew Bible, since he was preaching of the coming kingdom of God (*Washing in Water*, 186–87 n. 2; see Taylor, *The Immerser*, 3).

63. Robinson, "Baptism of John," 24. Ng puts it well: "Just as John the Baptist prepared the way for the eschatological Christ ([John] 2:23), his baptism anticipates salvific cleansing of the eschatological kingdom. So water anticipates the eschatological means of purification which the gospel eventually comes to reveal as the Holy Spirit (7:37–39)" (*Water Symbolism in the Fourth Gospel*, 68).

individuals were making the passage from divine judgment and death to a life approved by God as his elect. Third, water baptism could also carry the expectation of divine revelation. As at Sinai and before other acts of revelation and power, the people of Israel purified themselves. At Qumran, the faithful washed before prayer and perhaps even before study of the Torah in the expectation of divine ministration and insight. According to the Fourth Gospel, it is through baptism that the identity of the incarnate Word is revealed. Finally, a connection between water purification and eschatological hope is evident in both the scrolls and the Fourth Gospel. Through ritual ablutions, individuals demonstrated readiness for the future activity of God's Spirit, whether individually or corporately.

The understanding of water purification in the Fourth Gospel was not un-Jewish, but that does not mean it was an empty ritual or an antiquated rite that needed replacement. Rather, Qumran and other Jewish texts reveal that ritual ablutions among Jews in this period were used to express the need for cleansing simply because of one's impure status as a human being subject to moral failure and physical limitations, although these were not always distinguished clearly. Humility was the only correct approach to the deity, but with ritual purification and moral introspection one could gain confidence to enter the presence of God. Ritual ablutions provided an effective way of acknowledging that a person was on the side of sin and death and in need of rejuvenation and life. While this act of regeneration rested ultimately in the hands of God, water purification was a key in the hand of the human being to invite spiritual activity into the body of the penitent. Water made way for the Spirit.

What is unique about water baptism in the Fourth Gospel is not that it signified penitent individuals who were inviting and accepting the work of the Spirit, but that this activity would identify and then come to fruition in the person and work of Jesus. John's innovation lies in the idea that the figure of Jesus was able to fulfill the expectations of purification with water.

"Protect them from the Evil One" (John 17:15): Light from the Dead Sea Scrolls

Loren T. Stuckenbruck

The last monologue of Jesus regarding his followers in John 17 takes the form of a prayer. In this respect, Jesus' words differ from those of chapters 14–16, the content of which is presented as instruction given directly by Jesus to his disciples. This variation of form, however, cannot hide the fact that, together, chapters 14–16 and 17 comprise a "farewell discourse." Ultimately, this discourse has the readers of the Gospel in view: in chapters 14–16 the disciples, though formally addressed, are told about times and circumstances that anticipate realities to be faced at a later time, so Jesus' instructions to the disciples function also as instructions for the later readers (e.g., 14:12, 16–20, 26; 15:20–21; 16:1–4a). Equally, Jesus' prayer in chapter 17 concerns itself not only with his immediate devotees but also with those who will come after them (17:20–24). The communication strategy and form of John 14–17 thus carries certain analogies with the ancient testamentary literature which circulated so widely among ancient Jewish and early Christian circles.[1]

---

1. As is frequently observed, one can compare the final discourse and its literary context in John's Gospel with the recurring form in *Testaments of the Twelve Patriarchs*: (1) brief narrative about the patriarch drawing near to death and gathering his offspring; (2) exhortations which often take the patriarch's life as a model or paradigm and sometimes reinforced by *ex eventu* "predictions"; and (3) a closing narrative, usually brief, regarding the patriarch's death and burial. In John, the equivalent to (1) is more extensive, found in the introductory narrative to the last discourse in 13:1–31; the equivalent to (3), again much more extensive than its testamentary counterparts, is provided in the Gospel's passion narrative (chaps. 18–20). For a judicious comparison, see the still valuable discussion by Raymond E. Brown, *The Gospel according to John* (2 vols.; AB; Garden City, N.Y.: Doubleday, 1966–70), 2.581–604. It is, of course, very difficult to pin down a series of essential characteristics of ancient testamentary literature as a whole. For all its diversity, however, the communication by a patriarch to his followers or offspring remains a constant feature; cf. Nicolae Roddy, "Ultimate Reflections, Infinite Refractions: Form and Function in the Elusive Genre of Testamentary Literature," *Studia Hebraica* 3 (2003): 298–310.

The status of John 14–17 as "testamentary" instruction is straightforward. The voice of Jesus is Johannine: whatever continuity this voice may or may not have with the "historical Jesus," the words of instruction bear the stamp of Johannine language. Thus, like many testamentary writings of antiquity attributed to well-known figures, in some sense Jesus' message is "pseudepigraphic"[2]—that is, it is a communication attributed to Jesus, who cannot be shown to have instructed his disciples through these particular words. The status of these chapters as "testamentary," however, might appear more problematic if one adheres strictly to an understanding of a "testament" as "the farewell speech of a dying man" to his offspring.[3] One difficulty is acknowledged by Ernst Käsemann, who calls it "paradoxical" that in the Fourth Gospel the one who is "life" itself is put into the position of giving last instructions to his disciples before a death which the Johannine community knows is not ultimately going to be his death.[4] Nevertheless, if this is a "departure" at all, it is not clear that John's Gospel actually marks such a radical change from convention. An analogy presents itself in the early Enoch tradition: Enoch's last instructions (cf. 1 Enoch 81.5–82.4; 91.1–3; 92.1–5; 93.1–2; 108.1–2) are given by one who is about to depart—in this case, either for the first time or back from a temporary visit—and not actually about to die. Another difficulty is also only apparent. The inclusion of a prayer would seem to be out of place in a testamentary discourse; indeed, this very point led Käsemann, for all his insistence on the testamentary nature of chapter 17, to emphasize that these final words are not in fact a prayer at all. The distinction between a prayer and instruction should not, however, be pressed too far. Some of Moses' instruction to the people just before his death is, after all, formally couched in the form of a prayer called a "song" (Deut 32:1–43).[5] In addition, as we shall see in some of the passages considered below, prayers for one's progeny can occur at pivotal

---

2. The term here—Jewish "pseudepigrapha"—is misleading, as the writers are not actually presenting their works as such, but rather as an authentic voice and communication from the well-known figure.

3. Cf. Ernst Käsemann, *The Testament of Jesus: A Study of the Gospel of John in the Light of Chapter 17* (trans. Gerhard Krodel; London: SCM, 1968), 4.

4. Käsemann, *Testament of Jesus*, 4–5, who famously played down the theological significance of Jesus' death for the Fourth Gospel. For an early criticism of this one-sided emphasis on the spiritual Jesus, see Günther Bornkamm, "Towards the Interpretation of John's Gospel," in *The Interpretation of John* (ed. John Ashton; IRT 9; Philadelphia: Fortress, 1986), 88.

5. After recognizing the difficulty of considering John 17 as a prayer spoken "within the framework of farewell discourses," Rudolf Schnackenburg concluded that "[i]t is most closely related to the farewell words and the farewell blessing of the patriarchs in the biblical and Jewish tradition," that is, to the Song of Moses in Deut 32, Moses' prayer in *Jubilees* 1.19–21, Noah's prayer in *Jubilees* 10.3–6, and Abraham's blessing of Jacob in *Jubilees* 20–22; see *The Gospel according to St John* (trans. Kevin Smyth; 3 vols.; HTKNT; New York: Crossroad, 1980–82), 3.199.

moments of a narrative, including moments penultimate to a patriarch's departure from the scene.[6]

Since testamentary instruction is not necessarily in tension with the formal
use of a prayer, I would like to focus on the possibility that at least some of Jesus'
words in John 17 can be understood as a real prayer rather than, for instance,
a formal prayer which in fact is only meant to instruct. Here several elements
in Jesus' petition for his disciples may be illumined by a consideration of Jewish
traditions relating to the prayers of patriarchs for their offspring. As we shall see,
whereas the prayer of Jesus may, in very general terms, be illuminated by formal
points related to a testamentary setting, some of it emerges from a framework
that—even beyond what one formally encounters in testamentary literature from
the Second Temple period—circulated in the literature of pious Jewish circles,
especially as preserved among the Dead Sea Scrolls. This is not to play down
the special concerns of the Fourth Gospel itself. However, the parallels, both in
smaller and broader details, remind us of the degree to which the discourse of
the Fourth Gospel remains indebted to a formative Jewish matrix and, indeed,
assumes a certain familiarity with such a matrix among its readers in order to
communicate effectively.

The Petitions of John 17

In drawing attention to Jesus' petitions in John 17, we first briefly summarize the
chapter. The prayer of Jesus may be divided into four parts: (1) a series of declara-
tive statements about Jesus' and the disciples' special position and faithfulness in
relation to God (17:1–8); (2) petitions for Jesus' disciples (17:9–19); (3) a petition
for those who come to faith through the disciples' ministry (17:20–23); and (4)
statements that resume and build on selected elements of the foregoing prayer
(17:24–26). Limiting our observations to Jesus' petition for his disciples in 17:9–
19 (number 2 in the outline above), we may note several points of emphasis.

First, Jesus underlines the enmity or tension between his disciples and "the
world." This tension manifests itself in the hate the world shows toward his disciples (v. 14). Jesus' petition unambiguously takes the side of his disciples: he does
not pray for the world but for those whom God has given him (v. 9). Despite the
sharp distinction between the disciples and the world, however, Jesus does not
seek to resolve this tension by requesting that God remove the disciples from the
world (v. 15).

---

6. Significant here is *1 Enoch* 83–84, in which Enoch discloses to Methuselah his prayer
that a remnant will be saved from the coming destruction (the Flood) upon the earth (84.2–6).
Unlike the passages discussed below, however, the petition is not specifically concerned with
protection from demonic forces.

Second, formally, in 17:9–19 Jesus presents God with three petitions. First, in verses 9–13, God (addressed as "holy Father") is asked to "keep (τήρησον) them [the disciples] in your name which you have given to me" (v. 11). The basis for this request is provided by Jesus, who himself has "kept" (ἐτήρουν) the disciples "in your name which you have given me." The notion of "keeping" is reformulated in terms of protection by Jesus, who has "guarded" (ἐφύλαξα) his disciples so that none of them are lost (v. 12).[7] Initially, the petition is concerned with unity among Jesus' disciples: "in order that they may be one" (v. 11), a petition that is also brought to bear on later believers (vv. 20–23). At this point, the specific source of danger from which protection is needed is not clear. Implied, however, is the perception of a danger that threatens to splinter the community for whom Jesus is praying. Second, in verses 14–16, Jesus prays again for God to "keep" (ἵνα τηρήσης). Here, it is immediately clear that the petition is for protection: "I ask . . . that you keep them from the evil one" (v. 15). The reason for this need for protection lies, again, in a tension between Jesus' followers and "the world." Because Jesus is not of the world, those whose unity he has maintained are not from the world (v. 16), which has "hated them" (v. 14). Despite these conditions of alienation and enmity, Jesus refuses to contemplate removal (v. 15): the protection he requests assumes that the cosmos, as presently structured for the disciples, involves an open clash or conflict with "the evil one" who is "ruler of this world" (cf. 12:31; 14:30; 16:11). As in the first request, God's protection is related to protection by Jesus, who in 14:30 has already declared that "the ruler of the world has no power over me." Thus, the protection is required if Jesus' followers are living in a world and in an age dominated by "the evil one." The third petition of Jesus, in verses 17–19, is a request that God sanctify or make his disciples holy (ἁγίασον αὐτούς). Again, as with the first and second petitions just mentioned, the request is linked to Jesus' own status: because he has sanctified himself or rendered himself pure for the disciples' sake, they themselves can also be sanctified.

As a third point of emphasis, each of Jesus' petitions to God is a genuine supplication—that is, none merely borrows a formula of petition in order to accomplish something else. However, because the very basis for the divine response to these requests is already to be found in Jesus' activity, these petitions are replete with statements about himself in relation to both God and his followers. Thus, on the one hand, Jesus is *the one* sent by God (vv. 3, 21, 23, 25); he is *the one* entrusted by God with the divine name (vv. 6, 12, 26); *the one* who is being glorified by God (vv. 1, 5, 10, 22, 24); and, he and God are "one" (vv. 11, 22). On the other hand, the unity between Jesus and God (vv. 11, 22, "just as we are one") and Jesus' origin in God rather than in the world are determinative for Jesus' fol-

---

7. This function of Jesus echoes the shepherd imagery of John 10:7–16, though there the protection attributed to him is implied.

lowers who are aligned with him. Alignment with Jesus makes it possible for his followers to be "one" among themselves and, in their mutual belonging to God through Jesus, to be in tension with "the world" (v. 14).

The proclamations in Jesus' prayer—so much of the language attempts to shore up Jesus and his followers' identity—cannot hide the petitionary force of Jesus' words. The petitions are real, especially since the situation of Jesus is not entirely the same as that of his followers. Whereas Jesus' relationship to the world is already resolved—he is glorified, chosen "from before the foundation of the world" (v. 24; cf. v. 5) and on his way to God (vv. 11, 13)—the disciples remain "in the world," where they must contend with that which characterizes it: "the ruler of the world." The clearest example of this is provided in the petition of 17:15: "I do not ask that you take them out of the world, but that you keep them from the evil one." Significantly, the final phrase, ἐκ τοῦ πονηροῦ ("from the evil one"), is not to be taken as an abstract reference to "evil," but rather to a personified power who is in open conflict with God.[8] Though this personification occurs nowhere else in the Fourth Gospel—πονηρός otherwise refers to "evil" activity (3:19, 20; 5:27; 7:7; cf. 2 John 11; 3 John 11)—its force in this context is unmistakable: "the evil one" denotes the one who in other passages is called "the devil" (8:44; 13:2; cf. 1 John 3:8, 10), "liar" and "father of lies" (8:44), "Satan" (13:27), and "the ruler of the world" (12:31;14:30; 16:11). Of these other designations, the last mentioned, "the ruler of the world," is of particular relevance here: Jesus asks for protection from the evil one precisely because of the existing hostility between the disciples and the world.

Several considerations suggest that Jesus' petition in 17:15 has been shaped by tradition (which, in turn, illuminates how it links up with themes found elsewhere in John's Gospel). First, as noted above, "the evil one" as a designation for the devil occurs only here in the Fourth Gospel and thus seems uncharacteristic of the writer's language, which may have been expected at this point to refer to "the ruler of the world." Second, the phrase "that you may keep them from the evil one" is reminiscent of language found in Matthew's version of the Lord's Prayer (Matt 6:13) and in a declaration about God's faithfulness in 2 Thess 3:3.[9] Third, the verb "keep" (τηρεῖν), which in verses 11–12 is treated as a synonym for "protect, guard" (φυλάσσειν), may be an echo of the Aaronic blessing of

---

8. For the same use in the Johannine tradition, see 1 John 2:13–14; 3:12; 5:18–19.

9. Matthew 6:13: "But deliver us from the evil one" (ἀλλὰ ῥῦσαι ἡμᾶς ἀπὸ τοῦ πονηροῦ). In the Matthean context, the personified meaning of the expression is strengthened by a less ambiguous reference to "the evil one" in 5:37. See also 2 Thessalonians 3:3: "For faithful is the Lord, who will strengthen you and guard you from the evil one" (πιστὸς δέ ἐστιν ὁ κύριος, ὅς στηρίξει ὑμᾶς καὶ φυλάξει ἀπὸ τοῦ πονηροῦ). While it is possible to construe the phrase as an abstract reference to "evil," the foregoing mention of "the lawless one" in 2:8 strengthens the case for a personified meaning here. In 2 Tim 4:18, on the other hand, the writer—though possibly alluding to the Lord's Prayer—is not directly concerned with an evil being when he

Num 6:24: "may the Lord bless you and keep you" (MT: יברכך יהיה ורשמרך, LXX: εὐλογήσαι σε κύριος καὶ φυλάξαι σε).[10]

The main difference between the New Testament texts just mentioned and the Aaronic blessing lies in the absence of any reference in the latter to "the evil one." Admittedly, the Aaronic blessing simply concludes with the object of the verb ("you") without specifying what it is that Israel is to be kept or protected from. To be sure, in two adaptations of the Aaronic blessing in the Hebrew Bible, "evil" is added to the equation: 1 Chr 4:10: "Jabez called on the God of Israel, saying 'Oh that you would bless me and enlarge my border and that your hand would be with me, and that you would keep me *from evil* [MT: ועשית מרעה; the Greek presupposes a very different text] and harm!'"; Ps 121:7: "The Lord will keep you *from all evil*; he will keep your life" (NRSV; MT: יהוה ישמרך מכל־רע ישמר את־נפשך, LXX: κύριος φυλάξει σε ἀπὸ παντὸς κακοῦ φυλάξει τὴν ψυχήν σου). In neither of these cases, however, do the texts suggest anything about protection from an "evil one." The same seems to be the case in the later 2 Macc 1:25 (God is addressed as one who rescues Israel "from all evil"; ὁ διασῴζων τὸν Ισραηλ ἐκ παντὸς κακοῦ) and Wis 16:8 ("you persuaded our enemies that it is you who delivers from all evil"; σὺ εἶ ὁ ῥυόμενος ἐκ παντὸς κακοῦ).

Beyond the Matthean version of the Lord's Prayer and 2 Thessalonians, is there anything which may help us explain the background to John's petition for protection from personified evil? If there is, what might such a background tell us about the theological framework in which Jesus' petitions in John 17 are formulated? In the following section, we shall explore some ancient petitions, arguing that our closest link between the Aaronic blessing and its adaptations, on the one hand, and the narrative world of John 17, on the other, lies in sources for which the primary evidence is preserved in the Dead Sea Scrolls.

---

declares that "the Lord will rescue me from every evil work (ἀπὸ παντὸς ἔργου πονηροῦ) and save me for his heavenly kingdom."

10. In the Fourth Gospel, the term "keep" (τηρεῖν) operates with a double function: being "kept" or protected by God from adversity (whether "the evil one," wickedness, or adversity) varies directly with "keeping" God's words or commands; this not only avails in John (cf. 17:11 with 17:6 and 12:47; 14:15, 21, 23–24; 15:10, 20), but also in Revelation (cf. 3:10 with 1:3; 3:8, 10; 12:17; 14:12; 22:7, 9). In addition to further references given by Rudolf Bultmann, *The Gospel of John: A Commentary*, trans. G. R. Beasley-Murray, R. W. N. Hoare, and J. K. Riches (Philadelphia: Westminster, 1971), 301–2 n. 5; see *j.Peah* 16b: "if you keep the words of the Torah, I will protect you from the demons" (אם שמרתם דברי תורה אני משמר אתכם מן המזיקין), in which the motif of protection from the demonic represents much earlier tradition.

Protection from Demonic Powers: Early Jewish Traditions

Petitions to God for help in the Hebrew Bible and the Greek translations are attested in abundance,[11] but, in line with the few passages considered earlier, there is no single instance in the Hebrew Bible in which God is specifically invoked for deliverance against another deity. Prayers seeking divine protection from harm or help in neutralizing the effects of demonic power begin to surface, however, in literature from the Second Temple period, including a number of the Dead Sea documents. An overview of the relevant texts will provide a broader background for Jesus' petition in John 17.

The Community Rule (1QS)

Representative of this development is an adaptation of the Aaronic blessing within the Qumran community's covenant-renewal ceremony, which according to the *Serek ha-Yahad* was to take place year by year (1QS 2.19; the ceremony as a whole is described in 1QS 1.16–3.12). After an opening confession of wrongdoing and affirmation of divine favor by the community (1.23–2.1a), the liturgy is organized into a short series of blessings to be pronounced by the priests on "all the men of the lot of God" (2.1b–4) and two longer series of curses pronounced by the Levites against "all the men of the lot of Belial" (2.14–17). The language of both the blessings and curses, though reflecting contemporary concerns of the community, relies heavily on the Aaronic blessing. In particular, the benediction in Num 6:24, "May the Lord bless you and keep you," is reformulated in 1QS 2.2–3 in terms of contrasting activities of God, thus avoiding the possible implication that the verbs "bless" and "keep" are synonymous or complementary: "May he bless you with everything good, and may he keep you from every evil" (יברככה בכול טוב וישמורכה מכנל). While in comparison to 1 Chron 4:10 and Ps 121:7 (or even 2 Macc 1:25 and Wis 16:8) the reformulation does not seem to mark much of a conceptual shift from the Aaronic blessing, the larger context makes clear that the Qumran blessing is concerned with divine protection from Belial.[12] As the text following the liturgy suggests, it is precisely because the community knows itself to be living during a time of Belial's rule that the ceremony

---

11. Such prayers request divine help in relation to one's own shortcomings (Pss 27:12; 39:8; 51:14; 79:9); from dangers coming from opponents or enemies (Gen 32:11; Josh 2:13; Judg 10:15; 1 Sam 12:10; 2 Kings 21:14; 1 Chron 6:36; 16:35; Pss 6:4; 17:13; 22:20; 25:20; 31:1–2; 31:15; 40:13; 43:1; 59:1–2; 69:14, 18; 70:1; 71:2, 4; 82:4; 116:4; 119:134, 170; 120:2; 140:1; 142:6; 143:9; 144:7, 11; Isa 44:17); or from premature death or an unwanted afterlife (Job 33:24, 28).

12. The text's appropriation of Num 6:24 is on a trajectory that leads to the version preserved in *Targum Pseudo-Jonathan*: "may YYY bless you in all your undertaking, and may he guard you from the night demon, the vile demons, the children of the noon demons, the children of the morning demons, injurious and shadowy beings": יברכינך ייי בכל עיסקך ויטרינך

is necessary: "they shall do thus year by year all the days of the dominion of Belial" (1QS 2.19). Indeed, the ceremony counteracts the reality of life "during the dominion of Belial" because it is a time when it is possible for members to stray from the covenant on account of "fear or dread or testing" (1QS 1.17–18); likewise, the opening confession of sins is expressly understood as a measure to be taken by the community "during the dominion of Belial" (1QS 1.23–24). The expanded benediction that God "keep you from every evil," therefore, ultimately has protection from demonic powers that cause transgression in view. The repetition of the ceremony during the era when Belial exercises dominion implies that there will be a time when it is no longer necessary (cf. 1QS 4.19–21).

THE WAR SCROLL (1QM)

A similar perspective is reflected in other Dead Sea documents which, however, do not as explicitly formulate a need for divine protection as part of a blessing or petition. This is the case, for example, in 1QM,[13] where the sons of light declare that "during the dominion of Belial . . . you [God] have driven away from [us] his [Belial's] [de]struction, [and when the me]n of his dominion [acted wickedly] you have kept [or: protected] the soul of your redeemed ones (שמרתה נפש פרותכה)" (1QM 14.9–10; par. 4Q491 = 4QMᵃ frags. 8–10 1.6–7; cf. further 4Q177 = 4QCatenaᵃ frag. 3 8).

SONGS OF THE MASKIL

Of special note here is the document Songs of the Maskil, preserved in fragments of 4Q444, 4Q510, and 4Q511. In one of the songs, the sage initially declares the splendor of God's radiance "in order to terrify and fr[ighten] all the spirits of the angels of destruction, and the bastard spirits, demons, Lilith, owls and [jackals . . .] and those who strike suddenly to lead astray the spirit of understanding and to cause their hearts to shudder" (4Q510 1.4–6a; par. 4Q511 10.1–3a). This proclamation of divine majesty, which Armin Lange has described as a "hymnic exorcism,"[14] is then followed by an address to "righteous ones" in which the sage states:

מן לילי ומזייעי ובני טיהררי ובני צפרירי ומזיקי וטלני; cf. Robert Hayward, "The Priestly Blessing in Targum Pseudo-Jonathan," *JSP* 19 (1999): 81–101.

13. Thus, in the "Two Spirits Treatise," the Angel of Darkness, who has complete dominion over the sons of iniquity, is made out to be the influence behind the sins, iniquities, guilty deeds, and transgressions of the sons of light (1QS 3.21–24); see further 1QS 4.19: "then truth shall go forth forever [in the] world, for it has been corrupted in paths of wickedness during the dominion of iniquity."

14. See Armin Lange, "The Essene Position on Magic and Divination," in *Legal Texts and Legal Issues: Proceedings of the Second Meeting of the International Organization for Qumran*

You have been put in a time of the dominion [of] wickedness and in the eras of the humiliation of the sons of lig[ht] in the guilt of the times of those plagued by iniquities, not for an eternal destruction, [but] for the era of the humiliation of transgression. Rejoice, O righteous ones, in the God of wonder. My psalms [are] for the upright ones. (4Q510 1.6b–8; par. 4Q511 10.3b–6)

The *maskil*'s declarations about God, told in the third person (not in the second person in the form of prayer addressed to God), are regarded as potent enough to diminish or counteract demonic powers that are at work in the present order of things ("the dominion [of] wickedness"). While the text does not furnish a prayer for divine protection against these demons, it reflects a framework that holds two concurrent things in tension: the existence of a community of those who are unambiguously "righteous" and "upright," and the characterization of the present age as "a time of the dominion [of] wickedness." Analogous to the pronouncement of a benediction in the yearly covenant renewal ceremony in 1QS, the song of the righteous functions as an expedient measure that neutralizes the threats associated with demonic powers until the present age of wickedness is brought to an end.

Significantly, the documents just considered are arguably sectarian. The hostility between the group behind the writings and other groups may have been felt to such an extent that the world order, as a whole, could not be portrayed as anything other than inimical. But this notion of an eschatological tension between divine activity already being realized in a specially elect community and ongoing demonic activity was not entirely unique to the community associated with Qumran. Several prayers come down to us in documents preserved among the texts recovered from the Qumran caves that do not show any obvious signs of having been composed by or for the Yahad. Before turning to the Fourth Gospel, we may briefly review prayers for protection from the demonic preserved in four Qumran fragments from (1) "Prayer of Deliverance" (11Q5 19), (2) the Aramaic Levi Document (4Q213a = 4QTLevi^a frag. 1 1.10; par. *Jub.* 1.19–20), (3) the *Book of Jubilees* 10.3–6 and 12.19–20, and (4) the book of Tobit.[15]

Studies, Published in Honour of Joseph M. Baumgarten (ed. Moshe Bernstein, Florentino García Martínez, and John Kampen; STDJ 23; Leiden: Brill, 1997), 383, 402–3, 430–33. Lange also applies this classification to 1QapGen 20.12–18; *Jub.* 10.1–14; 12.16–21. On the problem of categorizing the passage from 1QapGen in this way, see Loren T. Stuckenbruck, "Pleas for Deliverance from the Demonic in Early Jewish Texts," in *Studies in Jewish Prayer* (ed. Robert Hayward and Brad Embry; JSSSup 17; Oxford: Oxford University Press, 2005), 60–62.

15. For a fuller treatment of these and other texts, see Loren T. Stuckenbruck, "Deliverance Prayers and Hymns in Early Jewish Documents," in *The Changing Face of Judaism and Christianity* (ed. Gerbern S. Oegema and Ian Henderson; Gütersloh: Gerd Mohn, 2005), 146–65.

(1) Prayer of Deliverance (11Q5 19)

This text, which is also extant through two of the six fragments belonging to 11Q6, comes to us as part of a larger manuscript that consists of psalmic texts known from the Hebrew Bible, other hymnic compositions, and a text that attributes a series of compositions to David.[16] Since both 11Q5 and 11Q6 are copied in Herodian hands, they provide evidence for the prayer at the turn of the Common Era, though the compilation itself is surely earlier.[17] The piece, significantly, is composed as a prayer per se, showing—perhaps as in 1QS 1–2 and the Maskil songs of 4Q510–511—that we are safe to assume that the text consists of words actually in use during the Second Temple period.

Of the originally twenty-four or twenty-five verses of the prayer,[18] some eighteen lines of twenty verses are preserved. In the opening extant lines of 11Q5 19 (lines 1–5), the writer declares that only living creatures can praise God, implying that God should therefore spare him from death (cf. Isa 38:18–19; Ps 6:4–5). In the next section (lines 5–12), the writer proclaims YHWH's faithfulness based on his own experience, and for this he offers YHWH praise. This praise of divine activity introduces a plea for forgiveness and purification from iniquity (lines 13–14), in place of which the one praying seeks to be given a "spirit of faith and knowledge" so as not to be dishonored in iniquity. The petition culminates in lines 15–16 as follows:

---

16. For a description of the contents of the six fragments of 11Q5, see James A. Sanders, *The Psalms Scroll of Qumrân Cave 11 (11QPs^a)* (DJD 4; Oxford: Clarendon, 1996), 5. See further Peter W. Flint, *The Dead Sea Psalms Scrolls and the Book of Psalms* (STDJ 17; Leiden: Brill, 1997), 190. According to Jan P. M. van der Ploeg, 11Q6 is an exact copy of 11Q5 ("Fragments d'un manuscrit de Psaumes de Qumran (11QPs^b)," *RB* 74 [1967]: 408–13). It is possible, in addition, that 4Q87 (= 4QPs^e) is a copy of the same collection; see Flint, *Dead Sea Psalms Scrolls*, 160–64.

17. Lange argues for a date as early as the first half of the second century B.C.E.; see "Die Endgestalt des protomasoretischen Psalters und die Toraweisheit: Zur Bedeutung der nichtessenischen Weisheitstexte aus Qumran für die Auslegung des protomasoretischen Psalters," in *Der Psalter in Judentum und Christentum* (ed. Erich Zenger; HBS 18; Freiburg, Germany: Herder, 1998), 108. If the treatment of Aramaic Levi Document below is correct, however, this prayer may go back to the third century B.C.E.

18. Sanders argues that the psalm probably began on the previous column 18 (*Psalms Scroll*, 76). Regarding the end of the prayer, see James A. Sanders with James H. Charlesworth and Henry W. L. Rietz, "Non-Masoretic Psalms," *The Dead Sea Scrolls—Hebrew, Aramaic, and Greek Texts with Translations. Vol. 4a: Pseudepigraphic and Non-Masoretic Psalms and Prayers* (ed. James H. Charlesworth and Henry W. L. Rietz; PTSDSSP; Louisville: Westminster John Knox, 1997), 193.

אל תשלט בי שטן ורוח טמאה מכאוב ויצר רע אל ירשו עצמי

Do not let rule [or: have power] over me a satan or an unclean spirit;
may an evil inclination not take possession of my bones.

The first thing to notice here is that the petition seeks divine help not to come under the rule or power of a demonic being. That being which would have sway over the one praying is designated as both "a satan" and "an unclean spirit," the latter expression possibly an echo of Zech 13:2.[19] However, in the present context it may refer to a disembodied spirit, that is, a being whose origin lies in the illegitimate sexual union between the rebellious angels and the daughters of men that resulted in the birth of the prediluvian giants.[20] If the Enochic material, known to us through the Book of Watchers (1 Enoch 10, 15–16) and the Book of Giants, lies in the background, the prayer presupposes a wider narrative that negotiates God's decisive intervention against evil in the past (i.e., through the flood and other acts of punishment) and the final destruction or eradication of evil in the future. The petition is therefore one that expresses confidence in God's control over the demonic (i.e., "do not allow" = hiph. verb. + "satan" and "unclean spirit" as direct objects), while recognizing the very real possibility that such power still leaves its mark in the present. As for the former designation, "satan," it is not clear whether the writer has a chief demonic ruler in view (i.e., "Satan") or uses the term functionally to refer to a being that plays an adversarial role. Its juxtaposition with "unclean spirit" may suggest that "satan" is not a proper name here.[21] What is clear, nonetheless, is that the use of the term reflects a development that has gone well beyond its use in the Hebrew Bible, where it denotes an angelic being that is subservient to God (cf. Num 22:22, 32; Ps 109:6; even Job 1–2 and Zech 3:1–2) or functions as a general designation for one's enemies (1 Kings 11:23, 25; Pss 71:13; 109:20, 29). In the Prayer of Deliverance of 11Q5, "satan" refers generally to an angelic being whose activity in seeking to rule over the human being runs counter to what the petitioner regards as the divine will.

---

19. See Armin Lange, "Considerations Concerning the 'Spirit of Impurity' in Zech 13:2," in Die Dämonen—Demons: The Demonology of Israelite-Jewish and Early Christian Literature in Context of Their Environment (ed. Armin Lange, Herman Lichtenberger, and K. F. Diethard Römheld; Tübingen: Mohr Siebeck, 2003), 254–55.

20. For discussions of a wider network of related references in 1 Enoch (esp. chaps. 10, 15–16) and the Dead Sea materials (inter alia Book of Giants, 4Q444; 4Q510–511; and 11Q11) see Philip S. Alexander, "The Demonology of the Dead Sea Scrolls," in The Dead Sea Scrolls after Fifty Years: A Comprehensive Assessment (2 vols.; ed. Peter W. Flint and James C. VanderKam; Leiden: Brill, 1999), 2.331–53; Loren T. Stuckenbruck, "The Origins of Evil in Jewish Apocalyptic Tradition: The Interpretation of Genesis 6:1–4 in the Second and Third Centuries B.C.E.," in The Fall of the Angels (ed. Christoph Auffarth and Loren Stuckenbruck; TBN 6; Leiden: Brill, 2004), 87–118, esp. 99–110.

21. This would, then, be in contrast with Jubilees 10.11, in which "Satan" is the named equivalent for Mastema as the ruler of demons on the earth; cf. also T. Dan 5.6.

Though further observations about the petition will be made below when we consider the parallel prayer text in the Aramaic Levi Document, a more general point about the compilation of psalms in which this petition is found should be made. Whereas James Sanders argued in his edition of the scroll that the compilation in 11QPs[a] was produced by the Qumran community,[22] Peter Flint has emphasized that the absence of peculiarly Qumranic expressions and the presence of calendrical affinities with those groups within which the early Enochic works and *Jubilees* were composed suggest that this collection probably predates the formation of the Qumran community and thus enjoyed a wider circulation.[23] If Flint is correct, and if the "Prayer of Deliverance" was in the psalmic compilation, then it is likely that its petition that YHWH act on behalf of the pious petitioner to disempower "a satan" and "an impure spirit" from ruling over him was probably not a single prayer written by and for an individual. It would have enjoyed some degree of circulation, and we perhaps may imagine that it was written as a model prayer for the pious to recite. This view is strengthened by our consideration of the following text.

(2) Aramaic Levi Document

The text in question (4Q213a = 4QTLevi[a] frag. 1 1.10) was initially published by Michael E. Stone and Jonas C. Greenfield,[24] and has been dated by J. T. Milik to the late second–early first centuries b.c.e.[25] However, the document itself was likely composed during the third, or perhaps even the late fourth, century b.c.e.[26] Since the wording of the Aramaic text corresponds closely to that of the more

---

22. Sanders in fact designated it the "Qumran Psalter"; see *The Dead Sea Psalms Scroll* (Ithaca, N.Y.: Cornell University Press, 1967), 158.

23. See the discussion by Flint in *Dead Sea Psalms Scrolls*, 198–200. While continuing to underscore the consistency between the ideas in the scroll and those of the Qumran community, Sanders has more recently adopted a less narrow view of its origins, arguing that the compilation was acquired by the community; see James A. Sanders, "Psalm 154 Revisited," in *Biblische Theologie und gesellschaftlicher Wandel: Für Norbert Lohfink S.J.* (ed. Georg Braulik, Walter Gross, and Sean McEvenue; Freiburg, Germany: Herder, 1993), 301–2.

24. Initially in "The Prayer of Levi," *JBL* 112 (1993): 247–66, and then in *Qumran Cave 4. XVII: Parabiblical Texts, Part 3* (DJD 22; Oxford: Clarendon, 1996), 25–36 and Plate II.

25. So J. T. Milik, "Le Testament de Lévi en araméen," *RB* 62 (1955): 398–408.

26. See esp. the thorough discussion and considerations offered by Henryk Drawnel, who dates the text to the early Hellenistic period, *An Aramaic Wisdom Text from Qumran: A New Interpretation of the Levi Document* (JSJSup 86; Leiden: Brill, 2004), 63–75. Other recent treatments have dated the work to the third and late third or very early second century b.c.e.; so, respectively, Robert Kugler, *From Patriarch to Priest: The Levi-Priestly Tradition from Aramaic Levi to the Testament of Levi* (SBLEJL 9; Atlanta: Scholars Press, 1996), 131–38, and Jonas C. Greenfield, Michael E. Stone, and Esther Eshel, *The Aramaic Levi Document: Edition, Translation, Commentary* (SVTP 19; Leiden: Brill, 2004), 19–22.

complete Greek manuscript from Mount Athos (Athos Koutloumous no. 39, at *Testament of Levi* 2.3), the latter may be used to reconstruct many of the lacunae in 4Q213a.[27]

The text with which we are concerned is part of a prayer spoken by the patriarch Levi just before he is granted a vision of heaven (cf. 4Q213a 2.14–18) and commissioned to become a priest (cf. the later *T. Levi* 2.5–4.6).[28] After Levi makes preparations through cleansing and gestures (4Q213a 1.6–10), a text of his prayer is given (Gk. vv. 5–19; Aram. 1.10–2.10). The prayer, according to Robert Kugler, may be loosely structured as follows: (1) In verses 6–9 (Gk.; Aram. 1.10–16), Levi prays that God would purify him from evil and wickedness, show him the Holy Spirit, and endow him with counsel, wisdom, knowledge, and strength, in order that he might find favor before God and give God praise; (2) in verse 10 (Gk.; Aram. 1.17), the patriarch petitions that God protect him from evil; (3) in verses 11–19 (Gk.; Aram. 1.18–2.10), the patriarch formulates a series of requests that resume themes touched upon during the earlier part of the prayer—namely, that God cleanse and shelter Levi from evil (Gk. vv. 12, 14), that wickedness be destroyed from the earth (Gk. v. 13), and that Levi and his descendants be placed in God's service for all generations (Gk. v. 18; 4Q213a 2.8–9). The wording in the petition for protection in 4Q213a 1.17 is remarkably close to that of the text from 11Q5 discussed above; with the help of the Greek, it reads as follows.

וא[ל תשלט בי כל שטן]לאטעני מן ארחך

And do not let rule[or: have power] over me any satan [to lead me astray from your path.

καὶ μὴ κατισχύστω με πᾶς σατανᾶς πλανῆσαί με ἀπὸ τῆς ὁδοῦ σου

And may no satan rule [or: have power] over me to lead me astray from your path."

The context suggests that the petition here is concerned with demonic threat. Earlier in the prayer, Levi has asked that God "turn away" (4Q213a 1.7 רחא; Gk. ἀποστρέψον) to a distance "the unrighteous spirit (Gk. τὸ πνεῦμα τὸ ἄδικον) and evil thoughts and fornication and hubris." He then asks, instead, to be shown "the holy spirit (Gk. τὸ πνεῦμα τὸ ἅγιον) and counsel and wisdom and knowledge and strength." Moreover, in a further petition not extant in the Aramaic but preserved

27. So, e.g., Stone and Greenfield, "Prayer of Levi," 257–58 (Aramaic and Greek texts, respectively, from which the citations here are taken); cf. Drawnel, *Aramaic Wisdom Text*, esp. 99, 101.

28. Unless otherwise indicted, my present comments follow the line numeration from 4Q213a, rather than the versification derived from the Greek text. However, the content is partially reconstructed by referring to the Greek, as in the eclectic translation of Stone and Greenfield, "Prayer of Levi," 259–60.

in the Greek (v. 12), Levi asks for protection as follows: "and let your shelter of power shelter me from every evil (ἀπὸ παντὸς κακοῦ)." Thus, in seeking protection from overpowerment from "any satan," the writer is referring to a being belonging to a category of demonic power rather than to a primary power of evil who is called "Satan."[29] This is even clearer here than in 11Q5 with the addition of "any" (כל).

Given the similarity between the petitions in 4Q213a and 11Q5, is there any genetic link? The parallel is strikingly similar to the text that comes down to us in Ps 119:133b:

ואל תשלט בי כל און ("and do not allow any iniquity to rule/have power over me," Grk: μή κατακυριευσάτω μου πᾶσα ἀνομία, "may no iniquity rule over me")

It is possible, therefore, that both texts, rather than being directly interdependent in one direction or another, draw on a "common interpretation" of Ps 119.[30] This view, if correct, (1) underscores that the writers of these texts and of the underlying tradition were personifying traditional references to evil, and (2) suggests that such a reinterpretation of biblical prayer was more generally widespread than the evidence preserved in 4Q213a and 11Q5 alone. Lange, however, has argued against a dependence of either text on Ps 119 and, instead, reasons as follows for a literary dependence between the two documents: (1) it is unlikely that both 4Q213a and 11Q5 col. 19 would have independently substituted the term "iniquity" of the Psalm with "Satan," and (2) both texts exhibit "extensive parallels in demonic thought."[31] More significant, Lange admits that there is a parallel between the petition in 11Q5 col. 19 and *Jubilees* 1.19–20,[32] in which Moses pleads that God not deliver Israel "into the control of the nations with the result that they rule over them lest they make them sin against you" and that *"the spirit of Beliar not rule them so as to bring charges against them* before you *and to trap them* away from every proper path so that they may be destroyed from your presence."[33] The text also shares language with the petition in the Aramaic Levi Document which, however, lacks the specificity of "Satan" as the inimical

---

29. Stone and Greenfield draw attention to the use of the same expression ("every satan") in 1QH isolated fragments 4 and 45 ("Prayer of Levi," 262).

30. So David Flusser, "Qumrân and Jewish 'Apotropaic' Prayers," *IEJ* 16 (1966): 196–97; Kugler, *From Patriarch to Priest*, 73; Stone and Greenfield, "Prayer of Levi," 263.

31. Lange, "Spirit of Impurity," 262. In favor of literary dependence, Lange argues that one would have expected the Aramaic verb in 4Q213a to be מלך rather than the cognate שלט. This point, however, is not persuasive; cf. Klaus Beyer, *Die aramäischen Texte vom Toten Meer* (Göttingen: Vandenhoeck & Ruprecht, 1984), 709–10, and idem, *Die aramäischen Texte vom Toten Meer: Ergänzungsband* (Göttingen: Vandenhoeck & Ruprecht, 1994), 422.

32. Beyer, *Aramäischen Texte*, 262 n. 38.

33. The translation is that of James C. VanderKam, *The Book of Jubilees* (CSCO 511; Louvain: Peeters, 1989), 5.

demonic power. The wording in *Jubilees* 1.20, as in the "Prayer of Deliverance," has no equivalent for כל and the mention of "satan" has been replaced by the more proper name in the designation "the spirit of Beliar" and reformulated as a verb that describes the activity of the demonic Beliar as an accuser of God's people.

These considerations suggest that both Levi's prayer in the Aramaic Levi Document and Moses' intercession in *Jubilees* 1.20 reflect the influence of a tradition that is extant through the "Prayer of Deliverance." If this is the case, however, their common concern with the bestowal of a "holy spirit" in the context of the petition (cf. Aramaic Levi Document Gk. v. 8; *Jub.* 1.21) suggests that the underlying tradition was not entirely in line with the petition as preserved in 11Q5. Moreover, if the text of Ps 119:133 is lurking in the background, by the time of *Jubilees*, at least, it lies well behind, and we may infer that the petition for protection from demonic power was beginning to acquire a life of its own. If this is correct, then we may offer two observations. First, the writers of these texts have adapted the generally formulated prayer text to suit the purposes of their narrative, doing so in different ways. Whereas the author of *Jubilees* has transformed the ambiguous "satan," perhaps from 11Q5, into a proper name Beliar while retaining his adversarial function, the author of the prayer of Levi retains "satan" as a type of demonic being that poses a threat. Second, the existence of the deliverance prayer in 11Q5 demonstrates that the attestation of the petitions for deliverance within larger narratives that have shaped them (i.e., in 4Q213a and *Jub.* 1) does not mean they bear no relation to religious practice. In fact, if the underlying tradition to the Aramaic Levi Document and *Jubilees* was independent from the petition in 11Q5, then we have to deal with a more widespread prayer than has previously been recognized.

In other words, in 4Q213a and *Jubilees* 1 we do not have prayers formulated in order to enhance a given storyline, so much as an independently circulating petition against demonic power which, due to its popularity, has been narrativized—that is, adapted into new literary settings. The adaptability of the petitionary prayer for protection is illustrated by two further passages in *Jubilees*. Though none of the passages from *Jubilees* discussed here is preserved among the fragments of at least fifteen manuscripts of this work among the Dead Sea Scrolls, it is the discovery of these materials which gives the considerations here firmer footing when it comes to describing the use of petitionary prayer during the Second Temple period.

(3) *Jubilees* 10.3–6

This text contains a prayer formulated as the words of Noah spoken after the Great Flood (10.1–2). The prayer comes at the request of Noah's sons, who complain that Noah's grandchildren were being led astray, being blinded and being killed by "demons." In response, Noah utters a petition to curb the activities of evil spirits. The text of the prayer is as follows:

> (v. 3) . . . God of the spirits which are in all flesh,
> who has acted mercifully with me and saved me and my sons
> from the water of the Flood
> and did not let me perish as you did the children of perdition,
> because great was your grace upon me,
> and great was your mercy upon my soul.
> Let your grace be lifted up upon my sons,
> and *do not let the evil spirits rule* over them,
> lest they destroy them from the earth.
> (v. 4) But bless me and my sons.
> And let us grow and increase and fill the earth.
> (v. 5) And you know that which your Watchers,
> the fathers of these spirits, did in my days
> and also these spirits who are alive.
> Shut them up and take them to the place of judgment.
> And do not let them cause corruption among the sons of your servant, O my God,
> because they are cruel and were created to destroy.
> (v. 6) And *let them not rule over* the spirits of the living
> because you alone know their judgment.
> And *do not let them have power over the children of the righteous now and forever.*[34]

Formally, the prayer has a two-fold structure. First, it opens with a declaration of all that God has done on behalf of Noah and his sons to save them from the destruction of the deluge (v. 3). Thus, the prayer initially assumes a posture of thanksgiving and praise. The second, more extensive, part of the prayer contains a petition in two parts: (1) Noah asks God to bless him and his sons in order that they might "grow and increase and fill the earth" (cf. Gen 9:1, 7);[35] (2) as almost a prerequisite for such a blessing, Noah asks God to punish "the spirits," the off-

---

34. Here I follow the translation by O. S. Wintermute in *The Old Testament Pseudepigrapha* (2 vols.; ed. James H. Charlesworth; Garden City, N.Y.: Doubleday, 1983–85), 2.75–76, which structures Noah's prayer into stichs (italics added).

35. Cf. the MT: "God blessed Noah and his sons, and said to them, 'Be fruitful and multiply, and fill the earth.'" With regard to intertextuality, Noah's prayer in *Jubilees* makes God's act of blessing Noah the object of the petition. Significantly, no such command is given in *Jubilees* to the first humans (see Gen. 1:28a). This implies that the demons pose an obstacle to the carrying out of God's command to "be fruitful and multiply" after the flood; cf. James C. VanderKam, "The Demons in the Book of Jubilees," in *Die Dämonen—Demons: Die Dämonologie der israelitisch-judischen und fruhchristlichen Literatur im Kontext ihrer Umwelt* (ed. Armin Lange, Herman Lichtenberger, and K. F. Diethard Römheld; Tübingen: Mohr Siebeck, 2003), 343.

spring of the fallen angels (v. 5). Because of their destructive activities toward humankind, the prayer asks that the spirits be consigned to a place of judgment. Then, in verse 6, the petition concludes with two reformulations of the initial petition for protection in verse 3, a formula reminiscent of *Jubilees* 1.20, "let them [the evil spirits] not rule over the spirits of the living" and "do not let them have power over the children of the righteous now and forever."[36]

With respect to its specific content, the petition has been recast to reflect the preceding and following narrative in *Jubilees*. The evil spirits referred to are those of the giant offspring of the Watchers and the women they deceived (v. 5; see 5.1–11; 7.21–24). Though they began as creatures with a human flesh (v. 3; cf. 5.8), they became spirits when they killed one another. And so, after the deluge,[37] Noah's descendants (his grandchildren) are being threatened by the activities of these impure spirits, who are now called "demons" (v. 2). The narrative following Noah's prayer describes God's response to the petition: God directs the angels to bind all of the demons (10.7). However, the divine judgment is not achieved with finality. Mastema, the chief of these punished spirits (mentioned here for the first time in *Jubilees*), begs God to permit him to exercise his (rightful) authority, given that the greatness of human sin is inevitable (v. 8). God responds by having nine-tenths of the spirits consigned to the place of judgment below (v. 9), while a limited number (one-tenth) may carry out Mastema's orders (cf. v. 9). In the end, Noah is taught various herbal remedies through which the afflictions brought about by the evil spirits on his offspring can be curbed or at least kept in check (v. 12).

In its position between the antediluvian catastrophes and the deluge, on the one hand, and the containment and punishment of malevolent forces, on the other hand, the prayer comes at a pivotal point in the storyline. Because of Noah's great piety, his prayer functions to set on course the temporary position of evil spirits until the eschatological judgment. God's response to his petition ensures that, from now on, the evil that is manifest on earth represents an essentially defeated power whose activity has already been subjected to a preliminary judgment. This strong link to the literary context means that the prayer is here really conceived as *Noah's* prayer and in its present form does not draw on a prayer that would have been uttered by anyone. Thus, the wording of the petition that God punish the demonic spirits is "narrativized"; that is, it takes into account what

---

36. This petition is also similar to texts in the Aramaic Levi Document and 11Q5 col. 19 mentioned above.

37. Similar to the Book of Watchers, the role of the flood as divine punishment against the rebellious angels and their progeny in *Jubilees* is unclear; whereas the Book of Giants seems to have given the deluge a more prominent role in this respect, *1 En.* 6–16 and *Jubilees* give the impression that when they describe the remaining demonic activity following God's initial judgment against the fallen angels and giants, they have post-diluvian times in view; cf. Stuckenbruck, "Origins of Evil," 111–12.

the author believed were the specific circumstances faced by the patriarch after the great flood. However, this is not merely a prayer composed *ad hoc*; the petition that God not permit evil spirits to have power over those who are pious was, as we have seen, in use outside the text. It is likely that early readers of *Jubilees* would have been familiar with such a prayer and would have recognized it as it is put into the mouths of Moses in 1.20 and of Noah in 10.3–6.

Not only would ancient readers have recognized the petition for protection, the content of the prayer itself widens the horizon beyond that of Noah and his grandchildren to embrace the implied readers of the author's own time. Two details in the prayer suggest this. First, at the end of the prayer, the plea to curtail the spirits' power no longer simply refers specifically to Noah's grandchildren. Though "the sons of your servant" could refer to Noah's immediate family, the mention of "the spirits of the living" and, in particular, "the children of the righteous *henceforth and forever*" opens the horizon to include all those who are pious after the time of Noah until the very end. In this sense, then, Noah's prayer is also a plea for protection on behalf of all righteous ones who come after him, and readers would have understood themselves to be included in this protection.[38] Second, the brief and conventional form of the conclusion to the prayer presupposes a certain familiarity with this sort of prayer among the readers. To attribute a petition that readers perhaps knew among themselves to Noah not only anchors their prayer within a pivotal point of the covenant story of Israel, but also strengthens their confidence in the effectiveness of their prayers for protection against demonic powers: though they lie behind the afflictions and iniquities suffered and carried by God's people, evil spirits are but defeated powers whose complete destruction is assured.

(4) *Jubilees* 12.19–20

In *Jubilees* yet a third figure is made to offer a petition for protection: Abram, whose prayer is given in 12.19–20.

(v. 19) . . . My God, my God, God most High,
You alone are my God.
You have created everything;
Everything that was and has been is the product of your hands.
You and your lordship I have chosen.
(v. 20) *Save me from the power of the evil spirits,*
who rule the thoughts of people's minds.
May they not mislead me from following you, my God.
Do establish me and my posterity forever.

---

38. The same may be implied by Moses' intercessory prayer in *Jub.* 1.19–20.

May we not go astray from now until eternity.[39]

Abram's petition shares the two-fold structure observed above in *Jubilees* 10.3–6. In the first part, the prayer extols God as the only God and the one who has created all things (v. 19). In the second part, the petition asks for rescue from the rule of evil spirits who would lead humankind astray from showing exclusive devotion to God.[40]

Again, as in the case of Noah's prayer in *Jubilees* 10, it is important to consider Abram's prayer in relation to its immediate literary context. Abram is made to utter his petition just prior to receiving God's promise that he and his descendants will be given a land. The petition, then, associates the promise of the land to Abram with God's power over evil, on behalf of Abram and his descendants. Earlier in the narrative, the path to the story about Abram is laid in chapter 11. After the flood, Noah's descendants became involved in violent and oppressive activities (v. 2); indeed, they had begun to make idols and thus were coming under the influence of those evil spirits which, under Mastema's rule, were allowed to lead people astray to commit sin and acts of impurity (vv. 4–5). The introduction of Abram into the narrative, beginning with 11.14, marks a shift in the midst of this post-diluvian corruption among humanity. Abram, at an early age, offers prayers "to the creator of all" and rejects his father's worship of idols (11.16; 12.2–8, 12–14). At one point, Abram even tells his father, Terah, not to worship idols fashioned by human hands, but rather "the God of heaven" who has "created everything by his word" (12.3–4). Therefore, Abram's prayer in 12.19–20, in its focus on God as creator (v. 19), expresses an objection to post-diluvian idolatry behind which lay the activities of malevolent demonic beings. As in the prayer of Noah, Abram's proclamation of God as "creator" shows how embedded the petition is within the story line.

If one links the first part of Abram's prayer back to the account of growing post-diluvian evil, it is possible to find the rationale for the petition to counteract the "evil spirits" in the second part. The reason for the mention of "evil spirits," however, need be neither so remote nor so implicit. As Lange rightly argues, since the prayer occurs while Abram is gazing at the stars by night (12.16), these spirits must be the stars linked with "astrology."[41] Abram, after all, recognizes that it is wrong for him to prognosticate on the basis of the stars; this even includes the weather—for example, whether or not it will rain—as the making of such predictions distracts from the conviction that meteorological events are to be left in

---

39. The text given follows the translation of VanderKam, *Book of Jubilees*, 72 (emphasis added).

40. As in 4Q213a, the prayers in *Jub.* 1.20 and 12.20 refer to demonic activity as "leading astray," a motif that occurs in the narrative before Noah's prayer in 10.3. The "Prayer of Deliverance" in 11Q5, however, makes no mention of this.

41. Lange, "Essene Position on Magic and Divination," 383.

God's control. In sitting alone at night, Abram thus finds himself resisting the temptation to adopt the instruction about "the omens of the sun and moon and stars within all the signs of heaven," which in the story has been attributed to the fallen angels and which has been rediscovered after the deluge by Noah's great-grandson, Cainan, who "sinned" because of it (8.1–4).

In the subsequent part of the Abraham narrative in *Jubilees*, several passages are illuminating: the angel's explanation of the significance of the law of circumcision (15.30–32); the account about the sacrifice of Isaac (17.15–18.19); and the blessings pronounced by Abraham over Jacob (esp. 19.27–29). In 15.30–32, the angel's instruction to Abraham about circumcision is explained as a means by which God rules over his people Israel, over whom "he made no angel or spirit rule" (v. 32). The rest of the nations, by contrast, are ruled by spirits who lead them astray (v. 31). The link already made in 11.4–5 between evil spirits and the worship of idols (cf. 22.16)[42] suggests that Abram's petition in chapter 12 for the establishment of his "seed" is one that is ultimately answered when God separates Israel from the nations of the earth to become the people he will protect (15.32). In 17.15–18.19, Mastema is identified as the one who sought to distract Abraham from obedience to God in the sacrifice of Isaac (17.16; 18.12). In 19.28, Abraham pronounces a blessing over Jacob: "may the spirit of Mastema not rule over you or over your seed in order to remove you from following the Lord who is your God henceforth and forever." Abraham's story thus exemplifies how his prayer for deliverance from the rule of "evil spirits" is answered: his obedience to God thwarts Mastema's plan to test his character, and God's separation of Israel as his elect people is God's response to Abram's prayer of deliverance (and perhaps also the prayers of Moses and Noah).

For all the connections between Abram's prayer in chapter 12 and the narrative, the subject matter of the petition itself remains conventional—that is, it is formulated in a way that is not fully bound into the literary context. The petition for deliverance from the rule of "evil spirits" (rather than, simply, from the

---

42. For the association of idolatry among the Gentiles with the influence of demonic powers, Deut 32:16–17 played a formative role: "They made him [God] jealous with strange gods (בזרים, ἐπ' αλλοτρίοις), with abhorrent things (בתועבת, ἐν βδελύγμασιν) they provoked him. They sacrificed to demons (יזבחו לשדים, ἔθυσαν δαιμονίοις), to deities they had never known, to new ones recently arrived, whom your ancestors had not feared" (NSRV). In the Hebrew Bible, the equation of demons and idols is more explicitly made in the Greek translation of Ps 96[95]:5a: "For all the gods of the nations are demons" (δαιμόνια; Heb. אלילים "idols"); cf. also Ps 106[105]:37 and Isa 65:11. *1 Enoch* 19.1 picks up this association in the third century B.C.E., followed in the second century B.C.E. by *Jubilees* (1.11, as well as at 22.16–18) and *Epistle of Enoch* (*1 En.* 99.7). After this, the idea becomes more widespread: see 4Q243 13.2; par. 4Q244 12.2, "demons of error" (טעותא שידי); *T. Jud.* 23.1; *T. Job* 3.6; *Sib. Or.* 8.47, 381–394 and frag. 1.20–22; Bar 4.7; 1 Cor 10:20; Rev 9:20; cf. Gal 4:8; *Ep. Barn.* 16.7; Ignatius, *Magn.* 3.1 (long recension).

rule of Mastema, as the story bears out) is formulated in general terms. As such, it is a petition by the pious that expresses the desire to stay away from idolatry. Moreover, similar to Noah's petition at 10.6, Abram's plea is concerned with all his progeny "forever," which includes the implied readers of the story. With perhaps the exception of the Abram-specific phrase "me and my seed forever," the prayer itself could be uttered by any of Abram's seed, that is, those whom the author regards as pious.

Regarding *Jubilees*, we may, in summary, note that the language of petition for protection from demonic evil occurs in a number of texts: 1.20; 10.3–6; 12.19–20; 15.30–32; and 19.28. As we have been able to note on the basis of 11Q5 col. 19 and the Aramaic Levi Document, the recurrence of such language in *Jubilees* picks up on a prayer formula that circulated prior to and independently from the setting within which the communication between its writer(s) and implied readers took shape. In *Jubilees*, to a greater degree than in the Aramaic Levi Document, a more widely known petition is placed in the mouths of patriarchs to whom formulations are attributed that include the community in relation to whom the work was composed.

JESUS' PETITIONS IN JOHN 17

In our review of Second Temple Jewish literature preserved in the Dead Sea Scrolls, we have discovered several things that may have an impact on the way one reads Jesus' petitions for his disciples and later followers in John 17. First, analogous to John 17, our Jewish traditions all construe prayer for protection in relation to demonic power, something which marks a development beyond prayers conveyed through the Hebrew Bible. Second, the texts we have looked at are not merely literary; they reflect a piety which in at least some Jewish circles was expressed through the offering of prayers for divine protection from the personified forms of evil (cf. 11Q5 19). Third, such petitions were adaptable. They could be narrativized into stories involving ideal figures from Israel's ancient past (Aramaic Levi Document; *Jubilees*). Thus, patriarchs would not only be presented as practitioners of the piety familiar to those who read about them, but also would be made to formulate petitions that sought God's protection for their descendants. In such cases, readers would have been able to find themselves addressed in the unfolding story line. Fourth, the petitions for divine help against malevolent power were based on a twinfold assumption that (1) the present age is under the dominion of evil (ruled by Belial/r, Mastema, or evil spirits), and (2) the powers which hold sway are essentially defeated and await certain eschatological destruction.

These texts contribute to our understanding of Jesus' prayer in the Fourth Gospel in at least three ways.

First, according to John's Gospel, "the world," which is under the dominion of "the ruler of the world," is completely opposed to Jesus and his followers because they are not of the world. While the hostility between the present age of wickedness and a future age of restoration has long been known through Second Temple–period literature produced by apocalyptic circles, some of the Dead Sea materials express this tension in language that comes closer to what meets us in John's Gospel.

Second, the confidence expressed in the petitionary prayers considered here, based on definitive acts of God in the past and the certain eschatological defeat of demonic power in the future, is reframed in John's Gospel around Jesus' death, through which the world is already judged. Though the inimical world order holds sway, its days are numbered, and it already stands condemned.

Third and finally, the petitions in search of protection are formulated in recognition that in the meantime a community which considers itself especially elect needs divine help in order to ward off the unabating influences of evil power. Such prayers would have been known to the pious, whether they were those who recited the "Prayer of Deliverance" preserved in 11Q5 col. 19 or members of the Matthean and similar communities who prayed to be delivered from "the evil one" in the Lord's Prayer (Matt 6:13; cf. 2 Thess 3:3). If such a petition was known to the implied readers of the Johannine community, then it is not without significance that in John's Gospel the petition that God protect Jesus' disciples "from the evil one" is placed on the lips of Jesus himself. In doing this, the writer of the prayer in John 17 would have been providing readers something that we have witnessed in some texts of the Gospel's Jewish predecessors: a prayer which readers may already have been reciting for themselves has been strengthened by having it spoken by the very one in and through whom their religiosity is determined. Therefore, just as the patriarchs' petitions against demonic evil are formulated as prayers for their descendants and spiritual heirs, so also Jesus' petition is concerned with his "descendants," that is, the disciples and "those who believe in me through their word"—members of the Johannine community who find themselves covered by its force.

THE FOURTH EVANGELIST AND THE DEAD SEA SCROLLS: ASSESSING TRENDS OVER NEARLY SIXTY YEARS

James H. Charlesworth

The sixtieth anniversary of the discovery of the Qumran Scrolls is a propitious time to assess how and in what ways, if at all, uniquely Essene or Qumranite ideas may have influenced the Fourth Evangelist or his community.[1] Research on the Dead Sea Scrolls has helped to clarify a number of important issues surrounding the Fourth Gospel. These include, but are not limited to, questions regarding the date of the Gospel, its possible Palestinian provenance, and its Jewish nature. These considerations, in turn, underscore the value of the Gospel for Historical Jesus research. Each of these topics will be briefly reviewed here. Following this survey of past research, I will comment on potential future avenues of inquiry, many of which have been anticipated by the essays in this volume.

QUMRAN AND JOHN IN JESUS RESEARCH

First, the *dating* of the Fourth Gospel has been significantly clarified by research on the scrolls. Virtually no scholar now dates this Gospel to the middle of the second century or later. The undeniable similarities between the Fourth Gospel and Jewish thought known to be influential in pre-70 C.E. Judaism (Second Temple Judaism) indicate that the work took definite shape no later than about 100 C.E. Most scholars rightly stress that the final version of the Gospel reflects earlier editions and some unique sources.

---

1. Along with most Qumranologists, I have concluded that Philo and Josephus were correct to report that there were two branches of Essenes and also to conclude that Qumran was the major center of the extremely conservative branch of the Essenes. A few Essenes did not marry and isolated themselves from all others (the Qumranites represented by the Rule of the Community), while other Essenes married and associated in some ways with other Jews (the Essenes behind the Damascus Document). See here James H. Charlesworth, "Have the Dead Sea Scrolls Revolutionized Our Understanding of the New Testament?" in *The Dead Sea Scrolls Fifty Years after Their Discovery* (ed. Lawrence H. Schiffman, Emanuel Tov, and James C. VanderKam; Jerusalem: Israel Explorations Society and the Shrine of the Book, 2000), 116–32.

Second, research on the scrolls has significantly affected our understanding of the *provenance* of the Gospel of John. Thanks to the study of Second Temple Jewish texts, especially the Dead Sea Scrolls, it is now certain that one does not have to look to Iranian texts or Greek philosophy to locate expressions and thoughts typical of the Fourth Gospel. What was once defined as uniquely Johannine terminology and ideology is now evident in Second Temple Judaism. Thus, research on the Dead Sea Scrolls has led many experts, like Herbert Braun and John A. T. Robinson, to conclude that the Gospel is both early and reflects Palestinian Jewish terms and thoughts.[2] Martin Hengel, a leading specialist on early Judaism and Christian origins, expresses the opinion of many current scholars, "The Qumran discoveries are a landmark for a new assessment of the situation of the Fourth Gospel in the history of religion." Hengel concludes that the Fourth Gospel took shape in Palestine: "[N]umerous linguistic and theological parallels to Qumran, especially in the sphere of dualism, predestination, and election also point to Palestine" as the provenance of the Fourth Gospel.[3] Leon Morris voiced the same judgment: The Dead Sea Scrolls "have demonstrated, by their many parallels to this Gospel both in ideas and expression, that our Fourth Gospel is essentially a Palestinian document."[4] F. F. Bruce agreed with these insights: "An argument for the Palestinian provenance of this Gospel which was not available to scholars of earlier generations has been provided by the discovery and study of documents emanating from the religious community which had its headquarters at Qumran, north-west of the Dead Sea, for about two centuries before AD 70."[5]

Eschewing any reference to a consensus (which might sink it), I shall add to these judgments solid conclusions that remain valid for today. In my assessment, John's knowledge of topography and debates within Second Temple Judaism, understanding of the Samaritans, and awareness of costly provisions for the Jewish rites of purification indicate that, at least in these areas, the Fourth Evan-

---

2. Herbert Braun, *Qumran und das Neue Testament* (2 vols.; Tübingen: Mohr Siebeck, 1966), 1.98; John A. T. Robinson, *The Priority of John* (ed. J. F. Coakley; London: SCM, 1985).

3. Martin Hengel, *The Johannine Question*, trans. John Bowden (London: SCM, 1989), first quote 111, second quote 281 (German original: *Die johanneische Frage* [WUNT 67; Tübingen: Mohr Siebeck, 1993]). Hengel holds that "die Qumranfunde" is "einen Markstein für die religionsgeschichtliche Einordnung." Note also the words of C. K. Barrett: "[T]wo circumstances have led to a strong reiteration of the Jewish background and origin of the gospel: on the one hand, the criticism, directed against Bultmann and those who follow him, concerning the relative lateness of the comparative material used to establish a Gnostic background of John; on the other, and more important, the discovery of the Qumran scrolls"; see *The Gospel of John and Judaism* (trans. D. Moody Smith; Philadelphia: Fortress, 1975), 7–8.

4. Leon Morris, *The Gospel According to John* (rev. ed.; NICNT; Grand Rapids: Eerdmans, 1995), 9.

5. F. F. Bruce, *The Gospel of John* (Grand Rapids: Eerdmans, 1994), 2.

gelist lives in the world of pre-70 C.E. Palestinian Judaism.[6] Stone vessels "for the Jewish rites of purification" are mentioned in an aside at John 2:6, but we now know that such stone jars almost always antedate 70 C.E. and have been found not only in Jerusalem's Upper City but also in Lower Galilee.[7] The Fourth Evangelist also seems to know the locations of Caiaphas's house and the *praetorium* (18:28). The Herodian Pool of Siloam has been discovered south of the temple mount, just where the Evangelist locates it. The Pool of Bethzatha is north of the temple, also where the Evangelist places it, and it does have five porticoes and two pools (cf. the Copper Scroll). While theological exegesis once sufficed to unlock the mysteries of the Fourth Gospel, we now need to include considerations of historiography and archaeology.

As a third significant implication of scrolls research, the *Jewish nature* of the Fourth Gospel has slowly been recognized by most leading scholars, as evident from, *inter alia*, the following data. (1) Sabbath observance by some Second Temple Jews is portrayed as excessive and fails to represent obedience to God's will as revealed in Torah (John 5:9–18).[8] (2) The Fourth Evangelist knows that influential Jews have judged that circumcision overrides Sabbath observance (John 7:22–23). (3) The Jewish festivals are integral not only to the composition of the Fourth Gospel but also placard its Jewish background.[9] (4) Jewish purity concerns appear throughout the Fourth Gospel and are assumed to be meaningful to the intended reader.[10] In her essay for this volume, Hannah Harrington demonstrates that a connection between water purification and the eschaton is not an innovation of the Fourth Gospel, and that purification was a fundamental tenet of the Qumran sect. (5) Stone vessels designated for the Jewish rites of purification and *miqva'ot* for ritual cleansing appear both on the surface of the narrative (John 2) and just beneath it (John 9). (6) Jesus' opponents in John, the Ἰουδαῖοι, are not always simply "Jews"; sometimes this Greek noun designates "some Judean leaders."[11] (7) The Johannine calendar may be aligned with the

---

6. I also am convinced that the context of the final editing of the Fourth Gospel is post-70 C.E. Judaism.

7. See esp. Peter Richardson, "Khirbet Qana (and Other Villages) as a Context for Jesus," in *Jesus and Archaeology* (ed. James H. Charlesworth; Grand Rapids: Eerdmans, 2006), 120–44.

8. See Martin Asiedu-Peprah, *Johannine Sabbath Conflicts as Juridical Controversy* (WUNT 2.132; Tübingen: Mohr Siebeck, 2001).

9. This new perspective has been brilliantly demonstrated by two recent monographs: Luc Devillers, *La Fête de l'Envoyé: La section Johannique de la fête des tentes (Jean 7, 1–10, 21) et la christologie* (EB n.s. 49; Paris: Gabalda, 2002); and Michael A. Daise, *Feasts in John: Jewish Festivals and Jesus' "Hour" in the Fourth Gospel* (WUNT 2.229; Tübingen: Mohr Siebeck, 2007).

10. See esp. Michael Newton, *The Concept of Purity at Qumran and in the Letters of Paul* (SNTSMS 53; Cambridge: Cambridge University Press, 1985).

11. James H. Charlesworth, "The Gospel of John: Exclusivism Caused by a Social Setting Different from That of Jesus (John 11:54 and 14:6)," in *Anti-Judaism and the Fourth Gospel:*

solar calendar of Qumran, *1 Enoch*, and *Jubilees*.[12] (8) The Johannine Jews (not Johannine Christians) are prohibited from attending synagogue services by some synagogal Jews.[13]

Before the 1960s, many scholars were persuaded that the Fourth Evangelist couched Jesus' words in terms of Greek thought, especially evident in the Stoic concept of Logos. In 1963, Peder Borgen demonstrated that the Fourth Evangelist shaped his exegetical discourses according to the ancient midrashim;[14] since then we have found the technical term *midrash* used as a title for a pre-70 C.E. composition (*Midrash Sepher Moses*). The Dead Sea Scrolls have caused a shift in Johannine studies that is acknowledged by scholars such as Paula Fredriksen, who notes that "the Scrolls incontrovertibly show that early first-century Judean Jews spoke and thought in similar ways [to the way Jesus speaks in the Gospel of John]. And an earlier, Jewish context of composition for John's Gospel then reopens the question of its historical value for reconstructing Jesus' life."[15]

Fredricksen's comment brings forward the importance of the Fourth Gospel in Jesus research. Many scholars are now voicing an awareness that the Fourth Gospel preserves history and is thus fundamental for Jesus research.[16] As D. Moody Smith states, the Fourth Gospel contains "an array of historical data" which have as good a claim to be historically reliable as passages in the Synoptics.[17] John Meier wisely uses the Fourth Gospel to obtain genuine historical information regarding the historical Jesus.[18] The advice of Gerd Theissen and Anne Merz is to be taken seriously: the Fourth Gospel is independent of the

---

Papers of the Leuven Colloquium, 2000 (ed. Riemund Bieringer, Didier Pollefeyt, and Frederique Vandecasteele-Vanneuville; Assen, Netherlands: Royal Van Gorcum, 2001), 479–513.

12. See Annie Jaubert, "The Calendar of Qumran and the Passion Narrative in John," in *John and the Dead Sea Scrolls* (ed. James H. Charlesworth; New York: Crossroad, 1990), 62–75.

13. See the pioneering work by J. Louis Martyn, *History and Theology in the Fourth Gospel* (3d ed.; Louisville: Westminster John Knox, 2003); 1st ed., 1968.

14. Peder Borgen, "Observations on the Midrashic Character of John 6," *ZNW* 54 (1963): 232–40.

15. Paula Fredriksen, *Jesus of Nazareth, King of the Jews: A Jewish Life and the Emergence of Christianity* (New York: Alfred A. Knopf, 2000), 5.

16. See esp. the contributions to *Jesus in Johannine Tradition* (ed. Robert T. Fortna and Tom Thatcher; Louisville: Westminster John Knox, 2001).

17. D. Moody Smith, "Historical Issues and the Problem of John and the Synoptics," in *From Jesus to John* (ed. Martinus C. de Boer; JSNTSup 84; Sheffield: JSOT, 1993), 252–67. See also idem, "John and the Synoptics: Historical Tradition and the Passion Narrative," in *Light in a Spotless Mirror: Reflections on Wisdom Traditions in Judaism and Early Christianity* (ed. James H. Charlesworth and Michael A. Daise; Valley Forge, Pa.: Trinity Press International, 2003), 77–90.

18. John P. Meier, *A Marginal Jew: Rethinking the Historical Jesus*, Vol. 1: *The Roots of the Problem and the Person* (ABRL; New York: Doubleday, 1991), esp. 44: "In short, our survey of the Four Gospels gives us three separate major sources to work with: Mark, Q, and John."

Synoptics and in places preserves "old traditions" that are "not worthless" historically.[19] The Qumran Scrolls have been the major catalyst for this emerging perception.

Essene Influence on the Gospel of John

Of course, one of the most significant points of contact between the Fourth Gospel and the scrolls in recent research relates to a reconceptualization of the nature and origin of Johannine "dualism." Specifically, recent Johannine scholarship, informed by Qumran studies, has located John's dualistic thinking squarely within a Jewish matrix, further indicating the Jewish provenance of the Gospel. Before proceeding further, it will be helpful to explore how unique Qumran dualism is as a way of clarifying the value of apparent parallels with the Johannine literature.

John Painter correctly emphasizes that, while dualism is regnant in the ancient world, a unique type of dualism is found in John and Qumran: "But we find no developed or systematic expression of a dualistic position in the Old Testament such as we find at Qumran and in Jn."[20] As Israeli Qumran specialist Devorah Dimant states, "One of the most striking elements in the Qumranic documents is *the dualistic doctrine* expounded by them. *Unique* in Early Judaism, this doctrine drew the attention of scholars from the earliest days of Qumran research."[21] If the dualism is *unique to Qumran* within the world of Second Temple Judaism, as most scholars have concluded, it is misleading and fruitless to find isolated and similar phrases in other early Jewish (and non-Jewish) texts. What is missing in these other early texts is a cluster of *termini technici* that constitutes a paradigm. Within the purview of the Fourth Evangelist, this paradigm is developed only in scrolls composed at Qumran and especially in the Rule of the Community.

Thus, to take but one notable example, John 12:35–36 was once incorrectly judged to represent the Evangelist's novel creativity.

> Jesus said to them, "The *light* is with you for a little longer. *Walk* while you have *the light, lest the darkness* overtake you; *he who walks in the darkness does not know* where he goes. While you have *the light,* believe in *the light,* that you may become *sons of light.*

19. Gerd Theissen and Annette Merz, *The Historical Jesus: A Comprehensive Guide* (trans. John Bowden; Minneapolis: Fortress, 1998), 36–37.

20. John Painter, *The Quest for the Messiah: The History, Literature, and Theology of the Johannine Community* (2nd ed.; Nashville, Tenn.: Abingdon, 1993), 37.

21. Devorah Dimant, "Dualism at Qumran: New Perspectives," in *Caves of Enlightenment* (ed. James H. Charlesworth; North Richland Hills, Tex.: BIBAL, 1998), 55, emphasis added.

Here, the Fourth Evangelist is obviously not developing, but rather inheriting, a dualistic paradigm and *termini technici*. Why did the Evangelist use such symbolism, such phrases and terms, and from what source did he inherit the technical term "sons of light"? As George Brooke notes in his essay for this volume, we should avoid elaborate theories of literary dependence; we should also note, however, that John 12:35–36 raises significant questions about the specific origin of the Fourth Evangelist's dualism, dualistic perception, and technical terms. I prefer to see some "direct" influence from the world of Qumran upon John. In my view, however, this influence should not be viewed in strictly literary terms. I never imagined that the Fourth Evangelist was working from a copy of the Rule of the Community; it seems to me more likely that he learned this uniquely Qumranic form of dualism through conversations with Essenes (perhaps some who joined the Palestinian Jesus Movement). Let me explain my position.

The most probable explanation for the shared dualism in the Qumran scrolls and the Fourth Gospel is that the Fourth Evangelist, and perhaps those in his group, were influenced by the light/darkness paradigm developed only in the Rule of the Community. That scroll identifies the "sons of light" (see 1QS 3.13, 24, 25) and introduces the phrase, "and they shall walk in the ways of darkness" (3.21; cf. 4.11). One passage in the Rule contains phrases and words that may sound "Johannine" to those who do not know that this scroll antedates John's Gospel by about two centuries.

> In the hand of the *Prince of Lights* (is) the dominion of all the *Sons of Righteousness; in the ways of light they walk*. But in the hand of the *Angel of Darkness* (is) the dominion of the *Sons of Deceit*; and *in the ways of darkness they walk*. By the *Angel of Darkness* comes the aberration of all the *Sons of Righteousness*; and all their sins, their iniquities, their guilt, and their iniquitous works (are caused) by his dominion, according to God's mysteries, until his end. And all their afflictions and the appointed times of their suffering (are caused) by the dominion of his hostility. And all the spirits of his lot cause to stumble the *Sons of Light*; but the God of Israel and his *Angel of Truth* help all *the Sons of Light*. He created *the spirits of light and darkness*, and upon them he founded every work. (1QS 3.20–25; my translation)[22]

Note the *termini technici* that are italicized in the excerpt above and the resulting dualistic paradigm. Except for "sons of darkness," all the following technical

---

22. See Elisha Qimron and James Charlesworth, "The Rule of the Community," in *The Dead Sea Scrolls—Hebrew, Aramaic, and Greek Texts with English Translations*, Vol. 1: *Rule of the Community and Related Documents* (ed. J. H. Charlesworth, F. M. Cross, J. Milgrom, E. Qimron, L. H. Schiffman, L.T. Stuckenbruck, and R. E. Whitaker; PTSDSSP: Louisville: Westminster John Knox, 1994), 16–17.

terms are found in a self-contained, short, memorable section of the Rule (e.g., cols. 3–4). Note the polarities:

light	darkness
Sons of Light	[Sons of Darkness; see 1QS 1.10]
Angel of Light	Angel of Darkness
Angel of Truth	Spirit of Deceit
Sons of Truth	Sons of Deceit
Sons of Righteousness	Sons of Deceit
spring of light	well of darkness
walking in the ways of light	walking in the ways of darkness
truth	deceit (or perversity)
God loves	God hates
everlasting life	punishment, then extinction

As Becker points out, the dualism in the Fourth Gospel is closest, in the ancient world, to that found in 1QS 3–4. The widespread recognition of some influence of Qumran or Essene thought on the Fourth Evangelist leads Becker to conclude that "the Johannine community must, after some undualistic phase, have come under the influence of a type of Qumran dualism."[23] David Flusser emphasized that the "flesh-spirit" dualism known to the Qumran authors reappears in, and perhaps influenced, the Fourth Gospel (John 3:6).[24] Raymond Brown similarly observed that "not only the dualism but also its terminology is shared by John and Qumran."[25] Those who focus only on how dualism operates differently in Qumran theologies than in Johannine Christology need to heed Fitzmyer's question, which is a warning against such myopic methodology: "[W]hy should we expect the light/darkness imagery to function in the same way in both bodies of literature?"[26]

As the preceding discussion has indicated, among all ancient writings, only the Dead Sea Scrolls disclose a type of thought, a developed symbolic language, and a dualistic paradigm with *termini technici* that are surprisingly close to the

---

23. Jürgen Becker, *Das Evangelium nach Johannes* (3d ed.; 2 vols.; Gütersloh: Gerd Mohn, 1991), 1.176.

24. David Flusser, *Judaism and the Origins of Christianity* (Jerusalem: Magnes, 1988), 61.

25. Raymond E. Brown, *The Gospel according to John* (2 vols.; AB; Garden City, N.Y.: Doubleday, 1966–70), 1.lxii. See also see Brown's posthumous "John, Gospel, and Letters of," in *Encyclopedia of the Dead Sea Scrolls* (ed. Lawrence H. Schiffman and James C. VanderKam; 2 vols.; New York: Oxford University Press, 2000), 1.414–17.

26. Joseph Fitzmyer, "Qumran Literature and the Johannine Writings," in *Life in Abundance: Studies of John's Gospel in Tribute to Raymond E. Brown* (ed. John R. Donahue; Collegeville, Minn.: Liturgical Press, 2005), 123.

Fourth Gospel.[27] Recognizing the unique genius and theological creativity of the Fourth Evangelist also leaves room, indeed demands, exploring what terms he inherited and from whom and how he inherited them. Was he somehow influenced by Qumran dualistic terms and concepts?

It is apparent to many Qumran scholars and New Testament specialists that in some ways the Fourth Evangelist has been influenced by Qumran's dualism and its terminology. He contrasts darkness with light, evil with truth, hate with love, and perishing with receiving eternal life. William Sanford LaSor was impressed with numerous phrases unique to Qumran that reappear only in the Fourth Gospel and the Johannine Epistles: "to do the truth" (1QS 1.5; 5.3; 8.2; cf. John 3:21); "walking in truth" (1QS 4.6, 15; cf. 2 John 4; 3 John 3); and, "witnesses of truth" (1QS 8.6; cf. John 5:33; 18:37).[28] As D. Moody Smith correctly reports, "[T]hat the Qumran scrolls attest a form of Judaism whose conceptuality and terminology tally in some respects quite closely with the Johannine is a commonly acknowledged fact."[29] John Painter also astutely concludes "that the context in which the Johannine tradition was shaped . . . is best known to us in the Qumran texts."[30] Craig Evans rightly judges, "The relevance of the Scrolls for Johannine studies can scarcely be doubted."[31] Barnabas Lindars rightly pointed out that the Qumran Scrolls, especially the Rule, contain "the clearest expression of the contrast between light and the darkness, which is a central theme of John." Lindars offered the following conclusion: "Some kind of influence of the sect on John seems inescapable."[32]

The experts who conclude that the Fourth Evangelist was influenced by the Qumran texts or Essenes have provided many conceivable scenarios. Scholarly reconstructions range from the suggestion that the Fourth Evangelist had been influenced by John the Baptizer (who in turn had some ties to the Qumranites in these scenarios) to the proposal that at one time the Fourth Evangelist him-

---

27. Some of the Hermetic tractates and Gnostic codices are strikingly similar to the Fourth Gospel, but the influence seems to flow from the Fourth Gospel to them.

28. William Sanford LaSor, *The Dead Sea Scrolls and the New Testament* (Grand Rapids: Eerdmans, 1972), 198.

29. D. Moody Smith, *Johannine Christianity: Essays on Its Setting, Sources, and Theology* (Columbia, S.C.: University of South Carolina Press, 1984), 26.

30. Painter, *Quest*, 29.

31. Craig A. Evans, *Word and Glory: On the Exegetical and Theological Background of John's Prologue* (JSNTSup 89; Sheffield: Sheffield Academic Press, 1993), 55.

32. Barnabas Lindars, *The Gospel of John* (NCBC; Grand Rapids: Eerdmans, 1972), 38. Lindars further suggests that Qumran's "ideas were probably widespread and influential." In fact, however, the only early Jewish document in which a dualism similar to Qumran's appears is the *Testament of the Twelve Patriarchs*, which may itself reflect Essene influence and may be related to the liberal branch of Essenism represented by the Damascus Document.

self had been an Essene.[33] At one end of the scale, Raymond Brown represents those scholars who contend that the influence from the Essenes on the Fourth Evangelist was "indirect." "[I]n our [Brown's] judgment the parallels are not close enough to suggest a direct literary dependence of John upon the Qumran literature, but they do suggest Johannine familiarity with the type of thought exhibited in the scrolls."[34] Brown elsewhere asserts that the "ideas of Qumran must have been fairly widespread in certain Jewish circles in the early first century A.D. Probably it is only through such sources that Qumran had its indirect effect on the Johannine literature."[35] By contrast with Brown, I myself have concluded in numerous publications that the influences are so deep and significant that some "direct" influence is more likely.[36] I should stress here that I never imagined the Fourth Evangelist visiting Qumran, studying the Community Rule, and taking notes from it.[37] In my opinion, Essene influence came to the Evangelist from Essenes who had memorized the dualism developed in the Rule of the Community, were disenchanted when Qumran was burned, and were attracted to the proclamation that Jesus had been raised by God and is the long-awaited Messiah.[38]

---

33. It is possible that the Baptizer had once been a member, or almost a member, of the community. See here William H. Brownlee, "John the Baptist in the New Light of Ancient Scrolls," in *The Scrolls and the New Testament* (ed. Krister Stendahl and James H. Charlesworth; New York: Crossroad, 1992), 33–53; also idem, "Whence the Gospel according to John?" in *John and the Dead Sea Scrolls* (ed. James H. Charlesworth; New York: Crossroad, 1990), 166–94; cf. Bo Reicke, "Nytt ljus över Johannes döparens förkunnelse," *Religion och Bibel* 11 (1952): 5–18; James H. Charlesworth, "John the Baptizer and the Dead Sea Scrolls," in *The Bible and the Dead Sea Scrolls: The Princeton Symposium on the Dead Sea Scrolls* (ed. James H. Charlesworth; 3 vols.; Waco, Tex.: Baylor University Press, 2006), 3.1–35.

34. Brown, *Gospel according to John*, 1.lxiii.

35. Raymond E. Brown, "The Qumran Scrolls and the Johannine Gospel and Epistles," in *The Scrolls and the New Testament* (ed. Krister Stendahl and James H. Charlesworth; New York: Crossroad, 1992), 206.

36. Essene affinities with the Fourth Gospel are recognized by the contributors to *John and the Dead Sea Scrolls* (ed. James H. Charlesworth; New York: Crossroad, 1991). John Ashton, not unfairly, has criticized my lack of precision on this point: "[I]t makes little sense to speak, as Charlesworth does, in terms of 'borrowing,' however right he may be, against Brown and Schnackenburg, to adopt a theory of direct influence. For what *kind* of borrowing is he thinking of? Does he picture John visiting the Qumran Library, as Brown calls it, and taking the Community Rule out of the repository, scrolling through it, taking notes perhaps, and then making use of its ideas when he came to compose his own work?" (John Ashton, *Understanding the Fourth Gospel* [Oxford: Clarendon, 1991], 236–37).

37. For a method to discern how one text may have influenced another, see James H. Charlesworth, "Towards a Taxonomy of Discerning Influence(s) between Two Texts," in *Das Gesetz im frühen Judentum und im Neuen Testament, Festschrift für Christoph Burchard zum 75. Geburtstag* (ed. Dieter Sänger and Matthias Konradt; NTOA 57; Göttingen: Vandenhoeck & Ruprecht, 2006), 41–54.

38. If Barnabas was a Levite from Cyprus (Acts 4:36), then other Levites, including those who were Essenes, were most likely attracted to the missionary fervor of the Palestinian Jesus

Going beyond my proposal, John Ashton argued that the author of the Fourth Gospel was a convert from Essenism (although he has now modified his view considerably).[39] Rucksthul contended that the Fourth Evangelist may have been an Essene living in the Jerusalem cloister,[40] and, in the present collection, Brian Capper's essay seems to imagine that the Fourth Evangelist, or at least the elusive "Beloved Disciple," may have been an Essene who joined the Palestinian Jesus movement.

The apparent consensus that the Fourth Evangelist was in some way significantly influenced by Qumran or Essene thought was not supported by an earlier generation of scholars, who followed the lead of Rudolf Bultmann. Such experts tended to view early forms of Gnosticism, as evident in the Dialogue of the Savior and the Apocryphon of James, as the source of Johannine dualism.[41] Still today, the consensus view of the influence of Qumran on John is challenged by some scholars. David Aune, for example, is not impressed by the uniqueness of Qumran dualism and sees the Fourth Gospel within its Hellenistic period.[42] Richard Bauckham also rightly notes the influence of Genesis on the Fourth Evangelist's interest in light and darkness.[43] It is appropriate now to respond, in a brief way, to these ongoing challenges to the consensus. While I cannot go into detail here, the following points are significant.

First, specifically in response to those who argue that Johannine dualism is derived primarily from the Old Testament (particularly Genesis) rather than the Dead Sea Scrolls, five points should be noted.

---

movement.

39. Cf. Ashton's earlier proposal in *Understanding the Fourth Gospel*, 199–204, with his more recent remarks in "Second Thoughts on the Fourth Gospel" (in *What We Have Heard from the Beginning: The Past, Present, and Future of Johannine Studies* [ed. Tom Thatcher; Waco, Tex.: Baylor University Press, 2007]), 1–2.

40. Eugen Ruckstuhl, *Jesus im Horizont der Evangelien* (SBAB 3; Stuttgart: Katholisches Bibelwerk, 1988), 393–95.

41. The well-known works of Koester, Robinson, and others do not need to be rehearsed here. See the analysis and judgment of James D. G. Dunn, "John and the Synoptics as a Theological Question," in *Exploring the Gospel of John: In Honor of D. Moody Smith* (ed. R. Alan Culpepper and C. Clifton Black; Louisville: Westminster John Knox, 1996), 303.

42. David E. Aune, "Dualism in the Fourth Gospel and the Dead Sea Scrolls: A Reassessment of the Problem," in *Neotestamentica et Philonica: Studies in Honor of Peder Borgen* (ed. David E. Aune, Torrey Seland, and Jarl Henning Ulrichsen; NovTSup 106; Leiden: Brill, 2003), 281–303.

43. Richard Bauckham, "Qumran and the Fourth Gospel: Is There a Connection?" in *The Scrolls and the Scriptures: Qumran Fifty Years After* (ed. Stanley E. Porter and Craig A. Evans; JSPSup 26; Sheffield: Sheffield Academic Press, 1997), 267–79, esp. 278. See also Bauckham's "The Qumran Community and the Gospel of John," in *The Dead Sea Scrolls Fifty Years after Their Discovery, 1947–1997* (ed. Lawrence H. Schiffman, Emanuel Tov, and James C. VanderKam; Jerusalem: Israel Exploration Society and the Shrine of the Book, 2000), 105–15.

1. Genesis presents only a dualism of light versus darkness, which is the most common dualism in antiquity. As Sverre Aalen noted long ago, the juxtaposition of darkness and light is the most primordial experience of the human.[44]

2. The dualism in Genesis lacks what is so prominent in the Fourth Gospel and in texts composed at Qumran: Genesis contains neither a dualistic paradigm nor a set of *termini technici*.

3. The text of Genesis and its interpretation evolved over numerous centuries. Within Second Temple Judaism, the final development is reflected at Qumran in many compositions, including Commentary on Genesis (A through B). Such wisdom teaching clearly influenced the composition of the dualistic paradigm that reached its high-water mark in the Rule of the Community (cf. esp. 1QS 3.15; 11.11).

4. One should be aware of the insights derived from canonical criticism. One cannot assume that, because Genesis is in our canon, it was therefore better known to the Fourth Evangelist than the dualistic teaching in the Rule of the Community. The dualistic teaching in the Rule was most likely memorized by those who became members of the Yahad (or Essenes). These Jews took with them wherever they went all that had been memorized and the paradigm for answering the human's perennial questions, sharing it during heated discussions regarding theodicy, the origin of the human, and the reasons why good people do bad things and bad people do good things.

5. It is not helpful to point out how many differences there are between the Qumran Scrolls and the Fourth Gospel. From the outset, those who perceived major similarities between Qumran and John also emphasized the amazing creativity of the Fourth Evangelist. As I myself stated in the late 1960s, John's genius forced potentially parallel lines of thought to be diverted as light that passes through a prism. All that he inherited, including Genesis and Isaiah, was sifted through his Christological convictions and perception that the Father had sent his Son into the world to save it, and that all who believe in the Son, Jesus, will have eternal life. Jesus, therefore, not the Spirit of Truth, is the "light of the world."

Second, those who posit that Johannine dualism does not reflect direct contact with Qumran/Essene thought, but rather that the similarities simply reflect the fact that both strains emerged from the same broad Jewish milieu, fail to adequately consider the common set of *termini technici*. In comparing the Qumran scrolls with the Fourth Gospel, it is imperative to see not only the dualism but also the distinctive terms and paradigm that developed within the Qumran community. As noted earlier, all these technical terms appear together in one circumscribed section of the Rule (cols. 3–4), a section that was most likely memorized by all who wished to cross over into the "New Covenant." The new recruits

---

44. Sverre Aalen, *Die Begriffe Licht und Finsternis im Alten Testament, im Spätjudenteum und im Rabbinismus* (Oslo: J. Dybwad, 1951).

were introduced to *termini technici* which together form *a paradigm*. If the same terms and paradigm shape the Fourth Evangelist's dualism, then it seems that the most likely source would be direct influence from Qumranites or Essenes. Since we now know that the Fourth Gospel is deeply Jewish and influenced by pre-70 Judaism, the Evangelist most likely inherited these concepts and terms from other Jews. He did not have to see or read a scroll; this line of dualistic thinking was available where Essenes were living, and Philo and Josephus report that they lived virtually everywhere in Galilee and Judea. This being the case, it is conceivable that the Evangelist discussed dualistic theology with Essenes in Jerusalem before 70 C.E. Perhaps some Essenes eventually became members of the Johannine community or school.[45]

NEW AVENUES FOR POTENTIAL EXPLORATION

Building on the above survey of past and recent research, and reflecting the collection of essays in the present volume, I will now point to a number of emerging paths in the study of the relationship between John and Qumran. These include new perspectives on the Johannine view of election and predestination; unity within the community; shared exegetical concerns; Christology and eschatology; views of the temple and worship; the sociology of sectarianism; and the relevance of archaeology.

ELECTION AND PREDESTINATION

Armin Lange has contributed to our understanding of wisdom and predestination at Qumran.[46] The Qumranites are distinguished in Second Temple Judaism by the development of the concept of election and the creation of a new concept in the history of ideas: "double predestination."[47] The perception that the Qumranites created the concept of double predestination needs to influence our work on the Fourth Gospel. As Fitzmyer states, in the broader context of creation theology, what the Qumranites ascribed to God's knowledge "is predicated

45. See Charlesworth, "Dead Sea Scrolls and the Gospel according to John," 65–97; idem, "A Study in Shared Symbolism and Language: The Qumran Community and the Johannine Community," in *The Bible and the Dead Sea Scrolls: The Princeton Symposium on the Dead Sea Scrolls* (ed. James H. Charlesworth; 3 vols.; Waco, Tex.: Baylor University Press, 2006), 3.97–152.

46. Armin Lange, *Weisheit und Prädestination: Weisheitliche Urordnung und Prädestination in den Textfunden von Qumran* (STDJ 18; Leiden: Brill, 1995).

47. See esp. Megan Broshi, "Predestination in the Bible and the Dead Sea Scrolls," in *The Bible and the Dead Sea Scrolls: The Princeton Symposium on the Dead Sea Scrolls* (ed. James H. Charlesworth; 3 vols.; Waco, Tex.: Baylor University Press, 2006), 2.235–46.

by the Christian evangelist of 'the Word,' and the double formulation is not to be missed."[48]

The Fourth Evangelist stresses the dynamic element in believing and knowing, using the verbs πιστεύω ("to believe") and γινώσκω ("to know") more than any other Evangelist.[49] At the same time, as a maestro, he avoids the nouns πίστις ("faith") and γνῶσις ("knowledge"). He thus brings to the fore the verbal, active element in believing that entails some choice. He cannot then be one who believes in election or predestination. Yet he regularly uses terms that reflect election and predestinarianism: only those who are born of God, the children of God, have the power to believe in Jesus (John 1:12–13); "no one can come to me unless the Father who sent me draws him" (6:44). If the Fourth Evangelist mirrors double predestination, then we should not be blind to what may be reflected in that mirror.

UNITY

At Qumran, all members of the community held possessions in common, as we know from the stipulations in the Rule of the Community. Jews who joined the community turned their backs on all other Jews, labeling them "sons of darkness." They formed a bonded unity, coining a new terminology: the Yahad. As Hartmut Stegemann claimed, the Qumranites were "the major Jewish union" within Second Temple Judaism.[50] The Qumranites believed they were all elected sons of light. They all shared the only means of understanding Torah, God's will, since "all the mysteries of the words of his servants the prophets" had been revealed only to the Righteous Teacher (1QpHab 7). They explained why they had "separated" from all other Jews (4QMMT Some Works of the Torah). This emphasis on separation and adherence to communal unity is unique in Second Temple Judaism: it is not advocated by the authors of any book in the Bible, the Apocrypha, the Pseudepigrapha, or the Jewish Magical Papyri, and it is not directly recommended by Philo or Josephus.

---

48. Fitzmyer, "Qumran Literature," 121.

49. The verb "to believe" appears ninety-eight times in John, compared to eleven times in Matthew, fourteen times in Mark, nine times in Luke, thirty-seven times in Acts, and fifty-four times in the letters attributed to Paul. The verb "to know" appears fifty-six times in John, twenty times in Matthew, twelve times in Mark, twenty-eight times in Luke, sixteen times in Acts, and fifty times in the letters attributed to Paul. See Robert Morgenthaler, *Statistik des neutestamentlichen Wortschatezes* (Zürich: Gotthelf, 1982).

50. Hartmut Stegemann, *The Library of Qumran: On the Essenes, Qumran, John the Baptist, and Jesus* (Grand Rapids: Eerdmans, 1998), 140–53. See also Stegemann, *Die Essener, Qumran, Johannes der Täfer und Jesus: Ein Sachbuch* (Herder Spektrum; Freiburg: Herder, 1993), 227–31.

A similar thought, however, is articulated in the Fourth Gospel, and this notion largely defines the farewell address. In chapter 15, the Fourth Evangelist portrays Jesus exhorting his followers to remain attached and united to him; he uses the imagery of a vine and argues that the branches and fruit receive life only so long as they remain one with the vine, namely Jesus. In this chapter, we find an odd mixture of "hate" and "love" that is reminiscent of the opening chapters of the Rule of the Community. In chapter 16, the Evangelist urges believers not to fall away because of those who have insufficient knowledge. He then introduces the concept of the terms παράκλητος and "the Spirit of Truth." At this point, many scholars rightly hear an echo of the Qumran chorus.[51] The Qumranite knows that God created two cosmic spirits and set them for humanity's dynasty: "the Spirits of Truth and Deceit" (1QS 3.18–19). The use of the Παράκλητος and the Spirit of Truth in the Johannine community is reminiscent of the Qumran thought. The latter affirms that "the God of Israel and his Angel of Truth help all the Sons of Light" (1QS 3.24–25). Similarly, the Fourth Evangelist has Jesus state that "the Spirit of Truth" shall "guide you [the Sons of Light] into all the truth" (John 16:13). The Fourth Evangelist shifts the theology to stress the importance of believing. Here as always, any comparison of the Fourth Gospel with any form of ancient Judaism requires one to recognize the genius of the Fourth Evangelist and his creative stress on believing that Jesus has come from above and was sent into the world by the Father. Finally, in chapter 17 the Evangelist portrays Jesus calling upon God so "that they [the disciples] may be one." As the Father is in Jesus, and Jesus in the Father, those who believe in Jesus are to be one: "that they also may be in us, so that the world may believe that you have sent me" (John 17:21). Perhaps we need to contemplate the source of the traditions being reshaped in chapters 15 through 17. In them we find reflected some of the brilliance that enflamed the Qumranites.

Shared Exegetical Concerns

Eschewing any literary relationship between the Qumran corpus and the Fourth Gospel opens up vast areas for a deeper perception of how important scriptural texts, like Genesis and Isaiah, were being interpreted by ancient Jews. Considering why Jews chose the same scriptural texts for comment is enlightening and has proved significant for studying the More Psalms of David at Qumran, Habakkuk for the Qumranites and Paul, and Isaiah at Qumran and in the Fourth Gospel. Different exegetical methods present at Qumran inform our understand-

---

51. Otto Betz concluded that John's association of the Paraclete and the Spirit of Truth indicates Qumran influence on the Fourth Gospel; see his *Der Paraklet: Fürsprecher im häretischen Spätjudentum, im Johannes-Evangelium und in neu gefundenen gnostischen Schriften* (AGSU 2; Leiden: Brill, 1963), 36–116.

ing of the variegated text types (i.e., psalms, prophetic texts, wisdom material, etc.) and the different exegetical methods developed by the biblical authors in order to understand the scriptures. Similar means of interpreting Scripture, with the assistance of the Holy Spirit and through a hermeneutic of fulfillment, may raise issues of some influence from Essenes on the Johannine community or school without suggesting direct literary relationships between John and the scrolls.

In his article for the present volume (and elsewhere), George Brooke indicates one such avenue for appreciating "shared exegetical concerns" without being burdened by a model of literary dependence. He wisely points out that our understanding of the 153 fish caught by Peter and the eleven disciples (John 21:21) may be enriched by examining a passage in the Commentary on Genesis A(4Q252): "And the waters prevailed upon the earth [for] one hundred and fifty day[s],until the fourteenth day of the seventh month on the third [day] of the week." Brooke observes that "although the number 153 does not occur in the text of 4Q252, it is clear that the ark comes to rest on Mount Ararat on the 153rd day after the start of the flood, on the seventeenth of the seventh month."[52] Brooke's insight strengthens the argument of scholars who have assumed that the number 153 must have had a symbolic or allegorical significance. The meaning of the number 153 takes on even deeper meaning when we observe that the Commentary on Genesis A links the number 153 with the Feast of Sukkoth, that this festival included a water libation (*t. Sukkoth* 3.3–8), and that the Fourth Evangelist mentions "rivers of living water" within a narrative that has a focus on Sukkoth (John 7–8). The study of numerology in the Fourth Gospel leads us not to the Pythagoreans but perhaps in some ways to Judaism, especially the Essenes.

CHRISTOLOGY AND ESCHATOLOGY

Recognizing that the background of the Fourth Gospel is the world of early Judaism indicates a need to reexplore the origin of titles and terms used by the Fourth Evangelist. The growing recognition that the Parables of Enoch are not only Jewish but probably anterior to the Fourth Gospel indicates that a reexamination of the concept of "the Son of Man" seems appropriate.[53] The Fourth Evangelist has Jesus declare that he is "the Son of Man" (John 9). What traditions shaped this declaration? The Fourth Evangelist also portrays Jesus confessing that he is "the Son of God" (Jn 10:36). This term is very important in Early Judaism,

---

52. See George J. Brooke, *The Dead Sea Scrolls and the New Testament: Essays in Mutual Illumination* (Minneapolis: Fortress, 2005), 286.

53. James H. Charlesworth, "Can We Discern the Composition Date of the Parables of Enoch?" in *Enoch and the Messiah Son of Man: Revisiting the Book of Parables* (ed. Gabriele Boccaccini; Grand Rapids: Eerdmans, 2007), 450–68.

developing out of an exegesis of Ps 2 and exploding with eschatological richness in An Aramaic Apocalypse (4Q246).[54] Further research into the scrolls could significantly enhance our understanding of the Johannine terminology.

H.-W. Kuhn disclosed that "eschatology" at Qumran, if that is the proper terminology for Semitic thought, is not only futuristic but being realized in the community.[55] The same is certainly true of the Fourth Gospel and, since in both Qumran and the Fourth Gospel "living water" is both salvific and eschatological, then we need to explore how and in what ways it is best to explain this shared emphasis.

TEMPLE AND WORSHIP

The Fourth Evangelist portrays Jesus saying to the Samaritan woman, "Believe me, woman, the hour is coming when neither on this mountain nor in Jerusalem will you worship the Father" (John 4:21). This is a complex claim; the rejection of worship in Jerusalem is startling and reminiscent of Samaritan and Qumran traditions. Jesus' comment about worship in Jerusalem is unique to this chapter in John. Earlier, Jesus refers to the temple as "my Father's house" (2:16). What are the traditions that have shaped John 4:21?

In 1960, Aileen Guilding indicated that the Fourth Evangelist may have known some Jewish lectionary readings focused on Hanukkah.[56] Brooke now contends that 4Q246 apparently confirms VanderKam's argument that the historical origins of Hanukkah, and the claim of Antiochus IV to be "god," created debates within Judaism that provide the historical background to the debate over blasphemy in John 10.[57] This insight helps curb Qumran fever, since the celebration of Hanukkah, if it became a celebration of the Hasmonean dynasty, would not have been appreciated by Essenes, who hated the Hasmoneans.

The Qumran texts help us comprehend that some Jews in the Johannine community may have imagined Jesus as the Nazarene who will build the new temple. As indicated by at least one extant Qumran scroll (4Q161), the צמח, the "Branch" (see Zech 6:12), is also the נצר, the Davidic Branch (the root behind the one from "Nazareth"; cf. Isa 11:1). There should be no doubt that צמח and

54. See Charlesworth, "Dead Sea Scrolls and the Gospel," 72–73.

55. Heinz-Wolfgang Kuhn, *Enderwartung und gegenwärtiges Heil: Untersuchungen zu den Gemeindeliedern von Qumran, mit einen Anhang über Eschatologie und Gegenwart in der Verkündigung Jesus* (SUNT 4; Göttingen: Vandenhoeck & Ruprecht, 1966).

56. Aileen Guilding, *The Fourth Gospel and Jewish Worship: A Study of the Relation of St. John's Gospel to the Ancient Jewish Lectionary System* (Oxford: Clarendon, 1960).

57. James C. VanderKam, "John 10 and the Feast of Dedication," in *Of Scribes and Scrolls: Studies on the Hebrew Bible, Intertestamental Judaism, and Christian Origins Presented to John Strugnell on the Occasion of his Sixtieth Birthday* (ed. Harold W. Attridge, John J. Collins, and Thomas H. Tobin; CTSRR 5; Lanham, Md.: University Press of America, 1990), 203–14.

נצר obtained messianic overtones by the early first century C.E. Since the Fourth Evangelist is the only Evangelist who labels what is written on the cross "a title" (*titlov*), then perhaps one should explore the possibility of echoes from Qumran on the Evangelist's Christology. Did some Johannine Jews think that the title declared that "Jesus, the Nazarene" is "the King of the Jews"?[58] It is obvious that, at Qumran, the temple was considered defiled and that the Holy Spirit had left the temple and resided at Qumran, the Holy House in which "the Holy Ones" and "the Most Holy of Holy Ones" lived with the angels. By what methods may we more accurately discern echoes of Qumran temple theology in the Johannine narrative?

SOCIOLOGY OF SECTARIANISM

The study of temple symbolism in the Fourth Gospel has led Kåre Fugsleth to explore Johannine sectarianism.[59] Both the Qumranites and the Johannine Jews represent sectarian sociological phenomena.[60] Each is recognized as distinct by a larger group and indeed persecuted by that establishment. The presence and abuse of power is often the cause of sectarianism,[61] and such sociological reasoning helps explain the sectarian nature of Qumran and the Johannine communities. We need to be very cautious, however, in postulating any influence from Qumran on John at this point; here we may be observing two independent reactions to a similar sociological crisis. As Painter has stated, "The Johannine community was born in a bitter schism. Before long that community was itself rent by a schism."[62] John Ashton's essay in the present volume urges us to recognize that both the Jewish sectarians at Qumran and the Johannine community "were apocalyptic both in the sense in which earlier scholars understood that

---

58. I am indebted here to the reflections of Mary L. Coloe, "Household of Faith (Jn 4:46–54; 11:1–44): A Metaphor for the Johannine Community," *Pacifica* 12 (2000): 326–33, and "Sources in the Shadows: John 13 and the Johannine Community," in *New Currents through John: A Global Perspective* (ed. Francisco Lozada Jr. and Tom Thatcher; SBLRBS; Atlanta: Society of Biblical Literature, 2006), esp. 70–71.

59. Kåre S. Fugsleth, *Johannine Sectarianism in Perspective: A Sociological, Historical, and Comparative Analysis of Temple and Social Relationships in the Gospel of John, Philo, and Qumran* (NovTSup 119; Leiden: Brill, 2005).

60. On Qumran and the Essenes, see Anthony J. Saldarini, "Sectarianism," in *Encyclopedia of the Dead Sea Scrolls* (ed. Lawrence H. Schiffman and James C. VanderKam; 2 vols.; New York: Oxford University Press, 2000), 2.853–56. On the Fourth Gospel, see Gail R. O'Day, "Johannine Theology as Sectarian Theology," in *What Is John?* Vol. I: *Readers and Readings of the Fourth Gospel* (ed. Fernando F. Segovia; SBLSymS 3; Atlanta: Scholars Press, 1996), 199–203.

61. See Hillel Newman, *Proximity to Power and Jewish Sectarian Groups of the Ancient Period: A Review of Lifestyle, Values, and Halakhah in the Pharisees, Sadducees, Essenes, and Qumran* (BRLJ 25; Leiden: Brill, 2006).

62. Painter, *Quest*, 31.

term and in the more specific sense of living lives shaped by a revealed mystery." This insight adds to our sociological investigations and is an area for fruitful discussion.

The Qumranites clarify that they have separated from the Jerusalem priesthood (Some Works of the Torah). The author of 1 John explains the schism that has split his community, insisting that those who left them were never part of them (2:19). The appearances of the term *aposynagōgos* in the Fourth Gospel mirror a social setting not only of polemics but also of sectarianism. We probably will never be able to prove to what degree the social setting of the Fourth Gospel derives from the Palestinian Jesus movement, from influences from Essenism, or from the tension among Jews after 70 C.E., but the parallels with Qumran should not be overlooked. The ingenious reflections by Brian Capper, both in the present volume and elsewhere, provide an important exploration of how and in what ways the concept of *sect* helps us grasp the interrelatedness and uniqueness of the Qumranites, the Essenes, and the Johannine Christians.[63]

I end this section with a caveat about the special problems associated with a sociological study of ancient texts and their putative social settings. Timothy Ling argues that a social analysis of the Fourth Gospel indicates that what has been called "Johannine sectarianism" should be relabeled a "religious order."[64] In the present book, Capper supports this nomenclature. Perhaps "religious orders" were represented in the world of early Judaism and the ascetic practices advocated by Palestinian Jews, including the Qumranites and Essenes. We should first be clear what defines a *sect* and distinguishes it from a *religious order*, and how that precision helps us to obtain a better perception of the social world of Qumran and the Fourth Evangelist.

ARCHAEOLOGY

The contributors to *Jesus and Archaeology* (2006) found that the Fourth Gospel preserves a remarkable number of architectural descriptions and topographical details that are lacking in the other canonical Gospels. Only the Fourth Evangelist mentions *gabbatha* and *lithostrōtos* (the large stones that would be typical of a palace) in connection with the Praetorium in which Pilate would have lived, which would be either the Hasmonean Palace in southern Jerusalem or more likely Herod's Palace near the Citadel (John 19:13). As the archaeolo-

---

63. Brian J. Capper, "Essene Community Houses and Jesus' Early Community," in *Jesus and Archaeology* (ed. James H. Charlesworth; Grand Rapids: Eerdmans, 2006), 472–502; also idem, "The New Covenant in Southern Palestine at the Arrest of Jesus," in *The Dead Sea Scrolls as Background to Postbiblical Judaism and Early Christianity* (ed. James R. Davila; STDJ 46; Leiden: Brill, 2003), 90–116.

64. Timothy J. M. Ling, *The Judaean Poor and the Fourth Gospel* (SNTSMS 136; Cambridge: Cambridge University Press, 2006).

gist who seems to know first-century Jerusalem best, Dan Bahat, states, "Only in John 19:13 is there . . . a detailed description . . . of the site (the Praetorium)."[65] Similarly, only the Fourth Evangelist notes the two five-porticoed pools of Bethzatha (Bethesda), which seem to have been healing pools in view of the fact that devotion to Asclepius (the god of healing) seems evident from archaeological discoveries, especially the Bethzatha Vase. And only this Evangelist mentions the Herodian Pool of Siloam, which was most likely the largest *mikveh* in pre-70 Jerusalem. These monumental pools were not created by John's theological needs; they have been unearthed just north and south of the temple area, respectively— precisely where the Fourth Evangelist locates them. Urban von Wahlde rightly reports that these references in the Fourth Gospel "are not symbolic creations, as was once thought, but are accurate and detailed references that reveal aspects of Jesus' ministry not otherwise known."[66] Few scholars would need to be reminded that the most sensational archaeological discovery, the Dead Sea Scrolls, enriched our perception of the landscape and context in and behind the Fourth Gospel.

QUMRAN AND THE JOHANNINE NARRATIVE

In view of the many potential avenues of inquiry into John and Qumran, a somewhat surprising reality seems to call for explanation. From the 1950s to the 1990s, scholars habitually appealed to the Dead Sea Scrolls and related Jewish texts to explain the origin of, and the theology found in, the Fourth Gospel. Yet, as Eileen Schuller points out in her introduction to the present volume, a review of recent research will quickly reveal that this emphasis has somewhat waned in recent years, most notably in North American Johannine scholarship. Why is this? While there is no easy answer to this question, I will intimate an explanation as we anticipate the next decade of scrolls research. Three causes seem to me primary.

First, the shift in interest is partly due to a lack of confidence in historical-critical methodologies for providing an accurate approach to biblical interpretation.[67] The shift in Johannine research can be largely traced to Alan

---

65. Dan Bahat with Chaim T. Rubinstein, *The Illustrated Atlas of Jerusalem* (trans. Shlomo Ketko; Jerusalem: Carta, 1990), 56. Bahat proceeds to emphasize that even the Fourth Evangelist provides us with a description that "is not sufficiently specific."

66. Urban C. von Wahlde, "The Road Ahead—Three Aspects of Johannine Scholarship," in *What We Have Heard from the Beginning: The Past, Present, and Future of Johannine Studies* (ed. Tom Thatcher; Waco, Tex.: Baylor University Press, 2007), 351.

67. See, e.g., the reflections by Sandra M. Schneiders, "Remaining in His Word: From Faith to Faith by Way of the Text," in *What We Have Heard from the Beginning: The Past, Present, and Future of Johannine Studies* (ed. Tom Thatcher; Waco, Tex.: Baylor University Press, 2007), 267–68.

Culpepper's magisterial *Anatomy of the Fourth Gospel*, which appeared in 1983.[68] Culpepper's study of literary theory, narrative texture, and rhetorical techniques in the Fourth Gospel was preceded by earlier studies of the rhetoric of the text. Since Culpepper's book, other Johannine experts have deepened our understanding of the Fourth Evangelist's use of such literary devices as irony and revelation. For purposes of the present discussion, however, it should be noted that Culpepper himself did not call for a focus solely on literary techniques in the Gospel. He continued to recognize the importance of the historical context of the narrative and the stimulus to research provided by research on the Dead Sea Scrolls. Culpepper's continuing interest in history and the background of the Fourth Gospel is evident in his recent claim that "the theory of a Johannine school still seems to me to be the best explanation for the origin of the Johannine writings," and his insistence that his "aim was never to replace historical criticism."[69] As Martinus de Boer states, "[H]istorical and literary approaches need not be mutually exclusive."[70] Indeed, the Qumran scrolls have helped in improving our comprehension not only of the historical context of the Fourth Gospel but also its literary complexities and brilliance.[71] Ultimately, while narrative criticism has proved helpful and at times exciting, one must keep in mind that the Fourth Evangelist did not write a drama; he composed a Gospel—a story that points back to the eternal significance of a Galilean Jew who was crucified publicly, but in a triumphant way.[72]

Second, a shift away from a preoccupation with the historical context of the Fourth Gospel may be the by-product of a different way of training young scholars. Before 1980, students interested in mastering the Gospel of John were urged to study numerous ancient languages—Greek, perhaps Coptic, and at least Hebrew and Aramaic. A shift has occurred: many students now attempt to master only Greek. If students find Semitic languages daunting, they will shy away from

---

68. R. Alan Culpepper, *Anatomy of the Fourth Gospel: A Study in Literary Design* (Philadelphia: Fortress, 1983).

69. R. Alan Culpepper, "Pursuing the Elusive," in Thatcher, *What We Have Heard from the Beginning*, first quote 111, second quote 113.

70. Martinus C. De Boer, "Narrative Criticism, Historical Criticism, and the Gospel of John," in *The Johannine Writings* (ed. Stanley E. Porter and Craig A. Evans; BibSem 32; Sheffield: Sheffield Academic Press, 1995), 106.

71. See esp. Aage Pilgaard, "The Qumran Scrolls and John's Gospel," in *New Readings in John: Literary and Theological Perspectives. Essays from the Scandinavian Conference on the Fourth Gospel (Århus 1997)* (ed. Johannes Nissen and Sigfred Pedersen; JSNTSup 182; Sheffield: Sheffield Academic Press, 1999), 126–42.

72. See esp. C. Clifton Black, "'The Words That You Gave to Me I Have Given to Them': The Grandeur of Johannine Rhetoric," in *Exploring the Gospel of John: In Honor of D. Moody Smith* (ed. R. Alan Culpepper and C. Clifton Black; Louisville, Ky.: Westminster John Knox, 1996), 220–39.

Qumranology and tend to despair of gaining expertise in research on this fore-boding collection of more than nine hundred manuscripts.

Third, and perhaps the most important reason for a decline in the study of Second Temple Judaism by students of the Fourth Gospel, are the overwhelming demands now made of the serious student interested in historical context. The vast amount of data to master causes a tsunami effect that makes it difficult to focus. In the early seventies, in teaching a course at Duke University's graduate school, I introduced students to seventeen Old Testament Pseudepigrapha and seven Dead Sea Scrolls. Now we must include at least sixty-five documents in the Pseudepigrapha and more than 940 Qumran scrolls—the latter number not including the ancient scrolls found in other caves. If biblical studies departments are divided between Old and New Testaments because sixty-six writings cannot be adequately mastered, how much more difficult is it to master more than 940 scrolls? Moreover, these texts are preserved, and sometimes misidentified, within more than two hundred thousand fragments that are difficult to read and in unfamiliar handwriting.

Against the trends noted above, the essays in this book herald a critical reevaluation of Qumran studies for the Fourth Gospel. It follows on a trend that Tom Thatcher rightly heralds, "the current revival of interest in the setting and historical value of the Fourth Gospel."[73] This trend may have begun just before 1990, when Martin Hengel rightly reported that "the Qumran discoveries are a landmark for a new assessment of the situation of the Fourth Gospel in the history of religion."[74]

SUMMARY

From 1954, when L. Mowry emphasized the importance of the Dead Sea Scrolls for an understanding of the Fourth Gospel,[75] until the present, many scholars have seen the various ways that the Fourth Evangelist may have been influenced by concepts, terms, and symbols that are apparently unique to the Qumranites. While some scholars judge that the relation is unimpressive, most experts have perceived the Qumran influences to be somewhat revolutionary for research on the Fourth Gospel. The influence has been judged to be indirect or direct (terms that can be misleading if not adequately defined), and some have even suggested that the Fourth Evangelist may have been an Essene. While the discussions of the relations between Qumran and John have tended to focus on dualism, there

---

73. Tom Thatcher, "The Fourth Gospel in First-Century Media Culture," in Thatcher, *What We Have Heard from the Beginning*, 159.

74. Hengel, *Johannine Question*, 111.

75. Lucetta Mowrey, "The Dead Sea Scrolls and the Background for the Gospel of John," *BA* 17 (1954): 78–97.

is much more to include as we seek to discern how and in what ways, if at all, unique Qumran thoughts and symbols have shaped the mind and writing of the Fourth Evangelist. Generally speaking, Painter rightly assesses that "the importance of the Qumran texts [for understanding the Fourth Gospel] is difficult to exaggerate."[76] If there are indeed Qumran influences on the Fourth Evangelist or the Fourth Gospel, then how significant are they, how modified were they by the Evangelist's creativity, and how were such influences transmitted from Essene circles to the Johannine community? As in most biblical research, sometimes the best answers appear in a polished question.

It is clearly unwise to imply that the Qumran scrolls present us with something like a preparation for "the Gospel" (a *praeparatio evangelium*).[77] These scrolls introduce us to a complex world. Before we can imagine the origins of the Palestinian Jesus movement, let alone a construct such as "Christianity," we must immerse ourselves in the world of Second Temple Judaism.[78] Then we will become sensitive to the problems in reconstructing texts, exploring their origins, and discerning the intentions of their authors. In the process, many will discern how and in what ways the Qumran scrolls have revolutionized our understanding of Second Temple Judaism and the emergence of the Palestinian Jesus movement.

76. Painter, *Quest*, 35.

77. See the judicious reflections by Casey D. Elledge, *The Bible and the Dead Sea Scrolls* (SBLABS 14; Atlanta: Society of Biblical Literature, 2005), esp. 115–20.

78. See Andre Paul, *Les manuscrits de la Mer Morte* (Paris: Bayard, 1997), 291–96.

BIBLIOGRAPHY

"100,000 Protestors Flood Streets of Rangoon in 'Saffron Revolution.'" No pages. Cited 24 September 2007. Online: http://www.novinite.com/view_news.php?id=85644.

Aalen, Sverre. *Die Begriffe Licht und Finsternis im Alten Testament, im Spätjudenteum und im Rabbinismus*. Oslo: Dybwad, 1951.

Abegg, Martin G., Jr. "Who Ascended to Heaven? 4Q491, 4Q427, and the Teacher of Righteousness." Pages 61–73 in *Eschatology, Messianism, and the Dead Sea Scrolls*. Edited by Craig A. Evans and Peter W. Flint. Grand Rapids: Eerdmans, 1997.

Abegg, Martin G., Jr., et al., eds. *The Dead Sea Scrolls Concordance: The Non-biblical Texts from Qumran*. Leiden: Brill, 2003.

Albright, William F. "Recent Discoveries in Palestine and the Gospel of St. John." Pages 153–71 in *The Background of the New Testament and Its Eschatology*. Edited by W. D. Davies and David Daube. Cambridge: Cambridge University Press, 1956.

Alexander, Philip S. "The Demonology of the Dead Sea Scrolls." Pages 331–53 in volume 2 of *The Dead Sea Scrolls after Fifty Years: A Comprehensive Assessment*. Edited by Peter W. Flint and James C. VanderKam. 2 vols. Leiden: Brill, 1999.

———. "Physiognomy, Initiation, and Rank in the Qumran Community." In *Geschichte–Tradition–Reflexion: Festschrift für Martin Hengel zum 70. Geburtstag*. Edited by Hubert Cancik, Hermann Lichtenberger, and Peter Schäfer. 3 vols. Tübingen: J. C. B. Mohr, 1996.

———. "The Redaction-History of Serekh ha-Yahad: A Proposal." *RevQ* 17 (1996): 437–56.

Alexander, Philip S., and Geza Vermes. *Qumran Cave 4 XIX: Serekh ha-Yahad and Two Related Texts*. DJD 26. Oxford: Clarendon, 1998.

Allegro, John. *The Dead Sea Scrolls and the Christian Myth*. 2d ed. Amherst, N.Y.: Prometheus Books, 1992.

———. *The Sacred Mushroom and the Cross: A Study of the Nature and Origins of Christianity within the Fertility Cults of the Ancient Near East*. Garden City, N.Y.: Doubleday, 1970.

Allison, Dale C. *Scriptural Allusions in the New Testament: Light from the Dead Sea Scrolls*. DSSCOL 5. North Richland Hills, Tex.: Bibal, 2000.

Alon, Gedalia. *Jews, Judaism, and the Classical World: Studies in Jewish History in the Times of the Second Temple and Talmud*. Jerusalem: Magnes, 1977.

Anderson, Paul N. "Beyond the Shade of the Oak Tree: The Recent Growth of Johannine Studies." *ExpTim* 119 (2008): 365–73.

———. *The Christology of the Fourth Gospel: Its Unity and Disunity in the Light of John 6*. WUNT 2.78. Tübingen: Mohr Siebeck, 1996.

———. *The Fourth Gospel and the Quest for Jesus: Modern Foundations Reconsidered*. LNTS. London: T&T Clark, 2006.

──────. "The Having-Sent-Me Father—Aspects of Agency, Irony, and Encounter in the Johannine Father-Son Relationship." Pages 33–57 in *God the Father in the Gospel of John*. Edited by Adele Reinhartz. *Semeia* 85. Atlanta: Society of Biblical Literature, 1999.

──────. "The *Sitz im Leben* of the Johannine Bread of Life Discourse and its Evolving Context." Pages 1–59 in *Critical Readings of John 6*. Edited by R. Alan Culpepper. BIS. Atlanta: Society of Biblical Literature, 2006.

Ansberry, Clare. "Sister Rosemarie Wants You." *The Wall Street Journal* 246, no. 132 (December 17–18, 2005), A1, A6.

Arnold, Russell C. D. *The Social Role of Liturgy in the Religion of the Qumran Community.* STDJ 60. Leiden: Brill, 2006.

Ashton, John. "Second Thoughts on the Fourth Gospel." Pages 1–18 in *What We Have Heard from the Beginning: The Past, Present, and Future of Johannine Studies.* Edited by Tom Thatcher. Waco, Tex.: Baylor University Press, 2007.

──────. *Studying John: Approaches to the Fourth Gospel.* Oxford: Clarendon, 1994.

──────. "The Transformation of Wisdom: A Study of the Prologue of John's Gospel." *NTS* 32 (1986): 161–86.

──────. *Understanding the Fourth Gospel.* Oxford: Clarendon, 1991.

Asiedu-Peprah, Martin. *Johannine Sabbath Conflicts as Juridical Controversy.* WUNT 2.132. Tübingen: Mohr Siebeck, 2001.

Aune, David E. *The Cultic Setting of Realized Eschatology in Early Christianity.* NovTSup 28. Leiden: Brill, 1972.

──────. "Dualism in the Fourth Gospel and the Dead Sea Scrolls: A Reassessment of the Problem." Pages 281–303 in *Neotestamentica et Philonica: Studies in Honor of Peder Borgen.* Edited by David E. Aune, Torrey Seland, and Jarl Henning Ulrichsen. NovTSup 106. Leiden: Brill, 2003.

Bahat, Dan, and Chaim T. Rubinstein. *The Illustrated Atlas of Jerusalem.* Translated by Shlomo Ketko. Jerusalem: Carta, 1990.

Baillet, M., J. T. Milik, and Roland de Vaux, eds. *Les 'petites grottes' de Qumrân: Exploration de la Falaise; les grottes 2Q, 3Q, 5Q, 6Q, 7Q and 10Q; le rouleau de cuivre.* 2 vols. DJD 3. Oxford: Clarendon, 1962.

Bailey, John Amedee. *The Traditions Common to the Gospels of Luke and John.* NovTSup 7. Leiden: Brill, 1963.

Bammel, Ernst. "Sadduzäer und Sadokiden." *ETL* 55 (1979): 107–15.

Barrett, C. K. *The Gospel according to St. John: An Introduction with Comments and Notes on the Greek Text.* 2d ed. Philadelphia: Westminster, 1978.

──────. *The Gospel of John and Judaism.* Translated by D. Moody Smith. Philadelphia: Fortress, 1975.

Barthélemy, D., and J. T. Milik. *Qumran Cave 1.* DJD 1. Oxford: Clarendon, 1955.

Bauckham, Richard. "The Holiness of Jesus and His Disciples in the Gospel of John." Pages 98–105 in *Holiness and Ecclesiology in the New Testament.* Edited by Kent E. Brower and Andy Johnson. Grand Rapids: Eerdmans, 2007.

──────. "Qumran and the Fourth Gospel: Is There a Connection?" Pages 267–79 in *The Scrolls and the Scriptures: Qumran Fifty Years After.* Edited by Stanley E. Porter and Craig A. Evans. JSPSup 26. Sheffield: Sheffield Academic Press, 1997.

──────. "The Qumran Community and the Gospel of John." Pages 105–15 in *The Dead Sea Scrolls Fifty Years after Their Discovery, 1947–1997.* Edited by Lawrence H. Schiffman, Emanuel Tov, and James C. VanderKam. Jerusalem: Israel Exploration Society and the Shrine of the Book, 2000.

Baumach, Gunther. *Qumran und das Johannes-Evangelium.* AVTRW 6. Berlin: Evangelische Verlagsanstalt, 1957.

Baumgarten, Albert I. "The Rule of the Martian as Applied to Qumran." *IOS* 14 (1994): 121–42.

Baumgarten, Joseph M. "The Calendars of the Book of Jubilees and the Temple Scroll." *VT* 37 (1987): 71–78.

———. "Does *TLH* in the Temple Scroll Refer to Crucifixion?" *JBL* 91 (1972): 472–81.

———. "Hanging and Treason in Qumran and Roman Law." *ErIsr* 16 (1982): 7–16.

———. "The Purification Rituals in DJD 7." Pages 199–209 in *The Dead Sea Scrolls: Forty Years of Research.* Edited by Devorah Dimant and Uriel Rappaport. STDJ 10. Leiden: Brill, 1992.

———, ed. *Qumran Cave 4 XXV: Halakhic Texts.* DJD 35. Oxford: Clarendon, 1999.

———. "The Qumran/Essene Restraints on Marriage." Pages 13–24 in *Archaeology and History in the Dead Sea Scrolls: The New York University Conference in Memory of Yigael Yadin.* Edited by Lawrence H. Schiffman. JSPSup 8. Sheffield: JSOT Press, 1990.

———. *Studies in Qumran Law.* SJLA 24. Leiden: Brill, 1977.

Bearman, Gregory H., Stephen J. Pfann, and Sheila I. Spiro. "Imaging the Scrolls: Photographics and Direct Digital Acquisition." Pages 472–95 in volume 1 of *The Dead Sea Scrolls after Fifty Years: A Comprehensive Assessment.* Edited by Peter W. Flint and James C. VanderKam. 2 vols. Leiden: Brill, 1998.

Becker, Jürgen. *Das Evangelium nach Johannes.* 3d ed. 2 vols. Gütersloh: Gerd Mohn, 1991.

Bengtsson, Håkan. "Three Sobriquets, Their Meaning and Function: The Wicked Priest, Synagogue of Satan, and the Woman Jezebel." Pages 183–208 in volume 1 of *The Bible and the Dead Sea Scrolls: The Princeton Symposium on the Dead Sea Scrolls.* Edited by James H. Charlesworth. 3 vols. Waco, Tex.: Baylor University Press, 2006.

Betz, Hans-Dieter. *Galatians: A Commentary on Paul's Letter to the Churches in Galatia.* Hermeneia. Philadelphia: Fortress, 1979.

Betz, Otto. *Der Paraklet: Fürsprecher im häretischen Spätjudentum, im Johannes- Evangelium und in neu gefundenen gnostischen Schriften.* AGSU 2. Leiden: Brill, 1963.

———. "Die Proselytentaufe der Qumransekte unde die Taufe im Neuen Testament." *RevQ* 1 (1958): 213–34.

———. "Was John the Baptist an Essene?" Pages 205–14 in *Understanding the Dead Sea Scrolls: A Reader from the Biblical Archaeology Review.* Edited by Hershel Shanks. New York: Random House, 1992.

Beutler, Johannes. "In Search of a New Synthesis." Pages 23–34 in *What We Have Heard from the Beginning: The Past, Present, and Future of Johannine Studies.* Edited by Tom Thatcher. Waco, Tex.: Baylor University Press, 2007.

Beyer, Klaus. *Die aramäischen Texte vom Toten Meer.* Göttingen: Vandenhoeck & Ruprecht, 1984.

———. *Die aramäischen Texte vom Toten Meer. Ergänzungsband.* Rev. ed. Göttingen: Vandenhoeck & Ruprecht, 1994.

Black, C. Clifton. "'The Words That You Gave to Me I Have Given to Them': The Grandeur of Johannine Rhetoric." Pages 220–39 in *Exploring the Gospel of John: In Honor of D. Moody Smith.* Edited by R. Alan Culpepper and C. Clifton Black. Louisville: Westminster John Knox, 1996.

Boccaccini, Gabrielle. *Beyond the Essene Hypothesis: The Parting of the Ways between Qumran and Enochic Judaism*. Grand Rapids: Eerdmans, 1998.

Böcher, Otto. "Johannes der Täufer." *TRE* 17 (1988): 172–81.

Boismard, Marie-Émile. "Qumrán y los Escritos de S. Juan." *CB* 12 (1955): 250–64.

———. "Saint Luc et la redaction du quatrième évangile (Jn iv, 46–54)." *RB* 69 (1962): 185–211.

Boismard, Marie-Émile, Arnaud Lamouille, and Gérard Rochais. *L'Evangile de Jean: Commentaire*. Paris: Editions du Cerf, 1977.

Borgen, Peder. "Observations on the Midrashic Character of John 6." *ZNW* 54 (1963): 232–40.

Bornkamm, Günther. "Towards the Interpretation of John's Gospel." Pages 79–98 in *The Interpretation of John*. Edited by John Ashton. IRT 9. Philadelphia: Fortress, 1986.

Bowley, James E. "Moses in the Dead Sea Scrolls: Living in the Shadow of God's Anointed." Pages 159–81 in *The Bible at Qumran: Text, Shape, and Interpretation*. Edited by Peter W. Flint. Grand Rapids: Eerdmans, 2001.

Braun, F.-M. "L'arrière-fond judaïque du Quartième Évangile et la Communauté de l'Alliance." *RB* 62 (1955): 5–44.

Braun, Herbert. *Qumran und das Neue Testament*. 2 vols. Tübingen: Mohr Siebeck, 1966.

Brooke, George J. "252. 4QCommentary on Genesis A." Pages 185–207 in *Qumran Cave 4.XVII: Parabiblical Texts, Part Three*. Edited by James C. VanderKam. DJD 22. Oxford: Clarendon, 1996.

———. "4Q252 and the 153 Fish of John 21:11." Pages 253–65 in *Antikes Judentum und Frühes Christentum: Festschrift für Hartmut Stegemann zum 65. Geburtstag*. Edited by Bernd Kollmann, Wolfgang Reinbold, and Annette Steudel. BZNW 97. Berlin: de Gruyter, 1999.

———. "Biblical Interpretation at Qumran." Pages 287–319 in volume 1 of *The Bible and the Dead Sea Scrolls: The Princeton Symposium on the Dead Sea Scrolls*. Edited by James H. Charlesworth. 3 vols. Waco, Tex.: Baylor University Press, 2006.

———. *The Dead Sea Scrolls and the New Testament: Essays in Mutual Illumination*. Minneapolis: Fortress, 2005.

———. "The Messiah of Aaron in the Damascus Document." *RevQ* 15 (1991): 215–30.

———. "The Scrolls and the Study of New Testament." Pages 61–76 in *The Dead Sea Scrolls at Fifty: Proceedings of the 1997 Society of Biblical Literature Qumran Section Meetings*. Edited by Robert A. Kugler and Eileen M. Schuller. SBLEJL 15. Atlanta: Society of Biblical Literature, 1999.

———. "The *Temple Scroll* in the New Testament." Pages 97–114 in *The Dead Sea Scrolls and the New Testament: Essays in Mutual Illumination*. Minneapolis: Fortress, 2005.

Broshi, Megan. "Predestination in the Bible and the Dead Sea Scrolls." Pages 235–46 in volume 2 of *The Bible and the Dead Sea Scrolls: The Princeton Symposium on the Dead Sea Scrolls*. Edited by James H. Charlesworth. 3 vols. Waco, Tex.: Baylor University Press, 2006.

Brown, Raymond E. *The Community of the Beloved Disciple: The Life, Loves, and Hates of an Individual Church in New Testament Times*. New York: Paulist Press, 1979.

———. *The Gospel according to John*. 2 vols. AB. Garden City, N.Y.: Doubleday, 1966, 1970.

———. *An Introduction to the Gospel of John*. Edited by Francis J. Moloney. ABRL. New York: Doubleday, 2003.

———. "John, Gospel, and Letters of." Pages 414–17 in volume 1 of *Encyclopedia of the*

Dead Sea Scrolls. Edited by Lawrence H. Schiffman and James C. VanderKam. 2 vols. New York: Oxford University Press, 2000.

———. "The Messianism of Qumran." *CBQ* 19 (1957): 53–82.

———. "The Qumran Scrolls and the Johannine Gospel and Epistles." *CBQ* 17 (1955): 403–19, 559–74. Repr. in Raymond Brown, *New Testament Essays* (Garden City, N.Y.: Doubleday, 1968), and *The Scrolls and the New Testament*, ed. Krister Stendahl and James H. Charlesworth (New York: Crossroad, 1992).

Brown, Tricia Gates. *Spirit in the Writings of John: Johannine Pneumatology in Social- Scientific Perspective.* JSNTSup 253. London: T&T Clark, 2003.

Brownlee, William H. "John the Baptist in the New Light of Ancient Scrolls." Pages 33–53 in *The Scrolls and the New Testament.* Edited by Krister Stendahl and James H. Charlesworth. New York: Crossroad, 1992.

———. "Whence the Gospel according to John?" Pages 166–94 in *John and the Dead Sea Scrolls.* Edited by James H. Charlesworth. New York: Crossroad, 1990.

Bruce, F. F. *The Gospel of John.* Grand Rapids: Eerdmans, 1994.

———. "Qumran and Early Christianity." *NTS* 2 (1955–56): 176–90.

———. *Second Thoughts on the Dead Sea Scrolls.* Grand Rapids: Eerdmans, 1956.

Bühner, Jan-A. *Der Gedandte und sein Weg in 4. Evangelium: Die kultur- und religionsgeschichtlichen Grundlagen der johanneischen Sendungschristologie sowie ihre traditionsgeschichtliche Entwicklung.* WUNT 2.2. Tübingen: Mohr Siebeck, 1977.

Bultmann, Rudolf. *The Gospel of John: A Commentary.* Translated by G. R. Beasley-Murray, R. W. N. Hoare, and J. K. Riches. Philadelphia: Westminster, 1971.

Burkitt, F. Crawford. *Evangelion da-Mepharreshe: The Curetonian Version of the Four Gospels.* 2 vols. Cambridge: Cambridge University Press, 1904.

Burrows, Millar. *The Dead Sea Scrolls.* New York: Viking, 1955.

———. *More Light on the Dead Sea Scrolls: New Scrolls and Interpretations with Translations of Important Recent Discoveries.* New York: Viking, 1958.

Campbell, Jonathan G. *Deciphering the Dead Sea Scrolls.* Oxford: Blackwell, 2002.

———. Introduction to *New Directions in Qumran Studies.* Edited by Jonathan G. Campbell, William John Lyons, and Lloyd K. Pietersen. LSTS 52. London: T&T Clark, 2005.

Capper, Brian J. "The Church as the New Covenant of Effective Economics." *IJSCC* 2 (2002): 83–102.

———. "Community of Goods in the Early Jerusalem Church." *ANRW* II, 26.2 (1995): 1730–74.

———. "Essene Community Houses and Jesus' Early Community." Pages 472–502 in *Jesus and Archaeology.* Edited by James H. Charlesworth. Grand Rapids: Eerdmans, 2006.

———. "Holy Community of Life and Property and amongst the Poor: A Response to Steve Walton." *EvQ* 80.2 (2008): 113–27.

———. "The New Covenant in Southern Palestine at the Arrest of Jesus." Pages 90–116 in *The Dead Sea Scrolls as Background to Postbiblical Judaism and Early Christianity: Papers from an International Conference at St. Andrews in 2001.* Edited by James R. Davila. STDJ 46. Leiden: Brill, 2003.

———. "The Palestinian Cultural Context of Earliest Christian Community of Goods." Pages 323–56 in *The Book of Acts in Its Palestinian Setting.* Edited by Richard J. Bauckham. BAFCS 4. Grand Rapids: Eerdmans, 1995.

———. "Two Types of Discipleship in Early Christianity." *JTS* 52 (2001):105–23.

———. "'With the Oldest Monks . . .': Light from Essene History on the Career of the Beloved Disciple?" *JTS* 49 (1998): 1–55.

Charlesworth, James. H. *The Bible and the Dead Sea Scrolls: The Princeton Symposium on the Dead Sea Scrolls.* 3 vols. Waco, Tex.: Baylor University Press, 2006.

———. "Can We Discern the Composition Date of the Parables of Enoch?" Pages 450–68 in *Enoch and the Messiah Son of Man: Revisiting the Book of Parables.* Edited by Gabriele Boccaccini. Grand Rapids: Eerdmans, 2007.

———. "A Critical Comparison of the Dualism in 1QS 3:13–4:26 and the 'Dualism' Contained in the Gospel of John." *NTS* 15 (1968–1969): 389–418.

———. "The Dead Sea Scrolls and the Gospel according to John." Pages 65–97 in *Exploring the Gospel of John: In Honor of D. Moody Smith.* Edited by R. Alan Culpepper and C. Clifton Black. Louisville: Westminster John Knox, 1996.

———. "The Dead Sea Scrolls and the Historical Jesus." Pages 1–74 in *Jesus and the Dead Sea Scrolls.* Edited by James H. Charlesworth. New York: Doubleday, 1992.

———. "The Gospel of John: Exclusivism Caused by a Social Setting Different from That of Jesus (John 11:54 and 14:6)." Pages 479–513 in *Anti-Judaism and the Fourth Gospel: Papers of the Leuven Colloquium, 2000.* Edited by Reimund Bieringer, Didier Pollefeyt, and Frederique Vandecasteele-Vanneuville. Assen, Netherlands: Royal Van Gorcum, 2001.

———. "Have the Dead Sea Scrolls Revolutionized Our Understanding of the New Testament?" Pages 116–38 in *The Dead Sea Scrolls Fifty Years after Their Discovery: Proceedings of the Jerusalem Congress, July 20–25, 1997.* Edited by Lawrence H. Schiffman, Emanuel Tov, and James C. VanderKam. Jerusalem: Israel Exploration Society and the Shrine of the Book, 2000.

———. "John the Baptizer and Qumran Barriers in Light of the Rule of the Community." Pages 353–75 in *The Provo International Conference on the DSS: Technological Innovations, New Texts, and Reformulated Issues.* Edited by Donald W. Parry and Eugene Ulrich. STDJ 30. Leiden: Brill, 1999.

———. "John the Baptizer and the Dead Sea Scrolls." Pages 1–35 in volume 3 of *The Bible and the Dead Sea Scrolls: The Princeton Symposium on the Dead Sea Scrolls.* Edited by James H. Charlesworth. 3 vols. Waco, Tex.: Baylor University Press, 2006.

———. *The Pesharim and Qumran History: Chaos or Consensus?* Grand Rapids: Eerdmans, 2002.

———. "The Priority of John? Reflections on the Essenes and the First Edition of John." Pages 73–114 in *Für und wider die Priorität des johannesevangeliums.* Edited by Peter Hofrichter. TTS 9. Hildesheim, Germany: Georg Olms, 2002.

———. "A Study in Shared Symbolism and Language: The Qumran Community and the Johannine Community." Pages 97–152 in volume 3 of *The Bible and the Dead Sea Scrolls: The Princeton Symposium on the Dead Sea Scrolls.* Edited by James H. Charlesworth. 3 vols. Waco, Tex.: Baylor University Press, 2006.

———. "Towards a Taxonomy of Discerning Influence(s) between Two Texts." Pages 41–54 in *Das Gesetz im frühen Judentum und im Neuen Testament: Für Christoph Burchard zum 75. Geburtstag.* Edited by Dieter Sänger and Matthias Konradt. NTOA 57. Göttingen: Vandenhoeck & Ruprecht, 2006.

———, ed. *Jesus and the Dead Sea Scrolls.* New York: Doubleday, 1992.

———, ed. *John and Qumran.* London: Chapman, 1972.

———, ed. *John and the Dead Sea Scrolls.* New York: Crossroad, 1990.

—, ed. *The Old Testament Pseudepigrapha.* 2 vols. Garden City, N.Y.: Doubleday, 1983, 1985.

Charlesworth, James H., Frank M. Cross, and Jacob Milgrom, eds. *The Dead Sea Scrolls— Hebrew, Aramaic, and Greek Texts with English Translations.* Vol. 1: *Rule of the Community and Related Documents.* PTSDSSP. Louisville: Westminster John Knox, 1994.

Chennattu, Rekha M. *Johannine Discipleship as a Covenant Relationship.* Peabody, Mass.: Hendrickson, 2006.

Chester, Andrew. *Messiah and Exaltation: Jewish Messianic and Visionary Traditions and New Testament Christology.* WUNT 207. Tübingen: Mohr Siebeck, 2007.

Chilton, Bruce. "Yohanan the Purifier and His Immersion." *TJT* 14.2 (1998): 197–212.

Cohen, Shaye. "Is 'Proselyte Baptism' Mentioned in the Mishnah? The Interpretation of m. Pesahim 8:8 (= m. Eduyot 5:2)." Pages 278–92 in *Pursuing the Text: Studies in Honor of Ben Zion Wacholder on the Occasion of His Seventieth Birthday.* Edited by John C. Reeves and John Kampen. JSOTSup 184. Sheffield: Sheffield Academic Press, 1994.

Collins, Adele Yarbro. "The Origin of Christian Baptism." *StudLit* 19 (1989): 28–46.

Collins, John J. "Apocalyptic Eschatology as the Transcendence of Death." *CBQ* 36 (1974): 21–43.

—. "The Eschatologizing of Wisdom in the Dead Sea Scrolls." Pages 49–65 in *Sapiential Perspectives: Wisdom Literature in Light of the Dead Sea Scrolls.* Edited by John J. Collins, Gregory E. Sterling, and Ruth A. Clements. STDJ 51. Leiden: Brill, 2004.

—. "The Mysteries of God: Creation and Eschatology in 4QInstruction and the Wisdom of Solomon." Pages 287–305 in *Wisdom and Apocalypticism in the Dead Sea Scrolls and in the Biblical Tradition.* Edited by Florentino García Martínez. Leuven, Netherlands: Leuven University Press, 2003.

—. "Qumran, Apocalypticism, and the New Testament." Pages 133–38 in *The Dead Sea Scrolls Fifty Years after Their Discovery: Proceedings of the Jerusalem Congress, July 20–25, 1997.* Edited by Lawrence H. Schiffman, Emanuel Tov, and James C. VanderKam. Jerusalem: Israel Exploration Society and the Shrine of the Book, 2000.

—. *The Scepter and the Star: The Messiahs of the Dead Sea Scrolls and Other Ancient Literature.* ABRL. New York: Doubleday, 1995.

—. "The Son of God Text from Qumran." Pages 65–82 in *From Jesus to John: Essays on Jesus and New Testament Christology in Honour of Marinus de Jonge.* Edited by Martinus C. de Boer. JSNTSup 8. Sheffield: JSOT Press, 1993.

—. "The Works of the Messiah." *DSD* 1 (1994): 98–112.

Coloe, Mary L. "Household of Faith (Jn 4:46; 11:1–44): A Metaphor for the Johannine Community." *Pacifica* 13 (2000): 326–35.

—. "Sources in the Shadows: John 13 and the Johannine Community." Pages 69–82 in *New Currents through John: A Global Perspective.* Edited by Francisco Lozada Jr. and Tom Thatcher. SBLRBS. Atlanta: Society of Biblical Literature, 2006.

Conzelmann, Hans. *Acts of the Apostles: A Commentary on the Acts of the Apostles.* Translated by James Limburg, A. Thomas Kraabel, and Donald H. Juel. Hermeneia. Philadelphia: Fortress, 1987.

Cross, Frank M. *The Ancient Library of Qumran and Modern Biblical Studies.* New York: Doubleday, 1958.

Cullmann, Oscar. "The Significance of the Qumran Texts for Research into the Beginnings of Christianity." *JB* 74 (1955): 213–26.

Culpepper, R. Alan. *Anatomy of the Fourth Gospel: A Study in Literary Design.* Philadelphia: Fortress, 1983.

———. "Pursuing the Elusive." Pages 109–22 in *What We Have Heard from the Beginning: The Past, Present, and Future of Johannine Studies.* Edited by Tom Thatcher. Waco, Tex.: Baylor University Press, 2007.

Daise, Michael A. *Feasts in John: Jewish Festivals and Jesus' "Hour" in the Fourth Gospel.* WUNT 2.229. Tübingen: Mohr Siebeck, 2007.

Daniélou, Jean. *The Dead Sea Scrolls and Primitive Christianity.* Translated by Salvator Attanasio. Baltimore: Helicon, 1958.

———. *Les manuscrits des la Mer Mort et les origines du Christianisme.* Paris: Editions de l'Orange, 1957.

Dauer, Anton. *Johannes und Lukas: Untersuchungen zu den johanneisch-lukanischen Parallelperikopen Joh 4,46–54/Lk 7,1–10–Joh 12,1–8/Lk 7,36–50; 10,38–42–Joh 20,19–29/ Lk 24,36–39.* FB 50. Würzburg, Germany: Echter, 1984.

Davies, Philip R. *Behind the Essenes: History and Ideology in the Dead Sea Scrolls.* BJS 94. Atlanta: Scholars Press, 1987.

———. "Death, Resurrection, and Life after Death in the Qumran Scrolls." Pages 189–211 in *Judaism in Late Antiquity, Part Four: Death, Life-after-Death, Resurrection, and the World-to-Come in the Judaisms of Antiquity.* Edited by Alan J. Avery-Peck and Jacob Neusner. Leiden: Brill, 2000.

Davila, James R., ed. *The Dead Sea Scrolls as Background to Postbiblical Judaism and Early Christianity: Papers from an International Conference at St. Andrews in 2001.* STDJ 46. Leiden: Brill, 2003.

———. *Liturgical Works.* ECDSS. Grand Rapids: Eerdmans, 2000.

De Boer, Martinus C. "Narrative Criticism, Historical Criticism, and the Gospel of John." Pages 95–108 in *The Johannine Writings.* Edited by Stanley E. Porter and Craig A. Evans. BibSem 32. Sheffield: Sheffield Academic Press, 1995.

De Jonge, Marinus. *Jesus, Stranger from Heaven and Son of God: Jesus Christ and the Christians in Johannine Perspective.* Missoula, Mont.: Scholars Press, 1977.

Delcor, Matthias. "Is the Temple Scroll a Source of the Herodian Temple?" Pages 67–90 in *Temple Scroll Studies: Papers Presented at the International Symposium on the Temple Scroll, Manchester, December 1987.* Edited by George J. Brooke. JSPSup 7. Sheffield: JSOT Press, 1989.

Destro, Adriana, and Mauro Pesce. "The Gospel of John and the Community Rule of Qumran: A Comparison of Systems." Pages 201–29 in volume 2 of *Judaism in Late Antiquity, Part Five: The Judaism of Qumran, a Systemic Reading of the Dead Sea Scrolls.* Edited by Alan J. Avery-Peck, Bruce Chilton, and Jacob Neusner. 2 vols. Leiden: Brill, 2001.

Devillers, Luc. *La Fête de l'Envoyé: La section Johannique de la fête des tentes (Jean 7, 1–10, 21) et la christologie.* EBib n.s. 49. Paris: Gabalda, 2002.

Díez, Luis Merino. "El suplicion de la cruz en la litertura judía intertestamental." *SBFLA* 26 (1976): 31–120.

———. "La crucifixíon en la antigua literatura judía (Período Intertestamental)." *EstEcl* 51 (1976): 5–27.

Dimant, Devorah. "Dualism at Qumran: New Perspectives." Pages 55–73 in *Caves of Enlightenment: Proceedings of the American Schools of Oriental Research Dead Sea Scrolls Jubilee Symposium (1947–1997).* Edited by James H. Charlesworth. North Richland Hills, Tex.: Bibal, 1998.

Dodd, C. H. *Historical Tradition in the Fourth Gospel*. Cambridge: Cambridge University Press, 1963.

———. *The Interpretation of the Fourth Gospel*. Cambridge: Cambridge University Press, 1953.

Drawnel, Henryk. *An Aramaic Wisdom Text from Qumran: A New Interpretation of the Levi Document*. JSJSup 86. Leiden: Brill, 2004.

Driver, Godfrey R. *The Judean Scrolls: The Problem and a Solution*. New York: Shocken Books, 1965.

Duhaime, Jean. "Relative Deprivation in New Religious Movements and the Qumran Community." *RevQ* 16 (1993–95): 265–76.

———. *The War Texts: 1QM and Related Manuscripts*. CQS 6. London: T&T Clark, 2004.

Dunn, James D. G. "John and the Synoptics as a Theological Question." Pages 301–16 in *Exploring the Gospel of John: In Honor of D. Moody Smith*. Edited by R. Alan Culpepper and C. Clifton Black. Louisville: Westminster John Knox, 1996.

———. "Let John Be John: A Gospel for Its Time." Pages 293–322 in *The Gospel and the Gospels*. Edited by Peter Stuhlmacher. Grand Rapids: Eerdmans, 1991.

Dupont-Sommer, André. *The Dead Sea Scrolls: A Preliminary Survey*. Translated by E. Margaret Rowley. New York: Macmillan, 1952.

———. "Observations nouvelles sur l'expression 'suspendu vivant sur le bois' dans le Commentaire de Nahum (4QpNah II 8) à la lumière du Rouleau du Temple (11Q Temple Scroll LXIV 6–13." *CRAI* 116 (1972): 709–20.

Elgvin, Torleif. "The Mystery to Come: Early Essene Theology of Revelation." Pages 113–50 in *Qumran between the Old and New Testaments*. Edited by Frederick H. Cryer and Thomas L. Thompson. Sheffield: Sheffield Academic, 1998.

———. "Wisdom and Apocalypticism in the Early Second Century BCE." Pages 226–47 in *The Dead Sea Scrolls Fifty Years after Their Discovery: Proceedings of the Jerusalem Congress, July 20–25, 1997*. Edited by Lawrence H. Schiffman, Emanuel Tov, and James C. VanderKam. Jerusalem: Israel Exploration Society and the Shrine of the Book, 2000.

———. "Wisdom at Qumran." Pages 147–69 in volume 2 of *Judaism in Late Antiquity, Part Five: The Judaisms of Qumran, a Systemic Reading of the Dead Sea Scrolls*. Edited by Alan J. Avery-Peck, Bruce Chilton, and Jacob Neusner. 2 vols. Leiden: Brill, 2001.

Elledge, Casey D. *The Bible and the Dead Sea Scrolls*. SBLABS 14. Atlanta: Society of Biblical Literature, 2005.

Emerton, John A. "The One Hundred and Fifty-three Fishes in John xxi.11." *JTS* 9 (1958): 86–89.

Eshel, Esther. "4Q414 Fragment 2: Purification of a Corpse-Contaminated Person." Pages 3–10 in *Legal Texts and Legal Issues: Proceedings of the Second Meeting of the International Organization for Qumran Studies, Cambridge 1995*. Edited by Moshe Bernstein, Florentino García Martínez, and John Kampen. STDJ23. Leiden: Brill, 1997.

Eshel, Esther, and Hanan Eshel. "Separating Levi from Enoch: Response to 'Enoch, Levi, and Peter: Recipients of Revelation in Upper Galilee.'" Page 458–68 in *George W. E. Nickelsburg in Perspective: An Ongoing Dialogue of Learning*. Edited by Jacob Neusner and Alan J. Avery-Peck. JSJSup 80. Leiden: Brill, 2003.

Esler, Philip F. *Community and Gospel in Luke-Acts: The Social and Political Motives of Lucan Theology*. Cambridge: Cambridge University Press, 1987.

———. *The First Christians in Their Social Worlds: Social-Scientific Approaches to New Testament Interpretation.* New York: Routledge, 1994.

Evans, Craig A. "Diarchic Messianism in the Dead Sea Scrolls and the Messianism of Jesus of Nazareth." Pages 558–67 in *The Dead Sea Scrolls Fifty Years after Their Discovery: Proceedings of the Jerusalem Congress, July 20–25, 1997.* Edited by Lawrence H. Schiffman, Emanuel Tov, and James C. VanderKam. Jerusalem: Israel Exploration Society and the Shrine of the Book, 2000.

———. "Jesus, John, and the Dead Sea Scrolls: Assessing Typologies of Restoration." Pages 45–62 in *Christian Beginnings and the Dead Sea Scrolls.* Edited by John J. Collins and Craig A. Evans. ASBT. Grand Rapids: Baker Books, 2006.

———. "'The Two Sons of Oil': Early Evidence of Messianic Expectation of Zechariah 4:14 in 4Q254 4 2." Pages 566–75 in *The Provo International Conference on the Dead Sea Scrolls: Technological Innovations, New Texts, and Reformulated Issues.* Edited by Donald W. Parry and Eugene Ulrich. STDJ 30. Leiden: Brill, 1998.

———. *Word and Glory: On the Exegetical and Theological Background of John's Prologue.* JSNTSup 89. Sheffield: JSOT Press, 1994.

Fitzmyer, Joseph A. "The Aramaic 'Son of God' Text from Qumran Cave 4." Pages 163–78 in *Methods of Investigation of the Dead Sea Scrolls and the Khirbet Qumran Site: Present Realities and Future Prospects.* Edited by Michael O. Wise et al. New York: New York Academy of Sciences, 1994.

———. "The Contribution of Qumran Aramaic to the Study of the New Testament." *NTS* 20 (1973–74): 382–407.

———. "Crucifixion in Ancient Palestine, Qumran Literature, and the New Testament." *CBQ* 40 (1978): 493–513.

———. *The Dead Sea Scrolls and Christian Origins.* SDSSRL. Grand Rapids: Eerdmans, 2000.

———. *Essays on the Semitic Background of the New Testament.* London: G. Chapman, 1971.

———. *The Gospel according to Luke.* 2 vols. AB. Garden City, N.Y.: Doubleday, 1981, 1985.

———. "Qumran Literature and the Johannine Writings." Pages 117–33 in *Life in Abundance: Studies of John's Gospel in Tribute to Raymond E. Brown.* Edited by John R. Donahue. Collegeville, Minn.: Liturgical Press, 2005.

———. *A Wandering Aramean: Collected Aramaic Essays.* SBLMS 25. Missoula, Mont.: Scholars Press, 1979.

Fletcher-Louis, Crispin H. T. *All the Glory of Adam: Liturgical Anthropology in the Dead Sea Scrolls.* STDJ 42. Leiden: Brill, 2002.

Flint, Peter W. *The Dead Sea Psalms Scrolls and the Book of Psalms.* STDJ 17. Leiden: Brill, 1997.

Flusser, David. *Judaism and the Origins of Christianity.* Jerusalem: Magnes, 1988.

———. "Qumrân and Jewish 'Apotropaic' Prayers." *IEJ* 16 (1966): 194–205.

Ford, Josephine Massyngberde. "'Crucify him, crucify him' and the Temple Scroll." *ExpTim* 87 (1975–76): 275–78.

Fortna, Robert T., and Tom Thatcher, eds. *Jesus in Johannine Tradition.* Louisville: Westminster John Knox, 2001.

Fredriksen, Paula. *Jesus of Nazareth, King of the Jews: A Jewish Life and the Emergence of Christianity.* New York: Alfred A. Knopf, 2000.

Freedman, David Noel, and Jeffrey C. Geoghegan. "Another Stab at the Wicked Priest."

Pages 17–24 in volume 2 of *The Bible and the Dead Sea Scrolls: The Princeton Symposium on the Dead Sea Scrolls*. Edited by James H. Charlesworth. 3 vols. Waco, Tex.: Baylor University Press, 2006.

Frey, Jorg. "The Impact of the Dead Sea Scrolls on New Testament Interpretation: Proposals, Problems, and Further Perspectives." Pages 407–61 in volume 3 of *The Bible and the Dead Sea Scrolls: The Princeton Symposium on the Dead Sea Scrolls*. Edited by James H. Charlesworth. 3 vols. Waco, Tex.: Baylor University Press, 2006.

———. "Zur Bedeutung der Qumran-Funde für das Verständnis des Neuen Testaments." Pages 33–65 in *Qumran–Bibelwissenschaften–Antike Judaistik*. Edited by Ulrich Dahmen, Hartmut Stegemann, and Gunter Stemberger. Einblicke 9. Paderborn, Germany: Bonifatius, 2006.

Fuglseth, Kåre Sigvald. *Johannine Sectarianism in Perspective: A Sociological, Historical, and Comparative Analysis of the Temple and Social Relationships in the Gospel of John, Philo, and Qumran*. NovTSup 119. Leiden: Brill, 2005.

Fujita, Neil S. *A Crack in the Jar: What Ancient Jewish Documents Tell Us about the New Testament*. Mahwah, N.J.: Paulist, 1986.

García Martínez, Florentino. *The Dead Sea Scrolls Translated: The Qumran Texts in English*. Leiden: Brill, 1994.

———. *Qumran and Apocalyptic: Studies on the Aramaic Texts from Qumran*. STDJ 9. Leiden: Brill, 1992.

García Martínez, Florentino, and Eibert J. C. Tigchelaar, eds. *The Dead Sea Scrolls Study Edition*. 2 vols. Leiden: Brill, 1997.

Garnet, Paul. "Cave 4 MS Parallels to 1QS 5:1–7: Towards a Serek Text History." *JSP* 15 (1997): 67–78.

Gerth, H. H., and C. Wright Mills, eds. *From Max Weber: Essays in Sociology*. London: Routledge and Kegan Paul, 1948.

Goff, Matthew. "Recent Trends in the Study of Early Jewish Wisdom Literature: The Contribution of 4qInstruction and Other Qumran Texts," *Currents in Biblical Research* 7 (2009): 376–416.

Greenfield, Jonas C., Michael E. Stone, and Esther Eshel. *The Aramaic Levi Document: Edition, Translation, Commentary*. SVTP 19. Leiden: Brill, 2004.

Grigsby, B. H. "Washing in the Pool of Siloam: A Thematic Anticipation of the Johannine Cross." *NovT* 27 (1985): 227–35.

Grossman, Maxine L. "Reading for Gender in the Damascus Document." *DSD* 11 (2004): 212–39.

———. *Reading for History in the Damascus Document: A Methodological Study*. STDJ 45. Leiden: Brill, 2002. Repr., Atlanta: Society of Biblical Literature, 2009.

Guilding, Aileen. *The Fourth Gospel and Jewish Worship: A Study of the Relation of St. John's Gospel to the Ancient Jewish Lectionary System*. Oxford: Clarendon, 1960.

Haenchen, Ernst. *The Acts of the Apostles: A Commentary*. Edited by Robert McLean Wilson. Translated by Bernard Noble, Gerald Shinn, and Robert McLean Wilson. Philadelphia: Westminster, 1971.

———. "Aus der Literatur zum Johannesevangelium, 1929–1956." *TRu* 23 (1955): 295–335.

———. *John: A Commentary on the Gospel of John*. Translated by Robert W. Funk. 2 vols. Hermeneia. Philadelphia: Fortress, 1984.

Halperin, David J. "Crucifixion, the Nahum Pesher, and the Rabbinic Penalty of Strangulation." *JJS* 32 (1981): 32–46.

Harrington, Daniel J. "Response to Joseph A. Fitzmyer, S.J., 'Qumran Literature and the Johannine Writings.'" Pages 134–37 in *Life in Abundance: Studies in John's Gospel in Tribute to Raymond E. Brown, S.S.* Edited by John R. Donahue. Collegeville, Minn.: Liturgical Press, 2005.

———. "Two Early Jewish Approaches to Wisdom: Sirach and Qumran Sapiential Work A." Pages 263–76 in *The Wisdom Texts from Qumran and the Development of Sapiential Thought.* Edited by Charlotte Hempel, Armin Lange, and Hermann Lichtenberger. Leuven, Netherlands: Leuven University Press, 2002.

———. *Wisdom Texts from Qumran.* London: Routledge, 1996.

Harrington, Daniel J., and Jacob Strugnell. "Qumran Cave 4 Texts: A New Publication." *JBL* 112 (1993): 491–99.

Harrington, Hannah K. *The Impurity Systems of Qumran and the Rabbis: Biblical Foundations.* SBLDS 143. Atlanta: Scholars Press, 1993.

———. *The Purity Texts.* CQS 5. London: T&T Clark, 2004.

Hayes, Christine E. *Gentile Impurities and Jewish Identities: Intermarriage and Conversion from the Bible to the Talmud.* Oxford: Oxford University Press, 2002.

Hayward, Robert. "The Priestly Blessing in Targum Pseudo-Jonathan." *JSP* 19 (1999): 81–101.

Heerkerens, Hans-Peter. *Die Zeichen-Quelle der johanneischen Redaktion: Ein Beitrag zur Entstehungsgeschichte des vierten Evangeliums.* SBS 113. Stuttgart: Verlag Katholisches Bibelwerk, 1984.

Hengel, Martin. *Die Johanneische Frage: Ein Lösungversuch.* WUNT 67. Tübingen: Mohr Siebeck, 1993.

———. *The Johannine Question.* Translated by John Bowden. London: SCM, 1989.

———. "Die Qumranfollen undeder Umgang mit der Wahrheit." *TBei* 23 (1992): 233–37.

Hill, Michael. *The Religious Order: A Study of Virtuoso Religion and Its Legitimation in the Nineteenth-Century Church of England.* London: Heinemann, 1973.

———. *A Sociology of Religion.* London: Heinemann, 1973.

———. "Typologie sociologique de l'ordre religieux." *Social Compass* 17 (1971): 45–64.

Hooker, Morna. "John's Baptism: A Prophetic Sign." Pages 22–40 in *The Holy Spirit and Christian Origins.* Edited by Graham N. Stanton, Bruce W. Longenecker, and Stephen C. Barton. Grand Rapids: Eerdmans, 2004.

Horsley, Richard A. "The Dead Sea Scrolls and the Historical Jesus." Pages 37–60 in volume 3 of *The Bible and the Dead Sea Scrolls: The Princeton Symposium on the Dead Sea Scrolls.* 3 vols. Edited by James H. Charlesworth. Waco, Tex.: Baylor University Press, 2006.

Hurst, D. L. "Did Qumran Expect Two Messiahs?" *BBR* 9 (1999): 157–80.

Hutchinson, John C. "Was John the Baptist an Essene from Qumran?" *BSac* 159 (2002): 187–200.

Jaubert, Annie. "The Calendar of Qumran and the Passion Narrative in John." Pages 62–75 in *John and the Dead Sea Scrolls.* Edited by James H. Charlesworth. New York: Crossroad, 1990.

Jeremias, Gert. *Der Lehrer der Gerechtigkeit.* SUNT 2. Göttingen: Vandenhoeck & Ruprecht, 1990.

Jeremias, Joachim. *The Rediscovery of Bethsada.* Louisville: Southern Baptist Theological Seminary, 1966.

Jones, Larry Paul. *The Symbol of Water in the Gospel of John.* JSNTSup 145. Sheffield: Sheffield Academic Press, 1997.

Käsemann, Ernst. *The Testament of Jesus: A Study of the Gospel of John in the Light of Chapter 17.* Translated by Gerhard Krodel. London: SCM, 1968.

Keener, Craig S. *The Gospel of John: A Commentary.* 2 vols. Peabody, Mass.: Hendrickson, 2003.

Kister, Menahem. "Wisdom Literature and Its Relation to Other Genres." Pages 13–47 in *Sapiential Perspectives: Wisdom Literature in Light of the Dead Sea Scrolls.* Edited by John J. Collins, Gregory E. Sterling, and Ruth A. Clements. STDJ 51. Leiden: Brill, 2004.

Klawans, Jonathan. *Impurity and Sin in Ancient Judaism.* Oxford: Oxford University Press, 2000.

Knohl, Israel. *The Messiah before Jesus: The Suffering Servant of the Dead Sea Scrolls.* Berkeley and Los Angeles: University of California Press, 2000.

Kugler, Robert A. *From Patriarch to Priest. The Levi-Priestly Tradition from* Aramaic Levi *to the* Testament of Levi. SBLEJL 9. Atlanta: Scholars Press, 1996.

———. "Making All Experience Religious: The Hegemony of Ritual at Qumran." *JSJ* 33 (2002): 131–52.

Kugler, Robert A., and Eileen M. Schuller, eds. *The Dead Sea Scrolls at Fifty: Proceedings of the 1997 Society of Biblical Literature Qumran Section Meetings.* SBLEJL 15. Atlanta: Scholars Press, 1999.

Kuhn, Heinz-Wolfgang. *Enderwartung und gegenwärtiges Heil: Untersuchungen zu den Gemeindeliedern von Qumran, mit einen Anhang über Eschatologie und Gegenwart in der Verkündigung Jesus.* SUNT 4. Göttingen: Vandenhoeck & Ruprecht, 1966.

———. "Qumran Texts and the Historical Jesus: Parallels in Contrast." Pages 573–80 in *The Dead Sea Scrolls Fifty Years after Their Discovery, 1947–1997.* Edited by Lawrence H. Schiffman, Emanuel Tov, and James C. VanderKam. Jerusalem: Israel Exploration Society and the Shrine of the Book, 2000.

Kuhn, Karl G. "Die in Palästina gefundenen hebräischen Texte und das neue Testament." *ZTK* 47 (1950): 296–316.

———. "Johannesevangelium und Qumrântexte." Pages 111–22 in *Neotestamentica et Patristica: Eine Freundesgabe, Herrn Professor Dr. Oscar Cullmann zu seinem 60. Geburtstag überreicht.* Edited by Willem C. van Unnik. NovTSup 6. Leiden: Brill, 1962.

———. "Die Sektenschrift und die iranische Religion." *ZTK* 49 (1952): 296–316.

———. "The Two Messiahs of Aaron and Israel." Pages 54–64 in *The Scrolls and the New Testament.* Edited by Krister Stendahl. New York: Harper, 1957.

———. "Zur Bedeutung der neuen palästinischen Handschriftenfunde für die neutestamentlishce Wissenschaft." *TLZ* 47 (1950): 81–86.

Kysar, Robert. *The Fourth Evangelist and His Gospel: An Examination of Contemporary Scholarship.* Minneapolis: Augsburg, 1975.

———. *Voyages with John: Charting the Fourth Gospel.* Waco, Tex.: Baylor University Press, 2006.

Lange, Armin. "Considerations Concerning the 'Spirit of Impurity' in Zech 13:2." Pages 254–55 in *Die Dämonen–Demons: Die Damonologie der israelitisch-judischen und fruhchristlichen Literatur im Kontext ihrer Umwelt.* Edited by Armin Lange, Hermann Lichtenberger, and K. F. Diethard Römheld. Tübingen: Mohr Siebeck, 2003.

———. "Die Endgestalt des protomasoretischen Psalters und die Toraweisheit: Zur Bedeutung der nichtessenischen Weisheitstexte aus Qumran für die Auslegung des protomasoretischen Psalters." Pages 101–36 in *Der Psalter in Judentum und Christentum*. Edited by Erich Zenger. HBS 18. Freiburg: Herder, 1998.

———. "The Essene Position on Magic and Divination." Pages 377–436 in *Legal Texts and Legal Issues: Proceedings of the Second Meeting of the International Organization for Qumran Studies, Published in Honour of Joseph M. Baumgarten*. Edited by Moshe Bernstein, Florentino García Martínez, and John Kampen. STDJ 23. Leiden: Brill, 1997.

———. *Weisheit und Präedestination: Weisheitliche Urordnung und Präedestination in den Textfunden von Qumran*. STDJ 18. Leiden: Brill, 1995.

LaSor, William Sanford. *The Dead Sea Scrolls and the New Testament*. Grand Rapids: Eerdmans, 1972.

Laurin, R. B. "The Problem of Two Messiahs in the Qumran Scrolls." *RevQ* 4 (1963–64): 39–52.

Lawrence, Jonathan David. *Washing in Water: Trajectories of Ritual Bathing in the Hebrew Bible and Second Temple Literature*. SBLAcB 23. Atlanta: Society of Biblical Literature, 2006.

Leaney, A. R. C. "The Johannine Paraclete and the Qumran Scrolls." Pages 38–61 in *John and Qumran*. Edited by James H. Charlesworth. New York: Crossroad, 1972.

Leroy, Herbert. *Rätsel und Missverständnis: Ein Beitrag zur Formgeschichte des Johannesevangeliums*. BBB 30. Bonn: Peter Hanstein, 1967.

Lesses, Rebecca Macy. *Ritual Practices to Gain Power: Angels, Incantations, and Revelation in Early Jewish Mysticism*. HTS 44. Harrisburg, Pa.: Trinity Press International, 1998.

Lichtenberger, Herman. "The Dead Sea Scrolls and John the Baptist: Reflections on Josephus' Account of John the Baptist." Pages 340–46 in *The Dead Sea Scrolls: Forty Years of Research*. Edited by Devorah Dimant and Uriel Rappaport. STDJ 10. Leiden: Brill, 1992.

Lincoln, Andrew T. *The Gospel according to St John*. BNTC 4. London: Continuum, 2005.

Lindars, Barnabas. *The Gospel of John*. NCBC. Grand Rapids: Eerdmans, 1972.

Ling, Timothy J. M. *The Judaean Poor and the Fourth Gospel*. SNTSMS 136. Cambridge: Cambridge University Press, 2006.

Lohse, Eduard. *Die Texte aus Qumran: Hebräisch und deutsch; mit masoretischer Punktation, Übersetzung, Einführung und Anmerkungen*. Munich: Kosel, 1971.

Maccoby, Hyam. *Ritual and Morality: The Ritual Purity System and Its Place in Judaism*. Cambridge: Cambridge University Press, 1999.

MacDonald, Ian. "What Did You Go Out to See? John the Baptist, the Scrolls, and Late Second Temple Judaism." Pages 53–64 in *The Dead Sea Scrolls in Their Historical Context*. Edited by Timothy H. Lim. Edinburgh: T&T Clark, 2000.

Maddox, Robert. *The Purpose of Luke–Acts*. FRLANT 126. Göttingen: Vandenhoeck & Ruprecht, 1982.

Martin, D. A. *Pacifism*. London: Routledge and Kegan Paul, 1965.

Martyn, J. Louis. *History and Theology in the Fourth Gospel*. New York: Harper & Row, 1968.

———. *History and Theology in the Fourth Gospel*. 3d ed. Louisville: Westminster John Knox, 2003.

Meeks, Wayne A. "The Man from Heaven in Johannine Sectarianism." *JBL* 91 (1972): 44–72.

——. *The Prophet-King: Moses Traditions and the Johannine Christology.* NovTSup 14. Leiden: Brill, 1967.

Meier, John P. *A Marginal Jew: Rethinking the Historical Jesus,* Vol. 1: *The Roots of the Problem and the Person.* ABRL. New York: Doubleday, 1991.

Metso, Sarianna. *The Serekh Texts.* CQS 9. London: T&T Clark, 2007.

——. *The Textual Development of the Qumran Community Rule.* STDJ 21. Leiden: Brill, 1997.

Milgrom, Jacob. *Leviticus 1–16: A New Translation with Introduction and Commentary.* AB. New York: Doubleday, 1991.

Milik, J. T. *Ten Years of Discovery in the Wilderness of Judea.* SBT 26. London: SCM, 1959.

——. "Le Testament de Lévi en araméen." *RB* 62 (1955): 398–408.

Milik, J. T., and Barthélemy, David. *Discoveries in the Judaean Desert: Qumran Cave 1.* Oxford: Clarendon, 1955.

Miranda, Jan Peter. *Der Vater, der mich gesandt hat; Religionsgeschichtliche Untersuchungen zu den johanneischen Sendungsformeln Zugleich ein Beitrag zur johanneischen Christologie und Ekklesiologie.* Europaische Hochschulschriften. Frankfurt: Lang, 1972.

Morganthaler, Robert. *Statistik des neutestamentlichen Wortschatzes.* Zürich: Gotthelf, 1982.

Morris, Leon. *The Dead Sea Scrolls and the Gospel of John.* London: Viking, 1960.

——. *The Gospel according to John.* Rev. ed. NICNT. Grand Rapids: Eerdmans, 1995.

——. *Studies in the Fourth Gospel.* Grand Rapids: Eerdmans, 1969.

Mowrey, Lucetta. "The Dead Sea Scrolls and the Background for the Gospel of John." *BA* 17 (1954): 78–97.

Murphy, Catherine. *John the Baptist: Prophet of Purity for a New Age.* Interfaces. Collegeville, Minn.: Liturgical Press, 2003.

Neirynck, Frans. *Jean et les Synoptiques: Examen critique de l'exégèse de M.-É. Boismard.* BETL 49. Louvain: Louvain University Press, 1979.

——. "John and the Synoptics: 1975–1990." Pages 3–62 in *John and the Synoptics.* Edited by Adelbert Denaux. BETL 101. Louvain: Louvain University Press, 1992.

——. "Q 6, 20b–21; 7, 22 and Isaiah 61." Pages 27–64 in *The Scriptures in the Gospels.* Edited by Christopher M. Tuckett. BETL 131. Louvain: Peeters, 1997.

Neufeld, Dietmar. "'And When That One Comes,' Aspects of Johannine Messianism." Pages 120–41 in *Eschatology, Messianism, and the Dead Sea Scrolls.* Edited by Craig A. Evans and Peter W. Flint. Grand Rapids: Eerdmans, 1997.

Newman, Hillel. *Proximity to Power and Jewish Sectarian Groups of the Ancient Period: A Review of Lifestyle, Values, and Halakhah in the Pharisees, Sadducees, Essenes, and Qumran.* BRLJ 25. Leiden: Brill. 2006.

Newsom, Carol A. "A Response to George Nickelsburg's 'Currents in Qumran Scholarship: The Interplay of Data, Agendas, and Methodology.'" Pages 115–21 in *The Dead Sea Scrolls at Fifty: Proceedings of the 1997 Society of Biblical Literature Qumran Section Meetings.* Edited by Robert A. Kugler and Eileen M. Schuller. SBLEJL15. Atlanta: Scholars Press, 1999.

——. *The Self as Symbolic Space: Constructing Identity and Community at Qumran.* STDJ 52. Leiden: Brill, 2004. Repr., Atlanta: Society of Biblical Literature, 2007.

Newton, Michael. *The Concept of Purity at Qumran and in the Letters of Paul.* SNTSMS 53. New York: Cambridge University Press, 1985.

Ng, Wai-Yee. *Water Symbolism in John: An Eschatological Interpretation.* StBibL 5. New York: Peter Lang, 2001.

Nickelsburg, George W. E. *1 Enoch 1: A Commentary on the Book of 1 Enoch*. Hermeneia. Minneapolis: Fortress, 2001.

———. "Currents in Qumran Scholarship: The Interplay of Data, Agendas, and Methodology." Pages 79–99 in *The Dead Sea Scrolls at Fifty: Proceedings of the 1997 Society of Biblical Literature Qumran Section Meetings*. Edited by Robert A. Kugler and Eileen M. Schuller. SBLEJL 15. Atlanta: Scholars Press, 1999.

———. "Enoch, Levi, and Peter: Recipients of Revelation in Upper Galilee." *JBL* 100 (1981): 575–600.

———. *Resurrection, Immortality, and Eternal Life in Intertestamental Judaism*. Cambridge: Harvard University Press, 1972.

O'Day, Gail R. "Johannine Theology as Sectarian Theology." Pages 199–203 in *What Is John? Volume 1: Readers and Readings of the Fourth Gospel*. Edited by Fernando. F. Segovia. SBLSymS 3. Atlanta: Scholars Press, 1996.

Paffenroth, Kim. *The Story of Jesus according to L*. JSNTSup 147. Sheffield: Sheffield Academic Press, 1997.

Painter, John. *The Quest for the Messiah: The History, Literature, and Theology of the Johannine Community*. 2d ed. Nashville, Tenn.: Abingdon, 1993.

Parker, Pierson. "The Kinship of John and Acts." Pages 187–205 in volume 1 of *Christianity, Judaism, and Other Greco-Roman Cults: Studies for Morton Smith at Sixty*. Edited by Jacob Neusner. 4 vols. SJLA 12. Leiden: Brill, 1975.

———. "Luke and the Fourth Evangelist." *NTS* 9 (1962–63): 317–36.

———. "When Acts Sides with John." Pages 210–15 in *Understanding the Sacred Text: Essays in Honor of Morton S. Enslin on the Hebrew Bible and Christian Beginnings*. Edited by John Reumann. Valley Forge, Pa.: Judson, 1972.

Parker, Robert. *Miasma: Pollution and Purification in Early Greek Religion*. Oxford: Clarendon, 1983.

Parry, Donald W., et al. "New Technological Advances: DNA, Databases, Imaging Radar." Pages 496–515 in volume 1 of *The Dead Sea Scrolls after Fifty Years: A Comprehensive Assessment*. Edited by Peter W. Flint and James C. VanderKam. 2 vols. Leiden: Brill, 1998.

Parry, Donald W., and Emanuel Tov, eds. *The Dead Sea Scrolls Reader*. 6 vols. Leiden: Brill, 2004.

Parry, Richard Lloyd. "Nuns Join Monks in Burma's Saffron Revolution." No pages. Cited 24 September 2007. Online: http://www.timesonline.co.uk/tol/news/world/asia/article2516773.ece.

Paul, Andre. *Les manuscrits de la Mer Morte*. Paris: Bayard, 1997.

Pesch, Rudolf. *Die Apostelgeschichte*. EKKNT 5/1. Neukirchen-Vluyn: Neukirchener, 1986.

Pfann, Stephen J. "The Essene Yearly Renewal Ceremony and the Baptism of Repentance." Pages 337–52 in *The Provo International Conference on the DSS: Technological Innovations, New Texts, and Reformulated Issues*. Edited by Donald W. Parry and Eugene Ulrich. STDJ 30. Leiden: Brill, 1999.

Piccirillo, Michele. "The Sanctuaries of the Baptism on the East Bank of the Jordan River." Pages 433–43 in *Jesus and Archaeology*. Edited by James H. Charlesworth. Grand Rapids: Eerdmans, 2006.

Pilgaard, Aage. "The Qumran Scrolls and John's Gospel." Pages 126–42 in *New Readings in John: Literary and Theological Perspectives. Essays from the Scandinavian Conference on the Fourth Gospel in Århus, 1997*. Edited by Johannes Nissen and Sigfred Pedersen. JSNTSup 182. Sheffield: Sheffield Academic Press, 1999.

Pixner, Bargil. "Mount Zion, Jesus, and Archaeology." Pages 309–22 in *Jesus and Archaeology*. Edited by James H. Charlesworth. Grand Rapids: Eerdmans, 2006.

Ploeg, Jan P. M. van der. "Fragments d'un manuscript de Psaumes de Qumran (11QPs[b])." *RB* 74 (1967): 408–13.

Popkes, Enno E. "About the Differing Approach to a Theological Heritage: Comments on the Relationship between the Gospel of John, the *Gospel of Thomas*, and Qumran." Pages 281–317 in volume 3 of *The Bible and the Dead Sea Scrolls: The Princeton Symposium on the Dead Sea Scrolls*. Edited by James H. Charlesworth. 3 vols. Waco, Tex.: Baylor University Press, 2006.

Preston, James. "Purification." Pages 7507–10 in *Encyclopedia of Religion, Volume 11*. Edited by Lindsay Jones. New York: Macmillan, 2005.

Price, James L. "Light from *Qumran* upon Some Aspects of Johannine Theology." Pages 9–37 in *John and Qumran*. Edited by James H. Charlesworth. London: Chapman, 1972.

Pryke, John. "John the Baptist and the Qumran Community." *RevQ* 16 (1964): 483–96.

Puech, Émile. "Fragment d'une apocalypse en araméen (4Q246 = pseudo-Dan[d]) et le 'royaume de Dieu.'" *RB* 99 (1992): 98–131.

———. "Quelques aspects de la restauration du rouleau des hymnes (1QH)." *JJS* 39 (1988): 38–55.

Regev, Eyal. *Sectarianism in Qumran: A Cross-Cultural Perspective*. RelSoc 45. Berlin: de Gruyter, 2007.

Reicke, Bo. "Nytt ljus över Johannes döparens förkunnelse." *Religion och Bibel* 11 (1952): 5–18.

Reinhardt, Wolfgang. "The Population Size of Jerusalem and the Numerical Growth of the Jerusalem Church." Pages 237–65 in *The Book of Acts in Its Palestinian Setting*. Edited by Richard J. Bauckham. BAFCS 4. Grand Rapids: Eerdmans, 2005.

Richardson, Peter. "Khirbet Qana (and Other Villages) as a Context for Jesus." Pages 120–44 in *Jesus and Archaeology*. Edited by James H. Charlesworth. Grand Rapids: Eerdmans, 2006.

Riesner, Rainer. *Essener und Urgemeinde in Jerusalem: neue Funde und Quelle*. BAZ 6. Giessen, Germany: Brunnen, 1998.

———. "Essener und Urkirche auf dem Südwesthügel Jerusalems (Zion III)." Pages 200–234 in *Laetare Jerusalem*. Edited by Nikodemus C. Schnabel. Münster, Germany: Aschendorf, 2006.

Robinson, James. Foreword to *John: A Commentary on the Gospel of John*, by Ernst Haenchen. Hermeneia. Philadelphia: Fortress, 1984.

Robinson, John A. T. "The Baptism of John and the Qumran Community: Testing a Hypothesis." Pages 11–27 in *Twelve New Testament Studies*. SBT 34. London: SCM, 1962.

———. *The Priority of John*. Edited by J. F. Coakley. London: SCM, 1985.

Roddy, Nicolae. "Ultimate Reflections, Infinite Refractions: Form and Function in the Elusive Genre of Testamentary Literature." *Studia Hebraica* 3 (2003): 298–310.

Rofé, Alexandre. "Revealed Wisdom from the Bible to Qumran." Pages 1–11 in *Sapiential Perspectives: Wisdom Literature in Light of the Dead Sea Scrolls*. Edited by John J. Collins, Gregory E. Sterling, and Ruth A. Clements. STDJ 51. Leiden: Brill, 2004.

Rosso-Ubigli, Liliana. "Deuteronomio 21, 22: Contributo del Rotolo del Tempio alla valutazione di una variante medievale dei Settanta." *RevQ* 9 (1977–78): 231–36.

Rousseau, John J., and Rami Arav, eds. *Jesus and His World: An Archaeological and Cultural Dictionary*. Minneapolis: Fortress, 1995.

Ruckstuhl, Eugen. *Jesus im Horizont der Evangelien*. SBAB 3. Stuttgart: Verlag Katholisch-esBibelwerk, 1988.

Rusam, Dietrich. "Das Johannesevangelium—eine 'Relecture' der synoptischen Evangelien? Intertextuelle Beobachtungen zu den 'Ich-bin-Worten' des Johannesevangeliums." Pages 377–90 in *Kontexte der Schrift. Band II, Kultur, Politik, Religion, Sprache–Text. Wolfgang Stegemann zum 60. Geburtstag*. Edited by Christian Strecker. Stuttgart: W. Kohlhammer, 2005.

Saera, Rafael Vicent. "La halaká de Dt 21, 22–23 y su interpretación en Qumrán y en Jn 19, 31–42." Pages 699–709 in *Salvación en la palabra: Targum, derash, berith. Homenaje al prof. A. Díez Macho*. Edited by Domingo Munoz Léon. Madrid: Ediciones Cristianidad, 1986.

Saldarini, Anthony J. "Sectarianism." Pages 853–56 in volume 2 of *Encyclopedia of the Dead Sea Scrolls*. Edited by Lawrence H. Schiffman and James C. VanderKam. 2 vols. New York: Oxford University Press, 2000.

Sanders, E. P. *The Historical Figure of Jesus*. London: Penguin, 1993.

Sanders, James A. *The Dead Sea Psalms Scroll*. Ithaca, N.Y.: Cornell University Press, 1967.

———. "Psalm 154 Revisited." Pages 296–306 in *Biblische Theologie und gesellschaftlicher Wandel: Für Norbert Lohfink S.J.* Edited by Georg Braulik, Walter Gross, and Sean McEvenue. Freiburg: Herder, 1993.

———. *The Psalms Scroll of Qumrân Cave 11 (11QPsᵃ)*. DJD 4. Oxford: Clarendon, 1965.

Sanders, James A., James H. Charlesworth, and Henry W. L. Rietz. "Non-Masoretic Psalms." Pages 155–58 in *The Dead Sea Scrolls—Hebrew, Aramaic, and Greek Texts with English Translations*, Vol. 4a: *Pseudepigraphic and Non-Masoretic Psalms and Prayers*. Edited by James H. Charlesworth, Frank M. Cross, and Jacob Milgrom. PTSDSSP. Louisville: Westminster John Knox, 1997.

Sandmel, Samuel. "Parallelomania." *JBL* 81 (1962): 1–13.

Schiffman, Lawrence H. "Purity and Perfection: Exclusion from the Council of the Community in the Serekh ha-'Edah." Pages 373–89 in *Biblical Archaeology Today: Proceedings of the International Congress on Biblical Archaeology, Jerusalem, April 1984*. Edited by Janet Amitai. Jerusalem: Israel Exploration Society, 1985.

———. *Sectarian Law in the Dead Sea Scrolls: Courts, Testimony, and the Penal Code*. BJS 33. Chico, Calif.: Scholars Press, 1983.

Schiffman, Lawrence H., and James C. VanderKam, eds. *Encyclopedia of the Dead Sea Scrolls*. 2 vols. Oxford: Oxford University Press, 2000.

Schiffman, Lawrence H., Emanuel Tov, and James C. VanderKam, eds. *The Dead Sea Scrolls Fifty Years after Their Discovery: Proceedings of the Jerusalem Congress, July 20–25, 1997*. Jerusalem: Israel Exploration Society and the Shrine of the Book, 2000.

Schnackenburg, Rudolf. *The Gospel according to St. John*. Translated by Kevin Smyth. 3 vols. HTKNT. New York: Seabury and Crossroad, 1980–82.

Schneiders, Sandra M. "Remaining in His Word: From Faith to Faith by Way of the Text." Pages 261–76 in *What We Have Heard from the Beginning: The Past, Present, and Future of Johannine Studies*. Edited by Tom Thatcher. Waco, Tex.: Baylor University Press, 2007.

Schofield, Alison. "Rereading S: A New Model of Textual Development in Light of the Cave 4 *Serekh* Copies." *DSD* 15 (2008): 96–120.

Schuller, Eileen. "4QHodayot^{a-e} and 4QpapHodayot^f: Introduction." Pages 69–76 in *1QHodayot^a*. Edited by Hartmut Stegemann and Eileen Schuller. Translated by Carol Newsom. DJD 40. Oxford: Clarendon, 1999.

———. *The Dead Sea Scrolls: What Have We Learned?* Louisville: Westminster John Knox, 2006.

———. "Women in the Dead Sea Scrolls." Pages 115–32 in *Methods of Investigation of the Dead Sea Scrolls and the Khirbet Qumran Site*. Edited by Michael O. Wise et al. New York: New York Academy of Sciences, 1994.

———. "Women in the Dead Sea Scrolls." Pages 117–44 in volume 2 of *The Dead Sea Scrolls after Fifty Years: A Comprehensive Assessment*. Edited by Peter W. Flint and James C. VanderKam. 2 vols. Leiden: Brill, 1999.

Scroggs, Robin. "The Earliest Christian Communities as Sectarian Movement." Pages 69–91 in *Social-Scientific Approaches to New Testament Interpretation*. Edited by David G. Horrell. Edinburgh: T&T Clark, 1999.

Shafaat, A. "Geber of the Qumran Scrolls and the Spirit-Paraclete of the Gospel of John." *NTS* 27 (1981): 263–69.

Shanks, Hershel, ed. *The Dead Sea Scrolls after Forty Years*. Washington, DC: Biblical Archaeological Society, 1991.

———. *The Mystery and Meaning of the Dead Sea Scrolls*. New York: Random House, 1998.

Silber, Ilana F. *Virtuosity, Charisma, and Social Order: A Comparative Sociological Study of Monasticism in Theravada Buddhism and Medieval Catholicism*. Cambridge: Cambridge University Press, 1995.

Smalley, Stephen S. "Keeping Up with Recent Studies; XII. St John's Gospel." *ExpTim* 97 (1986): 102–8.

Smith, D. Moody. "Historical Issues and the Problem of John and the Synoptics." Pages 252–67 in *From Jesus to John: Essays on Jesus and New Testament Christology in Honour of Marinus de Jonge*. Edited by Martinus C. de Boer. JSNTSup 84. Sheffield: JSOT, 1993.

———. *Johannine Christianity: Essays on Its Setting, Sources, and Theology*. Columbia: University of South Carolina Press, 1984.

———. *John among the Gospels: The Relationship in Twentieth-Century Research*. Minneapolis: Fortress, 1992.

———. "John and the Synoptics: Historical Tradition and the Passion Narrative." Pages 77–91 in *Light in a Spotless Mirror: Reflections on Wisdom Traditions in Judaism and Early Christianity*. Edited by James H. Charlesworth and Michael A. Daise. Harrisburg, Pa.: Trinity Press International, 2003.

Stanton, Graham N. *A Gospel for a New People: Studies in Matthew*. Edinburgh: T&T Clark, 1992.

Stegemann, Hartmut. *Die Essener, Qumran, Johannes der Täufer und Jesus: Ein Sachbuch*. Herder Spektrum. Freiburg: Herder, 1993.

———. *The Library of Qumran: On the Essenes, Qumran, John the Baptist, and Jesus*. Grand Rapids: Eerdmans, 1998.

———. "The Material Reconstruction of 1QHodayot." Pages 272–84 in *The Dead Sea Scrolls Fifty Years after Their Discovery, 1947–1997*. Edited by Lawrence H. Schiffman, Emanuel Tov, and James C. VanderKam. Jerusalem: Israel Exploration Society and the Shrine of the Book, 2000.

———. "The Qumran Essenes: Local Members of the Main Jewish Union in Late Second

Temple Times." Pages 83–166 in volume 1 of *The Madrid Qumran Congress: Proceedings of the International Congress on the Dead Sea Scrolls, Madrid, 18–21 March, 1991*. Edited by Julio Trebolle Barrera and Luis Vegas Montaner. 2 vols. STDJ 11. Leiden: Brill, 1992.

Steudel, Annette. "The Eternal Reign of the People of God—Collective Expectations in Qumran Texts (4Q246 and 1QM)." *RevQ* 17 (1996): 507–25.

Stone, Michael E. "Lists of Revealed Things in the Apocalyptic Literature." Pages 414–52 in *Magnalia Dei, the Mighty Acts of God: Essays on the Bible and Archaeology in Memory of G. Ernest Wright*. Edited by Frank M. Cross, Werner E. Lemke, and Patrick D. Miller. Garden City, N.Y.: Doubleday, 1976.

Stone, Michael E., and Jonas C. Greenfield. "The Prayer of Levi." Pages 25–36 in *Qumran Cave 4. XVII: Parabiblical Texts, Part 3*. Edited by George J. Brooke. DJD 22. Oxford: Clarendon, 1996.

Strugnell, John, Daniel J. Harrington, and Torleif Elgvin. *Qumran Cave 4. XXIV, Sapiential Texts. Part 2: 4QInstruction, 4Q415 ff., with a Re-edition of 1Q26*. DJD 34. Oxford: Clarendon, 1994.

Stuckenbruck, Loren T. "4QInstruction and the Possible Influence of Early Enochic Traditions: An Evaluation." Pages 263–75 in *The Wisdom Texts from Qumran and the Development of Sapiential Thought*. Edited by Charlotte Hempel, Armin Lange, and Hermann Lichtenberger. Leuven: Leuven University Press, 2002.

———. "Deliverance Prayers and Hymns in Early Jewish Documents." Pages 146–65 in *The Changing Face of Judaism and Christianity*. Edited by Gerbern S. Oegema and Ian Henderson. Gütersloh, Germany: Gerd Mohn, 2005.

———. "The Origins of Evil in Jewish Apocalyptic Tradition: The Interpretation of Genesis 6:1–4 in the Second and Third Centuries BCE." Pages 87–118 in *The Fall of the Angels*. Edited by Christoph Auffarth and Loren Stuckenbruck. TBN 6. Leiden: Brill, 2004.

———. "Pleas for Deliverance from the Demonic in Early Jewish Texts." Pages 55–74 in *Studies in Jewish Prayer*. Edited by Robert Hayward and Brad Embry. JSSSup 17. Oxford: Oxford University Press, 2005.

Sukenik, Elezar. *The Dead Sea Scrolls of the Hebrew University*. Jerusalem: Magnes, 1955.

Sutcliffe, Edmund F. "Baptism and Baptismal Rites at Qumran?" *HeyJ* 1 (1960): 179–88.

Taylor, Joan E. *The Immerser: John the Baptist within Second Temple Judaism*. SHJ. Grand Rapids: Eerdmans, 1997.

Taylor, Justin. 2004. *Pythagoreans and Essenes: Structural Parallels*. Collection de la Revue des Études juives 32. Louvain: Peeters, 2004.

Teeple, Howard M. "Qumran and the Origin of the Fourth Gospel." *NovT* 4 (1960): 6–25. Repr. in *The Composition of John's Gospel: Selected Studies from Novum Testamentum*. Edited by David E. Orton. RBS 2. Leiden: Brill, 1999.

Thatcher, Tom. "The Fourth Gospel in First-Century Media Culture." Pages 159–62 in *What We Have Heard from the Beginning: The Past, Present, and Future of Johannine Studies*. Edited by Tom Thatcher. Waco, Tex.: Baylor University Press, 2007.

———. *Why John Wrote a Gospel: Jesus–Memory–History*. Louisville: Westminster John Knox, 2006.

———, ed. *What We Have Heard from the Beginning: The Past, Present, and Future of Johannine Studies*. Waco, Tex.: Baylor University Press, 2007.

Theissen, Gerd, and Annette Merz. *The Historical Jesus: A Comprehensive Guide*. Translated by John Bowden. Minneapolis: Fortress, 1998.

Thiering, Barbara. *Jesus the Man.* New York: Doubleday, 1992.

Thomas, Joseph. *Le mouvement baptiste en Palestine et Syrie (150 av. J.C.–300 ap. J.C.).* Gembloux, Belgium: Duculot, 1935.

Thomas, Sam. *The "Mysteries" of Qumran: Mystery, Secrecy, and Esotericism in the Dead Sea Scrolls.* SBLEJL 25. Atlanta: SBL, 2009.

"Tibetan Monks: A Controlled Life." No pages. Cited 20 March 2008. Online: http://news.bbc.co.uk/1/hi/world/asia-pacific/7307495.stm.

Tov, Emanuel, ed. *The Dead Sea Scrolls: Electronic Reference Library 2.* Translated by Florentino García Martínez. CD-ROM. Leiden: Brill, 1999.

Tov, Emanuel, and Stephen J. Pfann, eds. *The Dead Sea Scrolls on Microfiche: A Comprehensive Facsimile Edition of the Texts from the Judean Desert.* Leiden: Brill, 1993.

Trafton, Joseph L. "Commentary on Genesis A." Pages 203–19 in *The Dead Sea Scrolls—Hebrew, Aramaic, and Greek Texts with English Translations, Vol. 6b: Pesharim, Other Commentaries, and Related Documents.* Edited by James H. Charlesworth and Henry W. Rietz. PTSDSSP. Louisville: Westminster John Knox, 2002.

Trever, John C. *The Untold Story of Qumran.* Westwood, N.J.: Fleming H. Revell, 1965.

Troeltsch, Ernst. *The Social Teaching of the Christian Churches.* Translated by Olive Wyon. 2 vols. London: Allen and Unwin, 1931.

VanderKam, James C. *The Book of Jubilees.* CSCO 511. Louvain: Peeters, 1989.

———. "The Demons in the Book of Jubilees." Pages 339–64 in *Die Dämonen—Demons: Die Damonologie der israelitisch-judischen und fruhchristlichen Literatur im Kontext ihrer Umwelt.* Edited by Armin Lange, Hermann Lichtenberger, and K. F. Diethard Römheld. Tübingen: Mohr Siebeck, 2003.

———. "John 10 and the Feast of Dedication." Pages 203–14 in *Of Scribes and Scrolls: Studies on the Hebrew Bible, Intertestamental Judaism, and Christian Origins Presented to John Strugnell on the Occasion of His Sixtieth Birthday.* Edited by Harold W. Attridge, John J. Collins, and Thomas H. Tobin. CTSRR 5. Lanham, Md.: University Press of America, 1990.

VanderKam, James C., and Peter W. Flint. *The Meaning of the Dead Sea Scrolls: Their Significance for Understanding the Bible, Judaism, Jesus, and Christianity.* San Francisco: HarperSanFrancisco, 2002.

Vermes, Geza. *The Complete Dead Sea Scrolls in English.* London: Penguin Books, 1997.

———. "The Etymology of Essenes." Pages 8–29 in *Post-biblical Jewish Studies.* SJLA 8. Leiden: Brill, 1975.

———. "Review of Barbara Thiering, *Jesus the Man.*" *The New York Review of Books* 41, December 1, 1994, 20.

Von Wahlde, Urban C. "Archaeology and John's Gospel." Pages 523–85 in *Jesus and Archaeology.* Edited by James H. Charlesworth. Grand Rapids: Eerdmans, 2006.

———. "The Road Ahead—Three Aspects of Johannine Scholarship." Pages 343–54 in *What We Have Heard from the Beginning: The Past, Present, and Future of Johannine Studies.* Edited by Tom Thatcher. Waco, Tex.: Baylor University Press, 2007.

Wacholder, Ben Zion, and Martin G. Abegg Jr. *A Preliminary Edition of the Unpublished Dead Sea Scrolls: The Hebrew and Aramaic Texts from Cave Four.* Washington, D.C.: Biblical Archaeological Society, 1991.

Wassen, Cecilia. *Women in the Damascus Document.* SBLAcB 21. Atlanta: Society of Biblical Literature, 2005.

Wcela, Emil A. "The Messiah(s) of Qumran." *CBQ* 26 (1964): 340–49.

Webb, Robert L. "John the Baptist and His Relationship to Jesus." Pages 179–229 in *Studying the Historical Jesus: Evaluations of the State of Current Research*. Edited by Bruce Chilton and Craig A. Evans. NTTS 19. Leiden: Brill, 1994.

———. *John the Baptizer and Prophet: A Socio-Historical Study*. JSNTSup 62. Sheffield: Sheffield Academic, 1991.

Weber, Max. "The Social Psychology of the World's Religions." Pages 267–301 in *From Max Weber: Essays in Sociology*. Edited by H. H. Gerth and C. Wright Mills. London: Routledge & Kegan Paul, 1948.

Whiteley, D. E. H. "Was John Written by a Sadducee?" *ANRW* II, 25.3 (1985): 2481–505.

Wilcox, Max. "'Upon the Tree'—Deut 21:22–23 in the New Testament." *JBL* 96 (1977): 85–99.

Wilson, Bryan. *Magic and the Millennium: A Sociological Study of Religious Movements of Protest among Tribal and Third-World Peoples*. New York: Harper & Row, 1973.

Wilson, Edmund. *The Scrolls from the Dead Sea*. New York: Oxford University Press, 1955.

Windisch, Hans. "Jesus und der Geist im Johannes-Evangelium." Pages 303–18 in *Amicitiae Corolla: Essays Presented to James Rendel Harris*. Edited by H. G. Wood. London: University of London Press, 1933.

Wink, Walter. *John the Baptist in the Gospel Tradition*. SNTSMS 7. Cambridge: Cambridge University Press, 1968.

Wise, Michael, Martin Abegg Jr., and Edward M. Cook. *The Dead Sea Scrolls: A New Translation*. San Francisco: HarperSanFranciso, 2005.

Yadin, Yigael. *The Temple Scroll*. 3 vols. Jerusalem: Israel Exploration Society, 1977–83.

CONTRIBUTORS

Paul N. Anderson is Professor of Biblical and Quaker Studies at George Fox University in Oregon. Anderson's research focuses on the Fourth Gospel's historical context, interconnections to other gospel traditions, and historicity. Anderson currently serves as co-chair of the John, Jesus, and History Group in the Society of Biblical Literature and is the author of *The Christology of the Fourth Gospel* (1996) and *The Fourth Gospel and the Quest for Jesus* (2006).

John Ashton formerly lectured at the University of Oxford and currently lives in Paris. He has written numerous books and articles on the New Testament and its historical setting, with particular attention to the Pauline and Johannine literature. His more significant titles include *Studying John: Approaches to the Fourth Gospel* (1998) and *Understanding the Fourth Gospel* (2007).

George Brooke joined the University of Manchester in 1984. Since 1998 he has been Manchester's Rylands Professor of Biblical Criticism and Exegesis. He has worked on the scrolls for more than thirty-five years, joining the international team of editors in 1992 with responsibility for editing the commentaries on *Genesis (4Q252–4Q254)*. Among many publications on the scrolls, his book *The Dead Sea Scrolls and the New Testament* was published in 2005.

Brian J. Capper wrote his doctorate at Cambridge University on the life of the early Jerusalem church in relation to Essenism and the Dead Sea Scrolls. He subsequently held two two-year research fellowships at the Institut Judaicum of Tübingen University. He is currently Reader in Christian Origins at Canterbury Christ Church University, England. He has published in *Revue de Qumran*, was a contributor to the *Encyclopedia of the Dead Sea Scrolls*, and has published on John and the Dead Sea Scrolls in the *Journal of Theological Studies*.

James H. Charlesworth is the George L. Collord Professor of New Testament Language and Literature and director and editor of the Princeton Theological Seminary Dead Sea Scrolls Project. He has written or edited more than sixty books. His most recent books are *The Historical Jesus: An Essential Guide* (2008), *The Serpent of Good and Evil* (2009). He has edited and contributed to the critical edition of the *Temple Scroll* (2009).

Mary L. Coloe is associate professor at Australian Catholic University, Melbourne. She has published a number of articles, essays, and two monographs, *God Dwells with Us: Temple Symbolism in the Fourth Gospel* (2001) and *Dwelling in the Household of God: Johannine Ecclesiology and Spirituality* (2007). She has also contributed to and coedited, with Rekha Chennattu, *Transcending Boundaries: Contemporary Readings of the New Testament* (2005).

Hannah K. Harrington is currently Professor of Old Testament and chair of the Department of Biblical and Theological Studies at Patten University, Oakland, California. She has written three books and numerous articles on ritual purity and holiness in the Dead Sea Scrolls and rabbinic literature. She received MA and PhD degrees in Near Eastern Studies from the University of California, Berkeley, under the mentorship of Jacob Milgrom and Daniel Boyarin.

Eileen Schuller is professor in the Department of Religious Studies at McMaster University, Hamilton, Ontario. She has edited the official edition in *Discoveries in the Judaean Desert, 4Q380 and 4Q38, Non-canonical Psalms* (DJD 11, 1998); *4Q427–432; Hodayot Manuscripts* (DJD 19 29, 1999); *4Q371–373, Narrative and Poetic Texts* (DJD 38, 2001); with Hartmut Stegemann, *1QHodayot* (DJD 40, 2009). She was an associate editor of the *Dead Sea Scrolls Encyclopedia* (2000) and on the editorial board of Dead Sea Discoveries. Her most recent book was *The Dead Sea Scrolls: What Have We Learned?* (2006).

Loren Stuckenbruck is the Richard S. Dearborn Professor of New Testament Studies at Princeton Theological Seminary and works as a specialist in Second Temple Judaism. He is on the editorial team that has published Dead Sea Scrolls for the Oxford Discoveries in the Judean Desert series.

Tom Thatcher is Professor of Biblical Studies at Cincinnati Christian University. The founding chair of the John, Jesus, and History Group in the Society of Biblical Literature, he is the author and editor of numerous books and articles on the Johannine literature and its historical context. His recent publications include *Jesus in Johannine Tradition* (2000), *Why John Wrote a Gospel* (2006), *What We Have Heard from the Beginning: The Past, Present, and Future of Johannine Studies* (2007), and *Greater Than Caesar* (2009). He is currently finishing commentaries on the Gospel of John and the book of Hebrews.

Subject Index

153 fish (John 21:11) 7 n 14, 44, 73–77, 74 n 19, 77 n 32, 175

Aaronic blessing 143–44, 145
Abraham 87 n 63, 122, 140 n 5, 156–59
Abraham's Prayer (*Jubilees* 12) 156–59, 157 n 40
accessible wisdom 59, 60, 60 n 32, 68
agency theme 16–17, 46 48
Alexander Balas 81
Alexandria 16, 30
Angel of Darkness (1QS 3–4) 79, 146 n 13, 166–67
angels 7, 33, 35, 66–67, 68, 79, 85, 121, 131–32, 134–35, 146, 149, 154–55, 155 n 37, 158, 166–67, 174, 177. *See also* "demons/demonic powers"
life among/of 7, 66–67, 121, 177
Antichrist (eschatological figure) 81
Antichrists (opponents in 1, 2, 3 John) 43, 71 n 10
Antiochus Ephiphanes 81, 84, 176
antiSemitisim 47, 47 n 75
apocalyptic(ism) viii, 7, 33, 53, 60, 60 n 32, 63, 67, 68, 70 n 4, 77 n 32, 100, 159–60, 177–78
archaeological periods at Qumran 4
archaeology
    and the Fourth Gospel 29 n 40, 40–41, 45, 45 n 71, 162–63, 178–79
    and Qumran 26–27, 27–28, 41
Asclepius 40, 179

astrology 157–58

baptism 20, 39–40, 76, 117–19, 123 24, 127–30, 129 n 37, 129 n 39, 130 n 40, 132, 134 n 54, 136–37, 136 n 60, 136–37 n 61, 137 n 62. *See also* "John the Baptizer"; "purification/ purity, water rituals"
    as initiation ritual 120–21, 120 n 8, 122, 122 n 12, 122 n 14, 126 n 29
    of Jesus 124, 128, 129, 136
    proselyte baptism 122–23, 123 n 15
    and repentance 125–28, 130 n 40
    and the Spirit 124–25, 130 n 42, 133–34, 136–37, 136 n 59, 136–37 n 61, 137–38, 137 n 63
Barnabas 85 n 60, 170 n 38
bathing (ritual). *See* "baptism"; "purification/purity, water rituals"
Bathsheba 131 n 46
Belial/Beliar 101, 145–46, 152–53, 159
Beloved Disciple 38, 39, 42, 48, 74, 110, 114–15, 170
Bethany ix, 95, 108–9, 109 n 36, 111–12, 115
Bethel 87–88
Bethesda/Bethzatha 40, 163, 179
Bethesda/Bethzatha Vase 179
Bethlehem 19, 109 n 36
blasphemy 84, 176
blindness (theme) 33, 44, 86, 135, 153

calendar 30, 75–76, 163–64

Index of Ancient Sources

OLD TESTAMENT

69:14	145 n 11	44:17	145 n 11
69:18	145 n 11	54:13	37
70:1	145 n 11	55:8–9	62
71:2	145 n 11	55:11	62
71:4	145 n 11	61	86
71:13	149	61:1	135
79:9	145 n 11	65:11	158 n 42
82	85		
82:4	145 n 11	Jeremiah	
82:6	82–83	2:13	123
96:5	158 n 42	17:13	123
106:37 158 n 42		29:11	62
109:6	149	32:17	60 n 31
109:20	149	32:27	60 n 31
109:29	149	51:29	62
116:4	145 n 11		
119:133	152–53	Ezekiel	
119:134	145 n 11	36:25	134
119:170	145 n 11	44:15	86 n 60
120:2	145 n 11	47:6–12	73
121:7	144, 145	47:8–9	119
131	60 n 31	47:10	74
131:1	60 n 31		
140:1	145 n 11	Daniel	
142:6	145 n 11	7	82, 84
143:9	145 n 11	8:9–14	84
144:7	145 n 11	8:23–24	84
144:11	145 n 11	11:36–37	84

Proverbs		Micah	
8	17	4:12	62
17:22	59		
30:18	61 n 3	Zechariah	
		3:1–2	149
Isaiah		6:12	176
10:20	88	12:10	37, 134
11:1	176	13:1	134
32:15	119	13:2	149
38:18–19	148		
40:3	39	4 Ezra	
40:8	62	6:6	62
44:2–3	123		
44:3–4	119		

Rabbinic and Related Texts

CPSIA information can be obtained at www.ICGtesting.com
264225BV00001B/9/P

7648

9 781589 835467